MENCKEN

and

SARA

MENCKEN

—— *a n d* ——

SARA

A LIFE IN LETTERS

*The Correspondence of H. L. Mencken
and Sara Haardt*

Edited by

Marion Elizabeth Rodgers

ANCHOR BOOKS

DOUBLEDAY

New York   London   Toronto   Sydney   Auckland

An Anchor Book
PUBLISHED BY DOUBLEDAY
a division of Bantam Doubleday Dell Publishing Group, Inc.
666 Fifth Avenue, New York, New York 10103

Anchor Books, Doubleday, and the portrayal of an anchor
are trademarks of Doubleday, a division of
Bantam Doubleday Dell Publishing Group, Inc.

MENCKEN AND SARA was originally published in hardcover by
McGraw-Hill in 1987. The Anchor Books edition is
published by arrangement with the author.

Book design by Mary A. Wirth

Library of Congress Cataloging-in-Publication Data

Mencken. H. L. (Henry Louis), 1880–1956.
Mencken and Sara : a life in letters : the correspondence of H. L.
Mencken and Sara Haardt / edited by Marion Elizabeth Rodgers.—
1st Anchor Books ed.
p. cm.
"Originally published in hardcover by McGraw-Hill in 1987"—
T.p. verso.
Includes bibliographical references and index.
1. Mencken, H. L. (Henry Louis), 1880–1956—Correspondence.
2. Haardt, Sara, 1898–1935—Correspondence.   3. Authors,
American—20th century—Correspondence.   4. Authors' wives—United
States—Correspondence.   I. Haardt, Sara, 1898–1935.   II. Rodgers,
Marion Elizabeth.   III. Title.
[PS3523.E43Z488   1992]
818'.5209—dc20   91-29717
CIP
ISBN 0-385-41980-5
PRINTED IN THE UNITED STATES OF AMERICA
FIRST ANCHOR BOOKS EDITION: FEBRUARY 1992
1   3   5   7   9   10   8   6   4   2

To my father and mother

Grateful Acknowledgement is made to the following firms for their permission to quote from previously published material:

The Baltimore *Sun*: Various "Monday Articles" and other columns by H. L. Mencken.

Delacorte Press: *The Constant Circle* by Sara Mayfield, Copyright © 1968 by Sara Mayfield.

Doubleday & Co., Inc.: *Southern Album*, by Sara Haardt, edited with a preface by H. L. Mencken, Copyright © 1936; *The New Mencken Letters*, Edited by Carl Bode, Copyright © 1976, 1977 by Carl Bode. Originally published by Dial Press.

E. P. Dutton, Inc.: *Days of the Phoenix: The Nineteen-Twenties I Remember*, by Van Wyck Brooks, copyright © 1957 by Van Wyck Brooks.

Harcourt, Brace, Jovanovich, Inc.: *The Sweeping Wind*, by Paul de Kruif, Copyright © 1962 by Paul de Kruif.

Holt, Rinehart and Winston, and Ray Hoopes: *Cain*, by Roy Hoopes, Copyright © 1982 by Roy Hoopes.

Alfred A. Knopf, Inc.: *Pistols for Two*, copyright © 1917; *Prejudices: First Series*, copyright © 1919; *Prejudices: Second Series*, copyright © 1920; *The Borzoi 1925*, copyright © 1925; *Prejudices: Sixth Series*, copyright © 1927; *Happy Days*, copyright © 1940; *A Mencken Chrestomathy*, copyright © 1949; *Minority Report*, copyright © 1956; *Innocence Abroad*, by Emily Clark, copyright © 1931; *Six Men*, by Alistair Cooke, copyright © 1956, 1977 by Alistair Cooke; *On Mencken*, edited by John Dorsey, copyright © 1980; *Mencken: A*

CONTENTS

INTRODUCTION

I

THE LETTERS IN THIS VOLUME chronicle the love story between H. L. Mencken, one of the most influential journalists, editors, and bachelors of the twentieth century, and Sara Powell Haardt, the young writer who would later become his wife. These are love letters, yet in each case neither the sender nor the recipient held a particularly high regard for love, and on the subject of marriage both had been cynical.

Mencken defined love as "the delusion that one woman differs from another," maintaining that "bachelors know more about women than married men. If they didn't, they'd be married too." On another occasion, he stated flatly: "If I ever marry, it will be on sudden impulse, as a man shoots himself." As for Sara, she expressed the same feelings as did the flappers in one of her novels: "I would advise any woman to wait. There is so much in life—so much for a woman to see and do—it would be a pity for her to miss it. Of course, marriage is a career, but it isn't life, it isn't everything!" Yet when H. L. Mencken married Sara Haardt in 1930 it was after a courtship that lasted seven years. During their courtship and subsequent marriage, they exchanged over seven hundred letters, a series beginning shortly after their first meeting in May 1923 and terminating twelve years later, a few days before Sara Haardt Mencken's early death of tuberculosis on May 31,

1935. The letters, recording Mencken's encouragement of Sara's writing and his growing love for her, were written against a background of America in the twenties and thirties. The Scopes Monkey Trial, Franklin Delano Roosevelt's election, F. Scott Fitzgerald, Clarence Darrow, Herman Mankiewicz, Hollywood in the age of silent film: in letter after letter are the events and people of a vanished era. Understandably, the letters cover a variety of subjects, ranging from the significant to the trivial. But beyond their value as the documentation of daily events they also reveal, step by step, how Mencken's influence upon a young Southern writer may have helped pave the way for the Southern literary renaissance, and how, in turn, Sara Haardt was able to reveal a hitherto unknown side of the "Bad Boy of Baltimore."

In light of both Mencken's and Sara's sense of privacy, it might well seem an intrusion to publish their letters. Yet strong arguments press for publication: few people know that Mencken married; fewer still know anything about his wife. If there are distortions about Mencken, Sara, and their marriage, these letters should help correct them. Although Mencken wrote that "a man seldom puts his authentic self into a letter," and that "it is rare, indeed, for a man to reveal himself, honestly and completely, to his correspondents," Mencken's lifelong reluctance to shed what Edmund Wilson called his "comic mask" gives unusual value to his correspondence as evocations of his most private feelings. The sheer volume of letters and the repeated confidences they contain support the notion that Mencken had fallen deeply, irrevocably in love.

Mencken's relationship with Sara Haardt was one more example of his lifelong habit of forming close friendships with fellow writers. In one of his notebooks he tells us: "I have been able, in my time, to give help to a good many young authors, male and female, and some of them have turned out very well. I often think of the immense number of others I might have aided if only I had known of them." The claim was justified, for he was as discriminating as he was helpful. "A bad writer," he insisted, "has no rights whatever. Any mercy shown to him is wasted and mistaken." Nonetheless, his rejections to authors were usually gently couched, accompanied by suggestions for their improvement and the names of other editors to whom they could send their material. (When editors received a direct note from Mencken, the net effect was a recommendation not to be ignored.) Mencken said he remembered too well his own efforts to sell material to magazines for him to be impolite to budding authors. It was the inevitable rule of *The Smart Set*'s office that all authors should be treated courteously, and this rule would be applied again when Mencken edited his next magazine, *The American Mercury*.

Long after the 1920s, when the question "What do you think of Mencken?" was a recurring phrase, it is hard to comprehend the magnitude of the impression of receiving a letter from the Sage of Baltimore. In his maturity, the writer Sherwood Anderson could remark in his memoirs: "We got the letters and the letters made us proud. 'Well, I had a letter from Henry Mencken today.' You said it casually, but in your heart, you felt that it was like being knighted by a king." It is easy to comprehend how Sara—as a writer, but also as a woman—experienced the same sort of elation as that of Sherwood Anderson and his contemporaries. She who had the habit, she confessed, of destroying all the letters she received, who often wrote the rough drafts of her articles and stories on the reverse side of letters from magazine editors, from friends, even one from her sister, never so disfigured any of those she received from Mencken. Every note, every card, every letter he wrote to her during the twelve-year period from 1923 to 1935 has been preserved. On the other hand, it is true that Mencken kept few of her communications, and this may account for the scarcity of letters that do survive, but then it must also be remembered that she was not as prolific a correspondent as he.

Mencken wrote over one hundred thousand letters during his lifetime. His usual output was sixty letters a day, but at one point, he told Alfred Knopf, he dictated as many as one hundred and twenty-five a day. There were letters to doctors, senators, movie stars, editors, and many of the intellectuals of the day. His letters to Sara are filled with admonishments. "Why don't you write? I never hear from you!" is a constant refrain. For Mencken, it was almost impossible not to write a short letter recording all that he saw or felt, or a note regarding a simple business transaction or meeting (like his contemporary Evelyn Waugh he hated the telephone).

Nonetheless, despite Sara's strict notions of privacy and propriety (standards matched only by Mencken's), she was more direct in revealing her love than he would have ever dared to be in print. It may be argued that if Sara had expressed herself in more frequent romantic outbursts than are collected here, this would have been the kind of letter that Mencken would have discarded; conversely, there is always the argument that if Mencken kept any love letters to Sara Haardt during their courtship ("love letters" of the type of, say, the rhapsodies of Robert Browning) he may well have destroyed them before bequeathing the entire collection to Goucher College, in Baltimore, where Sara studied and later taught. All of this, however, is mere hypothesis; it seems safe to assume that the collection of letters survives practically in its entirety, that the lack of effusiveness was in character. As one of his biographers, Carl Bode, has noted, Mencken "had a marked distaste for the rhetoric of emotion." Moreover, all of his friends—and this would have included Sara—led sane, systematic lives, their own personal code of conduct, like Mencken's, being based on the avoidance of extremes in both action and speech. Thus, while Mencken could say that he was "mashed" on Sara, the phrase "I love you" would not be used by him until after they were engaged. He must have at least given an indication of his feelings to exact from her the repeated confession of love in her own letters to him. But beyond that she does not go.

Outside of her private correspondence, Sara Haardt was creatively productive, but tuberculosis and general poor health ended her career prematurely. In forty short stories and two short novels, she examined the traditions, poverty, and prejudice that held many Southerners prisoner for several generations. Her death in 1935 interrupted the process of writing *The Plantation*, a novel she hoped would provide a greater understanding of the traditional Southern order and its effect upon those confined within it. *The Plantation* dealt with a South in transition, torn between the elder generation, gradually disappearing, and a new one searching to break through. In many ways, Mencken thought, the novel was a picture of her own life, in which she wished to give an account of what he later described as "the conflict which had gone on in her own soul—between the pull of rationalism on the one hand, and the almost irresistible fascination of the Southern scene." Sara was also planning to reprint some of her short stories in a collection to be entitled *Southern Album*, and her diary for 1935 reveals that she had begun work on their revision on February 18. (It was published posthumously in 1936.) Of her work, there were stories that, according to Mencken, "she turned out . . . to boil the pot and things . . .

involving great time and care." From the stories and articles Sara did complete, one is able to see in her one of the newer and more perceptive writers on the Southern scene. The challenge for the new Southern writer during the 1920s was to treat the Southern past—of slavery, recession, Civil War, defeat, reconstruction, decline, and Yankee-fication—with actuality, and not to continue an outworn tradition of fanciful historical romance. At the same time, this was not a literature of protest, but what Donald Davidson would later call "the literature of acceptance." In her novel *The Making of a Lady* and in the seventeen short stories Mencken gathered together in *Southern Album*, Sara was best at examining the effects of peculiarly Southern attitudes toward women, marriage, money, and race. Across her paper pass blacks and whites, old men and women and young children, rich and poor, all for the most part simple folk. While their idiom, gestures, and attitudes are those of the South, they are never types, but always individuals, with universal significance.

By the time Sara Haardt and H. L. Mencken were married in 1930, she had become a well-established free-lance writer and continued to write and publish under her maiden name. During the Depression, when Mencken's books and *The American Mercury* were selling slowly, he took special pride in Sara's writing. In a letter to his friend Philip Goodman he remarked: "Sara, whose chief market is the women's magazines, sold more stuff within the last month than she has ever sold before in a whole year. Moreover, she is beset with orders. Thus I hope she'll earn enough to support me with considerable decency."

H. L. Mencken met Sara Haardt during one of his annual lectures to Harry T. Baker's English class at Goucher College, on the evening of May 8, 1923.* The lectures were advertised as the esoteric comments on this or that philosophy, but the actual topic was always the same: How to Catch a Husband. During the lecture, Mencken spotted Sara in the audience—she was then twenty-four, the youngest on the faculty—and the next day, in a letter to Phil Goodman, he quipped: "Call me a liar if you will, but last night I lectured at Goucher College and discerned no less than 27 appetitizing [sic] cuties in the audience. It greatly astonished me; I always thought education ruined the com-

---

* Mencken first began (as he put it) "haranguing" the Goucher girls in December 1922.

plexions of women." That same evening Sara Haardt attended a dinner organized by Harry Baker, which included Sara Mayfield, the student who had won the contest for the best short story of the year by a freshman (a competition Sara Haardt had won only a few years previously), and H. L. Mencken. Most probably the group ate at Domenique's or at the Rennert, the latter of which Mencken regarded as the undisputed champion of Chesapeake shad roe and oyster pot-pie. * When, during the course of the dinner conversation, Mencken heard that besides teaching, Sara Haardt wrote short stories, he asked if he could see her work. Afterwards, she would boldly admit she had already been sending manuscripts to *The Smart Set* ever since she had been "big enough to lift a stamp." Nonetheless, she sent another sample to his office in New York.

She might not have expected an immediate answer. As she well knew, Mencken was very much sought after by both Baltimoreans and New Yorkers. He used to say that he was so infernally harassed by telephone calls from bores that he could never get any work done. Sara, intrigued by Mencken, was aware of this and puzzled as to how to approach him. Her first letter to Mencken reflects her bafflement: "How does one do it? I mean, see you." On May 29, 1923, Mencken arranged to meet her for lunch, a method which he and his coeditor, George Jean Nathan, utilized in order to encourage new authors to submit material to *The Smart Set*. After experiencing what she called "dog days" at Goucher College, Sara looked forward to their meeting as "the only inspiring thing that could happen."

The restaurant was Domenique's, a favorite haunt of Mencken's. As Mencken and Sara sat together, they undoubtedly discussed authors of mutual interest, and the new direction of Southern literature. Mencken, meanwhile, ate with gusto, while Sara, in typical fashion, ate, according to Mencken, "like an Armenian refugee," picking on "fruit salads and other cobwebs." Mencken was a Northerner, Sara a Southerner, a Confederate from Montgomery, Alabama, from a region Mencken had labeled "The Sahara of the Bozart."† He opened the doors to Northern progress and ideas; she was to evoke, in her stories, the

---

* In her book on those years, Sara Mayfield has written in *The Constant Circle* that the dinner was held at Schellhase's, when in fact the restaurant did not open until a good twelve months later, on April 1, 1924.

† "Bozart," of course, is Mencken's teasing on the term "beaux arts."

echoes of the late Confederacy, the other half of America—the mists, the magnolias, the honey sweetness of a Southern sky tinged with the melancholy of death. They were teacher and pupil, yet intellectual equals and although Sara sometimes retained what might seem, in these times, an overwhelming admiration for Mencken (as typified in a valentine inscription during their married life, "I worship you, Mr. Henry Mencken"), their correspondence indicates that the relationship grew into one of respect for each other's intelligence, wit, and culture. It was the beginning of a friendship. In this almond-eyed, delicate woman, Mencken was to find a soulmate.

Their romance developed slowly, in a courtship that was neither routine nor smooth. When they met, he was already a middle-aged bachelor and the most widely known editor and journalist in America. She was an unknown, eighteen years his junior. At first glance, it would seem that the friendship was not quite as important to Mencken as it was to Sara. His friends, editors and writers like Emily Clark, Louis Untermeyer, and Carl Van Vechten, believed he was "afraid of women, except the Broadway kind and the middle-aged intellectual ones." Then there was the episode at the Eastern Shore when Hamilton Owens, editor of the Baltimore *Evening Sun*, watched as Mencken, retreating from the advance of a particularly aggressive woman, almost fell backwards from a terrace and into the water. And what of Mencken's own statement that when he was in the mood to relax he preferred the company of men, preferably around the beer table?

The truth was that Mencken enjoyed the company of women. But he was nonetheless wary of women and their matrimonial aspirations. "No unmarried woman can be polite to a bachelor without beginning to speculate how he would look in a wedding coat," he stated, adding, "This fact, which is too obvious to need proof, makes friendly dealings with them somewhat strained." Incautiously, he remarked on another occasion, "That I have escaped . . . is not my fault, nor is it to my credit; it is due to a mere act of God. I am no more responsible for it than I am for my remarkable talent as a pianist, my linguistic skills, or my dark, romantic, somewhat voluptuous beauty." Mencken cultivated the image of bachelorhood, and his reputation as a bachelor reached legendary proportions. Because everyone was aware of his feelings in the matter there was nothing in his stance to offend even the most susceptible woman.

The truth, in fact, as his friend Joseph Hergesheimer observed, was that Mencken "concealed rigorously the details of a domestic, a filial, unmarried existence. He hid the fact that personally he was not less sensitive than an anemone. . . . It was his belief that there was no phase of marriage he wasn't familiar with; but there, actually, his understanding, his realism, failed; like practically all unmarried men older than forty he was an idealist about women. Henry tried to evade this by continually referring to the practical, the unromantic aspects of women; he had written a book [*In Defense of Women*] about their brutal practices on men; but every third line betrayed his incurable hopefulness, the charm of his private dream. . . ." In reality, Mencken had many female friends, women whom he encouraged with their writing or with whom he associated socially. Three days after he met Sara he was writing letters to Phil Goodman about his "new girl" in New York. And throughout 1925 and 1926 while he was helping Sara with her writing he was also helping another, equally attractive, young writer from Washington, D.C., named Beatrice Wilson. There was also the string of dancers and stage girls from the theater and nightclub circuit to whom Nathan introduced him and "blondes" who, according to the novelist Joseph Hergesheimer, would wait for him for hours, who called him "Menck," and who thought he was "sweet" and "adorable." And then there were the celebrated acquaintances: the ex-opera singer Gretchen Hood, writer Anita Loos, and the film actresses Lillian Gish and Aileen Pringle. Mencken always said he detested the company of stupid women, and his female friends were, for the most part, intelligent and quick-witted. Mencken kept up a running joke with Gretchen Hood that he would marry her after being elected president of the United States; Anita Loos's conversation and writing amused him (*Gentlemen Prefer Blondes* was inspired by Mencken); and even though he was averse to theater, he tried to see every play of Lillian Gish's if he was in the same town in which she was appearing.

Mencken was linked romantically in the gossip columns with Aileen Pringle. Aileen, whom he had met at one of Joseph Hergesheimer's parties, had already become a legend in Hollywood by the time Mencken met her in 1926. She enjoyed the company of literary men and women, and she was able to converse about books with what Gloria Swanson called "a scorching wit." Aileen was one with whom, in Mencken's words, he could "never be bored." Certainly Mencken's friendship with

Aileen was very different from that of his friendship with Sara Haardt, for he regarded the actress as an equal in terms of success and popularity. Theirs was the camaraderie of equally celebrated public figures. But it also seems fair to say that both recognized their friendship for what it was: a friendship. Their lives were too dissimilar, they moved in too different circles, for their relationship to develop into matrimony. Anyone who indulged in the news of gossip columns or in the frivolity of cocktail chatter—who assumed that their friendship was destined for a more serious relationship—should have realized that Mencken would never have left Baltimore, and, for her part, Aileen would never have left Los Angeles. Perhaps there was also a small part of Mencken that rebelled against the strong-minded Aileen. It was Aileen, after all, who changed his appearance by teasing him into wearing laced shoes instead of buttoned ones, suspenders instead of a belt, low instead of high collars, and who invariably lectured him on Bach and Beethoven. "You may resent it when she tries to run you, as she undoubtedly will," he wrote to James Cain upon Cain's impending marriage to the actress, "for there's a regular army general hidden in her soft and disarming exterior."

The most important woman in his life up to the time he met Sara Haardt had been Marion Bloom, with whom he had fallen deeply in love. They met in 1914, when Marion and her sister, Estelle (Theodore Dreiser's secretary), had visited Mencken in his office at the Baltimore *Sun*. Mencken often visited Marion at her home in Washington, D.C., while doing research for a book he dubbed his "Homo Sapiens book" (ironically, long after Marion had married, Sara Haardt would later travel to Washington herself to help Mencken with his research). The book was never completed; other projects crowded it out; perhaps it caused him too many painful memories. Marion Bloom was pretty, coquettish, and intelligent. She chided Mencken for not sending her a Christmas card and told him she was not beautiful enough to see him on certain days. He scolded her for casting "a sympathetic eye" on Nathan or for writing him when she was "drunk and feeling sorry" for herself. As with every woman Mencken met and liked, he urged her to become a writer, and for a while her writings appeared in the pages of *The Smart Set*. The letters Mencken exchanged with her are among the most romantic he ever composed, and inevitably they began to discuss marriage.

After Marion's return from France, where she served as a nurse during World War I, she became drawn toward the Christian Science religion. Mencken, the agnostic, found this turn totally repulsive. He wavered in his intentions toward Marion until finally, in the summer of 1923, she took the decision to marry another suitor, a Lou Maritzer. Her marriage to another man came as such a painful surprise to Mencken that it is little wonder that years later he was still cautious about expressing himself openly in his letters to Sara Haardt.

At first the tone of Mencken's letters to Sara is jaunty, as with his other correspondents. The letters record his talent for capturing the sharply observed scene or the fugitive absurdity. He assisted her in her writing, making suggestions for new topics or editing her material while traveling on the train between Baltimore and New York; he read her novel, encouraged her to continue her writing by reminding her that she was "a talented gal." He would often meet her at restaurants or else, more discreetly, at an old ruined mill, where, during Prohibition days, they would surreptitiously share a bottle of liquor or go on long walks.

Mencken's affection for Sara developed rapidly. She possessed that rare quality Mencken had always admired in people: a talent for listening. Even more valuably, she tempered her listening with insight, understanding, and wit. She regarded her fellow creatures with a common sense that verged on the cynical. Her later letters to Mencken conceal this aspect of her character. For the most part, they are docile. But her early letters to Mencken and her private notes to Sara Mayfield show a wicked sense of wit and fun. Mencken and his friends were continually impressed by her acumen. James Cain wrote that Sara could "see through most people." The writer and critic Jim Tully, meeting her in Hollywood, wrote her admiringly: "It is amazing how many young women try to solve life with fluttery questions. You don't."

As with his other female correspondents, Mencken concluded his letters with the ceremony "I kiss your hand 1,000 times," but with Sara there was something more. His letters to her began to be accompanied by love tokens: in one of them, a "modest bauble" he had bought in Berlin. (The bauble, it turns out, got lost in the mail. "Perhaps it is now hanging around the neck of the wife of the Postmaster General," complained Mencken. "I hope she comes down with smallpox.") He mixed his compliments with tender apology: "I suspect that you were trying to flirt with me this afternoon; hence the hollowness of my conversation. . . ." Finally, when she was away in Montgomery, he wrote: "Friend Sary, I miss you like hell." He was deeply impressed by the feeling Sara had for him and the fact that she expressed it without the coyness he had come to expect in women her age—the women he knew in New York. It was very important to him, knowing with what frequency he met people and what an influential position he had, to have someone he could trust. His reserve, his constant guarding of himself and his words in his correspondence, were equal to her own. Sara offered him the possibility, not otherwise available, of complete self-revelation, a source of great relief to a man as private as Mencken. It was to Sara that Mencken would write one of the first letters about his mother's death.

He did not reveal himself to Sara without difficulty. The letters of 1926 and some of those of 1927 seem to show a change in tone: they are a bit distant, certainly more reserved than his prior letters. Sara was spending most of her time traveling to upstate New York, where the summers were cooler than in Montgomery or Baltimore. And then, she too had her admirers. Indeed, there was much in her to attract others. There were her eyes, described by those who knew her as "luminous, piercing, beautiful" and "magnificently expressive," her wit, her infectious humor and throaty laugh. She possessed traits, they said, of both the *femme savant* and the *femme fatale*. When she entered a room, people took immediate notice of her.* She had, as Mencken noted, "a full measure of that indefinable, pleasant thoughtfulness which passes commonly under the banal name of Southern charm." It was this charm of manner that, said R. P. Harriss, one of her admirers, "in a less prosaic age inspired men to go out on the field of honor and

---

* Sara Haardt's beauty is seldom captured in photographs. One reason, as Mencken wrote in a letter to Sara Mayfield, may be because "the moment she [Sara] got before the camera she would screw up her face and the result was usually a horrible caricature." A more likely reason was that after several painful operations, Sara Haardt's appearance naturally seemed to have aged. In addition, her weight was kept high in the belief that it would help fight off any additional tubercular infections.

shoot each other full of holes." Robin Harriss, a young reporter with the *Evening Sun*, regularly sent her long-stemmed roses and love poems, and squired her to dinner, dances, and parties. James Cain, too, long before his own marriage, took Sara out for an occasional dinner. Nearer to home, Hudson Strode of the University of Alabama constantly plied Sara's younger brother John with "millions of questions" about her, as did Peyton Spottswood Matthis.

Matthis, one of Montgomery's young men about town, was believed to be the one great love of Sara's life, and there are stories in this connection circulating in Montgomery today that have reached Bunyanesque proportions. This was the same Peyton Matthis who is characterized as the "Dayton Bee" in John Kohn's book about Montgomery entitled *The Cradle*. He was, according to all who knew him, a man of many talents: successful with women, noted for his wit, and with a gift for making money. He is also the same ambiguous figure Sara Mayfield mentions in *The Constant Circle*, who is said to have boarded a train to Baltimore to propose to Haardt and, having "come to" in Charleston, proceeded to marry an unknown. But all these were rumors and, like all rumors of this kind, constituted in large degree what Mencken fondly termed "stretchers." Undoubtedly there is some truth that Peyton Matthis had indeed taken a strong liking to Sara, and it may well be true that during 1923 and 1924 Sara wrote him letters while she lived in Baltimore. It is not unlikely that during Sara's late teens she was infatuated with the witticisms and mellow tones of Peyton Matthis. Yet however seductive he may have been, years later she began to see him as a man who had all the questionable qualities of what she termed a "jellybean" (the Southern term for youth or town sheik) in her stories for *College Humor*.

She preferred Mencken. Robin Harriss reached the conclusion that she was committed to Henry and to him only. That Mencken was Sara's "special weakness" was also the realization that dawned on James Cain after their third dinner together. Her shyness and reserve may have been mistaken by Mencken and perhaps led him to believe that she did not care for him. Unlike most women of her age, Sara wholeheartedly agreed with Mencken's dim view of marriage. She believed that when a girl "gets the career germ in her system, the only sane thing for a man to do is to let her work it out. . . . What should you do? A great many men persuade girls to give up their careers and marry them, but it is a mistake, for no matter how good and kind the husband is, or how *generous*, she goes through life feeling she made a terrible sacrifice." In any event, Mencken had now met Aileen Pringle, and it may be that his attention was temporarily focused elsewhere. (However, it must be remembered that throughout his visit to Hollywood in 1926 he was giving interviews that said he could never hang on to two women at the same time, nor did he think it wise.)

The warmth of the relationship was renewed, however, when Sara moved back to Baltimore, and when she left for Hollywood in the autumn of 1927. The night before her departure they quarreled, but Mencken soon felt bad about what he considered his misjudgment of her. The letter written to her the next day was filled with remorse: "If I seemed idiotic yesterday, blame it upon the fact that it suddenly dawned on me that I'd not see you for weeks." Perhaps Mencken realized he had estranged a former relationship with Marion Bloom through similar quarrels and possessiveness, and did not want the same to happen with Sara. Whatever the motivation, the letters throughout the rest of the decade are full of encouragement, advice, and thoughtfulness. Finally, when Mencken and Sara are man and wife, they become genuine letters of love.

To some of Mencken's friends, Sara and he seemed complete opposites. She was a Southerner, from a region Mencken had publicly ridiculed (he had said the people, among other things, were "vegetables" who had "no more taste for Southern literature, or for any other arts, than a rutabaga"). To anyone observing the two of them seated at lunch, the sight must have seemed incongruous: the stocky, rotund man with wrinkled clothes (looking, as friends of Sara's would remark, as if they were made of tin), with the table manners of—as he himself put it—Cro-Magnon man; and the willowy, delicate, beautiful creature with a soft Southern drawl. But these differences were not irreconcilable, for Mencken had the habit of overlooking his prejudices once personal contact was established, and this held true in his attitude to Sara. Moreover, there were a great many links between the two. There were the moments when, as C. S. Lewis once remarked, someone who has till then believed his feelings to be unique cries out, "What? You too? I thought I was the only one." Mencken shared Sara's hatred for sports: under paternal pressure Mencken had been enrolled at the YMCA and from then on he refused to participate, in any organized or supervised athletics, while Sara had made a minor college career of avoiding sports throughout her four years at Goucher. Both were agnostics; both shared a sense of discipline and common sense (she was noted for her "cool, sane judgments"); both felt life was a human comedy (although Sara's outlook would remain, Mencken reflected, more "charmingly pessimistic" than his own); both enjoyed discussing philosophy and books. "We have substantially the same tastes. We like to do the same things," Mencken would tell a reporter upon his marriage to Sara. "One of them is to sit around at night and talk— just gabble. . . . We have spent many delightful evenings doing just that." Both shared a love of Baltimore. This was important to Mencken. Years later he would say he could never have married anybody who did not share the love for his city, with its sights and smells, its close community. He traveled every other week and spent two or three days working on *The Smart Set* or *The American Mercury* in New York, but he always breathed a sigh of relief when the train headed back in the direction of Baltimore. New York was a place "fit only for the gross business of getting money," Baltimore "a place made for enjoying it." He went on to say that he and Sara had "a great many Baltimore friends in common, people with whom we associate constantly," an important element in life, for "in human relationships that are so casual there is seldom any satisfaction. It is our fellows who make life endurable to us, and give it a purpose and a meaning; if our contacts with them are light and frivolous there is something lacking, and it is something of the very first importance." And he added: "What I contend is that in Baltimore, under a slow-moving and cautious social organization, such contacts are more enduring than elsewhere, and that life in consequence is more charming." Sara's attachment was shown by the fact that she left orders to be buried in Baltimore after her death.

Just as Mencken was steadfastly traditional about his attitude to home and friends, so too were his courtesy and standards of conduct soundly Victorian, as were Sara's. Notwithstanding Mencken's reputation and the immense influence he had on his contemporaries, he had naturally good manners and would treat some unknown writer or the assistant librarian of a public library with the same charming civility as if they were the most important persons in the world. Although Emily Clark once complained that sometimes Mencken "forgets and walks on the inside of the street," he was, to Sara, "the first Christian gentleman I have met since Mr. Baker took the oath of allegiance to Goucher College." Sara, with her traditional Southern upbringing, despite her independence and feminist point of view, was appealingly soft in her ways, and a fine example of those Southern women who Mencken maintained knew "how to handle a man." Successful friendships and marriage may be based on "animal magnetism" (Mencken said he wasn't attracted to any woman who lacked it), but those which last are formed out of a commonality of values, interests, humor, and conversation. Mencken and Sara also made a special point of being polite to one another. "Neither of us quarrels with other persons," Mencken observed. "So why should we quarrel with each other?" When they married in 1930 he told the press: "I am marrying one of the politest of women, and she is getting a husband whose politeness has the high polish of a mirror." What seemed to be the best rule for marriage was, they both felt, the best rule for all human relationships: mutual respect.

Finally, there was Sara's sickness, which helped bind them even closer together; tuberculosis, it turned out, ran in the paternal side of his own family.* William Manchester is right when he notes that Mencken was fascinated by the frailties of the human body—his own and everybody else's. Many of Mencken's friends were doctors, and he had much to talk over with them. He was constantly studying medical journals or visiting sick acquaintances who might not have seen him in years. (Doctors and nurses, once having discovered that *the* Mr. Mencken was visiting, constantly made up excuses to enter the patient's room to listen to the conversation.) Unlike Sara, he was forever analyzing his own persistent hay fever and recording in a huge journal (for the benefit of a study on allergies conducted by Robert A. Cooke but also, one imagines, for his own enlightenment) his temperature, his bouts of sneezing (sometimes as many as fifteen in a row at three o'clock in the morning), his coughs, and his sniffles.

---

* Harriet McClellan, the first wife of Mencken's grandfather Burkhardt Ludwig Mencken, died of TB.

Mencken and Sara's doctors were all deeply impressed by the courageous, patient way she faced suffering and pain. Her last six months in bed, Mencken realized, "must have been hideous, but she never uttered a syllable of complaint." Mencken's praise would have embarrassed Sara, for she was not a person to play the role of a martyr. As she put it simply: "People with tuberculosis learn to take things in their stride—with a minimum of howling; learn to extract the most pleasure from day-to-day living; adapt themselves to most situations, good or bad. . . ." Mencken's publisher, Alfred A. Knopf, and many of his friends thought Mencken had married Sara to take care of her, as he had enjoyed taking care of his mother. But they invariably missed one important factor: that they needed each other. Sara's illness logically struck a paternal chord in Mencken, but likewise, his violent sneezing and complaints of hay fever would have instinctively struck a maternal chord in Sara, and this, in turn, formed a special bond between the two.

What seems not to have crossed their friends' minds, then, was not that Sara was so dissimilar from Henry and that therein lay their mutual attraction, but that actually the two of them were basically alike. The points of contact even extended to the fact that in both cases their German ancestors had been scholars—and in one case actual colleagues. One of the Haardts had been a professor during the late seventeenth century, and an associate of Otto and Johann Burkhard Mencken at the University of Leipzig. Another surprising association came to light through the marriage of Sara's sister Philippa to T. M. McClellan, Jr., of Birmingham, Alabama, for it developed that Mencken's own paternal grandmother was Harriet McClellan of Kingston, Jamaica. "It always amazed Sara," Mencken wrote, "that she and her much loved sister Philippa should have both married men in whom ran the blood of the clan."

There still remains one other spiritual link which has not been mentioned in previous biographies, except William Manchester's *Disturber of the Peace*, where it has been only lightly touched upon: the coincidence of what one might call their dual allegiance. What the majority of his friends could not have known—for he hardly confided this to anyone—was that Mencken felt more German than American. To accuse Mencken of a lack of patriotism would be unfair. His book *The American Language* thrills with the spirit of America and independence. Nor did he hide the fact that he felt pro-German. Not only was Mencken's family of German descent, but in the early days of his youth Baltimore had a large German community. The first school he attended, the shops his parents patronized, the servant girls, the newspapers, the music they listened to, were all German. He put it succinctly in his "Autobiographical Notes": "I was born without a word of English, and didn't become a citizen of the United States until I was twenty-one years old." The statement is as clever as it is subtle. Until he was twenty-one he was, then, according to himself and unofficially at least, a German. He thought "my grandfather made a mistake when he came to America, and I have always lived in the wrong country." And yet, Mencken could never be one hundred percent German because, as he put it, he was a mixture of several bloods, "an intellectual mongrel." But he found it, as he said, "simply impossible to follow American patterns of thinking or to admire the American way of life." He was, in short, a German chauvinist who had grown up in an Americanized version of the German home. Mencken saw in traditional German bourgeois values all that was good, fine, and decent; he viewed German music as better than other music, German philosophy as more astute than other philosophies. As a journalist of German ancestry, Mencken suffered greatly during World War I; he was accused of a lack of patriotism. Throughout the war he stoutly defended the Kaiser, so much so that his writing had to be temporarily halted from appearing on the pages of the Baltimore *Evening Sun*. German Americans were often ridiculed and sometimes attacked in the streets; Mencken himself, because he was of German descent, because he kept on playing and defending German music, and because he thought America should have stayed out of a European war, was insulted, sneered at, and looked on as evil.*

---

* Mencken lost his following twice during his lifetime: when he did not line up for the left-wing causes during the 1930s; and when he did not recognize the true intent of Adolf Hitler. With the history of American anti-Germany hysteria in mind, Mencken was hesitant to believe the worst about *any* German. This does not mean, however, that he was neutral about the subject. In a letter of 1935 he wrote: "A very definite anti-Semitic movement is gathering force behind the door, and whenever a convenient opportunity offers it will bust out. At that time you may trust me to mount the battlements and holler for

Mencken's conflict was one which Sara Haardt could understand because, in a large part, it was also her own. In her case, she was a Southerner who could never feel one hundred percent Southern because her father and the relations who visited her home were of marked German descent. Although Sara's upbringing was not as intensely German as that of Mencken (her mother was distinctly a Southerner), Sara never felt at home in the South and yet she never felt herself to be a Northerner in the North; at the same time, she loved and dreamed of the Confederate tradition but wished to destroy some of its beliefs. In many ways, her own structure of thesis and antithesis would carry over into her writing, in paragraph and scene as well as in its more obvious opposites, such as North and South, male and female, father and mother, life and death. As a Southern writer and critic of the South, Sara was often criticized and insulted by her fellow Southerners. (Indeed, she was referred to as a "Menckenesque critic," something one can only surmise that she took as a compliment.) Both Mencken and Sara, then, like the Tonio Kröger of Thomas Mann, could say, "I stand between two worlds, I am alone in neither." One can imagine that the net effect was that they felt very much alone, and if not alone, at least different.

The question arises: who exactly was Sara Powell Haardt? There have been few studies on her; the only full-length work is *The Constant Circle* by Sara Mayfield. Yet even this piece approached Sara Haardt as the wife of H. L. Mencken and concentrated more on Mencken

---

the Chosen. Meanwhile, all I can say about Hitler is that he seems to be an idiot. That all other Germans are idiots I doubt gravely." And again, in 1936: "I should add I am entirely out of sympathy with the method used by Hitler to handle the Jewish question. It seems to me that the gross brutality to harmless individuals must needs revolt every decent man. I am well aware that reports from Germany have been exaggerated, but I am aware of the intolerable brutalities that have been practiced. I don't know a single man of any reputation in America who is in favor of the Nazi scheme. As it stands, Germany has completely lost the sympathy it had in the years following 1920." Unfortunately, Mencken's slurs—referring to those of Jewish faith or movie moguls as "Jews" or blacks as "coons" or "blackamoors"—have prevented contemporary critics from seeing what Mencken actually said. The truth is that Mencken despised the Nazi persecution of the Jews just as he condemned the suppression of civil liberties for blacks. Moreover, he saw both groups—and many others—as important contributors to the "cultural mosaic" of America.

himself. For the most part, Mayfield's recollections are unlikely to send many readers in search of Sara Haardt's writing. Failing to do that, the deeper and more valuable essence of her character—and what ultimately attracted Mencken to Sara—has never been explored.

I I

Sara was the firstborn of a couple for whom life was an everyday synthesis of foreign ideals and Southern heritage. On her father's side, Sara Haardt's forebears were among those who came to Montgomery from Germany seeking political freedom during the 1840s. Among the settlers who arrived in Alabama was Johannes Anton Haardt, a scholar from Otterberg, in the Rheinland-Pfalz, a district in Germany near Bavaria. In 1842, Johannes Anton emigrated to the United States, and in 1845, a scarce three years before Mencken's grandfather, Burkhard Ludwig Mencken, came to Baltimore, Johannes Anton settled in Montgomery and married a native from Otterberg, Phillipine Noreheimer, who bore him ten children between 1849 and 1866. Their son John Anton, born May 24, 1866, was to become Sara Haardt's father.

John Haardt was a man of keen business sense. Haardt Clothing, on Commerce Street, kept up a tradition of excellence for fifty years. On April 22, 1897, he married Venetia Hall, daughter of Joseph Newman Hall and Sarah Powell Farrar. John Haardt's new bride was a beautiful, brilliant, and strong-willed woman, known as "Queen Venetia" by her contemporaries. She had graduated as valedictorian from college, and her very manner commanded respect. Years later, there would be talk in Montgomery that the Venetia flower had been named after Venetia Hall.

Venetia's background was not German. The Farrars were related to a number of well-known Southern (especially Georgian and Virginian) families, including the Fields, Branches, Powells, and Jeffersons. The Southern connections of these families were never forgotten, and years later Sara Haardt, after her name had begun to appear in print, would hear frequently from distant relatives in the South. Sara, however, insisted that she was predominantly German and that the influence of Johannes Anton was particularly strong. She also thought, as she told Mencken, that her mixed ancestry was responsible for her early emancipation from the common run of Southern ideas. That Sara's vision of her native region was both obsessive and ambiguous is not surprising. Her German father had married a woman who had been raised as a true Southerner. The heritage of Johannes Anton was essentially liberal, skeptical, and tolerant; Venetia's was exactly the opposite: conservative, middle-class, and Episcopalian.

John Haardt and Venetia moved into a large corner house at 903 South Perry Street, at a time when it was considered to be one of the most prestigious neighborhoods of Montgomery. (Today, the old home is gone. What remains are two large oak trees, and in place of the old structure is Cook's Auto Repair.) There, Sara was born on March 1, 1898, and two years later Venetia gave birth to Ida, then John, Philippa, and Mary Kelley. But it was Sara whose birth was the most difficult. She was what they called a "blue baby"—born dead, according to her nurse. She failed to catch her breath after the usual spanking, even after the doctor had taken her by her heels and whirled her like a pinwheel in the air. Her doctor, Richard Frazer Michel, the first surgeon to enlist in the Confederate Army and who accompanied Beauregard to Fort Sumter at the very outbreak of war—literally breathed the first breath of life into Sara Haardt. He saved her a second time from death when she had smallpox, and a third time from typhoid. For the rest of her life Sara would battle against illness: from tuberculosis, from a lesion in her left eye, from appendicitis, and from the removal of a tubercular kidney. "When you've battled death since birth," she wrote, "and somehow weathered it through, it gives you a yen for the sweetness of life, that nothing short of death can take from you." For the next thirty-seven years this woman, whose frail body confined her to bed again and again, would try to live life to the fullest.

She was instilled with the spirit of the Southern way of life from the start. It was her mother, Sara wrote many years later, who "first taught me the charm of the South, the stranglehold it has upon every Southerner." Among the surviving photographs of Sara there is one which is as appropriate for Venetia as it was inappropriate for Sara. It was taken when Sara was three, when Venetia had enrolled her in a dancing school taught by Professor Weisner, a somewhat enigmatic figure: "the Gentiles thought he was a Gentile and the Jews thought he was a Jew; and no one could say where he came from or why a dancing master as talented as he could come to Montgomery." In the photograph Sara appears as a three-year-old, dressed in a long white dress, Empire style, wearing a leghorn hat trimmed in pink forget-me-nots and tied with pink saffron ribbons. Even the dancing slippers are exquisite—Venetia had painstakingly covered them with the same material as the dress. The picture tells us something about the South and about Venetia more than about Sara Haardt. Venetia, her daughter would write, was "fanatical about the South—its tropical beauty, Sherman's march to the Sea, the chivalry of Southern men." The truth is that, years later, Sara still could not bring herself to explain her reasons for not having remained in the South. When she compared herself to her mother, who completely identified herself as a Southerner, she contrasted her own "dark eyes and olive skin" with Venetia's green eyes, curly bronze hair, ivory and rose skin, and long pale hands, and felt "like an alien." For a long time Venetia had tried to instill in her daughter a love of the South, for a long time in vain.

If Sara sometimes found herself in silent conflict with her mother, life at the Haardt home was happy. Catherine Steiner, a close friend of the eldest siblings, Sara, Ida, and John, was often at their home and recalled the pleasant family atmosphere during mealtimes around the large dining room table. The conversation was warm and, with five children, boisterous. Their childhood was normal and, in many ways, Venetia tried to make it intellectual. After dinner, she would read stories aloud to all five children. It was not long before everyone recognized that it was Sara who was "the smart one." It is not surprising: her reading capacity was extraordinary; what is more, so was her comprehension and retention, for Sara was a gifted child who had spent the larger part of her life in books. She often sat on the front steps of the house, writing poems or helping her younger sisters and brother with the themes of their school compositions. Much of her poetry, like the photograph of Sara at Professor Weisner's dancing school, would be tied up in ribbons and stored in Venetia's trunk. The poetry not only shows Sara's romantic bent but also gives a foretaste of the themes she would explore in her later stories.

> Pressed butterfly,
> Embalmed death sentenced in your cell of glass,
> You of the pale, dream laden wings

Wan, golden prisoner of the past
Did your soul die, pressed butterfly?

What strange life-death,
Forever doomed to die, forever dead
You of the wonder painted hues
With wings uplifted and outspread
Do you want breath?
What strange life-death!

I broke the glass
to set you free. . .

Did your soul pass?
I broke the glass.

There were other poems, poems of magnolias and of the South, of which Mencken said that after reading them during the humid summers in Baltimore he immediately felt cooler. For the most part, however, Mencken considered poetry inferior to stories and novels, for he thought that poetry was simply the expression of the unbridled excesses of immature talent. None of Sara's poems was accepted for *The Smart Set*, so that she stopped submitting them in 1924 when Mencken initiated *The American Mercury*, contenting herself instead with collecting the poems of Alabama poets for the October 1926 issue of the magazine. Few of Sara's poems remain today. After Venetia died, Sara called Phillippa and requested her to take the poems out of their mother's trunk and return them to Baltimore so that she could have them burned.

When Sara was twelve Venetia enrolled her at the Margaret Booth School for Females, located on 117 Sayre Street. The Margaret Booth School was aristocratic, snobbish, and Victorian. Yet although it was a traditional school in a traditional city, it made some attempt to integrate the ways of the Old World with Northern progressivism. It had opened in 1914 with the aspiration of being a singular institution, accepting only those girls who showed enough promise to be college material. Nationally noted artists and speakers came to speak at a school which boasted the first student government and honor system in the state. It was a schoolhouse in a private home, limited in enrollment to one hundred girls, all from middle-class to upper-middle-class families. There, Sara was taught Latin, history of art, and French. Her reading included most of Shakespeare's plays, all of Charles Dickens, John Milton, and the essays of Emerson, with heavy emphasis on the English romantic poets, Shelley, Keats, and Wordsworth. Her teacher would later say that Sara was a "gifted girl," capable of excelling in many fields, but that in subjects that did not interest her "she did only enough not to be considered stupid." Her talent for writing was recognized at an early age; she was asked to compose the school song. The star pupil, she was encouraged by Margaret Booth to apply to the best colleges in the North.

Margaret Booth had strong ideas about discipline. Every morning, before class began, the pupils were obliged to recite the Lord's Prayer, then to sing the "Marseillaise" in French, and finally to answer roll call with quotations from Robert Browning. (Sara usually responded with tongue in cheek, "Only grant that I do serve/Else why want aught further of me. . ."). "Commencement," one of Sara's short stories, described life in the Margaret Booth School. It is a well-constructed piece, published in the August 1926 issue of *The American Mercury*, which tells us about Maryellen Thompson, the young girl who was "prettier, smarter than any girl in her class" but who was "doomed to stay in Meridian" because her father could not afford to send her to the school she deserved to attend. Sara used this story to express her own fear of a similar fate; when she was only seventeen her own father had died.

The death of her father was the beginning of difficult years for Sara. Besides suffering the social handicap of being German and thus not considered part of the *crème de la crème* of Montgomery society, the Haardts were now less affluent than they had once been. Sara Haardt was now obliged to live through the most trying of experiences and, at the same time, adjust to a melancholy house which had once been happy, close, and familiar. As in the case of many children growing up in this period, one's father was hardly seen, but his dominance and authority were keenly felt. It was Sara who fetched him his slippers after he came home from work, and who perched herself on his knee. The domestic authority of the house now rested on Venetia. And, although the senior John Haardt had left his family fairly well provided for, it was only thanks to the financial assistance of her maternal grandmother, Sarah Powell Farrar Hall, that Sara was not forced to remain in Montgomery as Maryellen in "Commencement" was "doomed" to stay in Meridian. Instead, Sara was to fulfill her dream of attending college in the North.

While Sara was still attending the Margaret Booth School, other changes were under way in Montgomery that would form a lasting influence upon her. Montgomery, which had looked upon itself as "the Paris of the South," a decorous city that kept control over lawless elements, was now undergoing a period of rapid change. Overnight, both industry and agriculture had expanded rapidly. By the end of the decade, the value of the city's manufactured products increased from three million dollars to nineteen. Construction projects were altering the city's appearance. Each new achievement seemed to bring profound economic and social upheavals to what had hitherto been a small, although bustling, genteel city. Finally, national attention was focused on Montgomery when the Wright brothers arrived in 1910 and founded a site for a flying school. Against "the powdery blue of an Alabama sky" Sara Haardt watched the Wright airplane "dip and glide like a drunken bird."

Despite all their commitment to tradition, Montgomerians could not escape the effect of the wrenching social upheavals brought by the new age. For Sara, these seemed "in some vague way, connected with my own secret ambitions, my escape from the sluggish South." Many factors precipitated the changes in social mores: increasing prosperity, a climate of doubt and uncertainty about old traditions, and a decline of moral standards brought on by the homogenizing effect of the First World War, with its mixture of regions and peoples. When the United States entered into the war in the spring of 1917, the government decided to establish an air depot to serve its southern training fields. Montgomery was chosen as the site because of its already existing airfields. The town immediately swarmed with soldiers: there were two aviation depots, and nearby Camp Sheridan with its 40,000 troops provided more than half as many men as were in the whole town itself. The arrival of thousands of soldiers and airmen from other regions left nothing unaffected, and for many, it altered life dramatically (as it would in the case of a friend of Sara's, Zelda Sayre, who would meet a young lieutenant named F. Scott Fitzgerald).

Montgomerians reacted to these newcomers in a multitude of ways.

If some resented the "Yankeeizing" of the capital of the Confederacy, others invariably became caught up in the expansive moods of patriotism and prosperity. Many of the young ladies welcomed the Northern men. In the ballroom of the Old Exchange Hotel, where Varina Howell, the wife of Jefferson Davis, was received as the First Lady of the Confederacy, Zelda Sayre, Sara Haardt, and "the first spirits of our generations" swirled in golden slippers and rainbow-colored skirts, dancing "from midnight until dawn at the thrilling dances of the holiday season." More frequent were the dances at the Oak Park Pavillion, given every Friday night. Among the belles who attended the dances to meet the newcomers were Catherine Steiner, Zelda Sayre, and Ida and Sara Haardt. All of them were accomplished dancers; Ida Haardt remembers Sara dancing nimbly up the steps with her partner and then down again. As more soldiers arrived in Montgomery, Venetia laid down a new set of rules for her girls: they were not allowed to come home separately on Friday nights because, she contended, it meant that they had been out on dates and not necessarily to the dance. Sara, Ida, and Catherine collaborated in a scheme whereby they used to meet under a tree at the edge of Oak Park and wait for each other. At the end of the evening they would come back to the house together, as if the party had just broken up. It worked for three weeks—"three good Fridays"—until Venetia discovered their ruse. The feeling Sara had (and which her contemporaries shared) was that they formed part of a new war generation. Zelda Fitzgerald summed up the new excitement of these times in an interview (never published) with Sara Haardt:

> Before 1905 or 1906, there was scarcely a ripple in our lives. Life itself seemed serene, almost smugly secure. . . .—and suddenly, almost the next day it seemed, everything was changed. Life had suddenly become exciting, dangerous; a crazy vitality possessed us. I felt it as I leaned over to fasten the straps of my skates the moment before I went sailing wildly down the middle of Perry Street hill, screeching at the top of my lungs and catching hold of the backs of automobiles as they dashed up the hill again. . . . then the war came and we had the inescapable feeling that all this beauty and fun—everything—might be over in a minute. We couldn't wait, we couldn't afford to wait, for fear it would be gone forever; so we pitched in furiously, dancing every night and

riding up and down the moonlit roads and even swimming in the gravel pools under that white Alabama moon that gives the world a strange, lovely touch of madness.

Throughout her life Sara would be able to draw upon the experience of these early days. Unlike her peers, the sobering side to the war— and, in turn, all wars—did not go unnoticed by Sara. By herself or with friends she wandered into the other half of Montgomery, into the neighborhoods "cut by railroad boards and quartered by cotton mills" where lived "the mill hands or white trash" and "the ratty, two-story section" of "weather cracked dwellings that was spoken of as 'a fairly nice good neighborhood.' " She ventured also into the black neighborhoods, where she observed children or the woman she named Callie Scott, a black woman who "shut herself in great loneliness, shunning everybody, except her flowers and the strange white men who visited the house occasionally after dark." More often, Sara wandered through the cool marble corridors of the Confederate wing of the Capitol, where the guards, "wearing the Confederate grey and the bronze cross of the UDC with especial reverence, took care not to miss the polished brass cuspidors," told her largely fabricated stories of the Civil War. Although General Pickett had remained behind a barn while his troops dashed to their death at Gettysburg, old Captain Faulkner had entertained her as a child on the capitol portico with accounts of Pickett's heroism.* Years later, she would realize that it was "a matter of pride and not of principle that held the guard into such irrevocable and bitter fiction." But at the time the words, "dron-

---

* Pickett's charge—the action which ended the battle of Gettysburg on July 3, 1863—has always been controversial. There is credence to the belief that General Pickett may have not led his troops but instead let them march on while he stayed at the Cordori Barn not 200 yards short of the goal. That Pickett did not stay with his troops seems to have been well known to many officers of both armies who were present at the battle, and it was apparently known by well-informed Confederate authorities. For further discussion, see: *The Third Day at Gettysburg: Pickett's Charge* (Alan M. Hollingworth and James M. Cox, New York: Henry Holt and Co., 1959); *Where was Pickett at Gettysburg?* (Monroe F. Cockrell, Atlanta: Emory University Library, December 10, 1949); *Pickett or Pettigrew?* (Captain W. R. Bond, Scotland Neck, N.C.: W.L.L. Hall, 1888).

ing like a bee in the honeysuckle," swept the young child into "a mystery darker and more deeply personal than the tragedy at Gettysburg." Here we have the picture of a solitary and sensitive girl, weighed down by a burden of the past, by the South's psychological and symbolic inheritance, nourished by a sense of moral guilt. In the most formative years of her life the somber realization of war is crystallized during one Memorial Day parade, when a minister, of corn-fed opulence, with square shoulders and a voice of brass, declares that the war of the Confederacy is not a lost cause. Sara would remember:

> I trembled ecstatically at his words, as Callie had said the flowers trembled when they drank in the dew and the sunshine; yet, at the core of my being, I felt that tangible, dreadful cold. I saw Callie's face in the deepening shadows, and I seemed to hear Callie's voice despairing. Under those hollow mounds and crumbling stones were dead soldiers in a lost cause! Stone dead they were, deader than last year's roses— not just sleeping. Their cause was not a guiding star but a muttering in old men's throats; its fury was no more than the thrashing of moth's wings in the dying light.

The burden of the past all Southerners ultimately identify with is finally realized. As the young girl turns away from the speaker, the mystery "darker and more deeply personal than the tragedy at Gettysburg" is unlocked:

> Through the web of light and shadow I saw Callie Scott walking swiftly, mockingly, like some vision that was woven of the mysterious texture of the night, and as I watched her it came to me clearly that if I had not extracted any secret from the past, I could never hope to know any in the future. Pain and pride, and death for my pain—these were my final heritage.

In the autumn of 1916, Sara Haardt left Montgomery and boarded the train for the long ride north to the heart of Baltimore, toward Goucher College, a mass of gray buildings through which passed generations of unusual American women. The pride of Goucher College was that it was one of the few women's colleges to stress a solid liberal education. Not without reason, its students felt offended if any outsider referred to it as a "finishing school." Then, as now, it was known to be a "quiet" school. "The characteristics of the Goucher undergraduate that has [*sic*] been more frequently commented upon than any other is the devotion of students to work," Sara would tell the Alumnae Council upon her graduation in 1920. It was also true that Sara, described by her friends as a "soulful high-brow," worked harder than most. She majored in history but also concentrated in English, psychology, and philosophy. (Perhaps it was just as well for her matrimonial future, for Mencken maintained that a steady diet of literature produced only "learned idiots.") During her college career, she was editor in chief of the school's three publications: the literary magazine (the *Kalends*), the newspaper (*The Weekly*), and the yearbook (*The Donnybrook Fair*). After her sophomore year, when her grandmother's death left her short of funds, Sara was forced to take a job as college postmistress in order to earn extra money. This must have made her feel somewhat apart from everyone else, not only from the girls of her hometown but also from those at Goucher. Many of her classmates saw only her serious side. They could not have imagined Sara dancing the Charleston, or up and down the stairs of the Oak Park Pavillion. She was not at all the flapper, as were some of the other Goucher girls. Instead, her classmates found her to be "a beautiful charming flower, just a little past its prime." Her coeditors at *The Weekly* found Sara to be an "individualist" who was not "wild about any groups." By the time Sara Haardt graduated in 1920 the two articles which appeared side by side in the society page of the Montgomery *Advertiser* did not surprise anyone: one announced Zelda Sayre's engagement to F. Scott Fitzgerald, the other Sara's election to Phi Beta Kappa.

Perhaps financial difficulties may, in part, have kept Sara from being in the height of fashion or in her "prime." A better explanation of her seriousness may have been, as she told Mencken years later, the Spartan wartime diet of the college. With it, her health began to fail. Easter vacation in 1917 coincided with the United States entering into World War I and in its own way the event exacerbated Sara's precarious health. At a meeting of the students' organization on April 12, 1917, Dr. Lillian Welsh, professor of physical education and hygiene, presented a plan which she said would aid the Goucher student, not necessarily for war, but for life. She said she wished each student would endeavor to form correct habits as to diet, and she requested Goucher women to abstain from eating needlessly between meals. The Goucher College

Plan was written in the form of a pledge (among them one for food conservation) and was enthusiastically adopted and signed by the students, who, as Sara wrote, were at this time caught up in the fervor of patriotism. The meals at dinner continued to be sparse. Contributing to the poor diet was a shortage of coal, which, in December 1917, forced many professors to hold their classes in the residence halls of the college.

If to her classmates she seemed a "loner" and "self-sufficient," it was because her pride made her deal with her anxieties about dwindling finances, a full work load, and ill health without demanding any sympathy or understanding. That was the basis of her courage, what Mencken referred to as her "gallantry" when she confronted painful operations and later her own death. Then, too, as with Mencken, when Sara felt dispirited or just simply, as she put it, ready to leap into the Chesapeake, she would disappear and would not reappear in public until she felt that she had regained her self-control. All this did not prevent Sara throughout her college years from being an active member of the sorority "Tri Delt," where she entertained her sorority sisters by playing the guitar and singing songs like "Danny Boy," "Willy the Weeper," and her favorite, "Frankie and Johnny." Late at night, when the women gathered in a friend's dormitory room and the lights were turned off, Sara would mesmerize her audience with chilling ghost stories. Or others might have found Sara and other members of her class at Bosley's Drug Store, on the corner of Charles Street, drinking a "dope" (Coca-Cola with an aspirin in it) and planning ways to recruit freshmen into activities. What remained engrossing about Sara was that underneath the languid seriousness was what Sara Mayfield called her "playfulness, a flash of ironic humor."

There were two sides to Sara. The surprise which filled many people upon meeting her derived from the extreme contrast from what one had been led to expect. Her friend Mary Parmenter summed up the duality of her character in an obituary of her friend: "Those who did not know her well sometimes did not understand her unique blend of 'realism' and 'romanticism,'—what in her sophomore days she used to call 'getting the low down' and 'decking the honeysuckle.' " There was her "wicked sense of the ridiculous," which contrasted with her "tragic feeling for beauty and the mutability of all things," the "keen tongue" alternating with "the soft voice." Because Sara felt free from the need of the approval of others, she was uninhibited in saying what she actually thought. In her religion class the students were horrified when Dr. Bell tried to reconcile the theory of evolution with the Holy Scriptures—but not Sara, who ridiculed her classmates for their simple, childlike faith, saying "you all want people to bring people out of their hats." (Incidentally, she received an *A*.)

To the coeds of Goucher, Sara was a genuine sophisticate. She was exotic, beguiling, fascinating. In later years she wrote about her "painfully happy" years at Goucher for a column that included F. Scott Fitzgerald's reminiscences on Princeton and George Jean Nathan's on Cornell. Sara had truly fond memories of Goucher, but at the same time one cannot avoid the suspicion that she was more of an observer than a participant. Her element of diffidence was noted as follows by Isabelle Diffenderfer Yates, a member of Tri Delt:

> Sara was always the lady—always proper, always reserved. She was certainly not smug, but she was a little bit superior, more than just aloof. After all, she had such a very fine mind, and she thought the rest of us who were interested in going to the Naval Academy hops, and so forth, were just childish. She was there to study and make good, which she certainly did.

The enigmatic element of Sara Haardt's character puzzled her fellow students, who felt, as one of them complained, "nobody got really close to Sara Haardt . . . no matter how friendly you were to her, she just had that aloofness to her nature, and you never felt you had your hands on the full Sara at one time."

Aloofness, this independence of spirit, naturally propelled Sara into forming friendships with older people. In her speech before the Alumnae Council she stressed that it was the relationship between faculty and student that had made her college years worthwhile. "Their relations stand for all that embodies confidence, inspiration, and understanding. She [the student] turns to them for this, but also more naturally, as friends." Those to whom Sara did turn were a primary force in leading her to become a writer. Miss Ola Elizabeth Winslow tutored her in writing and coached her for the freshman short story contest, which she won. Once "The Rattlesnake" had appeared in the

Kalends Sara became editorial assistant, ultimately rising in position to editor in chief and manager of a staff of twenty-two girls. In 1919 she took classes under Harry T. Baker. Baker, an eastern editor who had worked for *Cosmopolitan, Good Housekeeping,* and *The Smart Set,* led a solitary and gloomy life in Baltimore, which aroused the curiosity of the Goucher girls. Every year at commencement Baker would come to the ceremony with his travel bag in hand, and the instant it was over he would take off his academic robes and head for the railroad station. In the many years Baker taught at Goucher he never rose above the position of assistant professor of English; nonetheless, Sara and her classmates learned to have a deep respect for him. He possessed a fine critical sense and, rarer still, took an honest interest in his students. Sara never forgot his kindness, and, in later years, saw him and Ola Elizabeth Winslow frequently.

The four years at Goucher College had stimulated her curiosity and broadened her intellectual horizons. The return home to Montgomery for each summer vacation was now difficult for her. Years later, the letters she wrote to Mencken about staying home ("stuck," she called it) reflect a somber tone which Zelda Sayre echoed in the phrase "Nothing ever seems to happen" in her story "Southern Girl." But for Sara, it was more than a question of being free from the boredom of her hometown; it was rather a rebellion against a sense of human limitation. As part of a program that Mencken called her "revolt against the threadbare Confederate metaphysic" she spent her summer vacation in 1919 lobbying for Alabama politicians. There she headed Alabama's branch of the National Women's Party, and organized a campaign to persuade the legislature to enfranchise women. Montgomery's mayor and state senator, William A. Gunter, who had known her as a child, invited Sara and her friends to City Hall to speak on the issue. Eventually, however, they did not win enough votes to carry ratification. For her, with this introductory instance, politics provided a frustrating example, giving her the feeling that her talents were not put to their fullest use. She came to detest politics (years hence she would have to be dragged to the polls), and she knew that once the rallies were over, everything would remain the same. "How like the South that is," she wrote. "How irreconcilable!"

Meanwhile, her impatience with home life in Montgomery continued. On each visit home Sara found that nothing had really changed.

"It's like being buried alive," she scrawled on a scrap of paper. "The same old bore mouthing the same old platitudes. Nobody with any sense to talk to much less to have a date with . . . at least I don't pretend to be a lot of things I'm not." The social life of the well-to-do continued to be focused on the women's clubs, the ladies' literary clubs, the country club. Montgomery's economic boom may have changed the landscape, but in its place was a new plutocracy, a new society which, she observed, was "steadily reducing life to comfortable mediocrity." Less than ten years after she returned to Montgomery from her first visit to the North, she wrote:

> Indifference, insouciance, regardless—that is what the Confederacy is all over, never was there a country that argues less for its prophets. And it isn't a matter of principles, I may add, it is a state of mind. Prosperity, of course, the prosperity of a new and teeming society is the secret of it. Never has the South been so rich, so new, so splurgy. Every Southern state from the Carolinas to Texas are [*sic*] on the throes of a revolution, economic, political, and social. . . . As the land turns into money overnight, new cultures supplant the old, and the new cultures must be obvious and showy, easily capitalized—unaccountable! "Something spiffy," one literary lady put it, as she sought the novel of her taste in a rental library. Spiffy: . . . these are, you will observe, the very latest, startling in a way; the fad. . . .

Sara found that in the Southern literary renaissance there had been no real transformation of those pseudoliterary types of Montgomery who, according to their own principles, were the harbingers of good taste and culture. In one of her most acute essays, "Literary Life in the Cotton Belt," she described what she saw as the irresponsibility of that very class of citizens whose support and cultivation of new young writers the Southern literary renaissance depended upon.

Sara was now teaching history at the Margaret Booth School in Montgomery, where she became the chairman of its history department. Margaret Booth found that her former pupil possessed the unique power with the students of "interesting them in their work"—no small feat for a young woman directly out of college and with no teaching experience. To the underclassmen she seemed remote and mysterious, "a born writer who *looked* a born heroine." Many of them tried to imitate her slow, graceful movements; others, her large, legible handwriting. Montgomery at this time set a high priority on education. The city invested more money per student than either Mobile or Birmingham, and by 1930 Montgomery County could claim that it had the lowest rate of illiteracy in any county or metropolis in the South. So it must have been a cause of surprise to her friends that Sara did not remain in Montgomery to pursue a career in teaching in her hometown. However, instead of staying in Montgomery, Sara accepted an offer from Goucher College in 1922 to join the English faculty at $1500 a year. At age twenty-four, she was the youngest member of the department, teaching English composition and an introductory course in literature. At the same time she decided to study for an advanced degree in psychology at the Johns Hopkins University. She once said flippantly that she chose psychology because "I found it amusing," when what she was actually interested in was seeing how psychology and creative writing could interrelate. When she informed her mother of her decision, Venetia, with tears in her eyes (Sara would write that her mother was one of those rare women who could weep beautifully), told her daughter that the decision was an important and final one. "I did not say the word *forever* but she knew, as only she could know, that I meant it," Sara would write a few months after her mother's death. "There was no halfway measure possible to Southerners. You either live in the South or you leave the South. Forever." After this, they both knew Sara would never return to the South or view it in the same way again.

Nor did she. Never once did she seriously consider returning to Montgomery to live for any great length of time. Her self-imposed exile from the South was not chosen out of rebellion. That part of the country had simply become a past memory, a place, she would write to Mencken, of graves and "tombstones." Yet despite this reaction against the South, Sara never really freed herself of the fascination it held for her. On each visit home, she could become entranced anew with the region. Writing to Mencken in 1930, she commented on the Southern scene: "Darling: This morning I awoke in the deep South, and despite my lamentations, I confess that I was strangely excited. . . ." Again, some years later, she would write:

> Why this sentimentality about the South, about home? . . . The truth
> was that I could have latched on to the sweet moulding decay that

surrounded me, and convinced myself that it was brave, romantic. . . .
I loved the old war songs and the perfume of the magnolias, like any
other; and I could have lived my days talking about them and repining.

As a Southerner living in the north, she understood, more clearly and
deeply than most, that the conflict between the Old and the New
South continued unabated; as the product of two cultures, she realized
that this continuing battle was also being waged in her own self. Into
this self-contradicting world of an intellectual rejection of the South
and a sentimental attraction to "the damp rotting leaves and the bruised
petals of roses wired into grinning designs" now stepped the com-
manding figure of H. L. Mencken, who was so profoundly to influence
both her writing and her personal life.

III

It is interesting to speculate whether Sara Haardt would have been a
different writer if H. L. Mencken's essay "The Sahara of the Bozart"
had not been published. In it Mencken made the strongest of his early
attacks on Southern "Kultur," harshly denouncing the South, which
had been the seat of American civilization, for having become in 1917
"almost as sterile, artistically, intellectually, and culturally as the
Sahara Desert" despite all the "wealth and 'progress' it babbles of."
He mocked what he called this "vast plain of mediocrity, stupidity,
lethargy, almost of dead silence," a land of "barbarism" where "free
inquiry is blocked by the idiotic certainties of ignorant men." But he
reserved his attack for its literature. These criticisms were, of course,
hotly rejected in the South, which responded with a series of name-
callings labeling Mencken variously as a "cockroach," and a "jackass."
James Branch Cabell, writing from Richmond, observed that "a lynching party awaited H. L. Mencken at all points south of Maryland."
   However, Mencken's bemoaning the sterility of Southern literature
in 1917 did not prevent him from befriending and encouraging Southern writers and editors, a great many of whom began to ask themselves
whether perhaps there was not a great deal of truth in what he had to
say. "The Sahara of the Bozart" served as a catalyst, as, according to
Frederick C. Hobson, Jr. (in his study, *Serpent in Eden*), "an impetus for
Southerners to examine their native culture in a manner to which

Southerners had not been accustomed." It was followed in 1921 by
another of Mencken's essays, "The South Begins to Mutter." His
challenge, that the South needed criticism, gave evidence of his serious
interest in the new direction of Southern writing and identified specific
Southern groups which he felt would lead the way. Mencken was
especially interested in *The Reviewer*, edited by a Virginian named Emily
Clark. This magazine was rapidly becoming the kind of publication
Mencken had envisioned: it was publishing little-known Southern writers he had recommended—Julia Peterkin, Frances Newman, DuBose
Heyward, and, later, Sara Haardt, all of whom abandoned the South's
genteel tradition of romantic excesses and instead embraced Mencken's
mixture of realism and romanticism. Early in 1921, Mencken had
written to Emily Clark: "In general, your chief aim should be to develop
new Southern authors," and again, in 1922: "What is needed in the
South is a realistic discussion of Southern problems by Southerners."
Mencken's involvement with *The Reviewer* and also with *The Double
Dealer*, the two most prominent magazines of the early Southern renaissance, together with his support of several other literary endeavors,
suggests the importance of his role in developing Southern letters
immediately following the appearance of "The Sahara of the Bozart."

It should be noted that Mencken also perceived *The Reviewer* as a
proving ground for new writers who might be selected later for his
own magazine, a significant development in the career of Sara Haardt
in particular. "One might suggest," Frances Newman observed, "that
Mencken farmed out prominent young writers to *The Reviewer* just as
Mr. John J. McGraw farms out prominent young pitchers to Min-
neapolis and Birmingham, and then brings them out to his *Mercury*
when they are sufficiently experienced." By the mid 1920s many Southerners had come to hail Mencken as the principal instigator of the
revival of Southern literature. Frances Newman held this estimate in
the "Books" section of the New York *Herald Tribune*, in which she
described "the present literary activity in the late Confederate states"
as "almost certainly" the product of Mencken's indictment. She made
the same claim in the Atlanta *Journal*, where she added that Julia
Peterkin, Emily Clark, Mr. and Mrs. Julian Harris, and Sara Haardt,
"together with at least one half dozen other Southern writers, would
all, I am sure, happily acknowledge what Mencken has done for them."
Perhaps a literary renaissance would have occurred without Mencken's

help, but as Hobson has suggested, it is unlikely that any other critic would have been so influential. Mencken had become, in essence, "a mentor for those Southerners who were tired of their own genteel tradition." It is interesting to note that long before Sara had met Mencken she would be defending the value of his articles with her professors at Goucher.

In small, tentative steps, Sara Haardt started in earnest to explore her background as early as 1916 when, at Goucher College, she won the freshman English prize for her short story "The Rattlesnake." At that point, she had not yet developed, to an appreciable extent, her ironic view of her native Alabama. The motivation for the use of vague settings in her college fiction was explained thus in her 1918 editorial for the issue of *Kalends*: "A story does not have to have names. For a real story deals with the battering shuttle of fate." In another editorial, in the issue for April 1920, she modified this view somewhat, and also anticipated the direction of her own work, when she criticized the contributions to the magazine as "harmless and colorless and empty, primarily because of suppressed personality. Like the chameleon, the manuscripts are affected by every known life except the power of one's own individuality." Although in her case the setting of "The Rattlesnake" was vague, the choice of theme indicated that she would later return again to her native region for inspiration. The small-town atmosphere of the circus in "The Rattlesnake" is highly reminiscent of the small-town atmosphere Sara knew in Montgomery. Rejecting the view that the circus life was always exciting and colorful, Sara conceived of it rather as corrupt. "The Rattlesnake" expresses her impatience with the artificiality of this particular society's cultivation of appearance. This element of social criticism made her work particularly appealing to Emily Clark, and later to H. L. Mencken. By July 1922, *The Reviewer* had accepted a series of sketches Sara had written about small town Alabama men and women entitled "Strictly Southern."

Sara began to develop a new concept of form and subject after she had submitted two stories to Mencken, only to have them returned. According to his biographers, Mencken sent Sara a letter rejecting one of them on the grounds that he had far too many stories on spinsters already. But what is not generally known are the contents of the previously unpublished second half of the same letter of June 1923, in which Mencken made suggestions that undoubtedly profoundly inspired the aspiring young author:

> . . . It has a sort of second-hand air: you are looking at its people through a knothole in the fence, not living with them. Why don't you try to get a story or two out of the fair creature we discussed the other day—the flamingo on Main Street? What a picture! Montgomery must be alive with stories. Who is the town beau? Why not embalm him? The fashionable dentist? The leading amateur violinist?

The advice was important in encouraging Sara to write realistic fiction, utilizing her Southern background. Buoyed by his suggestion, Sara sent Mencken more stories and in her letter of June 24 expressed her enthusiasm for his suggestions: "I had a grand time doing it. This sort of thing does come more natural." She then sent him a new story, entitled "Joe Moore and Callie Balsingame." When this was accepted she again wrote Mencken to express "My joy over your taking 'Joe Moore and Callie Balsingame,' " a development, she admitted, that "was so perfect that I was afraid it was a dope dream. I have at least a hundred more that I want to do, including the town undertaker."

"Joe Moore and Callie Balsingame" was published in *The Smart Set* in October 1923; it was written only one year after Sara had left Montgomery, in her phrase, "to pluck up the roots and carve a career in the alien North," and it was her first story to be published in Mencken's magazine. Shortly thereafter, Mencken decided to leave *The Smart Set* and began editing a new magazine of his own creation. *The American Mercury*, Mencken wrote Sara, would be "something of a variety hitherto unknown in the Republic," for it would cover "the whole national scene—politics, education, the sciences, the fine arts," all in the aim of "setting up an organ of educated Toryism": in short, it was to be "the best damned journal in the Republic." It seemed natural to Mencken that at this time in American life such a magazine was desperately needed. Perhaps at no other time in their history did the American people undergo such profound changes in their ways of life and thought as they did in the years that began with the Armistice and ended with the stock market crash. When it began the horse and buggy still lingered. It ended with the roar of cars and airplanes. In the space of a decade industrial production increased almost 50 percent and the national income grew from 79.1 billion dollars to almost 88 billion. The Ku Klux Klan increased from a few hundred members before the war to more than 4 million in the mid 1920s. It was an era, wrote F. Scott Fitzgerald, in which "America was going on the greatest, gaudiest spree in history." He also wrote that "it was characteristic of the Jazz Age that it had no interest in politics at all." Harding's successor, Calvin Coolidge, was entirely sympathetic to American business, and "Coolidge prosperity" was to increase and last for seven years. Outside this general boom stood the farmers and other industries, notably coal and cotton, but most of America rejoiced at its prosperity and consumed and spent.

The post-World War I decade had presented Mencken with a unique opportunity: peace and prosperity had produced an atmosphere in which confidence was a veneer on top of confusion and conflict. Mencken, seeing through the superficiality, was among the first to criticize the suppression of civil liberties, the law, and the deterioration of the quality and traditions of American life. If there seems to be too much stress on Prohibition in Mencken's writings it was because, in the words of one of his biographers, Charles A. Fecher, Prohibition was to Mencken "the ultimate and grossest violation of those individual liberties which Mencken so cherished." The Scopes trial to him was not simply the case of a Dayton, Tennessee, schoolmaster being tried for teaching Darwin's theory of evolution, but a trial that concerned man's freedom of speech, and thus a trial that concerned every American. And so forth. No other periodical was as scathing or as thorough in its criticism of America. To have a copy of *The American Mercury* (albeit an old one) on the coffee table was considered a sign of culture. College students carried issues with them; discussion of its articles showed that one belonged in the world of modern ideas.

Undoubtedly there is a relationship between Mencken's demand for realistic fiction and Sara's subsequent stories and articles. In his letters to Sara through late July and August of 1923, Mencken tried to inspire articles of a social nature: "Anything that interests you: the South, the American university, the Anglo-Saxon, anything." He also added that she should not imitate the rest of his contributors, who are "a bit nervous, fearing that I shall advocate assassinating Coolidge in the first issue. After two or three numbers it will be easier. I resign Coolidge to God." Sara responded enthusiastically: "I am mad to do something on several Southern scenes of a social cast. . . . I am tremendously interested in the social phenomena hereabout and it would be wonderful to paint them." Unfortunately, the topics Sara had in mind—the Southern gentleman, women's suffrage, the university "as a small town on wheels but minus the usual small town thrills"—either were not used by Mencken or were not completed by her.

Shortly before Christmas, 1923, Sara had become so ill with tuberculosis that her writing was put to a temporary halt. She finally told herself: "I'm going to stop this three-ring circus I'm running. I finally found out you can't teach and study for an advanced degree and write a novel at the same time without one of them going bad on you." Her friends Marjorie Nicolson and Sara Mayfield took care of Sara in her room, but she begged them not to write home and worry her family. (One guesses, however, that she did not want to return to Montgomery and admit failure.) For the next year she stayed at the Maple Heights Sanitorium, fifteen miles from Baltimore, on a steep hill nicknamed "The Alp" by Mencken.

During the period of Sara's recuperation Mencken lent her books which he considered models of realism: the latest published work of Ring Lardner, Edgar Lee Masters, Ludwig Lewisohn, and especially Sinclair Lewis. It was the example of Sinclair Lewis's realism which Mencken would most impress upon Sara. Just one year earlier, Mencken had written in "Violets of the Sahara": "What the South needs, above all, is a Main Street—that is, a realistic presentation of its backward poor white society." To which he added: "The Confederate Sinclair Lewis will be lucky if he is not lynched. But appear he will, sooner or later" and "that day the Southern letters will be born." It is reasonable to suppose that Mencken was trying to set Sara in this direction, for many of her characters are poor whites. During his visits with Sara, they would discuss the books he lent her. Often, their literary conversation on the importance of realism in fiction would go on for so long that Mencken had to race down the Alpine hill of the sanitorium so as not to miss the train back to Baltimore.

Mencken's company not only afforded Sara an intellectual stimulus, it raised her spirits at an especially difficult time for her. At this time Lillian Welsh, medical advisor to Goucher College, wrote to Sara telling her that in view of her poor health, she need not return to teach at Goucher College the following semester. The letters from Miss Welsh and President William Westley Guth were a blow to Sara, for it meant she would have to find a different means of support in order to pay her bills at the sanitorium. Mencken's reaction was typical: he suggested they fire off President Guth and Lillian Welsh in a rocket and blow up the school. But beyond this facetious reaction, he was deeply concerned and attempted to send her a sum of money for her medical expenses. His attentiveness and protectiveness provided Sara with encouragement to continue her writing, even while hospitalized in the sanitorium. There she observed the nurses, the doctors, and the patients, all of whom would later emerge in a short story, "Licked," highly praised by the critics and, ironically, by President Guth himself. Her confinement put her into a mood of homesickness, of nostalgia for the comfort and security of her childhood in Montgomery.

It is not surprising, therefore, that the work which Sara submitted to the *The American Mercury* immediately following her seclusion at the Maple Heights Sanitorium all reflect her Southern heritage, using a critical approach recommended by Mencken. "Alabama" particularly reflects Mencken's guidance. In it, the author utilizes a specifically Southern background as a vehicle for a larger, generalized truth. Mencken was so pleased with it that he asked his other writers to write about their own states in the same manner, sending them copies of "Alabama" to follow as an example. "A Mendelian Dominant," written shortly thereafter, also demonstrates the influence of Mencken. That all its completeness of meaning should be expressed so subtly by someone who still considered herself an incipient author is little short of amazing. Mencken himself was highly impressed, writing Sara that he was so "won over by its high merits that I am slapping it into type at once," and a few days later he added that his assistant, Charles Angoff, was also "immensely pleased." The thematic treatment of "A Mendelian Dominant" is distinctly Southern.

It would be inaccurate to classify Sara Haardt as simply a realistic or naturalistic writer, a potential Sinclair Lewis or Theodore Dreiser of the South. She complained that Lewis lacked human soul, to which Mencken responded: "I never said that Lewis was a great artist. I said that he was a great technician—that he managed his novels superbly, especially 'Babbitt.' He is far more scientist than artist." On this there was not a contradiction: Mencken admired the naturalistic technique but rejected his belief that art could be an objective, scientific representation of life. In his reviews of various authors, he had remarked on the inability of the naturalist to do the one thing necessary to achieve the highest form of art: that is, to involve his reader emotionally with the central figures of his creation. In this aloofness was both the strength and weakness of Lewis as an artist. In his judgment of other novelists, Mencken was equally strict. His explanation of the inability of the British author Arnold Bennett to create memorable characters is in line with the comment in his letter to Sara about Sinclair Lewis: "The attitude of the author toward them remains, in the end, the attitude of a biologist toward his laboratory animals. He does not *feel* with them—and neither does the reader." Sara Haardt's own work described in naturalistic fashion the Southern settings and the men and women who were prisoners of their environment, but, like Mencken, she did not subscribe to exclusively naturalistic or realistic presentations. Her aim, instead, was to achieve those qualities Mencken had admired in Dreiser, who was able "not merely to record, but to translate and understand; the thing he exposes is not the empty event and act, but the endless mystery out of which it springs; his pictures have a compassion to them that is hard to separate from poetry." This insistence on poetic realism not only became the major theme of Mencken's criticism of the early 1920s but also served as a counterbalance to the kind of social satire fiction that he was helping to promote. He may have thought, with the passing of the "Genteel Tradition," with its idealism and sentimentality, that younger writers were swinging to the other extreme and depicting life as nothing but a farce. In Sara Haardt's case, her main goal was to achieve a balance between satire and sympathetic understanding. Under Mencken's guidance, she reflected in her stories two visions of the South: the romantic and the realistic. Her stories not only record the South as perceived through the sensibility of a Southern writer but depict the soul-searching of an author seeking to come to terms with her past in a pursuit of identity.

From short stories Sara Haardt turned to film. This was a field in which she had no experience. According to Mencken, however, this did not constitute any obstacle. After reading her ideas for scripts, he was particularly attracted to one that dealt with Confederate soldiers escaping to Brazil (*Way Down South*). Recognizing its originality and potential, he wrote enthusiastically of the project: "This, I think, is really a picture. It moves from the straight and is nine-tenths pure action. I think the chances it offers ought to stir up any movie man. He will probably suggest some flag waving in the end." That *Way Down South* would have aroused the interest of Mencken is not surprising, in view of the current state of cinema. Of the thousands of films made in the 1920s and of the hundreds of directors who made them, very few were memorable.

By 1927, the year Sara Haardt went to Hollywood, the industry was already in decline. The major complaint, to a large extent justified, was that too many people were staying home to listen to the radio. American exhibitors reported half-empty houses on the night the Jack Dempsey-Gene Tunney fight was broadcast. But it was not only that radio was a threat to the studio; the public had wearied of the quality of the productions offered by Hollywood and was losing interest in this form of entertainment. The silent film, depending basically as it did on mime, had reached a point of no return.

Early in the fall of 1927, Sara's writing had attracted the notice of a film company, Famous Players-Lasky, which would later become Paramount Pictures. The studio, established in 1912 by Adolph Zukor, had a reputation for producing big films. Zukor's first production was *Queen Elizabeth* starring Sara Bernhardt, for the then unheard-of price of eighteen thousand dollars. Through a campaign of lavish advertising, the film netted sixty thousand dollars. From then on the studio began to buy up the best plays and contracted a celebrated troupe of actors to work under the title of Famous Players, among them Mary Pickford and Charles Chaplin. By the 1920s, the Famous Players-Lasky Studio would contract writers for a five- to six-week stint, then retain their services if they provided usable material. The suggestion that Sara Haardt be invited to join was, as Mencken biographer Carl Bode has rightly said, a tribute both to her work and to Mencken's influence. She had already begun to be known for her short stories, and under Mencken's direction they had improved to the point that in 1924 she was included in the "Roll of Honor of American Short Stories" and in "The Best Short Stories" for that year. Mencken himself had suggested to his old friend, Walter Wanger, producer of Famous Players, that Sara be considered for one of their contracts. On April 27, 1927, Mencken typed a note to Sara, asking her to meet him in order to be introduced to a "movie man."

The "movie man" turned out to be Herman Mankiewicz, then an executive of Famous Players. Years later he would be known for his contribution to (some say authorship of) *Citizen Kane*. In those days, he read scripts and wrote titles to films and was Wanger's right-hand man. He had the ability to recognize fresh material when he saw it, and when Mencken relayed to Sara his reaction to her materials the tone was jubilant: "A letter from Mankiewicz says of you: 'Her stuff seems to be just what we're looking for. . . .' Hooray!" Sara promptly set off for Hollywood, encouraged by the enthusiasm of Mencken, whose prediction to her was that "you will go to Hollywood as a literary gal, and remain a screen star. When they see you there will be a riot." He advised her to stay at the Hotel Mark Twain, and to contact his friend the critic Jim Tully. "I'd rather be with him than any of the gaudy vacuums who infest Hollywood," he said.

It may seem odd that Mencken, who had a rather dim view of Hollywood writers, should have prompted Sara to work in Hollywood. Years earlier, he had written in *The Smart Set* that Los Angeles swarmed with literary aspirants of little worth:

> Every writer of movie scenarios out there is at work upon a novel, and nine tenths of the fair, frail and fat victims of the local swamis appear to have an itch for the short story. . . . The subject matter of this Los Angeles literature is not what gives it its distinction; the thing that genuinely marks it is its infernal badness. . . . The town really enjoys a vague eminence: it houses more bad authors than New York.

The same criticism continued in *Prejudices VI*, published the same year Sara went to Hollywood. In it Mencken maintained that the movie magnates who had put their faith in novelists and playwrights were taking "bad medicine." He continued his attack, arguing: "The fact that a man can write a competent novel is absolutely no reason for assuming he can write a competent film. The two things are as unlike as Pilsner and Coca-Cola." The fact that this did not prevent him from promoting the movie-making career of Sara is explained by the simple statement that he made to her that this would "bring enough money to let you do what you want." Privately, he wrote to Jim Tully: "If she could get together only a few thousand dollars it would enable her to write her novel. In view of her health it is hard for her to do hack work, and she has had a difficult time." In any event, had not Mencken maintained that starving artists do not produce good work, that it was far better to work at one film script than earn the equivalent (or less) for writing for a series of pulp magazines? And writing screenplays, he wrote Sara, was not necessarily synonymous with doing "trashy stuff." Instead, he said, one should approach the whole matter philosophically. Perhaps Maugham, Waugh, and Faulkner were able to exit, as Mencken advised Sara to do, like "Ring Lardner: laughingly." But this was the sort of work that could break the spirit of many a good writer, especially those who were in dire straits: it almost broke Sara's.

Sara saw in Hollywood the possibility of realizing what a struggling author most needed—not the glamour (she was less enraptured with it than Mencken had been on his visit with Hergesheimer the year before), the damning Hollywood standard—but something much more substantial: large amounts of money, which new writers could earn to subsidize their literary careers. What Sara detested most in Hollywood, more than its vulgarity, was its hypocrisy. "Her adventures there," Mencken wrote in his biographical preface to *Southern Album*, "were typically grotesque." For weeks she went to Mankiewicz with her script, only to be told to return the next day; when she did, she would be told to come back the next week; when she returned the following week, Mankiewicz paid no attention to her or else was not in his office. She wrote for months on end, never knowing if her work was being read, and in the meantime growing all the more homesick for the South. "The truth is that I confess to something like homesickness; for the South, or something of the South," she wrote. (To cheer her, Mencken wrote encouragingly: "It is capital that you are homesick for the South. You ought to try a couple of weeks in the Middle West! They would make you burst into sobs at the sight of an Alabama country ham. Some day you ought to take a look at New England.") Nevertheless, she continued to write, and to struggle feverishly night after night. ("This letter is insane! But I am so tired I can't think," she once scribbled at 3:00 a.m.)

Eventually Sara Haardt was able to sell the idea of her movie to James ("Jim") Cruze. By 1927 Cruze was the highest paid director in Hollywood, earning 7000 dollars a week. He had established his reputation in 1923 when he made his first western epic, *The Covered Wagon*, at a time when interest in the western had been on the wane. Although Cruze was never again to experience the same success he had enjoyed with this film (it would be overshadowed by another epic: John Ford's *The Iron Horse*, in 1924), he was well enough known to be taken seriously. After a succession of meetings with Sara Haardt during various dinner parties, Cruze became so enthusiastic with the subject of *Way Down South* that he offered her 20,000 dollars for the script, an amazing price, considering that most writers were being paid only 5000 dollars at the time. He promised her he would make it into a one-and-one-half-million-dollar production. "He's probably lying and exaggerating," Sara wrote Mencken, afraid to trust the good news. That same evening Cruze discussed scenarios with her and the next day introduced her to seven actresses, asking her which, in her opinion, would be best suited for the various female roles. Jim Tully told Sara that Cruze could talk of nothing else.

All of this was exciting to Sara, but there were serious problems. At one point the scenario writer Lawrence (*What Price Glory?*) Stallings heard of her offer from Cruze and claimed that she had stolen the idea from him. Another obstacle was that she was still under contract to Famous Players and while she remained so she was unable to sign any contract with Cruze. Mankiewicz continued not to read her material, although he did extend her contract. (In fact, at the last minute an emissary of the studio came to fetch Sara at the same moment she was entering into a taxi en route to the train station.) In the meantime, Cruze was becoming more and more impatient to begin filming in February, a mere two months later. He had already lined up the cast and now chose location spots for the crew. Finally, after much agony on Sara's part, Cruze paid her 1500 dollars for the script, and, tired, spent, and sick, she returned to Baltimore and later to Montgomery for Christmas. The other 18,500 dollars was to be hers in February on the filming of the movie. That year talking pictures revolutionized the industry. The film was never produced.

The homesickness Sara felt for Montgomery found an outlet in the short stories she proceeded to write on her return from Los Angeles. They are among her best work, sensitively written, the characters deftly drawn, the dialogue a faithful reproduction of vernacular speech. They were praised for their honesty and their close knowledge of Southern psychology. Those she submitted to Mencken stand out above the others and were honored three times by the compilers of annual volumes of short stories. Still others were used as models of style in student anthologies. Her other work—articles of literary criticism, book reviews for the Baltimore *Evening Sun* and the New York *Herald Tribune*, interviews with Jim Tully, Zelda Fitzgerald, Joseph Hergesheimer, and Ellen Glasgow—are also of a high literary level. Many of her nonfictional studies received critical accolades, as in Virginius Dabney's *Liberalism in the South* (1932). Indeed, Mencken often encouraged her to concentrate more on this type of writing. All too often, however, she yielded to the temptation to turn out work only for the income it would provide. This was what Mencken labeled as her "ephemeral work": articles on antiques or on seashells, sketches for *College Humor*.

The question then arises: in view of Sara Haardt's considerable talent, why is she not better known in American literature? The answer must reside in the influence of Mencken, at once stimulating and stultifying. Mencken felt that the aim of the novel was to describe the typical man, showing him in conflict with his environment. This idea clearly shaped the theme and tone of *The Making of a Lady*, in which the environment, Meridian (a real town, but her fictional name for Montgomery), dwarfs the protagonist, Beaulah, whom the critics consequently found to be a weak characterization. This excessive submission to the influence of Mencken is corroborated in correspondence between the two. When Sara expressed uncertainty as to what method to adopt, the following exchange took place:

(Sara):   First, I know about as much about the "structural principles" of the novel as a cat fish [sic]. This much: and you will say 'Thank God!'—I have never even had a "course" in the novel. I know even less about it than did Scott Fitzgerald. Must I continue to write madly on or should I stop and do a pack more of reading? You pulled me out of the gutter absolutely with the short-story and I wonder if there is anything that I should so take to heart with the novel. Any special thing? Or simply let the bad luck happen?

(Mencken):   Lay on! You have an excellent idea, and the less "structure" you put into the book the better. Simply

tell your story as you see it, and pay no attention
whatever to the form. Any story that moves is in good
form.

And then he added:

Get plenty of characters into it, and don't hesitate to
pause for episodes. The thing needs careful and
devilish writing; you must get into exactly the right
phrases. But don't let the job scare you: you can do it.

Just as had been the case with *Career*, Sara Haardt's first novel, the
author's inability to master the problem of structure continued to
plague her in *The Making of a Lady*, which she revised seven times
before she found it to her satisfaction. Yet, despite the revisions, the
novel was criticized for its unevenness and lack of transition between
episodes. Mencken complained that the reviewers were trying to attack
him through his wife's book. Yet it is not unwarranted to find their
assessment of *The Making of a Lady* as "somehow too full of details
after the manner of Mencken's favorite novelist, Dreiser," as one critic
put it, basically justified.

One factor in Sara's failure to be remembered today—as well as in
the lack of recognition of Mencken as a catalyst for the Southern literary
renaissance—was the inability of both Mencken and Sara to recognize
the change that was taking place in Southern literature. By 1929 the
writing of Southerners had taken a dramatic departure from the Menck-
enian direction of the 1920s. The new writers—Thomas Wolfe and
William Faulkner, as well as the new group known as the Fugitives
—expressed a sympathetic attitude to the South that for Mencken
would have been inconceivable. It can be said that the new phase of
the Southern literary renaissance began in the autumn of 1929 with
the publication of Wolfe's *Look Homeward Angel* and Faulkner's *The
Sound and the Fury*. Yet that autumn, in his discussion of the season's
books in *The American Mercury*, in which Mencken reviewed no fewer
than eighteen works, no reference was made to the novels of Wolfe
and Faulkner. In order to appreciate this blindness on Mencken's part
one must recall that his primary interest at this time was political;
this may account for his exclusive dedication to themes containing a
social message. Both Faulkner and Wolfe, on the other hand, were

writing out of a traditional South which Mencken had urged Southern writers, including Sara Haardt, to discard as subject material.

Would Sara Haardt have been a different writer without Mencken's influence? One can only surmise, bearing in mind that she was moving independently of Mencken in that direction, one that would be later followed by such writers as Eudora Welty, Carson McCullers, Harper Lee, and others. This in a large part is accomplished through a use of imagery, which compresses the entire story into telescoped form in one revealing moment. "Little White Girl," a story encapsulating a situation that is peculiarly Southern: the moment when black and white children realize their separateness in an adult world.* The focal image here is that of the flowers, arranged beneath a piece of glass and buried beneath a mound of dirt, which Susie Tarleton and her black playmate Pinky call their "Penny Poppy Show." The gentle beauty of the flowers is suggestive of Pinky, whose own skin, according to Susie, is as fragrant as magnolias. When Susie breathes in the aroma of the flowers as if it were the last time, it is a foreshadowing of the loss of friendship between her and her black friend.

This type of sympathetic recreation of the South at first conflicted with Mencken's anti-Southern conservatism. Sara Haardt's experiment with these styles, as evidenced in "Slade Jernigan's Woman," published in *The Southwest Review* in 1927, was called "a palpable failure" by Mencken. It was through this new literature as well as her own personal pleading that Sara Haardt sought to make Mencken revise his hardheaded ideas. He knew the South only vaguely before they met, he admitted; it was not until afterward that he began to understand how it looked to its own people. "I am being drilled in the Confederate catechism," he confided jokingly to Julian Harris in 1930, but three years later, in an article for the Birmingham *News Herald*, he was already making concessions to her point of view, even to an approval of Wolfe and Faulkner:

> I think the South is making great progress. Go back fifteen years when
> I wrote my "Sahara of the Bozart," then there was a mythical South:

---

* Mencken makes a reference to her story in one of his private notes (No. 295), gathered in *Minority Report* (New York: Alfred A. Knopf, 1956), p. 205.

the South of mint juleps and chin whiskers; and the Southern farmer was a planter, not a farmer, riding around in state and very much dressed up. No advance was being made in literature particularly. Northerners were writing about the South then. Today, the South is providing men and women who are intelligently picturing the South in fiction, who are completely of the South, fiction written by Southerners. Take for instance, William Faulkner, and Erskine Caldwell, and Julia Peterkin, Ellen Glasgow, T. S. Stribling, the late Frances Newman and Thomas Wolfe.

However, these retractions did not satisfy his critics. During the years 1930 to 1935 one of them, Donald Davidson, launched a scathing attack on the values that Mencken had advocated to Southern writers. In numerous articles he decried the "sociological linguistic" approach to Southern life, the investigative approach that had characterized the 1920s. The social program of modern Southern literature, he charged, had turned many Southern writers away from a proper relationship with their own people and had caused them to work under the handicap of painful self consciousness. It would almost seem that Sara Haardt, for example, was trying to embody the feminine ideals and yet the fatalism of two contrasting eras, "to be romantic in feeling and yet fatalistic in philosophy" (a trait which she admired in the Southern writer Ellen Glasgow). Sara had written that she liked to think of herself as an "enlightened Southerner"—which to a certain extent, she was—but she was also caught in a struggle between Mencken's iconoclasm and her own sentimentality. "For all her ironic intelligence, her perceptions of a hollow void behind the force of glamour, the mists of the South to some extent claim Sara Haardt," critics wrote. This she realized herself as she sought to overcome this contradiction. In her essay "Youth in the Cotton Belt" she wrote in admiration of the first signs of the renaissance in the work of the younger generations:

No overwhelming genius arose from the younger generations, but what vastly superior stuff they turned out! There was keen observation in it, a firm grip of materials, a feeling for composition. They wrote of Alabama woods, Alabama rivers, Alabama moons. In brief, they got next to Alabama and wrote Alabama poetry. As I say, there were no masterpieces that came out of it, but there were bright flashes of beauty, often a brilliantly clear picture, charming touches of genuine fancy.

For these were the goals she had set for herself. Perhaps it was at this point a somewhat self-conscious expression, but in many ways it was a necessary step toward the literature which would portray man in conflict with himself. It was a stage through which the new literature had to pass before a William Faulkner or a Thomas Wolfe could come into being. It was a renaissance that, in a large part, Mencken instigated.

IV

When the news was announced that Mencken and Sara would be married by the autumn of 1930, the headlines read, "Mighty Mencken Falls," mourning the impending loss of the sole survivor of "The Last Man Club." To the males of the world, Mencken had been the personification of noble bachelorhood, the patron saint of single men. Now, with the prospect of his wedding, one reporter wrote: "bachelors of the nation are aghast and sore afraid, like a sheep without a leader." Naturally, everyone was clamoring to know who was the young lady who had "subdued" "America's best known bachelor." The Mobile, Alabama, *News* provided an answer of sorts: "H. L. Mencken, who has been regarded as almost a professional bachelor, has at last succumbed to the charms of an Alabama girl, which only goes to show that if he had been in contact with some Alabama girls earlier he would have never been known as a bachelor, or even as an iconoclast." The marriage was the most notable and sensational since that of Anne Morrow to Charles A. Lindbergh a little more than a year before. Sara, now labeled "Baltimore's literary flapper" saw her photograph appear in all the newspapers. For weeks these publications quoted Mencken's statements ridiculing the institution of marriage, to which he replied with mock seriousness: "I formerly was not as wise as I am now . . . the wise man frequently revises his opinions. The fool, never." After years of bachelorhood, how had he known he was enough in love to contemplate marriage? "I can only say it was an intuition," he answered. "The Holy Spirit informed and inspired me. Like all other infidels, I am superstitious and always follow hunches: this one seemed to be a superb one."

There were those who had suspected the possibility of a match long before. Among Sara's friends, this belief was widespread: "Although you never spoke of him, I knew the feelings you had for him," one of them said, summing up the general feeling. Dorothy Hergesheimer, who often had seen them together, in August 1927 broached the possibility of such a denouement to a radiant Mencken, who responded with characteristic banter: "The idea is charming! Ah, that it could be executed! But I already have one foot in the cemetery, and spies hint that she is mashed by a rich Babbitt in Birmingham, Alabama." One reason for Mencken's delay in marrying Sara—and one which caused much speculation among his friends—may have been concern for his mother, a dominant figure in the Mencken household. Since his father was dead, his brother Charles married, and his other brother August constantly traveling, Mencken considered it his duty to be the provider for his mother and sister Gertrude, feeling strongly that it was his responsibility to take care of them. James Cain, who saw much of Sara during the early years, believed that the role of Anna Mencken explained many curious things, such as Mencken's nonmarriage until her death, August's permanent bachelorhood, and Gertrude's spinsterhood. Anna, he said, "was an extraordinarily good looking woman, something to write home about, and very possibly, as long as she lived, furnished the Mencken children with all they needed in the way of female emotion. . . ." Ever since Mencken had been a small child Anna had been the heart and mainstay of the household. She also "could think of more contingencies and catastrophes than anyone else I ever knew," wrote Mencken. "Whenever there was a peal of thunder in summer she took to rushing about the house in a violent manner, shutting down the windows. When guests were impending she anticipated every conceivable catastrophe, and not only suffered from them all in advance but made the rest of us suffer from them." She kept a house that not only looked as if it had stepped out from the pages of her favorite magazine, *Good Housekeeping*, but added the maternal touches, such as keeping a plate of sandwiches waiting for Mencken when he arrived home late at night. George Jean Nathan thus shrewdly summed up the matter to the press: Mencken hadn't married earlier because he had already been living the life of a married man.

Why had Mencken not married Sara immediately after Anna Mencken's death in 1925? It should be remembered that her death on December 13, occurring close to the anniversary of her husband's years before (on January 13, 1899), made the holiday seem gloomier than ever. The year 1926 began with Mencken trying to adjust to the fact that his mother was gone, a task rendered difficult by the fact that the house was still filled with her presence. To distract himself, Mencken traveled a great deal; during the course of his travels he struck up acquaintances with Gretchen Hood and Aileen Pringle, and made such friends as Lillian Gish, but his letters to Sara and to his friends indicate that his mind was already made up in 1927. In an article, "On Falling in Love After Forty," Mencken reflected:

> I see no reason why a man sliding into his forties should not marry satisfactorily, and make a good husband. His illusions may be gone, but if the lady he claps his eye on is really charming there may be a great many soothing realities. The plain fact of it is that many females of the species are lovely, and that their loveliness survives even the harshest of spotlights. They make pretty pictures, especially when completely made up. They have nimble wits, and are amusing. They are tolerantly cynical, and do not expect too much, either of God or of men. I can imagine the most hard-boiled of men falling for such a wench. In fact, I have seen them fall—and observed them happy afterward. . . . The genuinely charming woman remains charming at sixty. She can no more fade, in any real sense, than a diamond can fade. It is not necessary to fall in love with such a woman in order to appreciate her. Appreciating her is a function, not of the hormones, but of the higher cerebral centers. In other words, it is the function of men beyond thirty-five.

And yet for all this, Mencken balked at making the first move and the eventful date of his and Sara's union seems to have been postponed. During 1928 Mencken mentioned in a letter to Lillian Gish "my unfortunate love affairs." The year seems to have been a pivotal one. Marion Bloom had returned from France, where she had divorced her husband and had instigated a correspondence with Mencken, but he remarked to a friend that Marion had changed so much from the woman he once knew that he could hardly understand her. In a letter dated September 25, 1928, Sara Mayfield questioned Sara: "Do let me know what progress H. L. has achieved in 'making haste slowly,' " and a letter from Mary Parmenter to Sara Mayfield that following year comments on the relationship: "She and her boyfriend have been very realistic of late. At least she has been to him. Then she gets sorry she was mean, and him with bad sinus trouble."* Mencken wrote to Max Broedel that he would have been engaged long before if it had not been for Sara's illnesses. They had been many: in 1928 she underwent surgery for appendicitis and a cyst, and in 1929 she had a close brush with death when she had a tubercular kidney removed. That year they had already made arrangements to be married in the autumn, but now the doctors predicted that, at most, Sara would live only two or three more years. As he stood outside Sara's hospital room door, Mencken told Sara Mayfield: "I've promised to myself that I'll make them the happiest years of her life." One might naturally come to the conclusion that Mencken had decided to marry Sara out of pity. Not so. What is more likely is that, after years of loving Sara and postponing marriage for various reasons (his overzealous protectiveness of Gertrude; early feelings of rejection from Marion Bloom; that he was too old to take such a major step in his life; etc.), this major illness of Sara's was the one drastic measure that had finally made him come to terms with reality and spur him into action.

The date was officially set for September 3, 1930, but communicated only to the immediate families. ("Harry is worried about my being left alone," Gertrude wrote Sara on receiving the news, "but I tell him there is no need to worry at all.") Apparently, in an effort to avoid premature publicity, Sara hid the news from Sara Mayfield and her other friends and wrote that she was leaving her apartment on Read Street because the doctors told her she needed one with more light and that the reason she was buying furniture was that purchasing antiques was the only thing she could do to amuse herself in Montgomery.† Privately, however, she and her best friend, Anne Duffy, wife of the cartoonist Edward Duffy of the Baltimore *Evening Sun*, began the task of preparing a home for herself and Mencken.

The home of these two arch agnostics at 704 Cathedral Street was surrounded by churches. Located in a brownstone building that had

---

* Sara's good friends the Duffys went as far as to take Sara to dinner to meet John Owens, editor of the Baltimore *Sun*. "He is a widower with two children and said to be very eligible," Sara wrote to Mayfield in mid-1928, not very enthusiastic about the evening that stretched before her. "He will probably have a gold tooth."

† See Appendix.

once been the mansion of a Baltimore banker, the apartment contained seven spacious rooms with lofty ceilings and open fireplaces. It was on two levels: visiting rooms above, and then, seven steps down, Mencken's study and the bedrooms below. With the aid of Anne, Sara decorated the apartment in Victorian style with green satin wallpaper and antique furniture.* Mencken hated cut flowers, heavily scented, of the type his mother kept in vases on Hollins Street. So, instead, Sara arranged her collections of wax flowers and Victorian pin-boxes, three hundred pieces in all.†

The Menckens' new home was meant to reflect both the personality and taste of its prospective owners. Mencken brought his liquor and brewing equipment, a few paintings, and an enormous poster of the Pabst brewery plant, which would be displayed over the mahogany

---

* Sara's love of antiques stemmed back to her flapper days in Montgomery, where, on Saturday afternoons with "another adventurous spirit," she locked arms and sailed forth to visit the pawnshops. "Young ladies of my day and generation, of course, weren't supposed to know they existed; indeed, if they were forced to pass them, they drew their skirts about them and hurried by with the abstracted gaze they used to ignore barber shops and saloons." Every guitar she ever owned came out of the pawnshop, and whenever an especially good one was turned in, the pawnbroker called her up and she raced down to try it. " 'Try your 'Willie the Weeper' song on this one,' he would say," and invariably she would buy it. Her last one was of a dark, wine-colored wood that she took with her to Goucher, and despite the fact that she had three others, she "could have wept bitter tears" when her brother John "hauled it to the university with him and the jellybeans made off with it."

† Those who did not know Sara did not comprehend this obsession and found the knickknacks simply the tangible reflection of a matron. Sara had her own explanation of what she called this "curious perversity of mine." She wrote: "I like to remember that at a time when ladies in their hearts were sorely tired and troubled, they could fashion such charming trivia as lavendar baskets, wax flowers. . . .Far from a silly picture it is, it has, for me, a quiet heroism. If, as I have so often heard, knitting is soothing for the nerves, then surely the making of a nosegay of wax flowers must have concealed many a heartache. Whenever such a specimen of a lady's gallantry comes to my notice, I can almost never resist adding it to my collection. It may be my weakness is rooted in the fact that I lived through the active campaigning for women's suffrage; that I attended a women's college where the first course was given by a rabid, forbidding spinster; that I swallowed, indiscriminately, in those callous days, a great deal of stuff about women's careers, women's rights and women's destinies."

sideboard in the dining room. "Sara is moving the piano tomorrow," Mencken wrote Phil Goodman on August 4, "a heavy job for a frail girl. She tells me that Southern ladies were never expected to do hard manual work. I reply that what goes on in one place doesn't go in another." Actually, Mencken managed to bring along his own baby grand piano himself. ("The musical engineers dropped it two or three times," he wrote to Max Broedel, "so I suppose I'll have to have it tuned.") He came to the conclusion that getting married was a more "tedious" business than he had expected, especially having to deal with so many tradesmen. On the other hand, he was not averse to drawing some practical benefits from his new status. To his secretary, Edith Lustgarten, Mencken confided that he hoped his upcoming marriage would help promote the sales of *Treatise on the Gods*. "Outfitting a swell apartment turns out to be very expensive," he said, somewhat apologetically, advising her to tear up Sara's card in the index: "If she works for the magazine it will have to be for nothing!" The comments were made in jest, of course, probably to cover up whatever awkwardness he may have felt in preparing to take so big a step. And if Mencken would miss his familiar view of Union Park from Hollins Street, he did not complain. Although what was to be his new office overlooked a narrow courtyard, there was comfort in the fact that the apartment was surrounded by lots of greenery, and especially in the realization that he at last was providing a home for himself and for Sara.

Together, Mencken and his fiancee obtained their marriage license in Baltimore (where, the clerk noted, Mencken mumbled and blushed "like any young fellow"), and in a successful coup to avoid the Hearst papers, married quietly one week before the scheduled date, on August 27. The man who wrote that "being married with all your friends around you is as private and as discriminating as eating in the window of a restaurant" was finally able to have the "refined" wedding he had wanted. The entire wedding party consisted of eleven people: Sara's family, the Menckens, including his niece, Virginia, and Hamilton Owens and Paul Patterson of the *Evening Sun*. The bride wore a beige crepe ensemble and a brown felt cloche hat and carried a spray of green orchids as a bridal bouquet. For weeks beforehand Mencken had been writing his friends, requesting the loan of any sort of moth-eaten coat. Finally he took the advice of the Reverend Dr. Herbert Parrish, who advised him to "put on plenty of dog. Women like it, though they may pretend tactfully to encourage the opposite." Mencken then dressed in a pin-striped business suit and, as far as he was able, managed to look presentable (on ceremonial occasions, friends noted, Mencken dressed "like a plumber got up for church"). The expressions of both Mencken and Sara in their wedding photographs reveal their happiness but also a certain apprehension. Only when the groom and bride had escaped from the besieging reporters and found themselves at last at the Lord Nelson Hotel in Halifax, Canada, where they were greeted by blue skies and cool ocean breezes, were they finally able to relax. This did not prevent the indefatigable journalist in Mencken from continuing work. "Sara is out buying hand-painted sea shells, carved toothpicks, and other souvenirs," he wrote to Blanche Knopf. "I have spent the afternoon writing an article for the *Evening Sun* on the malt liquor situation in Quebec." Apparently, this did not bother Sara, who was blissfully happy. In postcards to her friends, she wrote glowingly: "You were right: I have the one perfect husband."

At least four biographies of Mencken describe his married life with Sara, and it is not my intention to repeat what has already been said. Suffice it to say that all of them agree that, though brief, Mencken and Sara's marriage proved to be a loving one. Although in the presence of reporters Sara remained gracious but appeared subdued, to those visitors who called at the Mencken household she was a rare spirit. And there were always visitors. The Darrows, Lillian Gish, the Hergesheimers, Ola Elizabeth Winslow, Benjamin Baker. Often, Sara's sister Ida would come to see them. "Ida, come tell me the *dirt* of Montgomery," Sara would say. As the two sisters talked in Sara's room they could hear Mencken's typewriter clacking down the hall in his office until, at one point, they would hear it stop. "Shh, Ida, lower your voice," Sara would say. *"Henry's listening."* There were, also, the early morning visits of F. Scott Fitzgerald, demanding they listen to portions of his new novel, *Tender Is the Night*. Often this would occur just when Sara had drifted off to sleep, and then Fitzgerald would write an apologetic note to "The Venus of Cathedral Street." The visitors who came to 704 Cathedral Street found a loving couple who held hands and called each other "darling," a man who was "as excited about having a wife as a child is with a new toy," and a woman who regarded him "with the amused and affectionate indulgence a mother accords a gifted and unaccountable son." Whenever he went out Mencken would return home with some surprise or another: almonds, fruit, or a joke that would amuse her and fill the apartment with what he called her merry and "easy laughter."

It was only natural that during this period Mencken paid more attention to his domestic life. Outside the walls of 704 Cathedral Street the Depression seemed remote and far away. In 1933 Mencken resigned as editor of the *The American Mercury*, and with it out of his life, Mencken found that he could concentrate on his revision of *The American Language* and could spend many quiet evenings at home with Sara. And there were many. Mencken would play the piano for her or brew his special beer. Beer in hand, he would talk to Sara about his projects while she sipped on her inevitable Coca-Cola and told him about her own articles. There were times when Mencken had to be in New York or at various political conventions, but he always made certain he plied her with calls and letters, and rushed home as fast as he could. From Chicago, where he was covering the Republican National Convention of 1932, he wrote: "I may be home a day sooner than I calculated. I have hired a preacher to pray for it. I love you." Once he was home, there were certain rituals from his former life that he still practiced, such as his weekly musical routine with the Saturday Night Club. ("My wife can always tell when I've been out drinking a lot of beer," Mencken would say, "because she says I come home and am very complimentary and bland.") Sara knew that as a bachelor Mencken had been accustomed to freedom and so she did not attempt to tie him down. She told reporters that she knew what she was getting into when she married Mencken, that although a bachelor was more thoughtful than most men, she recognized that he "is set in his ways," but the overall judgment was a favorable one: "I think it is pleasant to live with someone who knows what he wants." In her diary there appeared the forlorn entry: "alone," but outwardly she never complained. To all who knew her, she displayed a courage, cheerfulness, and sweetness that was almost incredible in someone who had been, and still was, so seriously ill. When Mencken was away traveling she was accompanied by Anne Duffy, Ola Elizabeth Winslow, or some of her other friends. She frequently spoke to her sisters on the telephone. In order to keep her entertained, Mencken bought her a radio (which, however, she never learned how to manipulate, and whose susurrous voices and music distracted her so much that she hesitantly told Mencken she thought it must be broken), and an even more useful present, a hospital-type desk on wheels, so that she could do her writing in bed. She also had a record player, on which she particularly liked to play her favorite record of a song by Werner R. Heymann. Years later, Mencken would write there had been something "prophetic" about the words of the refrain:

> It exists only once,
> It doesn't come again;
> It is too beautiful to be true . . .
> Perhaps it will be gone
>   tomorrow.

With Sara there was always the threat of illness, forcing her to remain a bedridden patient. Mencken was determined she should have many diversions, and, as the doctors recommended, as many changes of air as possible. There were visits to the Hergesheimers at Dower House, to the Knopfs, or to Sinclair Lewis's home in Vermont, where Lewis felt in Sara "a fineness and authentic sweetness as I have rarely known." In January 1932 the couple went to San Juan, Puerto Rico, on a two-and-a-half-week Caribbean cruise with the North German Lloyd line. Throughout Christmas they had felt run-down and when they finally did go on board they were both sick with the flu. As he boarded the ship, Mencken looked so worn-out that Sara asked the news photographers to caption their pictures "The Man Is Sick—Not Drunk." Sara arrived prepared for her maiden voyage with a suitcase full of apples and Coca-Colas. There were reasons for her to be apprehensive. For one, she was afraid of the water. When she was a little girl growing up in Montgomery she had refused to go out in the paddleboat in the park, no matter how much Venetia tried to coax her. Secondly, she didn't know how to swim. In her scrapbooks are notes from Lillian Welsh, the medical advisor of Goucher College, asking her to report for swimming lessons (she never went). There were days during the voyage from San Juan to Nassau when the weather was cloudy and other days when the ship rolled and pitched. Nonetheless, Mencken pronounced the voyage a success and his wife a good sailor. While she sat on a deck chair and enjoyed the sun, Mencken played shuffleboard, drank beer, and enjoyed the food. In their room, he sat under the fan in his B.V.D.'s and wrote articles for the Baltimore *Evening Sun* and for the ship's newspaper, the *Caribbean Caravel*. "Historical Notes," written "by our cruise member, Mr. Henry Mencken," gave the ficitious history of the North German Lloyd which, to Mencken's discomfiture, was taken too literally by the ship's captain, Captain Ahren. Mencken wryly observed to his friend Phil Goodman:

> The trouble with you and me is that we are never serious. As people say, we make a joke about everything. I suppose you have had the experience many times of having everyone swallow what you said in jest. Well, here is another case. I warn you so you won't swallow the enclosed yourself. I hear that the Captain did. He told the passengers who told other passengers who told me that, after working on the Lloyd for 15 years, and going through 175 horrible storms, each and every one of which was the worst in his experience, he is still learning something about the history of the line.

For the January 28 issue of the *Caribbean Caravel* Mencken wrote yet another article, entitled "Confidential Information," even more outlandish than the first. In it he gave the blueprint for a new German Lloyd (the *Doppelschraubenpostexpressluxuskolossalriesendampfer*) and wrote that it would have, among other things, a half-mile cinder track, a stadium seating two thousand people, Catholic and Protestant churches on the top deck, a space for Communists, and a half dozen speakeasies; the first-class accommodations would be, not cabins, but apartments, and of those, twenty would be penthouse apartments. (There would also be a fourth class for professors.) Finally, there would be a hospital equipped to extract fifty appendixes and five hundred tonsils a day. As the information circulated throughout the ship, one can only wonder about Captain Ahren's reaction. Under the burden of so many letters and articles Mencken's ailing Corona finally broke down and had to be fixed during the journey. "The business of taking it ashore to be repaired was really appalling," Mencken wrote. "It actually took me two hours to get permission . . . and I'd have failed if a fellow Cuban [*sic*], speaking good English, had not come to my rescue." This seemed to be the only untoward event, however, on the trip. Together, Mencken and Sara skipped the prearranged shore excursions and rented an automobile for trips of their own. On a cloudy, drizzly day in Curaçao

Mencken sat in the car for two hours while Sara shopped. ("The perfumes there, as everyone knows, are great bargains, or so it is said," he wrote to Phil Goodman. "I found a convenient alley, and so my bladder did not bother me.") They met Marcella DuPont and became good friends. (Mencken would seek Marcella's company on the first anniversary of Sara's death and would talk of her, seeking relief from his great loneliness and grief. Years before, Sara had told him: "If anything happens to me, Marcella will be a good friend for you to have.") On the whole, it was a successful voyage, and they returned home refreshed.

Later that same year Mencken and Sara visited Montgomery, which received them in a stagey, sycophantic way. Before the marriage, Montgomery was divided in its attitude to Sara Haardt. One powerful supporter was Grover Hall, editor of the Montgomery *Advertiser* and recipient of the 1928 Pulitzer Prize in journalism for his editorials against religious and racial prejudice. Nonetheless, there were others less understanding who indulged in what Sara referred to as the "usual unpleasantness." One of the unpleasantries not received directly by the family but loudly voiced nonetheless was from Marie Bankhead Owen, then the director of the Department of Alabama Archives and History and cousin of actress Tallulah Bankhead. On June 3, 1933, she had written to the head of the Department of Archives and History in Richmond, Virginia, to complain about Sara Haardt's article on General Pickett, recently published in *Harper's Bazaar*.

> Gentlemen: My attention has been called to a story by Sara Haardt . . . in which the courage of General Pickett is impugned. It occurred to me that if your attention were called to this statement that General Pickett hid behind a barn during the Battle of Gettysburg that you would take the matter up with the Editors of Harper's Bazzar and also Mr. Henry L. Mencken . . . husband of Sara Haardt. This is not the first time in some of her Confederate hero stories this author has traduced the courage of General Pickett in her writings. It is high time someone called her down.

Since there was actually no Department of Archives and History in Virginia, H. R. McIllwaine of the Virginia State Library answered that "Miss Haardt's article will be read only by a few, and her ideas

will not be concurred in by even those few." One can only wonder
whether this was enough balm to sooth the offended Owen.*

After Sara had married H. L. Mencken, local opinions became sup-
portive. The Birmingham *Herald* ran Sara Haardt's photograph with
the caption "Distinguished Visit . . . known to her hosts of admirers
in Alabama," and the leading hostesses of Montgomery welcomed the
Haardt family into their inner circle:

> Five o'clock tea in Montgomery is a lot more exciting than "dinner at
> eight" anywhere else. . . . The Henry Menckens were there, surrounded
> by people who were simply beside themselves to hear every word. . . .
> Mrs. Mencken is perfectly charming. . . . We somehow thought she'd
> be a little austere but she's anything else. She's stunning looking, in
> the first place. . . . We couldn't decide whether it was her voice, which
> reminds you of all your favorite actresses, or her eyes, or just a com-
> bination of qualities. . . . Mr. Mencken, of course, is somebody we
> don't even dare discuss in a flippant communication like this . . .
> besides, we have too worshipful an admiration for him. . . .

As Mencken would have undoubtedly observed, these reactions were
simply another example of "the stupendous farce of human existence."

The next voyage of Sara and Henry, in the spring of 1934, was a
five-week Mediterranean cruise in which they visited fourteen countries
and made thirty-eight stops. They made the usual tourist rounds,
buying the usual bottles of perfume and oils, leather goods, textiles,
silver, mother-of-pearl, and rare woods (for August, Mencken's younger
brother). Mencken became so absorbed in buying relics for friends that
he was usually late returning to the ship, and Sara was terrified it
would leave without them. In Alexandria they rode a camel (an animal
Sara didn't have the heart to tell Henry she didn't particularly *like*),
and from the ship they saw a glorious rainbow over the Sea of Galilee
(which Mencken said he hoped would give him good luck for ninety

---

* She was, incidentally, the same "Cousin Marie" who was shocked at Tallulah's
debut on the New York stage. After reading the headline "Society Girl Goes
on Stage," she wired Tallulah: "REMEMBER YOU'RE A BANKHEAD."
Through a slip in the telegraph office, the message Tallulah received read:
"REMEMBER YOU'RE A BLOCKHEAD." Needless to say, Tallulah was
delighted.

days). Once in Jerusalem, Mencken bought a plentiful supply of crucifixes and yarmulkas. Of the five articles Mencken sent to the Baltimore *Evening Sun*, two of them were on what is now Israel, his favorite country; his least favorite was Egypt. In a letter to his friend Raymond Pearl, he compared the two countries thus:

> As for Egypt, it is yours with my compliments. The air is full of desert dust and the streets are full of thieves. . . . The Holy Land, on the contrary, turned out to be swell. I have never seen more beautiful scenery, and everywhere there are good roads, and in Jerusalem a really first-class hotel. The Jews have spent millions developing some fine farm colonies. The Arabs retreat to the hills and wait. Armageddon is very handy.
>
> The cruise has been pleasant, but we have made too many stops. We called at every port in Africa from Casablanca in Morocco to Port Said. Always the same Arabs and the same desert dust. Between Tripoli and Beiroot a dust storm came out from Libya, 200 miles to the south, and dam nigh suffocated us. It lasted 36 hours, and when it was over the whole ship was white. This was naturally bad for tender sinuses, and the ship's doctor has been doing a landoffice business ever since. Those who went up the Nile came back bitten by flies, fleas, scorpions, lizards, etc. The professing Christians seemed to suffer worst.

The trip had, indeed, what Sara called "a blur of ports," and by the end of the cruise Mencken had lost five pounds and Sara fifteen. When they arrived in New York on April 5 Sara looked forward to settling down again in her comfortable apartment at 704 Cathedral, and Mencken to being back at his old stall at Schellhase's.

Once again, however, Sara fell ill, this time with a fever (the doctors diagnosed it vaguely as "something Mediterranean") and in August she went to Montgomery. Many times she had traveled the road from Maryland to Montgomery, but there was never a time as sad as this, for Venetia was dying. "I was going home to say goodbye," Sara wrote, not knowing that it would be her own farewell to the South. Venetia had not told anyone of the gravity of her condition. "That was like her," wrote Sara, "and so very Southern! *She* hadn't changed in the twenty years I had been away." The North was different; "there you not only talk about unpleasant things if they seem inevitable but you also attempt to rationalize them." She asked herself, "Why hadn't we spoken of this thing then? Why hadn't I talked of the momentous things that besieged my heart ever since I returned to the North again?" When Sara returned to Baltimore her infection had developed into pleurisy and she was hospitalized at the Johns Hopkins Hospital for three or four weeks and then bedridden throughout the fall. "She can read, write, bathe, eat, drink, holler, criticize, etc. OK," Mencken wrote to Marion Bloom's sister, Estelle. "While she is laid up I hate to leave her, for fear she will imagine burglars, etc. I could hire a nurse to stay with her, but that runs into money, for all the nurse gals here in Baltimore are very heavy eaters." On December 23 Venetia Haardt died and was buried on Chritsmas Day. Sara, too ill to attend the funeral, lay in bed, thinking of the violets blooming in Venetia's garden, remembering all too well they were in season. With Sara bedridden, Mencken suffering from a sinus infection, and the anniversary of their parents' deaths at hand, once again, he noticed, Christmas ran its usual infernal course.

By spring 1935 Sara continued to be ill. The discipline Margaret Booth had instilled in all of her pupils showed itself in Sara Haardt, for despite headaches and fevers she continued to write. It was when Mencken heard her start to type at her rolling desk, stop, then resume again only to stop entirely that he realized that Sara might have to be hospitalized. In the middle of May 1935 she was back at the Johns Hopkins Hospital with an undiagnosed condition. For a long time, however, no one was aware that she was gravely ill. On May 23 Mencken wrote Scott Fitzgerald that Sara had succumbed to what seemed to be "a mild flu." (To which Fitzgerald replied: "Dear Menck: I'm sorry as hell about all this nuisance to Sara. That's the hell of getting older.") Mencken and Sara made plans to purchase a house in Turtle Pond in the Adirondacks and have Sara stay there from June until September. It was an area she had visited during the first few years she had known Mencken, and to which she had always wanted to return with him. Mencken politely declined all invitations for himself and Sara, saying: "We all have hundreds of years of life ahead of us." Despite bouts of dizziness, Sara continued to write her own letters. In one of the last of these, written to Sara Mayfield, she spoke of wishing "we could see you in Alabam. I'm quite weary with my miseries and all." Life continued with its daily routine. On the evening of May 24 Mencken gave a lecture and spoke of his latest revision of *The American Language*. He wrote that he planned to be in New York on May 31.

When Sara showed no signs of improvement Mencken dropped all his activities to stay by her side. When the full nature of her illness was revealed, Mencken stood a death watch, steeling himself to his wife's swiftly approaching death. To his friend Max Broedel he wrote:

> Sara has meningitis, with t.b. bacilli in the spinal fluid. It is, of course, completely hopeless. She seems comfortable—at least far more comfortable than she was a few days ago. The horrible headache has passed off, and she sleeps peacefully all day long. She may be aroused for half a minute, but hardly for more. This is the climax of her long series of illnesses. It would be silly to say that I have not anticipated it; in fact, I have dreaded it constantly. But it is appalling to face.

Accompanied by Gertrude and August, he visited Sara in the hospital, watching her fight "magnificently in the shadows, with a strong heart and steady pulse." She died at 6:40 p.m. on May 31. To Mencken, it must have been a final irony that his wife should die at about exactly the same time as had his mother.

Sara had requested that her body be cremated and the funeral be held with no flowers or pallbearers. The ceremony was held on a beautiful spring day, and for Philippa, Ida, John, and Mary Kelley there was an acute pain in losing Sara so soon after their mother's death. Mencken summed up his years with Sara in a poignant comment to Hamilton Owens, his editor at the Baltimore *Evening Sun*: "When I married Sara," he said, "the doctors said she could not live more than three years. Actually, she lived five, so I had two more years of happiness than I had any right to expect."

V

Biography fails, Mencken once wrote, because it tries "to explain a man utterly, to account for him in every detail, to give an unbroken coherence to his acts and ideas," when actually

> it is by no such process of exhaustion we get our notions of the people we really know. We see them, not as complete images, but as proces-

sions of flashing points. Their personalities, so to speak, are not revealed brilliantly or in the altogether, but as shy things that peep out, now and then, from inscrutable swathings, giving us a hint, a suggestion, a moment of understanding. . . . Thus, by slow degrees, he accumulates an image . . . an image changing incessantly, and never more than half sensed.

It is, needless to say, the aim of the presentation of this collection of letters to identify such "moments of understanding," moments which, as in life, are sometimes revealed deliberately, but more often, as Mencken believed, disclosed "naively, surreptitiously, accidentally, by bold and scattered inferences."

But there is still one final image of Sara Haardt which is not contained in the letters, and which must be recalled; it is the account Sara wrote about her last visit to Montgomery in September 1934, where Venetia lay slowly dying. Mother and daughter sat talking, "as if nothing more than a casual caller was imminent" and spoke of the South, as they always did, because, as Sara said, "the South was uppermost in our minds." Inevitably, they spoke of Varina Howell, the wife of Jefferson Davis, a woman "who had known the South as no other woman of her time: brilliant youth; promise; love in a setting of rare roses; fame; then, inevitably, sorrow. Death." The story of Varina Howell was one which Sara had heard throughout her youth. Long years afterwards, when Jefferson Davis was dead, Varina Howell Davis moved to the North, to New York, which couldn't have been more different. "Even when I was young," Sara wrote, "I thought I understood why she went. She couldn't stand it here in the South where every fragrant flower reminded her of a strange tropical death." It created a scandal; they said Varina was hostile to the South, to her own people. "She heard what they said," noted Sara, "but she stayed; and she amused herself intelligently." It was history, of course, but to Venetia, it was a blueprint of her daughter's own life. She maintained that Sara was like Varina Howell in more ways than one, telling her "she was sentimental about the South less because she had buried her sorrows here than because she spent her youth here."

The nagging shadow of the past that Varina Howell felt was not unlike that which appears to have plagued Sara Haardt. Perhaps, as Venetia believed, Sara could have written realistically about the South as did Glasgow, Cabell, Faulkner, "and those people at Chapel Hill" if she had remained there. One cannot help but think that a few months before her own death Sara came to such a conclusion and set out to work on *The Plantation*, a work she hoped would, in some way, reflect her undying attachment to her origins. And some of her stories were good enough that, in the words from the *The New Republic*, "it is tantalizing to speculate on what might have been." Still, it must be admitted that the influence of H. L. Mencken on Sara Haardt was not simply negative, and it was not Mencken's influence that made the treatment of the themes of Southern identity, ambition, and spiritual isolation she strove to express largely unsuccessful, but her own un-resolved conflict. In her autobiographical sketch entitled "Dear Life," Sara wrote once more about the enormous problems facing the Southern writer who has so many inhibiting traditions to overcome in order to speak with an author's voice.

In order to be free to attain her aspirations, Sara had to reject the tradition which decreed that women must be ambitious not for their own sakes but on behalf of their husbands and that their own careers should be limited to marriage. As in the case of her fictional characters, it was not easy for Sara Haardt to find her own way, because she felt attracted to what she was led to believe was reprehensible. Mencken offered her the possibility of freedom and equality, without pretense. Had he played no part in the development of her fiction it might conceivably have been more consistent, less confused in its direction, but certainly not so ambitious or broad in its scope. Mencken deepened Sara's understanding of American society, and what Sara learned from her involvement with social criticism would be artistically realized by later writers of the Southern literary renaissance. In a different way from others of her contemporaries, she found that it was possible to forge links between the South and the North, and that past and present are not necessarily mutually exclusive. Of her abiding attachment to the South she wrote emotionally in "Dear Life,"

> At last I was beginning to understand what the South had bred into me. Birth, death, the flower gardens . . . all came to the same end, and the certainty of it gripped me with a kind of courage. I could never escape, either to the North, or the East, or to the West; I lived in the eternal mystery of the tropics, the memory of the tulip flowers wafting

down in the fragrant dusk, the soft kiss of the mists as they rolled over. The memory was sweeter than any escape I had imagined on earth. I wanted to live, I knew now, because life itself had a beautiful youngness; and youth was part and parcel of my affinity with the South.

As a writer, Sara Haardt unquestionably had her limitations. Within these limitations, however, there was achievement. It is generally acknowledged that Mencken's power as a critic was his intuitive understanding of good writing and his deep empathy for writers. Like Mencken, and through his example, Sara recognized and sought to encourage with every nerve of her being, the fine potential of the new Southern writers:

> . . . And yet, despite the signs, the renaissance is undoubtedly in progress; the Sahara is budding forth. After all, it isn't the older generations that count so much, or the very young ones, with their unassimilated tradition; the fact is that the South is getting educated, fast and furiously, and it is rare indeed that the moral certainty can stand long against education. Without a complete renunciation of the past, realism is springing up in the old citadels; in Birmingham, Chapel Hill, New Orleans, and Richmond. The movements have gone far in achieving the beginning of criticism. . . . The next twenty-five years, indeed, are bright with promise! For what else will the intelligentsia do, now that they have attained the outward hedges of economic prosperity—than turn to the arts? The Sahara is looking up!

Other writers began to replace Sara Haardt and what she has left is a lasting impression of the love she felt for H. L. Mencken, as he did for her: "If I had to live my life over again," Mencken would write in his preface to the first volume of his autobiography, *Happy Days*, "I don't think I'd change it in any particular of the slightest consequence. I'd choose the same parents, the same birthplace . . . the same wife." Sara Haardt was, as only she could be, what Lillian Gish has said, the only woman worthy of Mencken. For years Mencken would write to his friends that he hoped they would not forget Sara. "She is still tremendously real to me. I simply can't think of her as vanished." Every year Mencken visited her grave at Loudon cemetery, and every year his chronology seemed "to have gone haywire. There are days when it seems ten years have passed, and others when I can hardly believe that so much as a year has gone by." Through time, the loneliness he felt turned into bitterness and sometimes rancor, so that some years before his own incapacitating cerebral thrombosis, which left him unable to read or write, he could privately record this poignant thought: "I was fifty-five years old before I envied anyone, and then it was not so much for what others had as for what I had lost." In 1935, the year of Sara's death, it will be recalled that Mencken turned fifty-five. Curiously, in his "Autobiographical Notes" he does not further develop this train of thought, just as in *Heathen Days*, the third volume of his autobiography, he failed to mention Sara in his description of his 1934 voyage to Carthage and what is now Israel. What is too private and painful Mencken fails to dwell on, save, to some degree, in his letters. Perhaps he felt that people who knew him and his work would understand this reserve. Perhaps he felt he had left enough scattered allusions to his own sadness and torments to make direct comment unnecessary. Considering the special relationship that bound Mencken and Sara together, this reticence is not surprising. Sara Haardt's description of Varina Howell in her book review on *The First Lady of the Confederacy* for the New York *Herald* could well have been her own epitaph:

> The life of Varina Howell comes close to being an epic not only of the South but American womanhood. First of all, she was the perfect product of her times and her environment; she possessed a keener wit and a finer intelligence than most of the women of her generation, but she still clung to the ideals of their purposes. She possessed beauty and an enduring charm, and yet she loved and revered one man her whole life through. She was not a paragon . . . but she was a lady, with that secret impenetrable armour every lady wears before the world.

Theodore Dreiser's letter of condolence offered Mencken a solution for his sorrow: "As I see it, life furnishes just one panacea, if so much, for all the ills and accidents of life: it is work—and more work." It was exactly the way in which Mencken usually sought to conquer grief, but this time he was so heartbroken he found working an impossibility, and so in June he set sail for England with his brother August. When Mencken returned to Baltimore in the summer of 1935 he went back to 704 Cathedral Street, but when James Cain visited him there in

December he found Mencken wandering through the rooms, talking nonstop, almost mechanically. Living in the same surroundings proved to be too much for him, and finally Mencken gave away much of the furniture Sara had bought and moved back to 1524 Hollins Street, never to return. It was during these months that Mencken carefully arranged Sara's mementos from the Margaret Booth School, her Goucher College notebooks, and other papers, and had them bound in blue morocco leather. In his orderly way he wanted to document her life for posterity. He also selected what he felt to be her best stories and put them together for *Southern Album*, and neatly arranged her other work. In a preface to one of the volumes he typed the hopeful comment: "It may be that in the future some historian of Southern letters will want to go through her work with some care." On October 31, 1935, Mencken presented Sara's collection of five hundred volumes of literature and Southern history to Goucher College, along with several bound folios of her papers. Accompanying him was his old friend Joseph Hergesheimer, "to sustain me," Mencken wrote Dorothy Hergesheimer, "while I hand over Sara's books. How she would have larfed to see us!" Among the papers was a brown box, containing the letters which recorded the saga of their romance and literary relationship, and the years of their marriage. To these, we now turn.

EDITORIAL NOTE

~

THE COMPLETE AND UNABRIDGED letters of H. L. Mencken and Sara Haardt are preserved in the Mencken Collection at the Julia Rogers Library at Goucher College. Eighty-one abridged carbons of the originals (1923–1932) are at Princeton University Library. Most of Mencken's letters to Sara were typewritten on the familiar half-sheet stationary bearing the address "1524 Hollins St., Baltimore." Those letters which were handwritten by Mencken are rare and reflect him in a private moment, such as the anguished letter written one evening shortly after his mother's death; or a note hastily penned at the Hotel Algonquin (usually dated the same day he had dictated a rather formal business letter to Sara from his office on Forty-second Street, where he edited *The American Mercury*); or the quiet, thoughtful letters, professing his love for her, written after a long day reporting from the naval conference in London.

The few cases where the letters are entirely handwritten and signed by the writer are noted in the text by the initials ALS (Autograph letter signed). Sara's letters to Mencken were typed or (more often) written in her characteristically large and legible handwriting. Both Mencken and Sara were accurate spellers and followed the traditional rules of grammar. I have corrected the obvious misspellings where it seemed necessary, but in one or more instances, the mistake has remained (as the time when Mencken almost missed his train to "New Yrok" in order to type Sara a hasty note). I have also kept Sara's fondness for dashes and ellipses. When Mencken or Sara penned a correction in the letters, I have silently incorporated it into the text.

The customary signature for Mencken was "Sincerely yours, (signed) H. L. Mencken" or "Yrs., HLM," but his signature in his letters to Sara could almost relate their love story by its variation. The encircled "M," saved for his closest friends, was being used as early as 1924. "H" was an initial Mencken had used (outside of his family) during the years he courted Marion Bloom (he changed it back to "M" once she was married); when he buried his mother in 1925 and described his grief to Sara he signed the letter "H"; he used it again when he became engaged to Sara in 1930, and he would use this particular signature throughout that year and the subsequent years of their marriage.

The letters in this volume have never been published before. The exceptions are letters from which excerpts have been previously printed—a phrase or paragraph—but which seemed important to print in full. If there are two accounts of the same event, the most informative and enjoyable version wins. When information becomes repetitive, I have silently excised it, simply using ellipses widely spaced apart, not to be confused with Sara's own closely spaced ellipses. Every other intrusion into the text by me is enclosed in square brackets [ ]. Those letters which have been deleted are, for the most part, notes confirming a meeting for lunch or dinner at Schellhase's or some other meeting place. Also, Mencken's questioning Sara on her health appears in almost all of his letters to her—much of it has been excised so that the letters would not resemble each other. Some of Mencken's wittier postcards to Sara have been included. It should be noted that most of them were mailed with their postage stamp carefully pasted upside down: a code which, in those days, carried an additional message—that you were in love with the person you were sending your letter to.

Dates, usually noted by Mencken on the top right-hand corner and in the lower left-hand corner by Sara, have been made uniform, as have addresses. During the periods when Mencken and Sara were apart for long distances (as, for instance, Mencken and Sara's separate trips to Hollywood, or Mencken's 1930 voyage to Europe), the sequence of dates appears to be out of chronological order. Not so. Because of the irregularity of mail delivery, it became necessary to sequence the letters not by the date on which they were written but rather by the date on which Mencken or Sara received a letter and subsequently replied to it.

Because I wanted the letters to read like a continuous story, I have provided brief summary narratives at the outset of each year. The observations of Mencken and Sara's mutual friends have been inserted to link the years together and make the story complete. Annotations have been provided to identify names and events and to clarify otherwise obscure allusions. They are not aimed at the expert but at a younger generation. Mencken often accompanied his letters to Sara with clippings of the event he was then reporting (like the Republican and Democratic national conventions, or his description of the Scopes trial of 1925), and excerpts have been inserted at intervals to provide the reader with a little background material to which the letters themselves make no direct reference. These are quoted directly as Sara would have read them from the pages of the Baltimore *Evening Sun*, and not as they appeared in their revised form in *Making a President* or in the *Prejudices* volumes. For the most part, many of the articles so quoted have not been resurrected since their first appearance in the Baltimore newspaper. Upon reading them, the reader will marvel at how uncanny Mencken's predictions prove, and, one hopes, a newcomer will discover the fresh immediacy of his prose.

M.E.R.

THE AMERICAN MERCURY
730 FIFTH AVENUE
NEW YORK

OFFICE OF THE EDITORS   *George Jean Nathan and H. L. Mencken*

Nov. 10, 1924

Dear Sara:

Henry Cabot Lodge's
death is a great blow
to me. I am now the
oldest, handsomest and most
learned man left living
in America. And the
hardest worked. The last
three days have been
infernal.

I'll be back by
Thursday. When do we
meet?

Yrs
M

THE
Courtship Years

1 9 2 3 – 1 9 2 9

---~---

1923

H. L. Mencken first met Sara Haardt at one of his annual lectures at Goucher College on May 8, 1923. That evening they had dinner together, whereupon Mencken mentioned he would like to see a sample of Sara Haardt's short stories. Shortly thereafter, Sara wrote the famous critic the following note:

SARA HAARDT
GOUCHER COLLEGE

May the twentieth, 1923

Dear Mr. Mencken,

Before I get stuck in Alabama for the rest of the summer I want you to get me straight on this short-story business. My ideas, freshened by "Little Emma" and "Mamie Carpenter,"[1] and the old notions I had are squirming like a bucket full of bait. How does one do it? I mean, see you.

Thyra Winslow[2] has left me without a straw to lean on. But I admire her enough to resist imitation (seriously, I don't think it could be done) while at the same time I want right badly to write something and I am wondering if anything could come out of a Baltimore second-story back or a messing with elephant-eared academics.

Holy rhetoric! These "Suggestions" of yours would make a villain laugh. I wish to heaven you had fired a whole pack into the assembly. The young dogs, as Mr. Baker[3] dubs them, would have stuck them away in their Bibles—but only after you had autographed every single one of them![4]

Is there any time, then, when you are not too busy?

Cordially yours,
Sara Haardt

[1]"Little Emma," "Mamie Carpenter," two of the eleven short stories collected in *Picture Frames*, by Thyra Samter Winslow, published by Alfred Knopf in 1923.

[2]Thyra Samter Winslow began publishing stories and articles in 1922. She drew on her Arkansas childhood and later her experiences as a drama critic in New York.

[3]Harry Torsey Baker, an assistant professor of English at Goucher College, had been connected with *The Smart Set* (before Mencken's time), *Country Gentleman*, and *Cosmopolitan* magazines and subsequently enjoyed teaching writing to his students.

[4]Mencken had a habit of lifting Bibles from hotel rooms and presenting them to friends, inscribing them with "Compliments from the Author."

ALS

SARA HAARDT
GOUCHER COLLEGE

May the twenty-sixth, 1923

Dear Mr. Mencken,

I shall be at Domenique's[1] on Thursday at twelve-thirty unless I hear that that hour is not suited to your schedule. These have been dog days at college and I am looking forward to the meeting as the only inspiring thing that could happen.

Sincerely,
Sara Haardt

[1]Two doors away from Mencken and Sara's future home, on 702 Cathedral Street, Arrobbia Domenique, a proprietor of Marconi's restaurant, had opened "Maison Domenique." Its location in the fashionable district created a furor, and it closed after eleven months in December 1923.

H. L. MENCKEN
1524 HOLLINS ST.
BALTIMORE

May 29, 1923

Dear Miss Haardt:

I'll be delighted. Let us meet at Domenique's on Thursday at 12:30.

I am just in from Bethlehem, Pa., after hearing the Bach Choir and discovering excellent beer at 10 cents a glass![1]

Sincerely yours,

H. L. Mencken

[1]The Bach Festival, an annual two day celebration held on a Friday and Saturday in May, in Bethlehem, Pennsylvania, had begun as long ago as 1888. A varied program of Bach cantatas, motets, oratorios, and other numbers are presented in the afternoon and night sessions on the first day; on the second, Bach's *Mass in B Minor* (considered his greatest work) is presented in two parts.

This was Mencken's first visit to the festival, and he went accompanied by his friend, the novelist Joseph Hergesheimer, who showed up in a golden orange kimono with purple lining. The solo voices (and the brew) "singed" Mencken's kidneys, but nonetheless he returned year after year, often accompanied by his friend and publisher, Alfred A. Knopf. The next day Mencken's description of the festival appeared in the Baltimore *Evening Sun*; it would be the first of four different articles he would write praising the simplicity and beauty of the festival.

June the second, 1923

Dear Mr. Mencken,

I am forwarding you these manuscripts without more ado. In truth if I tampered with them in this atmosphere I would make them worse than they already are. I forward ANALOGY at Mr. Baker's suggestion. It is an old model. MISS REBECCA is after your recipe and I want you to test it before I try the next one. I will say this—that the other character-stories I have projected have a little more "story body." But is this one good enough in any respect and would it indicate that it would be worth while to go on with the others?

We are staging the usual commencement tail-spin these last days. All the cabbages have turned cauliflower and the Lord never heard of so many good chil'len. I told Mr. Baker that I envied him his Saturday night party and his company with the dogs of wit.[1] Heaven knows I need a bracer and I can't expect it on the New Orleans Limited.

I have prayed like everything that you wouldn't forget to capitalize that epigram on evolution![2]

Sincerely,
Sara Haardt

[1] Baker was invited to attend a meeting of the Saturday Night Club.

[2] Mencken's epigram, "The Row Over Evolution: A combat between men who believe that they are gorillas and gorillas who believe that they are men," would later appear in the September issue of *The Smart Set*.

H. L. MENCKEN
1524 HOLLINS ST.
BALTIMORE

June 5th, 1923

Dear Miss Haardt:-

If "Miss Rebecca" didn't deal with an old maid, I'd take it instantly.[1] It presents the character vividly, and it is very well managed, particularly at the end. But the old maid has been on the block so long that she is almost done to death, and Nathan and I made oath some time ago to give her a rest.

I think the "Miss Rebecca" sort of story is much more grateful to your manner than any other kind, and that you will find writing it much easier. "Analogy" is surely not badly done, but, after all, it has a sort of second-hand air: you are looking at its people through a knothole in the fence, not living with them. Why don't you try to get a story or two out of the fair creature we discussed the other day —the flamingo on Main Street? What a picture! Montgomery must be alive with stories. Who is the town beau? Why not embalm him? The fashionable dentist? The leading amateur violinist?

The poem I can't take, either.[2] We have 200 or 300 bales of poetry stored in Hoboken, in the old Norddeutscher-Lloyd pier. There are 360,000 poets in America, and at least 38,000 of them are good.

I enclose a copy of my tribute to the venerable Dulaney.[3] I have reserved the wheeze about the gorillas for the Smart Set.

It was a great pleasure to see you the other day. Let us have another palaver when you get back. Meanwhile, let me see whatever you do. I think you have a good novel in your head.

Temperature here: 95. I am about to swoon.

Sincerely yours,
H. L. Mencken

Baker didn't show up at the beer party—too busy packing. He missed a superb brew.

---

[1]Published in *The Reviewer*, July 1924.

[2]"On Reading Minor Poems," *The Reviewer*, January 1925.

[3]"The Siege of Genesis" (Baltimore *Evening Sun*, June 4), centering on Henry S. Dulaney's resignation from Goucher College.

520 SOUTH COURT STREET
MONTGOMERY, ALABAMA

June the twenty-fourth, 1923

Dear Mr. Mencken,

I hope this is some better. I swear it isn't about an old maid and it hasn't a sign of a plot. Furthermore, I had a grand time doing it. This sort of thing does come more natural.

I have been in the mills since the commencement series. I trolloped down to New Orleans upon landing here only to discover that Tulane was a summer school of 1500 cute cuties and that the best thing they offered was a revised course in Penmanship. So I came back—quick.

However, if I am not embalmed I do mean to wring a good story from the present wash. I am beginning to have hopes for them. An iconoclastic bookseller has installed a full shelf of your works and the literati have their teeth in your DEFENSE OF WOMEN. I heard a clerk in the "ribbon department" discussing it the other day and I was so sure of a new species that I almost asked the lady for her autograph.

I'll wager that Dulaney has concocted a fine Methodist ancestry for you and that all he digested was the first paragraph. Mr. Baker sustained me with remembered excerpts the hour before we paraded at commencement and for the time being I forgot all about having to listen to the public sing "America the Beautiful."

I wish I had the nerve not to enclose postage ...

I do hope that the thermometer has cooled off and that you are enjoying the respite ...

Sincerely,
Sara Haardt

520 SOUTH COURT STREET
MONTGOMERY, ALABAMA

July the seventh, 1923

Dear Mr. Mencken,

You started something I pray I can finish. I was having a beautiful time writing another story like you "told me to" when I discovered I couldn't stop. The thing is going to be a beaut and I am simply wild about it. I don't know where I began and I have no idea where I am going to stop but it's a glorious feeling. Seriously, it is going exactly like these last short stories, I hardly am aware that I am doing it. Just the same I am not at all sure and I wanted to bother you with a few things.

First, I know about as much about the "structural principles" of the novel as a cat fish. This much: and you will say 'Thank God!'— I have never even had a "course" in the novel. I know even less about it than did Scott Fitzgerald.[1] Must I continue to write madly on or should I stop and do a pack more of reading? You pulled me out of the gutter absolutely with the short-story and I wonder if there is anything that I should so take to heart with the novel. Any special thing? Or simply let the bad luck happen?

About the subject-matter: I am sticking to the only thing I know, the delineation of small town life from the viewpoint of a young girl who thinks she wants to get out of it, her subsequent career in one of the so-called "big" universities, the achievement of her Ph.D., and the delicious part—what she is good for and does when she gets it, namely, realizes that she is practically good-for-nothing and so snatches her last chance and returns and marries the one Babbitt in town who hasn't already married somebody else.

Is it all too terrible? I will never rest content until I can get off what I know about the university bubble. It is positively too good to keep. I am keeping my local color in psychology, too, because it is the craziest.[2] I must tell you some time about the prize bone that they pulled last year with an experiment on the Emotions. The Democratic Convention isn't in it. It would simply "break your heart with mirth." And these boobs actually think that they are doing something. My angle has been that there has been a big dab of small town in university and big city bright lights. In the end my damsel is going to beat it back to the real thing. But remember, she was small town to begin with.

What do you think?

I am just as crazy to get at some short stories that I have in the back of my head. I wonder if I hadn't better do those first. Your man of God would make a dog laugh. But that's nothing. I have a revivalist that beats Brigham Young[3] all to pieces. And I'm going to embalm him.

What have you done now? I am deprived of my Evening Sun and the New Orleans Picayune is the only foreign newspaper that the stands in this quarter carry but the dailies have devoted whole editorial columns to some vision of yours "On the South." I can't see you for the dust.[4]

My joy over your taking JOE MOORE AND CALLIE BLASIN-GAME was so perfect that I was afraid it was a dope dream.[5] I have at least a hundred more that I want to do, including the town undertaker. I actually feel emancipated. And I blush to think of my past dealings with "the plot" or whatever it was I was contaminated with.

I am working morning, noon, and night, in spite of the telephone and some really horrible weather. This would be a gorgeous place to live—if I could stand it.

Have you followed the Tuskegee affair?[6] I long for you to write an epic on the subject.

Sincerely yours,
Sara Haardt

[1]F. Scott Fitzgerald had by this time already published *This Side of Paradise, Flappers and Philosophers*, and *The Beautiful and the Damned*.

[2]Sara was pursuing a Ph.D. in psychology at Johns Hopkins University at the same time she was teaching English at Goucher.

[3]American Mormon leader and founder of Salt Lake City.

[4]Southern editorials were responding to Mencken's article "Below the Potomac," which dealt with labor, politics, and the Klan.

⁵Sara's short story to run in *The Smart Set*'s edition for October 1923.

⁶Robert Russa Moton, second president of Tuskegee Institute, led a national fight for employment of black doctors and nurses at Tuskegee VA Hospital. The NAACP and the National Medical Association played key roles in the struggle. The new policy set a storm of controversy, with opposition from Alabama governor William W. Brandon, state senator Richard H. Powell, and the Ku Klux Klan, which threatened, among other things, to burn every building on the Tuskegee campus to the ground. Three days before Sara's letter, a 40-foot cross was burned in the town of Tuskegee.

H. L. MENCKEN

1524 HOLLINS ST.

BALTIMORE

July 10th, 1923

Dear Miss Haardt:-

Lay on! You have an excellent idea, and the less "structure" you put into the book the better. Simply tell your story as you see it, and pay no attention whatever to the form. Any story that moves is in good form. What a chance for irony—the discovery that the college is simply a washed and ironed small town—that its loftiest dignitaries are simply third-rate Babbitts! Get plenty of characters into it, and don't hesitate to pause for episodes. The thing needs careful and devilish writing; you must get it into exactly the right phrases. But don't let the job scare you: you can do it.

I enclose a couple of clippings that may amuse you.¹ If the treatise on professors of English seems too harsh, God forgive me. The meeting I mention was at least partly devoted to denouncing me as a scoundrel for writing "The American Language."²

Let the short stories lie over; you can do them later. If, when the novel gets along, you want me to see it, send it to me as above. I may be able to detect some weak spots.

Confidentially, I am making plans to start a serious review—the gaudiest and damnedest ever seen in the Republic.³ But this is a secret for the present. I am sick of the Smart Set after nine years of it, and eager to get rid of its title, history, advertising, bad paper, worse printing, etc.

Sincerely yours,

H. L. Mencken

¹"The Vernacular" (July 2) and "Bogus Martyrs" (July 9), which appeared in the Baltimore *Evening Sun*.

²Both articles put down English professors and called for a study which would constitute a "full length investigation of the language that 110,000,000 Americans speak every day." Mencken's third revised and enlarged edition of *The American Language* had been released this same year.

³*The American Mercury*, first published in January 1924.

520 SOUTH COURT STREET
MONTGOMERY, ALABAMA

July the twenty-third, 1923

Dear Mr. Mencken,

I don't know when I have enjoyed anything like I have these knockouts of yours on the profession! . . To avoid Scott Fitzgerald I not only got the proverbial kick but passed out in a perfect hypnogogic state of joy. I almost clapped. When I came to I sent them on to Mr. Baker and the dear man crowned my confidence in him by being bowled over with sweet accord. He added that "these English professors are a dish of poor prunes." If you ever do anything like it again, please....

And, further, I know of nothing under the southern sun that would revive me like a shot in the person of the review set forth in your last. I may turn reformer and try to put through a bull declaring that all professors flying Ph.D.s wear the latest issue in their tool kits. Anyway, when your bills are ready, send me a couple of bales and let me bomb them over the sleeping and unprotected women and children.

I was dying for you to see this "novel" but I was afraid to ask you. I may send you a sample some time next month just to discover if you think it is worth going on with. I work at the thing morning, noon, and night until I can't see straight. And I would try to express some sort of decent appreciation but I honestly don't think it could be done. At least not strong enough. To put it stingily, you are "the first Christian gentleman that I have met since" Mr. Baker took the oath of allegiance to Goucher College.

Sincerely yours,
Sara Haardt

~

H. L. MENCKEN
1524 HOLLINS ST.
BALTIMORE

July 26th, 1923

Dear Miss Haardt:-

I enclose another canto of the Hymn Against Pedagogues.[1] Curiously enough, the suggestion for it came from exalted quarters at the Johns Hopkins. Some day they will offer me a D.D. and bring me down with rabies.

Let me see the novel,[2] by all means. I have paved the way for it with Knopf.[3] I haven't the slightest doubt that you can do a very good job. If you insert any plea for Service into it, however cunningly disguised, you will hear some colossal swearing.

Knopf, Nathan[4] and I, by the way, are starting a new review— something of a variety hitherto unknown in the Republic. Probable title: The American Mercury.[5] It will go, I hope, very far beyond the Smart Set. We should have the first issue ready by the end of the year. When the novel is finished, why not do an article for it? Absolute free speech will prevail—so long as it is annoying to right-thinking men. Keep this a secret for the present.[6] More anon.

Sincerely yours,
H. L. Mencken

[1] "The Higher Learning in Maryland," July 23, 1923. The University of Maryland was planning to set up a school of engineering at College Park, and Mencken suggested it should simply go as a new wing at Johns Hopkins University. "Two universities," he wrote. "Then Maryland needs two governors, two legislatures, and two debts."

[2] *Career*.

[3] Alfred A. Knopf, the American publisher.

[4] George Jean Nathan, Mencken's coeditor and drama critic of *The Smart Set*. Although Knopf had made the offer of "editor" solely to Mencken, Mencken insisted on bringing Nathan in, just as Nathan's support had earlier brought Mencken into *The Smart Set* as coeditor.

[5] After a series of titles, "The Defender," "The Other Man's Monthly," "The Inter-Continental Review," and "The New Review," George Jean Nathan suggested "The American Mercury." Mencken did not like it because he thought the title would confuse readers with *The London Mercury*, but the title remained.

⁶Actually, Mencken was writing sixty letters a day to several authors, from the sciences as well as the arts, in an effort to gather material.

520 SOUTH COURT STREET
MONTGOMERY, ALABAMA

August the thirteenth, 1923

Dear Mr. Mencken,

I got stuck on the novel and so gave vent to this—I only hope and pray that it is untainted by the atmosphere. Hell couldn't be any worse and I swear and pray simultaneously for breath until September . . .

Your séance on "Higher Learning" was simply delicious. I have folded it away to read every night next winter when I threaten to die by the hour for being fool enough to be coerced into writing a thesis. To write a sky rocket for your review is my dearest dream—I could even endure the Hopkins if I thought it would furnish an obituary.

If you don't hurry up and say that one about the gorillas it will be too late. I want it in black and white....

Sincerely yours,
Sara Haardt

H. L. MENCKEN
1524 HOLLINS ST.
BALTIMORE

August 17th, 1923

Dear Miss Haardt:-

A good idea, but it seems to me that you have failed to account for the last act sufficiently.¹ It surprised me that Scilla should run away with Dutch Spann. The foundation is not laid convincingly. Moreover, I have a feeling that the center of gravity of the story wobbles—that it is about the mother one minute and the daughter the next minute. Take a minute and prayerful look at it, and see if you can't pull it together better.

Incidentally, get yourself cured of the quotation-marks disease. You have quoted every fourth phrase in some paragraphs. It is a clumsy device, and unnecessary. Ruth Suckow[2] had it, and I had to use an axe on her to cure her.

The gorillas are in the Smart Set for September, page 56. A copy goes to you by this mail.

I am working day and night on the new review. We hope to get out the first number in December. Knopf is to be the publisher, and it will be a very sightly, and, I hope, dignified monthly. Probable name: the American Mercury. It will cover the whole national scene —politics, education, the sciences, the fine arts. Why not send me some ideas for it? Anything that interests you: the South, the American university, the Anglo-Saxon, anything. We'll pay more than the Liberal weeklies, and every contributor will be free.[3] Our aim, in brief, is to set up an organ of educated Toryism, avoiding the chasing of Liberal butterflies on the one hand and the worship of Judge Gary[4] on the other. I hope, in an early number, to print an article denouncing Abraham Lincoln, and another stating the psychological case for the Ku Klux Klan.

When are you coming back to Baltimore?

Sincerely yours,

H. L. Mencken

I am, of course, abandoning the Smart Set.

[1]Story missing.

[2]One of *The Smart Set* contributors who followed Mencken to *The American Mercury*. Mencken had discovered the writing of the Iowa native in 1921.

[3]*The American Mercury* paid two cents a word for prose, and little occasion was found to pay more, even though other magazines offered several times that much during the 1920s. The relatively low rate showed that the publication would rely on prestige rather than the size of its check. This policy was later followed by Ellery Sedgewick of *The Atlantic*.

[4]Elbert Henry Gary, jurist and chief organizer of the United Steel Corporation. The twelve-hour shift in industry had been in the news throughout 1923; every week one new organization declared that the twelve-hour day was dangerous, inhuman, and unnecessary, and every other week Judge Gary denied the charge and said the workmen favored it. He was finally forced to abolish the seven-day week and the twelve-hour day in the steel mills. The town of Gary, Indiana, laid out in 1906 by U.S. Steel, was named in his honor. Mencken scorned the deification of American business, of which "Judge Gary is its grand vizier as Cal [Calvin Coolidge] is its chief eunuch."

520 SOUTH COURT
MONTGOMERY, ALABAMA

August the twenty-second, 1923

Dear Mr. Mencken,

The gorillas were consoling.[1] And more, your piece on New York[2] and your sentiments about the country.[3] I hate to think of your giving up the Smart Set. I have been reading it and sending you manuscripts ever since I was big enough to lift a stamp. And I have a collection of every style of rejection slip that you ever issued.

The review I am simply wild about. If Knopf is to publish it it will be a knock-out. I still propose to go up in the air at the issuance of the first copy. For your bouquet to Lincoln I promise to bring you any brand that sparkles under this cotton moon. Just name it. As for the Ku Klux I will wager that even the *Hopkins News-Letter*[4] will honor you when you get through with it ...

I am mad to do something on several southern themes of a social cast. What do you think of my turning out a sampler on THE SOUTH-ERN GENTLEMAN? Such a being, of course, has never existed any more than there were angels of the Marne; but the fallacy is a dear one. And especially in the north and east. Naturally I would want to show that the type of gentleman who exists at all is the outcome of certain economic conditions. If the thing is worth doing have you a regulation word-limit?

I am tremendously interested in certain social phenomena hereabout and it would be wonderful to paint them. That one of yours—about the bottom rail being on top in southern society, the relation of Prohibition and Woman's Suffrage to Secession ideals, Education and the Boll Weevil—a dozen others—

As for the university—that needs primarily to be scalded out from the inside. My pet notion is that it is a small town on wheels but minus even the usual small-town thrills. First I would rather do a piece on the Psychology of the Rotary, Kiwanis Exchange, Lions, Pilot, Junior Commerce Clubs. I have some beautiful dope on those.

I am returning to Baltimore about the twentieth of September. I have a grand excuse to see you, too. I am saving what there is of the novel to mail to you after I arrive....

Sincerely yours,
Sara Haardt

¹Mentioned in previous letters. All of the following were in the September 1923 issue of *The Smart Set*.

²Mencken had been "plowing through" Fremont Rider's *New York City: A Guide to Travelers* ("Almost every conceivable fact about New York is here in one volume [although] I can find nothing about bootlegging, a very important matter to strangers who, with provincial shyness, hesitate to apply to the police") and used it as a springboard for his article "New York," a city "strangely lacking in physical charm. . . . the trees have a mangy appearance; the grass is like stable litter. . . . the whole place looks dingy. . . . Fifth Avenue, to me, seems to be gaudy rather than beautiful. What gives it distinction is simply its spick and span air of wealth; it is the only New York street that is clean."

³Entry number 6, "Bucolic in Prose," in Mencken and Nathan's regular feature, "Répétition Générale."

All three articles were in the September 1923 issue of *The Smart Set*.

⁴The newspaper of Johns Hopkins University.

H. L. MENCKEN

1524 HOLLINS ST.

BALTIMORE

August 24th, 1923

Dear Miss Haardt:-

Tackle the Southern gentleman, by all means. Let it run to any workable length—2,000, to 5,000 words. I'll be delighted to see it. Johnson, of the Greensboro News (the only intelligent editorial writer I know of, North or South),¹ has turned in a satirical article on the Northerner from a Southern viewpoint, and is at work on a serious treatise on the Ku Klux Klan, seeking to show its psychological springs. Do anything that strikes you. We'll come out once a month and there'll be plenty of room. Do you want to do a book review now and then?

Getting the new one together is a frightful job. Most of the writers I want to get into it are on holiday, and unreachable. Many of the rest are a bit nervous, fearing that I shall advocate assassinating Coolidge in the first issue. After two or three numbers it will be easier. I resign Coolidge to God.

Let me see the novel before you come to Baltimore, so that I may read it before we meet. The wop in Cathedral street has vanished, but his old cook is running a very good eating house in Saratoga street, bootlegging on the side.² If, without violating your conscience, you can smuggle me a small flask of the native corn I'll pay you back in any vintage wine you name. I want to try it, and write a scientific report on it. The last sample I had was brought to me by a Georgian, and was dreadful stuff. My brother and I tackled it, and both rued the day.

Write any or all of the articles you mention. I'll probably use most of them, and even if I don't you will have the makings of an excellent book.

Hay fever has been toying with me, but it seems very mild. I have booted out the medical faculty, and am treating-myself with lemon juice and bicarbonate of soda. It probably does no good, but it is a very pleasant dose.

Sincerely yours,
H. L. Mencken

[1]The reporting and editorial writing of Gerald W. Johnson of the Greensboro (North Carolina) *Daily News* had caught Mencken's eye in 1922, and by 1926 Johnson was to join Mencken on the Baltimore *Evening Sun* as an editorial writer until 1943, thus reigning as one of the leading native interpreters of the South.

[2]Marconi's, on 106 West Saratoga Street, had opened in 1920.

520 SOUTH COURT
MONTGOMERY, ALABAMA

September the fifth, 1923

Dear Mr. Mencken,

If by any miracle this should ever get into print I am afraid the Confederates are going to dig up my German ancestry—However, I am going to do another as soon as I get breath—

I would, above everything, like to do some reviews: how about letting me take a whack at some of the psychological literature? I might rake up some good dope at Hopkins.

On the sly, while I wait upon my dentist, I am devouring Fitzgerald's letters.[1] I have to do an essay on him some time during the winter for that preposterous volume that Mr. Baker probably told you of.[2] I chose Fitzgerald because I honestly believe old Omar has done more damage than any poem in the English language.

I have been seeing some delightful bootleggers. From the present crop I should say that there are at least three samples that you should speak intelligently of. Some of it, you may not believe, is not half bad. But I will bring you.

Sincerely yours,
Sara Haardt

¹Edward Fitzgerald, English writer and translator of *The Rubaiyat of Omar Khayyam. Some New Letters by Edward Fitzgerald*, edited by F. R. Barton, C.M.G., had just been published.
²Never published.

H. L. MENCKEN
1524 HOLLINS ST.
BALTIMORE

September 9th, 1923

Dear Miss Haardt:-

The treatise on the Southern gentleman somehow leaves me with an impression of insufficiency, but just what is the matter with it I can't make out. Let me give it some prayerful meditation; we can discuss it when you return to Baltimore. When is that to be? Certainly I hope you let me see you as soon as you get back. I'll be here pretty steadily for two weeks. Hay-fever, as usual, is hanging in the air. It reduces me to melancholy and moaning moods.

Baker told me nothing about any volume. You can't possibly overestimate the influence of "Omar" upon the Anglo-Saxon. It completely demoralized him. I believe thoroughly that it paved the way for jazz, Freudism, the rise in the divorce rate, and the sinful life of Greenbaum Village. There should be a monument to Fitz and Omar on the lawn of every country-club. From Edward Fitzgerald to F. Scott! Which suggests Mark Twain's theory that it was the Waverly novels that ruined the South.

I shall give that Southern corn liquor an exhaustive test in my laboratory.

Sincerely yours,
H. L. Mencken

520 SOUTH COURT
MONTGOMERY, ALABAMA

September the thirteenth, 1923

Dear Mr. Mencken,

You will now proceed to curse me black and blue. This bears the tidings that what there is of the novel is headed for you. I registered the package simply because the Republicans and Democrats in the local post office yammer and insult each other with such gusto that what there is of the mail usually perishes by the wayside. I am certain I have "blown up" over the business to the tune of all you see but I swear to you that it did cost me some pains. However, I leave it to you. You have a knack of saying a thing is rotten with such sweet poison that there seems nothing to do but make a fool of oneself once more.

Where did you come by the vivid sheet forwarded in your last? I want you to know that the southern beauty pointed out by you is none other than one Cheridah McLemore, a simple child of really respectable parentage, who has about as much business trying to get on the stage as a jack rabbit.[1] It was my duty to try to teach her history when I was incarcerated at the Margaret Booth School here. Her ambition, though, is not only to make the stage but to keep Montgomery from knowing that she is trying, with the climax that now it has gotten out on her that she has changed her name to Yates—she must surely; of course, have married....

I shall arrive in Baltimore on Monday, the twenty-fourth. Since I am looking forward so very much to seeing you I fully expect to hear that you have been buried in New York for the rest of my natural life or else struck dumb with hay-fever.

Pray, don't.

Sincerely yours,
Sara Haardt

[1]Cheridah later married a man named Chilton, a chemist for DuPont, and moved to Wilmington, and, much later, to Tuscaloosa, Alabama.

~

H. L. MENCKEN
1524 HOLLINS ST.
BALTIMORE

September 17th, 1923

Dear Miss Haardt:-

The MS is here and I shall fall upon in it a day or two. I'll be here, I think, the whole week of the 24th. As soon as you pass the customs let us have a palaver. I suggest lunch, if you can escape for it. If not, then dinner.

Cheridah, it appears, is not yet on the stage. That press-sheet is published by a theatrical agent who thus tries to get jobs for his clients. But I predict that she will get her chance and make a great success, and that the Montgomery Rotary Club will be giving her a welcome before three years have ebbed and oozed away.

The Mercury is keeping me jumping. I have had four nights on sleepers during the past 12 days. Friday night I came down from New York with a carload of Confederate sports who had gone up to see the Dempsey-Firpo fight.[1] These worthy men, it appears, had bet on the wop. They were buzzing all night; fortunately, I can sleep in a boiler-works.

Sincerely yours,
H. L. Mencken

[1]Jack Dempsey, the "Manassa Mauler," fought his title defense against Argentine heavyweight Louis Angel Firpo in Jersey City, with close to 100,000 people attending, and left a battered Firpo bleeding from the nose, mouth, and ears. No fight in the history of boxing had ever generated so much disgust, praise, controversy, or reform.

520 SOUTH COURT
MONTGOMERY, ALABAMA

September the nineteenth, 1923

Dear Mr. Mencken,

"On Victuals" is the most delightful piece that has met my eye since you applauded the English-teaching tribe.[1] Your thesis was worthy of an epic and, when mingled with some terrible memories I suffer, I could hardly read for joy. However, I cannot forgive you the cold fish in jelly.[2] That description was something terrible. Lord!

The other enclosure reduced me to a state of tears. The photograph belongs to the Pleistocene Period and I would promise to do anything if they would leave it alone. The last time I was casually mentioned as a Professor I was cursed, berated, scolded, informed, and made to understand by the whole rank that it was my professional and ethical duty to put a stop to such journalistic outrages. Seriously, they honestly suspected that I had ogled and then tipped the entire reportorial staff.

I am past thanking you for the reading of the manuscript. It was noble of you. What I fully expected was for you to advise me to take it and wade into the Chesapeake, suspecting that I could not swim. If you say so I shall attack it prayerfully again.

Indeed, yes, I can escape for lunch. I am not scheduled for classes at Goucher until Friday. But, even so, all the king's horses and so forth couldn't stay me.

The mercury is roaring at ninety-nine in the shade. You can't imagine it and I'm glad you can't. Baltimore—I shall be ever so glad to see!

Sincerely yours,
Sara Haardt

---

[1]"On Victuals," September 17, 1923, the Baltimore *Evening Sun*.

[2]"Perhaps the best French eating-house in New York is the Brevoort Hotel, on lower Fifth Avenue. . . . I went in one evening for dinner, saw cold fish in jelly on the bill-of-fare, and insanely ordered a rasher of it. . . . The dish is basically German, but with Yiddish overtones. It is prepared perfectly only by *Kosher* cooks, thoroughly grounded in Old Testament theology. When they put their minds to the business, they make a dream of it. But the more a Frenchman puts his mind to it, the worse it becomes. The honest *cuisinier* of the Brevoort converted it into something quite horrible. He chose a fish that had suffered, apparently, from diabetes, and he made the jelly obscene by dyeing it pink! The spectacle was revolting, and the flavor was that of second-rate shaving cream. As I say, I departed after one mouthful, and ran all the way to Luchows to ease my pyretial gullet. The cook there was an unflinching nationalist, with no weakness for the exotic. He gave me Rinderbrust mit Meerrettig. It was superb."

ALS

2326 NORTH CHARLES STREET

September the twenty-fifth, 1923

Dear Mr. Mencken,

The President[1] has roped me in for official duty on Wednesday and I dare not refuse. Could it be Thursday at the same hour?

I arrived from Alabama carrying several of your flasks and I wonder how I am to get it to you. In spite of my faith in Mr. Baker I would hesitate to ask him to get it to you and I know of no jellybean[2] whom I could trust in these parts. Perhaps, under cover of darkness, I could manage the package but that hour might be inconvenient for you.

I shall certainly rejoice to see you.

Sincerely yours,

Sara Haardt

[1]William Westley Guth, president of Goucher College.

[2]Southern nickname for "town sheik" or (as in this case), simply, a young person.

H. L. MENCKEN

1524 HOLLINS ST.

BALTIMORE

September 25th, 1923

Dear Miss Haardt:-

Too bad! Thursday, I fear, is hopeless, but what of Saturday? I suggest the same time and place: 12:15 at the wop's in Saratoga street.

God will reward you for bringing those flasks. Hold them securely and we'll discuss transporting them when we meet. Don't trust anyone, and especially not Baker. He is a heavy drinker.

Sincerely yours,

H. L. Mencken

I am, a la Babbitt, sending two copies of this letter, to be sure of reaching you.

~

2326 NORTH CHARLES STREET

October the seventh, 1923

Dear Mr. Mencken,

Your contribution to the *Southern Literary* was the best thing I've experienced these past days.[1] I should rather see that in the hands of the Confederates than the Apostles' Creed. When the old dears come to, every God-endowed 'Episcopalian' college of the Black Belt is going to crown you with a first degree. On that hinges the tale that when I tried to procure one of your volumes in Montgomery this summer the bookseller informed me with a lofty air that he was "out," his reason being—that the work was a best-seller. It seems that he had sold you out during the commencement season—Well, I forgive you.

I know one thing: that for a mortal with a sense of humor you are the most perfect gentleman I have ever seen or heard tell of. After leaving you in a fainting condition last Saturday, I returned here and re-read the manuscript. The colossal imbecilities therein, including the one on the Thirty-sixth Amendment, would have brought tears to the eyes of even a Professor of English. For restraint you would put a college president in the shade. You may delight to know that I have ogled, prayed with, beseeched, even gone to the movies with impossible dotards, from no less than six legislatures of my native state in the interest of the aforementioned Nineteenth. I can't even lay it to Mathematics, which I declare is the root of all evils, since even I can add that two times nineteen does not make thirty six—or wouldn't—

As for the liquor, if you are still in the mood for it,—let me bring it down town to you, say, to the corner above the Stafford,[2] or the end of the bus line, wherever that is, or any other place you could conveniently reach. I could come in the morning of Monday, Wednesday, or Friday, if you would rather, or in the afternoon of the same days, or Saturday. If you wanted to wait until late in the afternoon, just before you went home to dinner or something, I could meet you then. I would be coming down town, anyway, so don't fuss about it.

I am fixing up the novel at the weak spot sighted by you and I swear the damsel is leaving the home-town for a reason that will swell even your heart with pity. Also, I attended the first meeting of the seminar on the Psychology of Religions last Friday and if I am not disappointed I shall be the very Spirit of the worm before the year is out.

Sincerely yours,

Sara Haardt

¹The *Southern Literary* magazine, published in Atlanta, had just published Mencken's article "Is the South a Desert?" for its October 1923 issue.

²Long a landmark in the Mount Vernon area, the Stafford Hotel was located at 716 Washington Place.

H. L. MENCKEN

1524 HOLLINS ST.

BALTIMORE

October 8th, 1923

Dear Miss Haardt:-

God will reward you! Could we meet for lunch on Wednesday? My conscience troubles me about letting a Refined Women tote moonshine through the streets of a great Christian city. Couldn't I call for you, conceal the jugs in my baggage, and then make off with you to the wop's studio?¹ If not, where shall we meet and when? If Wednesday is impossible, I suggest Saturday.

I spent the week end on the Eastern Shore,² along with two other Baptists, one of them a judge. The local gentry turned out Saturday night to drink us under the table, but when the smoke cleared away all save four or five of them were dead on the field of honor. A great place for eating and drinking, but I saw only one pretty gal, and she was a New Yorker. A sad scene. The native *Junker*³ can't keep up their estates, and so all the best land is falling into the hands of profiteers from the North and West.

Sincerely yours,

H. L. Mencken

¹Marconi's restaurant.

²Mencken often visited his friend, the lawyer Daniel M. Henry, of Easton, Maryland, an undisputed authority on cooking canvasback duck and diamondback terrapin. On this particular occasion, Mencken ate from a 35-pound ham that

took him back to the days of the pre-Noachian monsters, and drank peach brandy out of gourds.

³Gentry.

2326 NORTH CHARLES STREET

October the ninth, 1923

Dear Mr. Mencken,

I could die, gladly, after hearing your sentiments on the moonshine. The thought is a beautiful one, and almost furnished me with a thesis, but—let me meet you at Marconi's, at 12:15, on Saturday. I can arrive safely and will not disillusion you....

If you were deaf, blind, and foolish, I believe that you would still have the impeccable taste to insist upon having a pretty nurse. It is an everlasting joy to weigh you against the academics. I hear that at the Hopkins not long ago a royal debate was staged on the subject of the Probable Effects of a Ph.D. on you. God perish the thought! I would rather see you dead by the chiropractors than to project you in to such a possibility.

Remember, too, that I flatter you to the extent of insinuating that "a small flask" would not have startled even the ghost of a shadow of a sensation; and, hence, all this—

Saturday, then?¹

Sincerely yours,
Sara Haardt

¹Sara Haardt brought the corn liquor in her typewriter case.

H. L. MENCKEN

1524 HOLLINS ST.

BALTIMORE

October 16th, 1923

Dear Miss Haardt:-

I have waited for the report of the medical examiners before reporting myself. They say that there is no permanent damage. After the first swig my blood pressure jumped to 170, but that is not alarming at my age. There ensued a great ringing in the ears, with flashes of orange light. Then a slight hemiphlegia, with sensations as of star shells exploding in the head. Then gradual anaesthesia, with coma and Cheyne-Stokes breathing. Then recovery. A potent refresher. I shall try some of it on my pastor.

Your Corona case goes back to you by parcel post. My very best thanks. It was a great pleasure to see you again, but I fear I talked you deaf. Well, I run on and run on. What an audience!

I am off for New York in a few days to dry Knopf's tears. The Mercury will be the death of him. Do we meet when I get back? Is Saturday your best day for lunching downtown?

Sincerely yours,
H. L. Mencken

2326 NORTH CHARLES STREET

October the seventeenth, 1923

Dear Mr. Mencken,

If I had not heard by high noon of this very day I should have sent up one more heavenly message, confessed the blood to Mr. Baker, paid him off in Coca Colas, and winged him after you. My prayers, whole gilt-edged flocks of them, have been attending you all this while. You promised, though, that you would whistle and I was pondering that if your sins were lofty ones God would surely punish you by turning you into a policeman—for spite, of course—and I was wondering....

Saturday happens to be my best day for lunching downtown for as you witness I can stay until you put me away. Some day, or night, try to talk me deaf or even to tears. Tonight, now I was plain wishing. . . .

Will you send me the *Calvinism* that I didn't get to finish?[1]

Sincerely yours,
Sara Haardt

[1]Mencken had written two articles on Calvinism for *The Outlook* (London): "Calvinism: New style," September 29, 1923, and for the Baltimore *Evening Sun*: "Calvinism (Secular)."

H. L. MENCKEN
1524 HOLLINS ST.
BALTIMORE

October 18th, 1923

Dear Miss Haardt:-

I am back to normalcy, as Baker can testify. He was at my house last night, and I showed only a few tremors. Saturday of this week, unluckily, I have some visiting literati on my hands, and I don't know at the moment whether I'll have returned from New York by the Saturday following. But the chances are that I'll be here. May I write to you from New York? The American Mercury, confidentially, is in a frightful mess, with make-up day fast approaching. I begin to lose confidence in prayer. It will be a fearful sweat getting it on its legs. But nothing, of course, is impossible to one who has Vision and the spirit of Service in him. Soli Deo gloria!

I enclose the Calvinism piece. As you will note, it is almost identical with a version I printed in the Evening Sun.

Sincerely yours,
H. L. Mencken

H. L. MENCKEN
1524 HOLLINS ST.
BALTIMORE

November 1st, 1923

Dear Miss Haardt:-

Something is wrong with this story.¹ The device whereby Judith snares the good doctor is made a bit too simple; it somehow becomes improbable. I see what you are driving at: that the imbecilities of the flappers drive him upon her fly-paper, but it seems to me that cause and effect are not made sufficiently clear. He falls altogether too quickly. Such a fellow, as a mere matter of routine, would at least make *some* effort to escape. He is certainly not a novice; he has been bathed in trained nurses for four years, and their technique is extremely competent. But let us go over the MS. when we meet again.

When is it to be? What of Saturday of this week? Will you let me know? I have discovered a place where first-rate beer is on draught,

but it serves no cocktails. We had better stick to the wop. He will
be in jail soon.

Sincerely yours,
H. L. Mencken

¹"The Smartest Girl in Town," never published.

H. L. MENCKEN
1524 HOLLINS ST.
BALTIMORE

November 1st, 1923

Dear Miss Haardt:-

Since I wrote to you this morning I have had a telephone call from
the office in New York and must go there by sleeper tonight. I won't
get back until after Saturday noon. What of Saturday week?

Sincerely yours,
H. L. Mencken

H. L. MENCKEN
1524 HOLLINS ST.
BALTIMORE

November 3rd, 1923

Dear Miss Haardt:-

Your note, just received on my return to Baltimore, gives me a
skeer. Didn't you receive my second letter? If you didn't, and the
result was that you went to the wop's and then damned me to 1,000,000
years of hell for failing to show up, I can only fall on my face and
offer my most profound apologies.

I was yanked to New York suddenly by a melodramatic emergency,
of which more when we meet.¹ Will it be next Saturday? I hope so.
I found poor Knopf with a pulse of 245 and his forehead cold and
clammy.

Sincerely yours,
H. L. Mencken

¹William P. Rossiter, the head of Rumford Press of Concord, Maine (which
also printed *The Atlantic*), suddenly notified Knopf that he refused to print the
Mercury because he thought some of the material was offensive. (The article in
question was James Cain's "The Labor Leader," which later appeared in the

February issue.) Knopf switched to the Haddon Press of Camden, New Jersey. "Working with a printer full of the delusions that he had authority to censor the magazine would have been extremely uncomfortable," Mencken wrote years later in his "Autobiographical Notes." It would later prove to be a step well taken.

H. L. MENCKEN

1524 HOLLINS ST.

BALTIMORE

November 12th, 1923

Dear Miss Haardt:-

Crystal is very persuasive, but she quite forgets the Christian doctrine that one of the aims of connubial bliss is to punish both parties.[1] I doubt that the rev. clergy will ratify her scheme. It is altogether too romantic, and, perhaps I may add, improper. I can't rid myself of the suspicion that she regards her husband as, in some sense, a lover. This is surely not to be countenanced by right-thinking Americans. I am passing on the article to a woman who has gone her one better. This fair creature lives in Paris; her husband in New York. They see each other once a year.

The chances are that I'll be on my way to New York Saturday. The Mercury is down with 35 different diseases, all apparently fatal. But I'll surely be back by Saturday a week. What of lunch together then? I suggest avoiding the wop until he returns to normalcy. There is a marvellous beer-house in Saratoga street, highly respectable outwardly but with a superb Dunkles on tap.[2] Or let us try the Southern Hotel, where a loud orchestra plays Massenet at meals and the drummers entertain the lady white goods buyers.[3] Or the Rennert, where the ceilings are 18 feet high but the food is excellent.[4]

Yours,

H. L. Mencken

[1]Story missing.

[2]Fritz Baum's restaurant, at 320 West Saratoga Street, between Howard and Eutaw streets, had become a landmark and rendezvous for the theater crowd and for musicians. There was one large dining room and several smaller ones for private parties. On the walls were decorations depicting legendary elves from folklore. The restaurant specialized in German cooking and beer was the drink, day and night (those misplaced souls who preferred to drink highballs with their *hasenpfeffer* were admitted, but talked about in the kitchen).

[3]The Southern Hotel, on the northeast corner of Light and Redwood Streets, was the third building to occupy the historic site of the colonial Fountain Inn, which became a favorite stopping place for George Washington on his journeys between Mount Vernon and the seat of government in Philadelphia. The hotel, with its 324 guest rooms, main ballroom, parlors, and roof garden, opened at the end of World War I and closed in 1964.

[4]Baltimore's leading hotel, on Saratoga and Liberty Streets, attracted politicians and socialites alike into its spectacular, elegant dining room. Today it is a parking garage.

H. L. MENCKEN
1524 HOLLINS ST.
BALTIMORE

November 15th, 1923

Wohledle, Hochehr- und Tugenbelobte und auch Hochgelehrte Fräulein[1]:-

Don't forget that I, too, have a talent for politesse. Auf Englisch: truly noble, highly honorable, for virtue praised and also high learned puella. My own legal title, by the way, is Herr Geheimrat. In conversation it is abbreviated to Herr Rat.

What of *this* Saturday? I find that I can get loose at lunch time, and the Saturday following I may still be in New York. If you are free I suggest that we meet at the wop's. I begin to fear that the beer-house, because of the current police raids, will be dry. I'll bring a drink to the wop's that will be better than his Bacardi.

Will you let me know about Saturday? A letter mailed tomorrow (Friday) will reach me in time.

Ihr Ergebener![2]
H. L. Mencken

[1]Very Noble, Highly Honorable Virtuous and Highly Learned Miss.
[2]Yours devotedly!

H. L. MENCKEN
1524 HOLLINS ST.
BALTIMORE

November 26th, 1923

Dear Miss Haardt:-

By dint of powerful prayer and the direct intervention of SS. Joseph and Bonaventura, we got the first number of the Mercury made up

Saturday afternoon. I spare you the accidents of the last week; they would make you sob. My yells and curses could be heard a block.

Such adventures make a man crave the Civilizing Influence of Lovely Woman. If you have any Missionary Zeal you will resort to the wop's with me on Saturday. What do you say?

Sincerely yours,

H. L. Mencken

H. L. MENCKEN
1524 HOLLINS ST.
BALTIMORE

November 28th, 1923

Dear Miss Haardt:-

Then we meet on Saturday at 12:15. Excellent! Dunlap's[1] discoveries affect me greatly—particularly that filling the right ear with hot water rotates the eyes to the left. A fine piece of research. I am tempted to put it into "Americana."[2]

All that remains is to psychoanalyze the morons. But more of this when we meet.

Yours,

H. L. Mencken

[1] Knight Dunlap, professor of psychology at the Johns Hopkins University, was also Sara's professor.

[2] The "Americana" section of *The Smart Set* comprised excerpts from foolish speeches, sermons, books, or passages of stupidity or prejudice from a newspaper. First a state was mentioned, then came a short ironical introduction by the editor further defining the source of the folly, and finally a brief passage was excerpted. The first "Americana" appeared in *The Smart Set* as early as 1914; then "Major Owen Hatteras, D.S.O." (Mencken and Nathan's joint pseudonym) began the "Americana" section in the May 1923 issue of *The Smart Set* and transferred it, without change, to *The American Mercury*. An imitation of "Americana" can be seen in current issues of *The New Yorker* magazine.

H. L. MENCKEN

1524 HOLLINS ST.

BALTIMORE

December 6th, 1923

Dear Miss Haardt:-

Where is the MS? If it is not already dispatched, bring it along on Saturday. I'll meet you, God willing, at the old ruined mill at 12:15.[1] I begin to tire of gin, which killed nine of my uncles. What do you say to Bacardi for a change?

I may have to depart early, but we can eat fast.[2]

Yours,

H. L. Mencken

[1]Timanus Rock Mill, an old stone structure that still stands to the south of the Cedar Avenue Bridge on the fringe of Druid Hill Park, was three to four miles away from Sara's apartment and north of the old campus of Goucher College. The abandoned grain mill was in a state of ruin in the 1920s, but it was rustic and scenic, affording a place to sit and watch a gurgling stream while being practically lost within the city. Here, during Prohibition times, Mencken and Sara would exchange a sip of liquor.

[2]*The American Mercury* went to press on December 6, 1923, with a first-copy printing of 5000 copies. It would be distributed on the newsstands on Christmas Eve.

H. L. MENCKEN

1524 HOLLINS ST.

BALTIMORE

December 9th, 1923

Dear Miss Haardt:-

As I feared, this Malone[1] turns out to be a cataloguer. What is accomplished by his toilsome division of the verbs into categories with a clumsy name for each? Absolutely nothing. Everything he says is already known, and it is not worth knowing. He somehow reminds me of the sort of man who knows the names and addresses of all the Democratic leaders in the counties of Maryland. What a waste of the human cerebrum!

It was a great pleasure to see you yesterday. I only hope that cocktail didn't cause you to repine later on. Last night the musical brethren sat at my house until 1 o'clock, and it was 2:15 before I got the smoke pumped out and the bottles washed. But no diligence in the cause of Art is too much. We played Richard Strauss' "Tod und Verklärung" and made all the neighbors regret that the war was over and the Department of Justice no longer functioning. During the war secret agents used to stand outside, waiting for us to play "Die Wacht Am Rhein." Several times we actually played it in G minor and they didn't recognize it.

God knows when I'll get back. But I'll read the MS before the end of the week.

> Yours,
> H. L. Mencken

[1]Later regarded as America's foremost Old English scholar, Kemp Malone, a graduate of Emory University and the University of Chicago, had at this time just become an assistant professor at Johns Hopkins University.

ALS

THE AMERICAN MERCURY
220 WEST FORTY-SECOND STREET
NEW YORK

December 12, 1923

Dear Miss Haardt:-

The novel is an excellent piece of work—really distinguished. I like it very much. But the last 2 or 3 pages drag fearfully. I believe they should be changed. The job is small—perhaps 2 hours. I offer my reasons when we meet.

When may that be? I'll probably find myself up to the ears if I get back to Baltimore by Saturday. What of Wednesday? Or some other day?

> Yours
> H. L. Mencken

~

ALS

H. L. MENCKEN
1524 HOLLINS ST.
BALTIMORE

December 23, 1923

Dear Miss Haardt:

Let me hear that you are getting well—and keep out of the fog and wind! It was heroical to come out today.

I got home to find news that one of my aunts had died at noon[1]—in the full hope, I take it, of a glorious resurrection. Monday the funeral. This is the fifth year running that I have gone to a funeral in Xmas week!

Yrs.,
H. L. Mencken

[1] Mencken's paternal aunt, Jane Mencken.

ALS

THE AMERICAN MERCURY
220 WEST FORTY-SECOND STREET
NEW YORK

December 27, 1923

Dear Miss Haardt:

I am dreadfully sorry to hear of it! But now you simply *must* stay in bed, and get well. My conscience is not silent. I should have taken you home on Saturday the moment you appeared. Going out in that fog was almost insane.

I'll be here on Saturday morning. Where are you? In the infirmary?[1]

Yrs.,
H. L. Mencken

[1] Sara was in her "2 × 4 room . . . with practically no food and not even enough cover on the bed," Sara Mayfield wrote home. "Why she hasn't died I don't see because the food she has had would kill a person much less a sick one."

~

H. L. MENCKEN
1524 HOLLINS ST.
BALTIMORE

December 31st, 1923

Dear Miss Haardt:-

You go into my card catalogue: human beings NEVER learn by experience. First, a day of fog floors you, and now you go out again, with a cold wind blowing. I can only hope that God overlooks it. To such dark and irrational intelligences the Republic looks for light and leading. Think of your responsibility to the Confederacy!

But I am delighted that you are better. When may I have a view of you? Are you on exhibition in the Krankenhaus,[1] or must I wait until you are able to come downtown? I'll be here all week.

Yours,

H. L. Mencken

[1] Hospital.

~

1924

When students came back to Goucher College from Christmas vacation in early January, they found that Sara Haardt had been sick in bed throughout the holidays with acute bronchitis bordering on pneumonia. On January 5 Sara got out of bed to meet Mencken at the old ruined mill, but as luck would have it, Baltimore weather took a turn for the worse, and that day the thermometer plunged to as low as 9° F, with a high gusty wind.

H. L. MENCKEN
1524 HOLLINS ST.
BALTIMORE

January 2nd, 1924

Dear Miss Haardt:-

It is excellent news that you are well enough to escape. I suggest that we meet at the old ruined mill at 12:15 on Saturday. I'll be present in advance, along with my jug. His old rival having been disposed of, the wop should be in excellent humor.

My niece[1] has departed, and now I hope to get some sleep. I only hope you are quite well, and not taking chances again with this infernal weather. This morning it was 18 degrees and the lather froze on my jowls.

We have had to reprint No. 1 of the Mercury. Knopf has bought eight new chrome yellow neckties and a carved Weichsel-wood walking stick.[2]

Yours,
M.

[1]Virginia Mencken, daughter of Mencken's brother Charles.

[2]By December 28 a second printing of *The American Mercury* had been prepared, and then a third, with a total of 22,000 copies quickly sold. In January Alfred Knopf sponsored a series of literary parties to celebrate the unusually prompt success of the magazine. By the end of 1924 it was at 42,614 copies, and after only two years of existence the magazine had gone up to 62,323.

H. L. MENCKEN
1524 HOLLINS ST.
BALTIMORE

January 15th, 1924

Dear Miss Haardt:-

Miss Nicolson writes that your temperature is disappearing, for which the Holy Saints be thanked.[1] My one hope is that you do not now poke your finger into the Eye of Omnipotence by going out too soon. Miss Nicolson hints that the Goucher Appendix to the White Slave Act forbids me to wait upon you until you are under steam again. But I'd certainly like to see you some time without your hat on. I'll be here all week, but next week I'll probably be in New York. By this mail I am sending you a book. My chaplain is lame in both knees.

Sincerely yours,
H. L. Mencken

[1] Dr. Marjorie Hope Nicolson, assistant professor of English at Goucher, went through the first siege with Sara. She had always looked upon Sara as "my little sister" and felt responsible for her; now, she vainly shopped around the general practitioners "who were all we could afford." Later, it would be Mencken who made it possible for Sara to see his own doctors.

~

H. L. MENCKEN
1524 HOLLINS ST.
BALTIMORE

January 18th, 1924

Miss Sara Haardt,
2326 N. Charles St.
City

Dear Miss Haardt:-

Zu befehl, Fräulein Oberst![1] I am at your orders Saturday.[2] But I protest very violently, as a lay member of the faculty, against your leaving the house with a temperature still running. It is, in such weather, extremely dangerous. I was particeps criminis to your last folly; I refuse to be so again. Stay in bed until you are back to normalcy. The x-ray can wait. If a shadow shows now, it will alarm you, and yet it may be of no significance whatever.

All I ask is that, when I come to judgment on the dreadful Resurrection Morn, the fact be remembered that I sent you no flowers while you were ill.[3]

I am going to New York on Tuesday, and shall be here on Monday, God willing.

Yours,
H. L. Mencken

[1]"At your orders, Miss Colonel!"
[2]Mencken was planning to take Sara to the doctors himself, but she was unable to make it.
[3]Mencken hated cut flowers, and their heavy perfume reminded Sara of death.

H. L. MENCKEN
1524 HOLLINS ST.
BALTIMORE

Sunday, January 20, 1924

Dear Sara:-

I enclose a card to Dr. Kahn.[1] You may see him any morning at 905 N. Charles Street, between 9 o'clock and noon. He is instructed to make x-ray plates of your upper works, and to pass you on to Sloan[2] for a physical examination and to Collenberg[3] for any laboratory work that may be necessary. Go to him on Monday and do whatever he tells you to do. He and his associates are very competent.

The more I think of it the more astonishing it seems that Guth should turn you out.[4] In fact, I doubt that he would do it if he knew all the circumstances. More, I doubt that he would do it in the face of a word from your doctor, as a member of his board. Why don't you tell him what the situation is—that is, the doctor? Or does he know it? What noble Christians the Methodists are!

I'll be back in Baltimore on Saturday night. Will you let me have a note telling me where and when I may see you on Sunday? I see no reason whatever for alarm. The chances are at least 10 to 1 that there is nothing worse to deal with than a post-bronchitis cloudiness. Even if there is a lesion it is very new and very small, and may be disposed of quickly.[5]

I kiss your hand.

Yours,
HLM

[1]Max Kahn, nonplaying member of The Saturday Night Club, and radiologist.

[2]Martin Francis Sloan, widely known authority on the treatment of tuberculosis, had in 1924 become president of the Maryland Tuberculosis Association. It was through his efforts that free chest clinics were established throughout the state.

[3]Harry T. Collenberg, leading clinical pathologist, who established the clinical laboratory at St. Agnes Hospital.

[4]President Guth of Goucher College and Lillian Welsh, professor of physiology and hygiene, had decided that, in view of Sara's illness, she not be allowed to teach at Goucher.

[5]When Sara had her X-ray, the doctors discerned a spot as big as an orange located near the back of her left lung.

~

ALS

H. L. MENCKEN
1524 HOLLINS ST.
BALTIMORE

January 21, 1924

Dear Sara:

Will you let me know what Kahn reports? I'll be at the Algonquin Hotel, 59 West 44th st., until Saturday. I'll call you up as soon as I get back. A brave gal you are indeed! I hadn't suspected half your difficulties. But don't let it bother you too much. The illness, whatever it is, can be disposed of quickly, and the money will be found somehow. I doubt that Guth will have the brass to put you off; it would cause a great scandal.

I kiss your hand. Write to me at once, will you?

Yrs,
HLM

ALS

THE AMERICAN MERCURY
220 WEST FORTY-SECOND STREET
NEW YORK

January 23, 1924

Dear Sara:

I hope you do whatever Sloan and Kahn recommend. If Sloan says go to Lubillasville,¹ go as soon as you can. You will be comfortable and contented in two days, and as you begin to put on weight you'll probably actually enjoy it. The place is not far from Baltimore. It is a first-rate hospital, run by good men, and you will be under Sloan's eye. Kahn says that a complete cure is certain.

God knows, I wish I were near enough to see you today. I'll be in on Saturday and shall call you up as soon as I arrive.

I kiss both hands.

Yrs.,
HLM

¹Lubillasville was Sloan's private clinic, but because of financial difficulty Sara opted to go to Maple Heights Sanitorium, in Sparks, Maryland, only 15 miles from Baltimore, on top of a steep hill.

By 1923 the national death rate in tuberculosis was 94 for each 100,000 persons. It was an affliction that caused considerable anxiety. Sara Haardt's siege at Maple Heights would not end until twelve months later, until she was, as Mencken said, "at the dead center of boredom." She described it in an article years later: "I had lived through tortures in this room, and now it was mine in a sense that nothing else had been mine my whole life. . . . From here I had stared out of the windows by the hour. Winter. Spring. Summer. And now Autumn. The months had slipped by so swiftly that I was scarcely aware of their coming and going. But now I remembered, absurdly, that in winter the snowflakes reminded me of the white petals of flowers, and in the spring the white petals of the apple blossoms reminded me of the snowflakes. In such pitiful ways had I diverted myself." For the first month she was not allowed to write or have any visitors. In spite of Sara's weakness, the urge to write persisted. "The only solution was to induce my nurse to give me a supply of pencils and paper so I could write to my heart's content." After a few more weeks, Mencken was allowed to visit.

H. L. MENCKEN
1524 HOLLINS ST.
BALTIMORE

Wednesday, February 6, 1924

Dear Sara:-

At last you emerge from the horse-blankets! I can only be Polonius and urge you to submit docilely. The aim of the rest cure is to break the temperature; there is no other way to get rid of it. William James used to argue that perhaps a temperature of 100 would be more favorable to spiritual growth than the normal 98.6. But I doubt it; it runs the machine amok. Perhaps no gentleman should mention it, but I feel it may be my duty to tell you that, when you were running 100 the other night, you used the word "damn" and tried to kiss me. This would make a scandal if it were known.

There is absolutely no reason why you should be uneasy. Count the six months as lost, and look ahead. You are young enough to be able to lose them. The whole adventure is precisely like breaking a leg, or having a baby, or going to jail. Once the temperature is knocked out you will feel perfectly normal, and begin to put on weight rapidly.

The stuffing is really not bad. I kept it up for several years. It will cure you permanently of victualling on fruit salads and such cobwebs. I suspect that this is what gave the bronchitis its chance. When you get out I shall order a dinner for you that will stagger the waiter.

I assume that you'll be forbidden visitors so long as you are in bed. As soon as you sit up let me hear of it and I'll wait on you. What do you feel like reading? Novels? I am tempted to send you "Heliogabalus,"[1] but maybe you have read it already, and in any case it would cause another scandal. I shall be in New York next week (we are moving),[2] but I'll be back by Sunday.

Ich kuss die Hand.

Yours,
HLM

[1]*Heliogabalus: A Buffoonery Written in Three Acts* was a play cowritten by Mencken and George Jean Nathan and published by Knopf in 1920. It had quickly sold out, and for years American stage companies vainly sought for the rights to put it on stage. When Mencken finally did mail the book to Sara on February 8, he warned her: "Don't let it circulate in the prison. Some of the other inmates may be Methodists, and we'll both go in jail. It is extremely irreligious, and depicts a Christian maiden as a nuisance."

[2]*The American Mercury* was moving from 220 West Forty-Second Street into a section of Alfred Knopf's new suite in the Heckscher building, a conspicuous tower at 57th Street.

THE AMERICAN MERCURY
220 WEST FORTY-SECOND STREET
NEW YORK

February 12th, 1924

Dear Sara:-

I am off for Babylon, to be gone until the end of the week. We are moving on Friday, and I must haul the booze in person. Now that Christianity is in the Constitution it is impossible to trust anyone. The job will take me half a day and cost me $10 in taxi fares. I only hope that hi-jackers do not hold me up. Last night two bootleggers fell into a dispute at the corner of the square in front of my house, and one of them murdered the other. My mother, hearing the shots, rushed to the window, and was in time to see the pursuit and capture of the murderer. This is the seventh or eighth murder in my neighborhood in historical times. We are looking up.

When you get the chance let me know what treatment you are suffering and how your fever curve is running. As soon as I am permitted to wait upon you, I shall sneak a look at your chart. You should be free of fever very shortly and begin to put on weight. When your sentence expires you will be a very bulky gal, but not too bulky. I shall kiss your hand anyhow—that is, so long as you are under 200 lbs.

Yours,
M

H. L. MENCKEN
1524 HOLLINS ST.
BALTIMORE

February 18th, 1924

My dear Sara:-

What is the news with you? And when may I come out to see you? No word from you for a week! I want to hear that the temperature is busted and that you are putting on weight. Certainly I must see you at least once while you are still svelte.

We finished moving in New York and are now at 730 Fifth avenue, the swellest building ever heard of. Our office walls are covered with mahogany panels. I crave the honor of showing you all this gaudiness when you graduate.[1]

Ich kuss die Hand.

Yours,
HLM

[1] The new offices, with a luxurious black-and-white tiled floor, well-upholstered library, and neatly arranged desks, were businesslike compared to the ones Mencken and Nathan had left behind from *The Smart Set* days.

THE AMERICAN MERCURY
220 WEST FORTY-SECOND STREET
NEW YORK

Saturday, February 23, 1924

Dearest Sara:-

Our long and interesting discussion of Hegelism this afternoon made me forget to warn you about that wine. It has been in my cellar five years, and in that time anything is apt to happen. If, when you open it, it turns out to be corked, heave it out of the window. There is no way to determine the condition of red wine exactly without pulling the cork. It looked good, but sometimes looks are deceptive. Red wine is delicate, and sometimes grows senile and undrinkable.

I got down the hill in 57 seconds, counting two flops on my caboose. At the bottom I ran into a Paleozoic stratum full of bones of sword-tooth tigers, cave hyenas and Neanderthal man. The mud came up to my knees. But what is mud to a hero of the wars? I fought my way out, and had a long palaver with the watchman at the crossing, a very amiable wop. He told me that there were many stills in the vicinity. God knows what is to become of the Constitution.

I refuse to believe that you are ill. Today you looked superb. I suspect that I am mashed on you; nevertheless, my eyes are still reliable. Ich kuss die Hand!

Yours,
HLM

H. L. MENCKEN
1524 HOLLINS ST.
BALTIMORE

February 25th, 1924

Dear Miss Haardt:-

The article on slavery goes into type at once.[1] It is excellent stuff and I am delighted to have it. The enclosed I like also, but it leaves me with a doubt that The American Mercury is the proper magazine for it.[2] I think it ought to be printed in some periodical of specifically literary purpose, and maybe I should add one somewhat more serious in tone than The American Mercury. The best of them is The Saturday

Review. I therefore suggest that you submit it to Dr. Canby.³ You ought to be writing for him anyhow.

Sincerely yours,

H. L. Mencken

¹"The Etiquette of Slavery" would not be published until the May 1929 issue of *The American Mercury*.

²A short story Sara had written. Mencken was beginning to discourage writers from sending short stories and encouraged them instead to write articles dealing with social issues. No doubt Mencken kept a carbon of this letter in his office in New York to have a record of it; hence, the formality.

³Henry Seidel Canby, critic, author, and editor of *The Saturday Review* from 1924 to 1952. The magazine, subtitled "of Literature," emphasized literature and the arts.

ALS

THE AMERICAN MERCURY

220 WEST FORTY-SECOND STREET

NEW YORK

February 27, 1924

Dear Sara:

The printer is drinking again, our beautiful stenog has quit us, and so I am up to my ears and probably won't get back to Baltimore until late on Saturday. May I have the honor of waiting on you next week? What days are visiting sociologists admitted beside the two Sabbaths?

The damned stenog left us cold, with no notice and the office in horrible confusion.¹ This after 10 years! In Hell God will punish her. We had a new one but she is still almost useless. She is of the intelligentsia and reads Guillaume Apollinaire² and Remy de Gourmont.³

Your hand is kissed.

Yrs,

HLM

¹Not to be confused with Edith Lustgarten, who had been a secretary to Mencken since *The Smart Set* and who remained with *The American Mercury* until 1935, two years after Mencken had retired.

²Guillaume Apollinaire de Kostrowitsky (1880–1918), French man of letters associated with advanced literature and artistic movements.

³Remy de Gourmont (1858–1915), French writer, on the staff of *Mercure de France*.

H. L. MENCKEN
1524 HOLLINS ST.
BALTIMORE

Friday, February 28, 1924

Dear Sara:-

I simply brought the wrong wine. Next time it will be sherry, which *never* gets corked. Moreover, sherry is capital with milk and eggs: a tablespoon full is enough to disguise the taste. When am I to wait on you? Is every day visiting day? . . .

But if you mention Hegel again I shall jump out of the window. Such debates have a fascination, but I can't sleep after them. Nor, I bet, can you. If you could, why should you be writing prayers? I shall go to Fourteen Holy Martyrs' Church tonight, and slip the one you sent into the poor box.

Snow again. But in ten days it will be Spring, and you'll be out on the porch, and listening to the bulbuls. I crave the honor of kissing your hand.

Yours,
HLM

H. L. MENCKEN
1524 HOLLINS ST.
BALTIMORE

March 3rd, 1924

Dear Sara:-

Barring acts of God and the public enemy, I'll wait on you on Saturday. There is a small chance that this may be impossible: a Sun meeting impends. If so, I'll come out on Tuesday. The trains on Sunday look hopeless.

Don't mention Wordsworth. He was an immoral fellow. It is dreadful to think of a Christian carrying on in such a manner. I'd like to have seen his blushes when he faced the Judgment Seat at last. Since hearing of his scoundrelism I have been unable to read his so called poetry.

You send no news? What of your alleged fever? Has it disappeared? And how much weight have you put on? I could see last week the outlines of your future bulk. You will be a buster! Well, did you ever notice that fat gals are always handsome, in a dignified, Romanesque way? So do not repine. Remember what every pound is costing you!

I am sending you a Baptist paper to give to Dr. Sloan. It contains a complete digest of all the heresies prevailing in Arkansas. I am glad to note that the use of oyster crackers at the Lord's Supper is not one of them. This seems to be confined to Florida.

I had a fearful time of it in New York. The Smart Set corpse emerged from its grave and began to dance. [1] But I believe that it will now rest in peace.

Ich kuss die Hand.

Yours,
HLM

[1] The magazine had been sold to Eltinge F. Warner, who owned most of the stock, with the provision that if he resold it within a year, Mencken and Nathan could share in the new sale. Despite his previous refusal, after long negotiations it was sold to Hearst.

H. L. MENCKEN
1524 HOLLINS ST.
BALTIMORE

March 5th, 1924

To:
Miss Sara Haardt,
Maple Heights Sanitarium,
Sparks, Md.

Dear Sara:-

Unless you forbid it absolutely I'll present myself on Saturday and offer my respects. Your letter is somewhat occult: am I forbidden to come? And shall I bring the jug of sherry, or are you offen the stuff? Oh, you wimmen! You are right about the assault on the poor peasants: it was very fair invective. [1] But how am I to write another unless I am refreshed? May I say with all respect that if you don't know the process of ideational genesis in an artist then you are a hell of a psychologist? I have to *talk* the stuff out first, and you are the victim.

Don't let a few fights on the reservation worry you. Sanitarium life is usually full of dreadful scandals, and no wonder!

Ich kuss die Hand!

In Xt.,
HLM

¹"A Government of Laws," the Baltimore *Evening Sun*, March 3, 1924, where Mencken continued his outrage over the Teapot Dome scandal.

H. L. MENCKEN
1524 HOLLINS ST.
BALTIMORE

March 7th, 1924

To:
Miss Sara Haardt,
Maple Heights Sanitarium,
Sparks, Md.

Dear Sara:-

If you hear a sound like a washing-machine's at 2:30 tomorrow it is a sign that I am coming up the hill and making heavy weather of it. I inquired for a Fjord the last time, but could find none in the village. But I'll try the wop again.

I reserve the kissing of your hand until we meet.

Yours,
HLM

H. L. MENCKEN
1524 HOLLINS ST.
BALTIMORE

March 8th, 1924

Dear Sara:-

I suspect that you were trying to flirt with me this afternoon; hence the hollowness of my conversation, against which you justly complained. Well, if you would have discourses worthy the ear of a lady savant, then you must not look so charming. You really had a very blooming look, and I am sure that you are quite well, and could escape tomorrow without damage. But a few more weeks of rest will simply clinch it.

If I can be of any aid to your brother when he comes to Baltimore, I hope he calls on me.[1] My telephone is Gilmor 1512-w. But don't go home with him yet. The Spring will open next week, and your long boredom will end. If I knew how to play mah jong I'd buy a set and bring it out to play with you.[2] But in this world of falling values and moral chaos, a man must cling, after all, to a few principles, and so I eschew gambling. I have tried all of the other standard crimes, and find them all pretty dull. My uncle Gustav was ruined by cards. His end was very melancholy, and both widows tried to throw themselves into his grave. The Elks held them back.

Nachmal [sic] ich kuss die Hand![3]

Yours,
HLM

[1] Sara's younger brother John had written Sara, expressing his desire to help her out in her finances.

[2] By 1923 the craze for Mah-Jongg was on, and it remained popular throughout the winter of 1923 to 1924. Dozens of manufacturers leaped into the business; $500 sets were sold; a Mah-Jongg League of America was formed. Joseph Hergesheimer would recall: "Mencken never pronounced the word golf without regarding me with a positively insane glee; and for a whole year I hid from him the fact that I played, and liked, mah-jong. To Henry golf and mah-jong and idiocy were slightly different forms of one word, of one state."

[3] Once again (nochmal) I kiss your hand.

H. L. MENCKEN
1524 HOLLINS ST.
BALTIMORE

March 13th, 1924

Dear Sara:-

I advised that poor woman[1] to divorce her husband and marry a sound Christian business man. They make the only good husbands. All else is dross.

I can't fathom your parleys with your family. Why not let your brother come to see you? Your mother is probably chiefly shocked by hearing about you through strangers.[2] Tell her all the facts, and she will feel better. After all, there is absolutely no reason for alarm. Stick to the treatment and you will get well infallibly. If you could get complete rest and proper nourishment outside I'd advise you to leave the sanitarium at once. But it is always hard to manage in a private house.

The infernal gale of Monday and Tuesday set me to wheezing, and I feel a bit rocky still.[3] The wind here was fearful: what must it have been on your Alp! But Spring is on the way. All the wild flowers are up in my yard.

Ich kuss die Hand!

Yours,
HLM

[1] A patient in the sanitorium that Sara had met.

[2] Sara undoubtedly did not want to worry her mother, nor did she want to return to Montgomery and, in so doing, admit that her aim in "carving a career" as an independent woman in the North had been a failure. She had already cautioned her friends, including Sara Mayfield, not to disclose her true illness to the Haardt family.

[3] This had been the coldest and wettest spring in Baltimore history since 1917. March 1924 was cold, wet, and windy. Despite the wind, snow, hail, and rain which plagued Baltimore from January to June, Mencken still found himself able to battle the elements and visit Sara at Maple Heights.

H. L. MENCKEN
1524 HOLLINS ST.
BALTIMORE

March 17th, 1924

Dear Sara:-

I am sending to you today a modest bauble bought in Berlin a year ago. I put it into storage, waiting for the appearance of a gal beautiful enough to wear it. Yesterday I unearthed it, and the fact dawned on me that the hour had come. It is barbaric, to be sure, but you can manage it. It will make you look like the Empress Theodora.

What is the news? Is any temperature left? And how is your weight? Let me have these pathological details. I have been in a low state all week, entertaining a mild bronchitis, the effect of the steady high wind. It is now passing off. When I'll go to New York I don't know: probably toward the end of the week. Nathan is laid up there with the flu. He has it regularly twice a year, and always believes that he is dying. I have sent him the usual Bible. He now has 22 of them.

Ich kuss die Hand!

As ever,
HLM

H. L. MENCKEN
1524 HOLLINS ST.
BALTIMORE

March 18th, 1924

Dear Sara:-

You are very vague about that sudden pain. Where was it—if a Pure Woman may tell a bachelor? I still suspect that you had pneumonia at Christmas, and that resolution is still in progress. The next time I come out I shall find Sloan and hear what he has discovered. That he has made no microscopic examination seems remarkable. It is a routine procedure. When is Sloan on the scene? Coming out on Saturday will probably be impossible, alas, alas! Some literary visitors are due here, and I must see them on business. I shall go to New York on Sunday. But I'll be back before the end of the week.

My bronchitis amounts to nothing. I got it in the great gale of a week ago. My whole family has it. It is very mild, and will pass off as the weather grows milder. All the wild-flowers are up in my yard, but it is still damp and chilly here in town.

Tell Baker I shall vote for Daugherty[1] at the Phi Beta Kappa election. If I were Guth I'd quit pedagogy and go in for bootlegging. It has been done by a number of college presidents.

I must go to the annual banquet of the Sun carriers tonight and address them on the issues of the hour.[2] Let me have your prayers.

Your hand is kissed!

Yours,
HLM

~

¹Henry M. Daugherty, an Ohio lawyer who had helped maneuver Harding into the White House and who was now his attorney general, had been banking huge funds that had caused a sensational Senate investigation. The Teapot Dome scandal almost caused his resignation, but he was not tried and acquitted until 1927.

²*Sun* carrier routes could be bought and sold, and their carriers created a new *Sun Carrier's Association* in 1919. It was represented in its dealings with the circulation manager of the *Sun* by a Carrier Council of seven members, and it held a banquet every year.

THE AMERICAN MERCURY
220 WEST FORTY-SECOND STREET
NEW YORK

March 21st, 1924

Dear Sara:-

I undoubtedly mailed that gaud on the 17th, in a small box, first-class. And I equally undoubtedly failed to register it. Perhaps it is now hanging around the neck of the wife of the Postmaster General. I hope she comes down with smallpox. But let us be patient. It may bob up yet. . . .

My bronchitis is practically gone, despite the infernal weather. Now I am lame in the left hoof, God knows why.¹ The fact is that I am gradually breaking up.

May I have the honor of waiting on you next Saturday, the 29th? If not, I kiss your hand anyhow. But I'll be there.

Yours,
HLM

¹A growth had appeared on the ball of Mencken's left foot, causing some disorder in the small front arch. Walking became difficult and painful: "like having a pebble in the shoe," he wrote to a friend.

~

H. L. MENCKEN
1524 HOLLINS ST.
BALTIMORE

Friday, March 28, 1924

Dear Sara:-

I can't imagine what could have happened to that bauble. It was addressed very plainly. Unluckily, I neglected to put my own address on it: the package was small and the front crowded. Well, some honest letter carrier's wife is now posturing before her mirror as Mme. Du Barry[1] or the Harlot of Babylon. I shall inquire of the Superintendent of Mails at the Sparks Postoffice the next time I visit that great city.

By the direct unfriendly act of God it may not be tomorrow. I hobbled around New York all week with a temporary bandage on my hoof. This morning a surgeon[2] put on a real one—at least 200 yards of adhesive tape, etc. It is very uncomfortable, and navigation is difficult. But it may be all right by tomorrow morning. If it is, I'll surely come out on the 12:30 train to wait on you. But if I don't show up within 20 minutes after the train is due at Sparks it will be a sign that I have either perished on the way, or not started.

Yours,

H. L. Mencken

[1]Comtesse Marie Jeanne Becu, 1746(?)–1793, mistress of Louis XV of France.
[2]Joseph Colt Bloodgood, surgeon and associate professor at Johns Hopkins Hospital and specialist in cancer and tumors.

H. L. MENCKEN
1524 HOLLINS ST.
BALTIMORE

April 5th, 1924

Dear Sara:-

Three whoops! Now you will return to normalcy quickly. Don't try to rush the novel. You have plenty of time, and it deserves to be done slowly. Make Otis a bit eloquent toward the end.[1] After all, he has God on his side. Certainly there is nothing in the Bible counselling a young woman to become a Ph.D. Her duty is plainly stated there: it is to cherish some honest man and fill the house with his heirs and assigns.

The enclosed[2] is submitted to your eye in the utmost confidence. Return it, or be forever damned. I believe that you have begun to poison Montgomery. Nathan answered the letter, and sent the writer a picture postcard of Grant's Tomb.

My hoof is still lame, but Bandage No. 2 seems to be better than No. 1 was. I can only pray, and hope for succor. The Knopfs were down here early in the week and I took them the round of the eating houses. When I passed our old pew at the wop's I dropped a tear. But pretty soon we'll be sitting in it again. The wop turned out some superb cocktails and a very good bottle of Chianti.

Where is the Jewish gentleman buried?[3]

> Yours,
> HLM

[1]Character in Sara's novel, *Career.*

[2]Now lost.

[3]A sick patient who apparently died within a few days of his entry to the sanitorium. Sara would later portray him as the character Isidore Kaplan in her story "Licked," which Mencken printed in the September 1927 issue of *The American Mercury.*

H. L. MENCKEN
1524 HOLLINS ST.
BALTIMORE

April 9th, 1924

Dear Sara:-

Nathan has sent Mrs. Cook a portrait of himself, showing him reading a book with his extended forefinger resting upon his left zygoma. If you lack anatomy, ask one of the nurses what a zygoma is; if she knows, let me know, and I'll send her a diamond necklace. Montgomery, I fear, is growing intellectual, and will lose its character.

Since when has Bright quit the Hopkins?[1] It is news to me. Getting rid of him must have been a terrific job. Do you mean to hint that our fair friend[2] is mashed on Malone? If so, then I can only marvel again at the taste you enlightened and cultured gals display. Shopgirls show more sense! If Malone is the Malone who wrote to me a couple of years ago, he is a desperate pedant.[3]

Why don't you send me some news about yourself? How is your weight? How do you feel? And what has Sloan to say, if anything? The novel has my prayers. And I kiss your hand.

Yours,

HLM

[1]James Wilson Bright, professor of English at the Johns Hopkins University, was world-renowned for his research on the origins of the English language and a pioneer in the study of Anglo-Saxon. He was editor in chief of *Modern Language Notes* and of the Albion series of Anglo-Saxon and Middle English poetry, and was regarded by many as the foremost authority in his field in America. He had been associated with the English faculty of Hopkins for forty years when his eyesight began to fail in 1924, forcing him to remain in his room at the University Club much of the time. In 1925 his eyesight forced him to retire, and he died May 28, 1926.

[2]Marjorie Nicolson; however, in 1927 Malone married Inez Rene Chatain of Richmond, Virginia.

[3]Mencken's poor opinion of Malone later changed into one of admiration. In 1935 Mencken would ask Malone to look over one of his chapters for a revised version of *The American Language*.

H. L. MENCKEN
1524 HOLLINS ST.
BALTIMORE

April 10th, 1924

Dear Sara:-

I had hoped to ask the honor of seeing you this Saturday, but God wills it otherwise. The secretary of the Saturday Night Club[1] notifies me that it is my turn to entertain it; moreover, Joe Hergesheimer is coming in from Richmond, maybe with some of his customers from that region. So I'll be on the jump all afternoon. When the club comes to my house I usually finish mopping up the debris by 2 o'clock Sunday morning. I have to put on an electric fan to suck out the smoke.

I am sending you William McFee's new novel by this mail.[2] It is probably very good. He is doing excellent work. I hope you let me come out some time next week. Your hand is kissed.

Yours,

HLM

¹Heinrich Ewald Buchholz was librarian and secretary of the Saturday Night Club. During Prohibition days the club met at the homes of the members, but with repeal they went back to Hildebrandt's shop and then to the Rennert for supper. After a few trial meetings, they ended up playing in a private room at the Schellhase's.

²The widely traveled British born writer had just come out with *Race*, which portrayed middle-class London life in the late nineteenth century. McFee was a frequent contributor to *The American Mercury*, writing articles on Latin America and the Caribbean.

H. L. MENCKEN
1524 HOLLINS ST.
BALTIMORE

April 12th, 1924

Dear Sara:-

Nevertheless, you ought to be a proud gal to have such a beau! Regard the enclosed.¹ Give a look, especially, at Thyra. She is, alas, somewhat more bulky in reality—in fact, a bit buxom. Return the clipping, or suffer forever in the lowest dens of hell!

I have got the first chapter of Prej. IV done at last and feel much better.² It is a treatise on the Anglo-Saxon: how he looks to a man of an older, more intellectual, more noble and more godly race. It will be a sufficient answer to his protest against the kissing of hands, an art practiced by us Huns for 1,000 years. The Anglo-Saxon is against it because when he attempts it his women fear he is going to bite them, and so commonly poke their fingers into his eye.

Why don't you send me some news? What has Sloan to say? What of the temperature? Spring seems to be here at last. You will be doing a week's wash in a few months. A good spell of ironing would make you feel as good as new.

Yours,

M

¹Six days prior to this letter the Sunday edition of the New York *News* had published an article called "The Three Most Fascinating Men of the United States." Almost without exception, a jury of ten women (among them Mary Pickford, Fannie Hurst, and Thyra Samter Winslow) had chosen the Prince of Wales and John Barrymore and then disagreed on the third. Thyra Winslow

chose the Sage of Baltimore, insisting that "all the women of New York are crazy about Mencken."

[2]"The American Tradition."

H. L. MENCKEN

1524 HOLLINS ST.

BALTIMORE

April 14th, 1924

Dear Sara:-

May I have the honor of waiting on you next Saturday? My hoof is so far recovered that I could now almost tackle the hill. But not while peasants loll about in Fords, hungry for money. I shall come up in state.

My Corona[1] is sick and this is a substitute. Forgive it as I do. Ich kuss die Hand.

Yours,

HLM

[1]Mencken's faithful (albeit ailing) portable Corona would accompany him across land and sea, up until his last reporting stint at the Republican and Democratic National Conventions of 1948, four months before Mencken's stroke would leave him unable to read or write.

H. L. MENCKEN

1524 HOLLINS ST.

BALTIMORE

April 17th, 1924

Dear Sara:-

Saturday, then. I'll climb the hill or bust.

Carl Schon, one of my venerable beer brothers, died day before yesterday.[1] He was, I regret to say, a disbeliever in the Divine Word, and left orders that no —— —— clergyman should be admitted to his funeral. So I have got the job of pontificating. We shall shove him into the crematory at 2 P.M. So they pass! In our club of 12 men we have had four funerals in three years.

I'll bring you Edgar Lee Masters' new novel, the damndest thing I have ever read.[2] It will make you howl. Parts of it read almost like "Daisy Ashford."[3]

Yours in Xt.,

(The Rev) HLM

¹Carl Schon, a member of the Saturday Night Club, was also a craftsman who made jewelry of fine metal objects: "sea horses and flyers, covered with gold, old rings, breastplates, bangles, and so on," wrote Mencken. "Many of his designs were far more ingenious than useful, but now and then he hit on something really fine."

²*Mirage.* "It seems to me to be one of the most idiotic and yet one of the most American novels that I have yet read," Mencken would write. By 1924 Masters found it impossible to match the success of his *Spoon River Anthology* (1915), and Mencken was forced to admit his decline in his review of *Mirage* in the June 1924 issue of *The American Mercury*, and again in the October 1925 issue.

³*Daisy Ashford, Her Book,* a collection of the remaining novels of the author Angela Ashford.

ALS

THE AMERICAN MERCURY
730 FIFTH AVENUE
NEW YORK

April 22, 1924

Friend Sara:

Having a swell time in this burg. Wish you was here.
With kind regards.

Yours truly
M

H. L. MENCKEN
1524 HOLLINS ST.
BALTIMORE

April 25th, 1924

Dear Sara:-

You become the sole and solitary White Hope. The Suckow novel came in during the week—and turned out to be 225,000 words long! Unless she can cut it down to 95,000 words it will remain in MS.¹ Next day came Tanaquil's novel.² Very excellent stuff, but so loud that Knopf would go to jail for 20 years if he published it. Tanaquil has been in Europe so long that he has forgotten every last American Ideal. So the way is clear for the sad story of Otis. Prayer works wonders.

What is the news with you? Are you out of bed yet? And will I be permitted to wait on you next Saturday? I got hold of 24 quarts of noble Scotch in New York during the week, and have brought some of it to Baltimore. But you get none of it. It is too strong for invalids.

As ever,

HLM

¹*Odyssey of a Nice Girl.* A letter from Blanche Knopf to Ruth Suckow said that it was much too long and that 90 thousand words would be sufficient to "get this girl between the covers" and advised her to take six months and cut the work.

¹Paul Tanaquil (Le Clercq, Jacques Georges Clemenceau), the Austrian-born educator, poet, and authority on French literature and romance languages, was also a regular contributor of short stories to *The Smart Set* and *The American Mercury*.

[POSTCARD]

April 26, 1924

The flag marks the spot where I landed in 1889.

M.

H. L. MENCKEN
1524 HOLLINS ST.
BALTIMORE

April 28th, 1924

Dear Sara:-

I'll surely wait on you on Saturday, barring acts of God. Kahn tells me that Sloan's five or six examinations have showed no sign of tuberculosis bacilli, and that he now regards you as substantially cured. His diagnosis, it appears, was made from the clinical picture. It certainly justified suspicion, but I believe that there was never any actual infection. However, you obviously needed preventive treatment, and it has been a great success. The important thing now is to keep your weight around 130.

My hoof is still painful and I have had it x-rayed. The plate shows nothing serious. But it is an infernal nuisance to be lame. Prayer seems to be unavailing.

Don't rush your MS. There is plenty of time. I must now break the news to Tanaquil that I have advised Knopf against doing his book. Inasmuch as it is dedicated to me the business presents difficulties. But courage, Camille! Nothing has been heard from La Suckow. Why she ran so wild I don't know.

Contain yourself! You will have the honor of kissing my brow on Saturday. And of hearing me swear.

Yours,
M

H. L. MENCKEN
1524 HOLLINS ST.
BALTIMORE

May 1st, 1924

Dear Sara:-

Don't let the Alpine light alarm you. If I may venture upon such a remark to a refined woman, the best thing that could happen to you would be to be well sunburnt all over. The effects of intense sunlight are superb. It clears up lingering low infections, and greatly stimulates the whole organism. After months in bed you need it. When you are paroled it will build up your vigor.

Barring divine intervention, I'll see you on Saturday.

Yours,

M

H. L. MENCKEN

1524 HOLLINS ST.

BALTIMORE

Friday, May [2], 1924

Dear Sara:-

I note the change in the train schedule. I'd have been on time anyhow. My grandfather used to get to the station at least an hour before his train started. He would first make sure that the locomotive was in good working order and the engineer well, and then he would drink a few glasses of beer and eat maybe two or three sandwiches. A Hunnish custom. In Germany the whole crowd is aboard at least half an hour before the train starts, and everyone takes some nourishment. I have cut the time down to 15 minutes, which would have got me in just under the wire.

If it is warm tomorrow and I have to march up the hill I'll take off my collar. Even last time it got wilted, and now the weather is warmer. But I hope to find a peasant with a flivver. Last time I asked the storekeeper to get one for me. He took so long that I started off a-foot.[1] When I got back to the station the car was waiting! Such is the Bauer!

I kiss your hand twice.

Yours,

M

[1]Pasted to the letter was a clipping from *Hygeia Magazine*: "A man over 45 should not run after trains or street cars."

~

[POSTCARD]

May 2, 1924

This is sure a swell town. Sorry you ain't with us. Have had a swell time sure. Kind regards from all

Otis[1]

[1]Character from Sara's novel.

H. L. MENCKEN
1524 HOLLINS ST.
BALTIMORE

May 6th, 1924

Dear Sara:-

I am sending you all of the books save "The American Language" by this mail.[1] Of the latter I find that I have no copy. I'll get one and it will follow later. In return I am to get a copy of that snapshot made by the bootlegger. If you refuse then I'll bring out a photographer myself. "The American Credo" is also missing.[2] I'll get it within a week. . . .

On the porch! Har! I knew that Sloan would not keep you in bed much longer. You will be navigating the countryside in a few weeks, and driving the yokels crazy. You know their tastes: they like a solid, vigorous gal, able to milk 200 cows a day. When you touch 150 I shall send you a Bible.

I am enclosing a copy of Ludwig Lewisohn's new book.[3] There is a portrait of him in it. Gaze upon it, and then ponder the fact that two women, one of them fair, are now struggling in the courts for him.[4] Then read my chapter in "A Defense of Women" on the aesthetic sense of women.[5] And then give yourself an hour of soul-searching.

My surgeon is a scoundrel. I am still lame—and I must go downtown today and hoof around for a couple of hours.

Ich kuss die Hand, gnädige Fräulein, zweimal![6]

Yours,

M

[1] Mencken sent Sara several of his own books, including Theodore Dreiser's *Jennie Gerhardt*, with Mencken's inscription: "This is 'Sister Carrie' done over again—but how much better!"

[2] *The American Credo, A Contribution Toward the Interpretation of the National Mind.* Mencken wrote the preface, and George Jean Nathan the credo.

[3] *The Creative Life.*

[4] Lewisohn was married to Mary Arnold Crocker, twenty years his senior, but their marriage would not be dissolved until 1937. In 1924, while still married to Mary Crocker, Lewisohn ran off with Thelma Spear, a young singer, to Europe, where they maintained residence for a decade.

[5] *In Defense of Women.* The chapter Mencken is referring to is the first, "The Feminine Mind."

[6] "I kiss your hand, gracious mademoiselle—twice!"

H. L. MENCKEN

1524 HOLLINS ST.

BALTIMORE

May 9th, 1924

Dear Sara:-

Dr. Jackson I know very well. He is one of the leaders of his Race. His income from the Institute, unluckily, is so small and uncertain that he has to supplement it by bootlegging. Cabell is a member of the Institute, and so is Josephus Daniels.[1]

Your loss of weight is due to abandoning the stuffing. Back to milk and eggs! The ideal is 165 lbs. Onward and upward!

Finishing Prejudices IV has left me very stale—and now I must do two months writing for the Mercury in one in order to get free for the national conventions![2] A dreadful life, indeed. God help us all.

Ich kuss die Hand.

Yours,
M

Have the books reached you?

[1]"The Colored Institute of America," a nonexistent institution which regularly sent out letters advising its members of meetings (on stationery boasting an engraving of a black George Washington), was actually Mencken's invention. Sara had apparently received one such typical letter, inviting her to a meeting at the institute's national headquarters in Washington, D.C. James Branch Cabell was the well-known Southern writer, Josephus Daniels the retired U.S. secretary of the navy, and unbeknownst to Sara (as well as to Cabell and Daniels), the Honorable Rev. Hannibal L. Jackson, A.B., A.M., Ph.D., LL.D., D.D., was Mencken himself.

[2]The Republican and Democratic national conventions were a scarce four weeks away. Despite Mencken's criticisms of conventions, each one was, he admitted, "nonetheless, not without its charms to the connoisseurs of the obscene." As it turned out, the approaching event would not disappoint him.

H. L. MENCKEN

1524 HOLLINS ST.

BALTIMORE

May 12th, 1924

Dear Sara:-

I hope you are making elaborate notes. All sanatariums are alike. Life in them is always one long series of catastrophes and scandals. A true novelist neglects nothing! When my brother[1] was incarcerated he used to telegraph to me ever and anon that they were starving and killing him. At one time he had to take to the mountains and hunt rabbits in order to eat. At another time the professor gave him too large a dose of antitoxin, and he was non compos for four days. Has the janitor yet tried to kiss you? It is coming! Also, you say nothing about the nurses getting drunk. What is the matter with them? Again, nobody has yet stolen your shoes. Be patient!

Ass that I am, I missed your symbolism. Is it too late to ask forgiveness and crave the privilege of kissing your hand? Did I ever send you Carl Van Doren's "Many Minds"?[2] If not, I have a copy. I have just finished the new Ring Lardner book.[3] It made me yell. Lardner is the best of them all. He knows more about writing the short story than 200 head of Edith Whartons.

I shoved Prejudices IV to a finish by sheer mule-power. It was a dreadful job. And now, as usual, I itch to rewrite it. But I shall let it stand as it is. There is some drivel in it, but here and there it is not bad. The opening chapter, on the Anglo-Saxon, will at least stir up the animals. It depicts him as an ignoramus and a poltroon. There is also some very fair stuff on Christian evidences. I must now write "On Democracy"[4]—in plan like the woman book.[5] Then for "Homo Sapiens"![6]

My hoof is lamer than ever, and I have just sent a note to the surgeon, bawling him out. He will no doubt bring in another quack. If the two fail then I'll have a horrible time at the two national conventions. There is not much chance to sit down while they are on. The alert reporter keeps to his legs.

Will you be at home on Saturday?

Yours,
HLM

[1]August Mencken.

[2]While balancing his teaching at Columbia University with acting as literary editor of *The Century*, Carl Van Doren had written *Many Minds*.

[3]*How to Write Short Stories*, a title suggested by Lardner's close friend and fellow writer, F. Scott Fitzgerald.

[4]*Notes on Democracy*. Mencken had first started making notes for the book in 1910, and the actual writing began in 1923. He finally resumed writing it in November 1925 and finished it in June 1926.

[5]*In Defense of Women*.

[6]Mencken would continue working on his Homo Sapiens book until 1927, but it was never completed.

H. L. MENCKEN
1524 HOLLINS ST.
BALTIMORE

May 13th, 1924

Dear Sara:-

I am sending you three books by this mail. "A Hind Let Loose" is yours if you want it, but the Fergusson[1] and the Lardner must come back. I'll pick them up some time. Unluckily, I begin to fear that I'll be unable to wait on you on Saturday. Half a dreadful nuisances show up. But I'll know more definitely in a day or two.

The American Mercury now has its first libel suit. Let Rome howl! Ich kuss die Hand!

Yours,
HLM

[1]Throughout the 1920s Mencken saw to it that Washington newspaperman Harvey Fergusson's novels were published and that their dust covers were adorned with enthusiastic blurbs. Fergusson's new book, *Women and Wives*, was a fictional study on the marriage arrangement and why it seems less and less feasible in the modern world. The Lardner book was *How to Write Short Stories*. Mencken was planning to review both books for the upcoming July issue of *The American Mercury*.

H. L. MENCKEN
1524 HOLLINS ST.
BALTIMORE

May 17th, 1924

Dear Sara:-

It is an old saying that women are the ruin of men. When I got back to the place of beginning I simply gave that shark my watch and took ten cents in change. Well, I don't repine. It was worth $17.40 to see you looking so lovely. I only hope Sloan liberates you from bed and lets you prowl and graze the adjacent fields. They were gorgeous. Upper Baltimore county, in fact, is a very tasty region.

Let me see the short story as soon as you type it. I'll find out what the Knopfs think of the novel on Monday, and let you know. My guess is that they will do it. I think it will sell, for it aims a padded dart directly at the most copious of novel readers: the fair creature who has nabbed her Romeo and settled down. It will annoy the intelligentsia.

I kiss your hand.

Pro Christo et Ecclesia,
M

ALS

THE AMERICAN MERCURY
730 FIFTH AVENUE
NEW YORK

May 22, 1924

Dear Sara:-

The Knopfs hem and haw—and incidently [sic] make a few excellent suggestions. I'll read the MS again from A to Z and try to determine whether they are right. More anon. I'll leave here tomorrow.

Excuse poor pen!

Yrs.,
M

H. L. MENCKEN
1524 HOLLINS ST.
BALTIMORE

May 29th, 1924

Dear Sara:-

. . . Don't let the Guth business worry you. You were in error about him before, and you may be in error again. Nor is the loss of your degree a serious matter. If you print a couple of novels and they get some attention you will be much more secure in the groves of learning than if you had a dozen Ph.D.'s. Goucher is not the only college in this great free Republic.

If you hear from Perkins,[1] tell him in your reply that you want to revise "Career" before it is set up, if it is. It needs some coopering here and there. He is writing to you at Goucher.

Ich kuss die Hand.

Yours,
HLM

¹Maxwell Perkins, the editor and director at Charles Scribner's Sons, influential in helping the careers of such writers as F. Scott Fitzgerald, Thomas Wolfe, Ring Lardner, and Ernest Hemingway.

H. L. MENCKEN

1524 HOLLINS ST.

BALTIMORE

May 24th, 1924

Dear Sara:-

Guth is an idiot. You will be quite as effective after you get out as you were a year ago. Why not ask Sloan to see Guth and tell him so? True enough, you will have to avoid washing and ironing for a year or so, and had better avoid excessive drinking, but otherwise you will be absolutely normal. He talks as if teaching were as onerous a job as driving a truck. What an ass! . . .

Knopf irritated me yesterday, and I took the MS. away from him. But don't let it concern you. If you get a letter from another publisher, don't answer it until I have seen it.

The short story comes so very near being a first-rate job that I want to spend a few days studying it. More anon.

Ich kuss die Hand.

Yours,

M

H. L. MENCKEN

1524 HOLLINS ST.

BALTIMORE

June 2nd, 1924

Dear Sara:-

God knows what will be the result of Sloan's letter to Dr. Welsh and the noble Christian, Guth. Against the chance that it may be nothing it might be well to cast about for something else in September. I know nothing in that line. How are such things managed? I doubt that full-time teaching would be advisable, as in a high-school or private school. Sloan told me, by the way, which I forgot to mention, that he believed Montgomery would be all right for you in cool weather.

Thus you might consider the plan of resting there awhile after you are released. Such a rest, of course, would be excellent physically. It would enable you to consolidate your gains, settle down to a natural weight, and get back upon the track, solidly and securely.

Our literary conversation diverted me from the question of finances. You always evade it when we meet. But it ought to be talked out realistically. If Scribner takes your novel he may pay a few hundred dollars advance royalties, but you won't get any of its actual earnings until next May, at the earliest. But once you were out of the sanatorium you might do a good deal of miscellaneous writing, and get something from it. I'll tackle the short story at the first chance. Going to Bloodgood's office every morning knocks out my day. He keeps me an hour and a half or more, soaking my hoof and experimenting with bandages. Who was your agent? It is possible that there may be some serial rights in "Career."

I am sending you by this mail a book of "best" newspaper stories[1]—an imitation of the idiotic O'Brien collections.[2] It is interesting for one thing: it shows what dreadful drivel gets into the newspapers. I am writing a long review of it.[3]

You looked very lovely yesterday. What a gal, indeed! Never go under 130 lbs.!

I kiss your hand.

Yours,
M

[1] *The Best News Stories of* 1923, edited by Joseph Anthony.
[2] Edward J. O'Brien began issuing his series of best short stories of the year in 1915.
[3] "The Reporter at Work," *The American Mercury*, August 1924.

H. L. MENCKEN
1524 HOLLINS ST.
BALTIMORE

June 3rd, 1924

Dear Sara:-

Give all the brutalities I have performed upon this MS. your prayerful regard.[1] I believe that they uncover some weaknesses that you ought to try to correct. You hook clauses together rather too recklessly, and you are sometimes careless otherwise. I suggest rewriting the whole story with the enclosed in front of you. The end, it seems to me, could be improved a bit. You should explain, in a sentence, how Archie gets his money. You should make rather more of Marshall's discovery that he is about to weaken: a line or two of dialogue there would help.

Rule No. 653: Never quote a phrase if you can help it! It is the hallmark of bad newspaper reporters.

God save us all, say I. And kiss your hand.

Yours,
M

¹"The atheist."

H. L. MENCKEN
1524 HOLLINS ST.
BALTIMORE

June 4th, 1924

Dear Sara:-

In brief, Guth is a swine! Well, you are lucky, in the long run, to escape his shambles. When we meet again, let us go into the matter of your finances. In case Scribner takes the book it may be possible to get some advance royalties out of him. But the amount will not be large, and if he doesn't offer them it will be unwise to ask for them. However, I'll work out some scheme for you. What you need first of all during the next year is rest. If you take on two much work there will be danger of a relapse. You must consider yourself under treatment for a year, at least. But what is a year at twenty-five? No more literary gossip when we meet again! Business first!

Don't get yourself into the position of exaggerating the horrors of a year in Montgomery. It may be, after all, the easiest solution. You got away once, and you can get away again. I believe, as I have told you, that your book offers a better chance of escape than teaching. It will get a publisher inevitably, and I believe that it will be a success. Meanwhile, if you were clear of teaching you could start another, and do some short stories.

When I'll be able to get to Sparks I don't know. It may not be for several weeks. I am off for Cleveland on Friday or Saturday, and shall have but a few days here between the two conventions. I must do all my Mercury work at odd moments. In addition, there is some writing to do, including an article for the Nation, long promised. It is on the Sex Question! I shall give them some good Biblical doctrine.[1]

You mention clippings. What clippings? Do you mean the odds and ends that come in for Americana? If not, what? Your literary style has its obscure moments.

I hope you tackle "The Atheist" at once, and try to tease up its ending. I thought you had an agent. I distinctly remember getting a letter from an agent, a year or two ago, about your short stories. The best one I know is Otto Liveright, 2 West 43rd street, New York. Tell him I recommended him.

I kiss your hand.

> Yours,
> HLM

[1]"Sex Uproar," *The Nation*, July 23, 1924. This was Mencken's letter in answer to an attack by Bernard Sobel, "Mr. Mencken and the Sex Comedy," October 22, 1923.

H. L. MENCKEN
1524 HOLLINS ST.
BALTIMORE

June 7th, 1924

Dear Sara:-

Throw these away when you have given them your eye. I am off for Cleveland tonight.[1] My address will be the Statler Hotel. If the convention is over by Thursday I shall go to Mt. Clemens to drink the waters as a patient of the Dr. Rickel[2] whose note is within. Old Bridges[3] is writing to me twice a week. If the time offers I may also drop in on him at Ann Arbor, where he is marooned among the morons. Then to Pittsburgh to see my niece,[4] and then home.

The canonization of Cal will make a superb show. I am very eager for it.

And I kiss your hand.

> Yours,
> M

¹The Republican national convention, held in Cleveland, June 9–13, 1924. The Democratic national convention was held in New York, June 23–July 9. The opponents were Calvin Coolidge (Republican), John W. Davis (Democrat), and Robert M. La Follette (Progressive).

²Harry Rickel, lawyer from Detroit.

³Robert Seymour Bridges, English physician, philogist, and poet laureate of Great Britain, had taken the chair in Ann Arbor, Michigan, as professor of English poetry.

⁴Virginia Mencken.

HOTEL STATLER

CLEVELAND

June 9th, 1924

Dear Sara:-

This is the usual obscenity. But for the first time in history the delegates and alternates are sober. They appear very strange.¹ The average diameter of the lady politicians present is one meter.

Today I spent two hours with a delegate from North Dakota, a piano tuner by profession.² He turned out, as might be expected, to be a very intelligent man.

So no more at present from your sincere admirer who kisses your hand.

Yours,

M

¹A few days before, Mencken had ventured the guess that bad Scotch would sell for $15 a bottle and more than one delegate would go home in a baggage car, "a victim to methyl alcohol." Instead, what greeted him at the Republican national convention in Cleveland was "as appalling and as fascinating as a two-headed boy": the first *dry* national convention in human history. Parched throats, Mencken found, precluded whooping: Coolidge may "freeze a sober man into solace, but could it freeze a man kissed by the grape? I doubt it." He went on: "A man who could be a Coolidge fanatic could also be a fanatic in double entry bookkeeping. Even the sworn men and partisans of the President—the men who brought him up to his present arctic eminence and will have charge of his campaign after he is nominated—even these professional Coolidgestas carry on

their business with the air of grocery clerks wrapping up packages of ginger snaps."

²The piano tuner was actually from South Dakota.

H. L. MENCKEN
1524 HOLLINS ST.
BALTIMORE

June 18th, 1924

Dear Sara:-

Didn't you ask me to send you my Cleveland dispatches?¹ Here they are. Please send them back. The other clippings may be thrown away.

I am going to New York Saturday morning. Wednesday night at 9.30, as my train passed Sparks coming down from Harrisburg, I sent you a vibration. I only hope you didn't sleep through it.

Ich kuss die Hand!

Yours,
M

¹If the behavior of the delegates and alternates seemed strange, the actual nomination of Coolidge was stranger still. As Mencken described it in his dispatch for the Baltimore *Evening Sun* on June 13: "The spell–binder put up to offer the name of Dr. Coolidge to the delegates was a very good one, and he made an excellent speech, but the theme he struggled with was too much for him. What he essayed to prove was, as he said himself, that the eminent candidate was and is a human being. The thesis apparently amused not a few of the delegates: they laughed somewhat indelicately at some of the learned speaker's illustrative anecdotes. What is more, he was constrained to laugh, at times, himself, and so the whole transaction took on a jocosity that was appropriate but disconcerting. . . . But for all his eloquence he could not make it thrilling, and the fact became horribly apparent the moment he discharged the name of the candidate. . . . It is the custom at national conventions to hold back the name until the last instant, and then to snap it out dramatically, for the sound of it is the signal for the formal demonstration to begin. But this time, for the first time in political history, no demonstration followed. There was a feeble round of applause, a few delegates began parading the aisles with their State standards and then the whole thing died. Three minutes after it began there was absolutely no sound in the hall save the shuffling of feet.

"Perhaps the man in charge of the lights and music was partly to blame for this unprecedented fiasco. He should have started the band to playing 'The Star-Spangled Banner,' 'Yes, We Have No Bananas,' or some other such stimulating tune; instead he kept it silent for at least five minutes. He should have turned on all the spotlights and bathed the delegates with great beams of blinding light; instead he turned on dim reds and blues, appropriate only for a funeral parlor.

"When, after what seemed to be a geological epoch, the band began to play at last, it played 'Onward, Christian Soldiers.' It was too late. The crowd in the galleries essayed to sing, but at once got out of tune with the band. Then the pipe organ horned in—out of time with both the band and the galleries. A YMCA song leader, hurriedly rushed to the platform, tried to lead all three, but made a mess of it. The singing died down as quickly as the applause, and again there was an appalling silence.

"In 10 minutes it was all over and the seconding speeches began. They quickly converted tragi-comedy into burlesque. A fat woman from Kansas, swathed in apricot-colored silk of dazzling brilliance, mounted the platform, squared off like a heavy-weight ready for the gong, and bawled 'Mr. Chairman' into the amplifier in a voice so raucous that the crowd yelled. Then a colored intellectual from New Jersey, with the beard of a Harvard professor, climbed into the pulpit and was riotously booed down. Then came the Hon. Isaac M. Meekins, of North Carolina, a chunky, bald-headed fellow in horn-rim spectacles and an alpaca coat. The Hon. Mr. Meekins planted himself firmly in front of the amplifier, cleared his throat and launched head-first into the following lofty and mellow stuff. . . .

"To the best of my knowledge and belief, this gem of Kiwanis poetry was never shot into the amplifier. I sat no more than fifty feet from the talented speaker, and I strained my ears to hear him, but all I got was a hurricane of guffaws and cat calls, and a voice from the gallery yelling, 'When do we eat?' "

H. L. MENCKEN
1524 HOLLINS ST.
BALTIMORE

June 18th, 1924

Dear Sara:-

Courage, Camille! There are plenty of other publishers. As the next candidate I suggest Eugene F. Saxton, of the George H. Doran Company, 244 Madison avenue, New York City. I am writing a note to him by this mail. Send him the MS. as soon as it comes in. If it is dogseared, retype the first page.

I got in last night and found 200 letters and more than 100 MSS, accumulated. This business will keep me jumping until I go to New York on Saturday, but I'll probably be able to get to "The Atheist." It is a good story and saleable, despite Liveright.

My hoof bore up very well, but it will need attention after the New York convention.

I am worried about your department of the treasury. Why not let me know exactly how you stand?[1] How much money do you owe now, and how much will you need until the end of the Summer? I wish I could come out and cross-examine you, but it looks hopeless this week, and once I get to New York I'll probably be there for ten days, at least. Damn politics!

The Coolidge show was the last gasp! If it had been any worse God would have sent down a pillar of fire from heaven and destroyed the whole assembly.

I kiss your hand!

Yours,

M

[1]Goucher had decided not to pay Sara for the year she had missed. Instead, Ola Elizabeth Winslow, Marjorie Nicolson, and others from the English faculty taught Sara's classes for a year, and in return Goucher paid Sara her year's salary.

H. L. MENCKEN
1524 HOLLINS ST.
BALTIMORE

June 20th, 1924

Dear Sara:-

Liveright is an ass. This story is undoubtedly saleable. But I think you can still improve the last page. The final speech of Peters rather spoils it. You want to get over the notion that he is irresolute at the end, or, rather, that Marshall is suddenly afraid that he is irresolute. He should say something equivocal—something reasonably to be interpreted as a doubt, a beginning recantation. He should make a gesture of appeal for help, utter a word or two, maybe only something inarticulate, a gutteral sound. Marshall half hears "God." Then in with the morphine. Isn't this your idea? The "saline" I can't understand.

Send the story to the following in order:

The Atlantic Monthly, 12 Arlington street, Boston.

Carl Van Doren, The Century, 353 Fourth avenue, New York.

Harper's Magazine, 49 east 33rd st., N.Y.

The Red Book, Chicago, Ill.

McCall's Magazine, New York.

Put a blank sheet of paper behind the last page, to protect the MS. If it gets dogs-eared, recopy the first page.

May I be permitted, in conclusion, to praise you for the neatness of your MS.? A small thing? Don't believe it. It always makes a great impression on editors. Imagine plowing all day through MSS written with worn-out ribbons, and full of bad errors and untidy corrections? It is to curse!

I am off for New York in the morning. I kiss your hand.

As ever,

HLM

ALS

THE BILTMORE

NEW YORK

June 22, 1924

Dear Sara:-

Don't let a small set-back alarm you. It comes almost invariably in the last stages. You will recover from it quickly, and without a pneumo-thorax. But I see no objection to the latter, even now. The infiltrated air is absorbed in a week or two, and so there is no damage. Take Sloan's advice absolutely. He has had a lot of experience, and knows what he is doing. Certainly his treatment so far has been a big success. A small flare-up almost *always* follows the first effort to return to normalcy. You have been leading an artificial life, and coming back is difficult. But once you get squarely on your legs you will be quite all right.

Send me a note about the money business as soon as you can. I'll come out to see you as soon as I get back.

Ich kuss die Hand

Yrs.,

HLM

ALS

New York, Wednesday June 25, 1924

Dear Sara:-

No news from you in the matter of ways and means. . . .

The weather here is infernal and the show, so far, is very poor. But I believe the Ku Kluxers will give it a lift tomorrow.[1]

Yrs.,

HLM

[1]The 1924 Democratic national convention in New York's old Madison Square Garden was the longest in American history, spanning seventeen days. At the time of this letter, the convention was only one day old. The major issue was the racist Ku Klux Klan, which split the convention fifty-fifty. The result was a bitter battle over the platform and a compromise plank which indirectly deplored the Klan.

ALS

THE AMERICAN MERCURY

730 FIFTH AVENUE

NEW YORK

June 27, 1924

Dear Sara:-

Old Welsh, despite everything, shows a certain sagacity.[1] If this adventure delivers you from pedagogy it will not be in vain. I defy you to imagine teaching as a steady job. It would drive you crazy. In ten years you will be thanking God for Welsh, Guth, the little bacilli, and all the rest of his masterpieces.

What you need, obviously, is a year to loaf, write and gather your wits. That is what we must discuss when I get back. It can be arranged without doubt. As for the set-back, don't let it alarm you, I prithee. Such things happen almost invariably. It is a hard job to change back from the life of a silk-worm in a cocoon to the active life of every day. But it can be done.

I kiss your hand.

Yrs.,

HLM

[1]Three days earlier, Lillian Welsh had written Sara a letter stating that she had been "entirely responsible for advising against your return to college next

year. It has not been an easy matter for me to give such advice, but I have considered both your future and the good of the college. . . . You know that my feeling for you has always been one of admiration for your ability and pluck. I have never, however, thought you had any real regard for the conditions which you were bound to live under if your health was to be preserved. I think in all probability you have learned a much needed lesson. . . ."

THE AMERICAN MERCURY

730 FIFTH AVENUE

NEW YORK

July 2, 1924

Dear Sara:-

. . . This combat of gorillas begins to be exhausting. The sessions last all day and all evening, and leaving the hall is very risky.[1] I laid off late this afternoon in order to take a look at my mail. The usual mountain! Just before I left Bryan made an idiotic speech.[2] The old jackass is really pathetic. I felt like throwing a lily at him—and then an egg. He prays daily—and God always fools him. Let us trust the Devil, who is more honorable.

I'll probably be back in Baltimore early next week.

Yrs.,

HLM

[1] The Democrats had begun raising issues that changed the delegates from a unity into a howling, raging mob. The issues which divided them were the League of Nations, the repeal of Prohibition, "oil-tainted" Democrats, and the Ku Klux Klan, but the fights also carried over to the naming of a presidential candidate. William Gibbs McAdoo, the son-in-law of Woodrow Wilson, had his chances ruined because of his connection with oil; Prohibition and Roman Catholicism ruined the chances of Governor Alfred Smith of New York; and Oscar Underwood of Alabama was destroyed by his criticism of the Klan.

[2] Admidst the booing of Al Smith supporters, William Jennings Bryan got up on the platform and launched a dramatic appeal for William G. McAdoo.

~

ALS

THE AMERICAN MERCURY
730 FIFTH AVENUE
NEW YORK

July 4, 1924

Dear Sara:-

This obscenity passes far beyond my hopes. The Ku Kluxers have ruined the Democratic party, finally and forever. You can't imagine the ferocity of it. I am among witch-burners 18 hours a day, and enjoying it. My desk is directly in front of Georgia. What faces!

But so much work, at my advanced age, is probably not salubrious. If I perish I leave you my Bible and 1,000,000 marks.

On account of the holiday no mail has been forwarded from Baltimore. I pray our Redeemer that you are top side up again, and full of Hegelian fury.

And kiss your hand!

Yrs.,
HLM

THE AMERICAN MERCURY
730 FIFTH AVENUE
NEW YORK

July 8, 1924

Dear Sara:

God knows when this convention will end. I begin to suspect that I am doomed to remain here all summer. The morons tried to come to an agreement on Saturday, but today it turns out they are further apart than ever. It is not at all inconceivable that they may wobble along all week. But I pray our Redeemer may inspire them to call it off tomorrow. I have on my last shirt and must go naked if they continue.

Your fellow Alabamans are giving a superb show. They have voted for Underwood unbrokenly for nine ballots and every time they are called on the Governor of the state answers in a voice of brass. The whole crowd now rises with him and gives him a cheer when he finishes.

What is news with you? I assume that it is very hot in Maryland. How are you standing it?

Sincerely yours,
M

HLM:L

'Typed by Edith Lustgarten.

HOTEL ALGONQUIN
NEW YORK

Friday. July 10, 1924

Dear Sara:-

The buffoonery being over at last, I seize the opportunity to pen you a respectful line. God, I believe, has delivered the Democratic party, but only to the Devil. Imagine a ticket with one leg in the Morgan spittoon and the other in the swill trough!' I shall vote for Cal, and advocate him with the utmost violence.

If I may ask the question without impertinence, why in hell don't you let me have word from your Treasury? You keep me in a sweat of fear that you may be in hock. I'll be back in Baltimore by Sunday or Monday, and shall come out to wait on you during the week. Are visitors barred absolutely on non-visiting days? Let me have a note to Hollins street.

A great mass of accumulated work confronts me here, but I think I can knock it out by Sunday. The last two days of the convention were rather strenuous. Night before last I didn't get to the hay until 4.30 A.M. and last night I was agog until after 3. But it was small devotion to give to my country. The last two hours, early this morning, were superb farce. When they put over Bryan II the whole press-stand roared and rocked with mirth. It was worth waiting for.

Entirely as a matter of Southern politeness and without committing myself to anything I kiss your hand.

Yours in Xt.,
A Life-Long Democrat

'Finally, after an all-time record of 103 ballots, the exhausted Democrats gave up on the prolonged and bitter contest between Smith and McAdoo and turned instead to a compromise candidate, John W. Davis, who was hampered at the opening of his campaign by the fact that he had been an attorney for Morgan and Company. The vice presidential nominee was Governor Charles Bryan of Nebraska, the brother of William Jennings Bryan.

H. L. MENCKEN

1524 HOLLINS ST.

BALTIMORE

July 13th, 1924

Dear Sara:-

Have you seen the enclosed?[1] If not, you may while away a dreadful hour looking through them. Some of the later dispatches are incomplete. But I'll never be able to get the late editions of the paper. You will notice a few prophecies that did not come true.[2] Such is journalism!

I had hoped to wait on you this afternoon, but it turns out to be impossible. My office is piled mountain-high with mail and other stuff, and I must do an article for The Evening Sun. Tomorrow I shall go to see the surgeon and find out what is to be done about my hoof.

I should be on my legs again by the end of the week. More anon.

Yours,

M

[1]Mencken's articles in the Baltimore *Evening Sun* describing the convention. The next day, in "Post Mortem," Mencken would conclude: "For there is something about a national convention that makes it as fascinating as a revival or a hanging. It is vulgar, it is ugly, it is stupid, it is tedious, it is hard upon both the higher cerebral centers and the *gluteus maximus*, and yet it is somehow charming. One sits through long sessions wishing heartily that all the delegates and alternates were dead and in hell—and then suddenly there comes a show so gaudy and hilarious, so melodramatic and obscene, so unimaginably exhilarating and preposterous that one lives a gorgeous year in an hour." What had thrilled Mencken most of all, of course, was that several "professors" had come to "ridiculous ends," especially William Jennings Bryan, making "all the long sessions, all the lost sleep, all the hard usage of the *gluteus maximus*" worth it. "He had sworn a mighty oath to prevent the nomination of Davis . . . [and in the end] they not only shoved his arch-enemy, Davis, down his throat; they shoved his brother, the Nebraska John the Baptist, after Davis, and so made it impossible for him to yell."

[2]Mencken had written, "Everything is uncertain in this Convention but one

thing: John W. Davis will never be nominated." As Malcolm Moos tells the story: "Informed that Davis had been nominated for president a few seconds after filing his story, Mencken, stunned for the moment, quickly snapped back: 'Why that's incredible! I've already sent off a story that it's impossible.' Then, as an afterthought: 'I wonder if those idiots in Baltimore will know enough to strike out the negative.' "

H. L. MENCKEN
1524 HOLLINS ST.
BALTIMORE

Friday, July 18, 1924

Dear Sara:-

Just a line at the heel of the day. I put in the afternoon brewing a noble keg of beer. It is a gift. Before you go to Montgomery I shall instruct you in the art, and assemble a full outfit of materials. The introduction of sound beer would be the saving of Alabama. Even old Brandon would be improved by it.[1]

Ich kuss die Hand.

Yours,

M

[1] William Woodward Brandon, who had served three terms in the House of Representatives and was a probate judge, now served as governor of Alabama.

H. L. MENCKEN
1524 HOLLINS ST.
BALTIMORE

July 19th, 1924

Dear Sara:-

Saxton[1] writes that he was tempted, but resisted the temptation. I begin to believe that there must be a hole somewhere in the MS.,[2] probably where the new ending begins. Let me see it again when it comes back. I'll give it a prayerful reading. If it turns out to need repairs, you can tackle it when you get home, and then I'll take it to Holt myself. Or to Harper. Got mit uns![3]

Phil Goodman[4] is coming down from New York this evening for a crab party. He will eat and drink so much that I'll have to get a doctor for him in the morning.

I kiss your hand.

Yours,

M

[1]E. P. Saxton, editor of the George H. Doran Publishing Company.
[2]*Career.*
[3]God be with us!
[4]Philip Goodman, author, theatrical producer, and publisher of some of Mencken's early books.

H. L. MENCKEN
1524 HOLLINS ST.
BALTIMORE

July 25th, 1924

Dear Sara:-

. . . Don't give away this Institute of Arts and Letters wheeze. I have a lot of fun with it. Cabell and Hergesheimer are both invited to the annual banquet, and both are full of indignation.

I kiss your hand.

Yours,

M

You never send me any news. What is your temperature?

H. L. MENCKEN
1524 HOLLINS ST.
BALTIMORE

August 6th, 1924

Dear Sara:-

The Johnson is a handsome gal,[1] and her beads are very nobby.[2] I incline to taking a look at her when she gets back. Is Dunlap jealous? If so, then you may hear of fisticuffs at Homewood.

Is it possible that you haven't got "A Book of Burlesques"? Surely you must be in error. If not, let me know, and I'll send it at once. It contains some very tasty stuff.

The proofs went to you last night. Don't return them. You will find plenty of errors in them, all now corrected. Such jobs wring the soul. I also had to make an index. Ah, that we two were Maying!

The weather has reduced me to a pulp. Today I must go downtown and take a Southern customer to lunch. I recall his name, but can't find him in my files and so don't know who he is. I'll have to feel my way.

Would it be forward in me to say that I think you are a very handsome and charming gal?

I kiss your hand.

Yours,

M

¹Buford Jeannette Johnson, professor of psychology at Johns Hopkins University, had just been given the distinction, on May 6, 1924, of being the second woman at Hopkins to be promoted to a full professorship.

²Expression meaning "her achievements are very nifty."

H. L. MENCKEN

1524 HOLLINS ST.

BALTIMORE

August 8th, 1924

Dear Sara:-

Convinced at last that you have no copy of the burlesques book, I am sending you one by this mail.¹ Cherish it fondly! It will probably outlast all my other works, save the one you know about,² and if you ever blab about that one then all I can say is that I hope you suffer in hell forever, which would be a small punishment for giving away so good an idea, when a man is lucky if he has one in a lifetime, the way things go in this world. The best things in the book are "Death" and the piece about Cheops and the pyramid.

As for La J., I refuse to be warned off. I shall tackle her in the grand manner as soon as she gets back. Her beauty inflames me. No wonder the whole place rocks with scandals. One such woman is enough to ruin a whole kingdom.

I doubt your forgiveness. There is a mental reservation in it. I have

set myself a penance: to read a chapter of Holy Writ every night for
40 nights.

Ich kuss die Hand.

Yours,
HLM

[1]*A Book of Burlesques.*
[2]The Homo Sapiens book.

H. L. MENCKEN
1524 HOLLINS ST.
BALTIMORE
August 11th, 1924

Dear Sara:-

It might be a good idea to try "The Atheist" on Nathan. He reads
all fiction that comes in in the regular course. Simply address it to
The American Mercury, 730 Fifth avenue, and send no letter with it.
Let us see how it strikes him.

Sloan will be ready for the coroner after two numbers of the magazine. Some very subversive stuff is due shortly, including an article
by the eminent Aframerican, Dr. W.E. Burghardt DuBois,[1] predicting
war to the death between coon and Saxon.[2]

The first kiss of hay-fever is on me. It takes the form of a dreadful
lethargy. I loll about all day, and no work gets itself done. This always
follows a very hot spell. It is due to acidosis. I am guzzling sodium
citrate and trying to get rid of it. . . .

I kiss your hand.

Yours,
M

[1]Editor of *Crisis* magazine, DuBois read Mencken with care and urged his
readers to do the same, saying that Mencken's recommendations for realism would
help the Harlem literary renaissance.

[2]The attitude that appeared in his article "The Dilemma of the Negro" (*The
American Mercury*, October 1924)—and one that Mencken had urged blacks to
express at the outset—was the issue of black superiority. Although blacks were

forced to go to separate schools, they often created educational institutions that were a cut above those attended by most whites. And yet, no matter how well educated, these blacks were denied access into the white world.

H. L. MENCKEN
1524 HOLLINS ST.
BALTIMORE

August 14th, 1924

Dear Sara:-

News comes that my niece is to bang into town tomorrow, to spend the week-end. It is a beautiful experience to receive her, but somewhat exhausting. At her age, nine years, there is little understanding of the fatigues which overcome senile uncles. She uses her legs as if she had a thousand of them. Let me have your prayers.

Have you read the Prejudices proofs? If so, how does Chapter I strike you? I wobble between the notion that it is too vicious and the fear that it may seem too mild. The Anglo-Saxon is my oyster henceforth. I shall perform upon him at least four times a year. The book is now in press, and I should have a copy within a month.[1]

The time approaches for you to come to town. When? I was at the wop's yesterday with my old boss, Lynn Meekins.[2] The same old Bacardi cocktails are on tap—not for you until you reach 160 lbs! And the victuals are just as good as ever. The cook came out of the kitchen and shook hands with me. He inquired after the beautiful lady of last Winter. I told him she had married a labor leader and gone to live in Altoona, Pa.

I kiss your hand.

Yours,
M

[1]Prejudices IV was about to be released that December.
[2]Young Mencken's superior at the Baltimore *Herald*, Meekins had taught Mencken more about newspaper reporting and literary writing than anyone else.

~

ALS

THE AMERICAN MERCURY
730 FIFTH AVENUE
NEW YORK

August 25, 1924

Dear Sara:

God is still trying to annoy me. When I got off the train yesterday I found that some anonymous woman had made off with one of my bags, leaving her own in place of it. I thus arrived at the Algonquin *on a Sunday night* without any clothes save those on my back. So far the Pullman Company has been unable to recover the bag. Loss: a suit of clothes, ½ a doz. shorts, the MS. of a novel, several American Mercury MSS. and my address book. But your *MS.* was in my other bag, and thus is safe. You are better regarded above than I am.

Ich kuss die Hand.

HLM

ALS

THE AMERICAN MERCURY
730 FIFTH AVENUE
NEW YORK

August 27, 1924

Dear Sara:

Excellent news! I believe that a holiday in Baltimore would be still better.[1] I shall prepare the wop!

That hussy brought my baggage back the next day. And hay fever seems to be very mild.[2] I am booked for St. Agnes Hospital Sunday, but even that will be trivial. I expect to be back home by Monday afternoon. On your knees!

Yrs.,

M

Ich kuss die Hand!

[1]Sara had been planning to leave Maple Heights and go to Asheville or Montgomery.

[2]Once again, hay fever had Mencken by the snout. "The worst of it is the depression," he commented to Sara. "I feel almost like a Christian."

H. L. MENCKEN
1524 HOLLINS ST.
BALTIMORE

August 31st, 1924

Dear Sara:-

This is the best story you have yet done—at all events, the best I have seen.[1] It is quite free of the mannerisms that I bawled against in the first draft of "The Atheist." I suggest that you send it to Carl Van Doren, of The Century, 353 Fourth avenue, New York. I believe that he will take it. If he doesn't, send it to Harper's. There ought to be an apostrophe before the name of Lasses, thus 'Lasses.

Whether I'll be able to travel to Sparks after I get out of St. Agnes I don't know.[2] Probably all locomotion will be difficult for 10 days. Is there any chance of your coming to Baltimore toward the middle of the month? I want to have a session with you about "Career." God has vouchsafed me several revelations about it.

I kiss your hand, and, if the Polizei were not around, would attempt to give you a hug.

Yours,
HLM

[1] Story missing.
[2] When Mencken finally went to St. Agnes Hospital to have the tumor removed from his foot he discovered that it had turned out to be a harmless wart. "What started it, God alone knows," he commented in a letter to a friend. But he still called it a "tumor" in front of Sara.

H. L. MENCKEN
1524 HOLLINS ST.
BALTIMORE

September 3rd, 1924

Dear Sara:-

I escaped in 24 hours, on two sticks, but with the toe reprieved. The tumor is now out. I can barely hobble, but I should be on my legs again in a week or so. On Saturday, in all probability, I'll still be moving ½ a knot an hour, but I hope to get downtown to see the surgeon, in Charles street. Could we meet for lunch? It sounds fabulous!

If you can manage it, name the time and place. My thirst remains as ever!

One day in hospital made me think of your long imprisonment. Well, soon you will be out.

Yours,
M

H. L. MENCKEN
1524 HOLLINS ST.
BALTIMORE

September 5th, 1924

Dear Sara:-

I'll certainly be here next Saturday. Let us meet then. I suggest lunch at the wop's studio. By that time I should be rid of the crutches and possibly of the hay-fever also. It is much better today. A few days of cool weather would finish it. It runs with the temperature. Last night I had to drink two large high-balls in order to get any sleep. If this went on, I fear, I might become an addict to drink.

I believe that you would improve faster by a change of base. You are simply Kriegsmüde—tired of the battle in one trench. Cain, of the Sun, went to Lubillasville three months ago, and is already getting week furloughs. He tells me that the other patients keep him amused, and that there are movie shows and other such divertissements. He has a good private room, with a sleeping porch.[1]

Yours,
M

[1] James ("Jim") M. Cain, a reporter for the Baltimore *Sun* (later known for *The Postman Always Rings Twice* and other novels), had been battling inactive tubercular bacilli since 1918, when he was rejected by the draft board. In 1924 doctors spotted an active lesion the size of a quarter in the apex of his right lung.

~

H. L. MENCKEN
1524 HOLLINS ST.
BALTIMORE

September 6th, 1924

Dear Sara:-

I am all right. The wound is healing nicely, there is no pain, and the stitches are holding fast. If I can get through next week without squashing it I'll be safe. I am sticking to the crutches to avoid putting any strain on it. There is no pain whatever.

What of next Saturday? Let me hear of it as soon as you make your plans. I went downtown today by taxi without difficulty. I am to have another dressing on Tuesday and then one on Saturday. Let us, if God wills it, meet at the wop's for old time's sake. But you are offen them cocktails! I'll have him make you a little one in a demi tasse. As for me, I shall order one in a beer seidel.

I wrote to Baker yesterday, trying to shake him out of his pedantry.[1] But it is probably hopeless. Beardsley had an idiotic article about me in yesterday's Evening Sun.[2] I shall duck him if possible.

The enclosed is my favorite portrait. It was made on a stencil by McKee Barclay.[3]

I kiss your hand!

Yours,
M

[1]Harry T. Baker was submitting articles to Mencken for use in *The American Mercury* but Mencken found all of them to be too pedantic.

[2]Wilfred Attwood Beardsley had just written an article entitled "A Spanish Mencken Revealed in Person of de Unamuno," comparing Mencken to the Spanish philosopher and writer Miguel de Unamuno.

[3]Chief cartoonist for the Baltimore *Sun*, Barclay was also a good reporter.

~

H. L. MENCKEN
1524 HOLLINS ST.
BALTIMORE

September 15th, 1924

Dear Sara:-

The MS. of "Career" goes to you by this mail. In the matter of the dialogue, I have made some corrections in the first chapter which sufficiently indicate what I think ought to be done to it. There are too many dashes. The result is that the speeches all seem broken. I believe it would be better to adopt a more usual punctuation.

The question of tagging the principal characters we discussed. It should be done to both the girl and Otis. At the end I believe that there is room for a soliloquy by the girl, making her volte face a bit clearer. But otherwise, the book is sound. And it will get a publisher. Don't be concerned about that.

Hay-fever has got me into so low a state that I can scarcely work. It always ends with just such a depression. I must have been gloomy enough Saturday, despite my joy at seeing you. You looked superb. Forget Sloan! You are quite well, and will discover it when you get out of the hospital.

Ich kuss die Hand.

Yours,
HLM

H. L. MENCKEN
1524 HOLLINS ST.
BALTIMORE

September 16th, 1924

Dear Sara:-

What nonsense! You were very silent, but very charming. I only hope you escape from Sparks by the end of the month. I believe that you have a bad case of hospital weariness, and that you'd do much better in Baltimore. But don't fight Sloan. So long as you are in his hands, let him decide.

Hay-fever has got me in a dreadful state. I simply can't work. I have none of the common symptoms—sneezing, etc.—but my head feels like a lump of clay, and I am very depressed. But this will pass off quickly. I hope to get to New York at the end of the week. A lot of work is piled up there. Meanwhile, I must try to knock out 6 pages of book reviews.[1]

Don't try to copy "Career." Simply rewrite it. I'll have my stenog copy it when the time comes.

Yours,
HLM

[1]As time progressed, Mencken found himself becoming irritated with his job at *The American Mercury*. More often than not, he found himself tied down to the necessary routine of watching the printer or the makeup man, thus being led further away from the job he was supposed to do—tracking down ideas, manuscripts, and authors. As he wrote to Nathan: "If I get out of contact with the office for three days my desk is a chaos." More often than not, Mencken found a sympathetic listener in Sara and began confiding his worries to her.

H. L. MENCKEN
1524 HOLLINS ST.
BALTIMORE

September 19th, 1924

Dear Sara:-

The Most High has healed me. Hay-fever is passing off, and my foot is almost back to normalcy. I walk with no limp, and there is only a slight tenderness left. I shall see the surgeon for the last time tomorrow. Now for his bill!

Is Baker a Ph.D.?[1] I ask because he has sent in a short article on the Ph.D.'s of the English faculty—old stuff, but coming from one of the lodge it might be worth printing. Don't ask anyone if you don't know.

I think you are ready to escape from the Zuchthaus.[2] You will get on quite as well in Baltimore as on that hill-top, and probably much better. Let me hear what Sloan says of it.

I kiss your hand!

Yours,
HLM

[1]Harry Torsey Baker had arrived at Goucher College as assistant professor of English in 1919 and served the college continuously as assistant professor until

his death in 1939. A Phi Beta Kappa student from Wesleyan University, he also received his M.A. there. He did not have a Ph.D.

²Tail.

ALS

MAENNERCHOR HALL RESTAURANT
EAST 56th STREET
NEW YORK

Friday, September 20, 1924

Dear Sara:

. . . I suggest that, when you escape, we make a bomb and blow up Goucher College. Guth would make a beautiful sky rocket.

I kiss your hand.

Yrs.,
HLM

THE AMERICAN MERCURY
730 FIFTH AVENUE
NEW YORK

September 30th, 1924

Dear Sara:-

The trouble with this is that it is not a short story at all, but a scene in a novel or novelette. It has no ending. A short story must lead up to a definite climax. You simply stop, and then add a tag.

It is excellent news that your imprisonment is near its end. I think that you have got all the benefit that is to be obtained from a sanitarium. What follows is in your own hands. If you stick to the cure for a year or so, you will begin to forget the whole adventure. It is not difficult to keep well, once you get a fair start.

Beardsley is calling me up again, suggesting a session. He now proposes to bring Baker. I have told him to come next week. I may learn something from him.

Hold this paper to the light, and observe the water-mark. Isn't it tasty? I delight in it.

Prejudices IV should reach you by the end of the week.

I kiss your hand!

Yours,
M

H. L. MENCKEN
1524 HOLLINS ST.
BALTIMORE

October 9th, 1924

Dear Sara:-

Your cell is so small that I must have brushed against you yesterday. At all events, I detect what seems to be perfume on my coat. The truth is that we both take up more space than we used to. I now weigh 180 lbs. But I got a plate for my hoof this morning, and now I should be able to get some exercise, and so reduce. But not you! You look perfect now. You are a very handsome gal.

I am sending you a copy of the Smart Set as it is under Hearst.[1] It will make you yell. I am glad that the change is so violent. Now nobody will ever suspect that I still have a hand in it. I haven't. But I had to take some bonds in payment.

It was gaudy to see you walking down the lawn. Now for the grand escape. When you get to town the wop will have his instructions. The dinner must be his masterpiece.

Did I kiss your hand yesterday? If I forgot, then I do it now.

Yours,
M

[1]William Randolph Hearst had bought the rights to *The Smart Set* for $60,000. The October issue featured an article by the Reverend Billy Sunday; a poem by Edgar Guest; pictorials on the girls of the Ziegfeld Follies, Rudolph Valentino, and Marion Davies; and articles entitled "Is Marriage an Aid to Success?" "The Life Story of a Leading Lady," and "When a Man Laughs at Love."

H. L. MENCKEN
1524 HOLLINS ST.
BALTIMORE

October 13th, 1924

Dear Sara:-

At 9 P.M. Friday throw yourself on your knees and give God a yell. Baker and Beardsley will arrive precisely at that moment. I'll probably give them fusel oil at once, and then shove their remains into the fire.

The Eastern Shore party turned out to be very pleasant. The native gentry drink peach brandy out of gourds. But they are a very agreeable lot. There was a continuous service from Friday to Sunday.

Maybe you are right: delusions are among the symptoms. I also note: a rising blood pressure, crying spells, religion and a ringing in the ears. But I have none of these. I note that La Calkins is also the author of "The Good Man," 1918.[1] I hope she had me in mind.

Now I must write bread-and-butter letters to four or five hostesses whose names I know only vaguely.

Ich kuss die Hand.

Yours,
M

[1]Mary Whiton Calkins, American philosopher and psychologist, and author of *The Good Man* and *The Good: Or the Introduction to Ethics*.

H. L. MENCKEN
1524 HOLLINS ST.
BALTIMORE

October 14th, 1924

Dear Sara:-

I pass the enclosed on to you. Please represent me. Paul is a young man who once worked on the Herald here, my old paper, and then on the Atlantic Monthly. He has blown up. Reading essays by the younger Gelehrten ruined him.[1]

Prejudices IV came wandering in at last this morning. I sent you a copy forthwith. It looks dreadful on its birthday, but maybe it will gain comeliness later on.

Have you fixed the date of your escape? I'll probably go to New York Sunday or Monday and remain away a full week. I am due at West Chester, Pa., to visit Hergesheimer, on Saturday and Sunday, the 25th and 26th. Then no more week-ending until the Spring.

Yours,
M

[1]Gilman Paul had become treasurer of the Poetry Society of Maryland. Mencken had sent Sara a membership blank and an invitation to attend its October meeting.

H. L. MENCKEN
1524 HOLLINS ST.
BALTIMORE

October 19th, 1924

Dear Sara:-

The MS. is here, and I shall give it my eye as soon as I get back from New York. Going through it will take prayer: I may be at it for weeks. Then to the stenog, and then to Harpers.

The horned-rim specs are lovely. My niece has a doll that they will fit.[1]

The Mercury boil, I fear, is about to bust. A palaver is called for Wednesday, and there will be a great row.[2]

Ich kuss die Hand!

Yours,
M

[1]Two evenings earlier, Mencken had had a "bout" with professors Baker and Beardsley, who had arrived at his house at 9:00 p.m. and remained talking until 1:30 a.m. "Trying to keep up with their flow of ideas was a dreadful strain," Mencken wrote to Sara. Apparently, Sara had sent Mencken a pair of spectacles that would befit a "Herr Professor."

[2]As the magazine gained in popularity, tension between Mencken and Nathan increased. Whereas Mencken believed that *The American Mercury* should be a general magazine, with literary concerns subordinated to other interests, Nathan held the opposite opinion. Mencken's focus was on the political and sociological issues of the day, Nathan's on literature and Broadway. The day Mencken wrote to Sara, expressing his anxiety, was also the same day he had written a long letter to George Jean Nathan, expressing his dissatisfaction with having to attend to all the detail work of the magazine himself, and also his doubt that both he and Nathan could remain as joint editors with such different interests.

ALS

THE AMERICAN MERCURY
730 FIFTH AVENUE
NEW YORK

October 23, 1924

Dear Sara:

This job becomes grotesque. My desk is under 4 feet of MSS., and this morning I dictated 42 letters. It was 11:15 last night before I got to the beer-hall.[1] Boyd,[2] who had been waiting for 3 hours, was already so far gone in malt that his conversation revolted me. What a world!

If you encourage me to crime God will punish you!

Yrs.,
HLM

[1]Mencken habitually was at the beer hall at 10:00 p.m.

[2]Ernest Boyd, critic and essayist, and author of *H. L. Mencken* (1925), a biography released the following year.

H. L. MENCKEN

1524 HOLLINS ST.

BALTIMORE

November 5th, 1924

Dear Sara:-

I perform at Mardal Hall at 8.15 precisely.[1] After the show, I suppose, I shall be in the hands of Baker and Beardsley, as heretofore, and my Scotch will suffer a boozeorrohage.

The News correspondent at the college broke the agreement, and printed a notice of my performance in The News of yesterday. This will get me into a great deal of trouble. My excuse for refusing to lecture before the Ladies' Aid Societies of Zion Church, the First Baptist and Oheb Shalom is now gone. I have written to Baker, suggesting that he call the culprit into his studio, bend her over his knee, and break a butter-paddle over her gluteus maximus. Or is corporal punishment forbidden by Guth?

I'll get in a little ahead of 8:15 and crave the honor of kissing your hand. Don't fail me!

Yours,
M

[1]Mencken's first lecture to the Goucher College women of Harry T. Baker's writing class took place in the fall of 1922. Once again he was to lecture to a new set of ears in the main building of the campus.

H. L. MENCKEN
1524 HOLLINS ST.
BALTIMORE

November 6th, 1924

Dear Sara:-

Tomorrow's soirée must be called off. I have to go to New Yrok
[sic] tonight unexpectedly, and won't get back until the middle of
next week. These few lines in haste.[1]

Yours,
M

[1]Even though Mencken was rushing to New York to discuss the Mencken-
Nathan decision, he nonetheless found time to type Sara this hasty note.

ALS

THE AMERICAN MERCURY
730 FIFTH AVENUE
NEW YORK

November 10, 1924

Dear Sara:

Henry Cabot Lodge's death is a great blow to me.[1] I am now the
oldest, handsomest and most learned man left living in America. And
the hardest worked. The last three days have been infernal.

I'll be back by Thursday. When do we meet?

Yrs.,
HLM

[1]Author and senator Henry Cabot Lodge had died the day before in Boston.
Lodge was not only a scholar who had published historical studies and several
distinguished biographies (*George Washington* and *Daniel Webster* among them),
he was also a leading opponent of Prohibition—which, among other things,
would have endeared him to Mencken.

~

H. L. MENCKEN
1524 HOLLINS ST.
BALTIMORE

November 13th, 1924

Dear Sara:-

I suspect that your tonsils have been to blame all along. They sufficiently account for your rise in temperature. Get them out, and all the rest of your troubles will vanish. I had mine chopped out eight or ten years ago, and with superb effect. The operation is not serious. You will be all right in three days.[1]

I assume that the business is to be done today or tomorrow. I'll wait on you on Saturday. Courage, Camille!

Yours,

M

After three days and three nights of struggle in New York, all the questions at issue were settled satisfactorily.[2]

[1]Mencken long held the belief that what bothered Sara was not in her lungs at all, and in this respect he was partially correct. Approximately one-tenth of clinically recognizable tuberculosis is nonpulmonary, instead, the tuberculous infection is passed through the bloodstream and becomes scattered throughout the body, affecting areas such as the lymph nodes, kidneys, and other organs. For the next eleven years Sara would undergo the complications of nonpulmonary tuberculosis, including "all the minor ills human flesh is heir to," she would write, admitting to a "somewhat complicated clinical career."

[2]This statement was an oversimplification; the conflict with George Jean Nathan would last much longer. Knopf chose to support Mencken, his original choice as editor, and Nathan was persuaded to vacate his position as coeditor.

H. L. MENCKEN
1524 HOLLINS ST.
BALTIMORE

November 16th, 1924

Dear Sara:-

You must have misunderstood Sloan. Kahn told me last night that your x-ray plate showed a very remarkable improvement. There was never any shadow in the apex of your lung, the almost invariable site of tuberculosis. Now the lower part is almost completely clear. This means, in fact, completely clear. It is impossible to detect very small congestions by the x-ray: they often appear when they do not exist in fact. Don't tell Sloan that Kahn told me this: it would only start a row. But it is the fact.

Your sore throat will pass over by the middle of the week, and with it your fever. If you are not back to normalcy by Wednesday I agree to have myself immersed by the First Baptist Church.

Ich kuss die Hand.

Yours,
HLM

H. L. MENCKEN

1524 HOLLINS ST.

BALTIMORE

November 20th, 1924

Dear Sara:-

Malone came to my house last night and we put in three hours over the jugs. He seems a very amiable fellow; more, he knows a great deal. I hope to get something from him for The American Mercury. He spoke of Miss N.[1] very enthusiastically. As soon as Bright is called to Jesus, which will probably be very shortly, Malone will get his chance. He is surrounded by idiots at the Johns Hopkins.

I am to get a whack at Knight Dunlap's next book for the Mercury—there may be an article or two in it.[2] This is a secret. I have proposed to Baker that my conference be set for Wednesday, December 3rd, and suggested to him that he invite you and Miss N. This will smoke him out. I have further provided that Beardsley is not to be admitted unless cold sober. God help us all!

What of the temperature?

Yours,
M

[1]Marjorie Nicolson.
[2]*Social Psychology*, which Mencken did not review.

H. L. MENCKEN
1524 HOLLINS ST.
BALTIMORE

November 22nd, 1924

Dear Sara:-

I refuse to get into the tank. I suspect that Sloan keeps inaccurate thermometers. Are you in bed? I hope not. If you don't appear for the seance at Goucher I shall refuse to go on the stage. The subject is not announced, but after the first question I shall sound the old motif in F sharp minor.[1] The gals are not interested in literature. They are too intelligent.

The enclosed, I trust, will make you respect me. It shows that I am at last getting some encouragement in the Confederate States.[2]

I have the club at my house tonight: the brethern will drink a dozen large jars of beer. Tomorrow morning, New York.

Ich kuss die Hand.

Yours,

M

[1]Mencken's speech on writing (alias "How to Catch a Husband") for Harry Baker's class.

[2]The Columbia (South Carolina) *Record* had published an article on November 9, announcing that Mencken had joined the staff of *The Sunday Record* and would write a weekly article for the book page. "Above all things Mencken hates dullness," the article concluded, "and not for one moment is Mencken himself ever dull. He may have his faults but dullness is not one of them."

H. L. MENCKEN
1524 HOLLINS ST.
BALTIMORE

November 28th, 1924

Dear Sara:-

The soirée is set for Wednesday at 8.15, at Mardal Hall. Baker replies that you are invited, but doesn't mention Miss N. Let us see what we shall see. I may bring along Governor Ritchie[1] and Jeff Coogan, my bootlegger. God help us all!

Don't think I have forgotten "Career." My worst spell of labor is now over, I hope and pray, and I shall have at the MS. next week. Then to the stenographer with it.

No news from you. What of the temperature? I suspect that it has no more to do with your lungs than with Coolidge's. There is probably some very low infection somewhere else, maybe in the nasal passages. What of the tonsil wounds? Are you comfortable?

Yours in Xt.,
M

[1]Maryland Governor Albert C. Ritchie was a close friend of Mencken, regularly passing along the rough drafts of his speeches for Mencken's critical eye. Mencken supported Ritchie's views throughout his articles for the Baltimore *Evening Sun*.

H. L. MENCKEN
1524 HOLLINS ST.
BALTIMORE

December 1st, 1924

Dear Sara:-

It all seems absurd to me. Kahn says that your x-ray plate shows immense improvement. I believe that what you need most of all is a change of base. You are simply hospital-weary, and no wonder. Once you escape from that hillside you will forget all of Sloan's alarms. If you stay until Saturday in Baltimore, then certainly we must meet. What of lunch together, Thursday, Friday or Saturday? If the weather is foul Wednesday, don't come in. You will hear a very bad lecture, and you may catch cold. A fearful wind is blowing today and it is very cold.

To hell with the pneumothorax. Ten days after you get home you will wonder what it was all about. You now know how to take care of yourself. Find out a good doctor in Montgomery and see him once a month—no oftener. And throw away your thermometer! The scales and your mirror show that you are well.

Yours,
M

H. L. MENCKEN
1524 HOLLINS ST.
BALTIMORE

Friday night, Dec. 5, 1924

Dear Sara:-

What a joy to see you looking so well! I forgot to ask you when you will come to Baltimore on Friday. Will there be time for us to have dinner together? I surely hope so. But maybe you are in Miss Winslow's hands. If so, bring her along. Don't neglect to get your reservation in time. Shall I look after it for you? Or after your baggage? Consider me your baggage-master.

I have put in two hours tonight on a MS. by Edgar Lee Masters— a long sketch in praise of Altgeld.[1] It is a superb piece of writing— something genuinely distinguished. Now for "Career." A lucky evening! I should finish the MS. by the middle of the week. It will go to the stenog at once. Maybe I'll give her half on Monday.

I refuse to repent. Praise God from Whom all blessings flow!

Yours,

M

[1]"John Peter Altgeld" (February 1925 *Mercury*). Altgeld, the Chicago lawyer who wrote *Our Penal Machinery and Its Victims* (1884), and the governor of Illinois, was also the subject of Vachel Lindsay's poem "The Eagle That Is Forgotton" and of Howard Fast's novel *The American*. Altgeld believed that American judicial systems were weighted against the poor, and he pardoned three anarchist leaders convicted of fostering the Haymarket Riot. He was defeated for reelection in 1896 because of his alleged radical sympathies.

H. L. MENCKEN
1524 HOLLINS ST.
BALTIMORE

December 11th, 1924

Dear Sara:-

I have been following you on the map, and find that your geography, like your physiology, is full of gaps. Montgomery is not north of Atlanta, but to the southward. For shame! I surely hope you have made a safe journey of it, and that it has not exhausted you. Lie low for a few days, and throw your clinical thermometer away. Once a month is often enough to use it.

Edward Bok, the eminent editor of the Ladies' Home Journal, is in town, and I am to meet him in an hour. I am all a-tremble. Not often has it been given to this paw to grasp such eminent hands. Bok is almost the perfect 100% American. One more ohm or kilowatt, and he would sprout wings.[1]

Ich kuss die Hand!

Yours,

M

[1]E. W. Bok had become the living caricature of the American Dream. The award of the Pulitzer Prize in biography in 1920 to his autobiography, *The Americanization of Edward Bok*, was less a recognition of Bok as an author than a tribute to the American hero-tale of the Poor Boy Who Makes Good. The previous year he had offered $100,000 as an American Peace Award for the best plan for cooperation between the United States and other countries to prevent war.

H. L. MENCKEN

1524 HOLLINS ST.

BALTIMORE

December 19th, 1924

Dear Sara:-

Half of "Career" is in the hands of the virtuous copyist, and she should have the rest by Christmas. I told her not to rush it. She is to make one fair copy and a carbon. The two, with the original, will go to you at New Years or thereabout.

. . . La Clark sold the Reviewer to Paul Green[1] at the University of N. Carolina. They paid her $2 for it. They will, I think, make a success of it. She wanted to sell because of her marriage. Her husband is a rich Philadelphian.[2] I advised her to get rid of the magazine: she had done enough for it. There were various bidders, but she chose the North Carolinians.

Your story, crowned by O'Brien, was not bad, but good.[3] He is occasionally intelligent—more so, in fact, every year. His list for this year surely shows some sense. Observe the portrait of La Suckow. It flatters her grossly.

Beware of too much excitement and exercise. No hoofing! You should resume physical activity very slowly. Above all, eat plenty of honest hog meat and hominy, and get plenty of sleep. Also sprach Zarathustra![4]

I am just back from New York after a laborious week, with two pink spots. One day I had lunch with Stokowski, conductor of the Philadelphia orchestra, and found him a capital fellow. The next day I lunched with Lillian Gish,[5] and found her truly incredible. She looks and talks like an Epworth League leader in a town of 200 people. She is a friend of Hergy's.[6]

My usual troubles mount up. My brother announces that he is to arrive with his wife and daughter on Dec. 31—and I must be in New York that day for a business meeting. My sister must go to hospital in two weeks to get some old appendectomy adhesions repaired. My mother is also ill, but not seriously. I am myself worked to death and in a very low state.

So I kiss your hand and close.

Yours,
HLM

[1]Professor at University of North Carolina at Chapel Hill, and later a recipient of a Pulitzer Prize for his play *In Abraham's Bosom*. Critical acclamation ranked him in the 1920s as second only to O'Neill among American playwrights.

[2]In 1924, Emily Clark, age thirty-one, surrendered the editorship of *The Reviewer* to make a spectacular marriage. Her husband, sixty-eight-year-old Edwin Swift Balch, a wealthy Philadelphian statesman and author of books of Arctic exploration, had financed the last few issues of *The Reviewer* and had taken Emily back to his palatial home in Philadelphia. Like her friend, Joseph Hergesheimer, at Dower House, Emily now held huge weekend parties where her friends served themselves rare wines from the Balch cellar while Edwin Balch looked on, fascinated and pleased by this new array of people. He lived only three more years, however, and at his death left Emily a rich woman.

[3]"Miss Rebecca," the story Mencken had rejected, had made the Roll Call of Honor for *The Best Short Stories of 1924*, edited by Edward J. O'Brien.

[4]*Also Sprach Zarathustra*, Friederich Nietzche's book which tried to present the whole of his thought.

[5]The silent film actress Lillian Gish, discovered by D. W. Griffith and made

famous in *Birth of a Nation* (1914), had at this time just returned from Florence, where she had been filming the title role in *Romola*.

⁶By the end of 1925 Joseph Hergesheimer would have been closely involved in six films. He was a close friend of several directors (including D. W. Griffith, who had planned to make a film of Hergesheimer's novel *Java Head*) and several stars, among them Lillian Gish (whom he portrayed in the character "Mina Raff" in *Cytherea*).

H. L. MENCKEN
1524 HOLLINS ST.
BALTIMORE

December 22nd, 1924

Dear Sara:-

You are escaping dreadful weather. The temperature dropped below 20 last night, and there was a wind. I darn nigh froze on my sleeping porch. I'd have come in, but I have no bedroom in the house, and sleeping on a couch in my office would have been worse, for the very books sweat tobacco smoke.

It delights me to hear that you are leading a quiet life, and not engaging in wholesale hoofing. The usual Christmas invitations are pouring in here. If I retain my faculties over the New Year it will be a miracle. Knopf is giving a grand and gaudy party New Year's Eve, and I must go to New York for it.¹ Hergesheimer will be there in his new $350 dinner jacket. I suspect that the whole gang will be unable to navigate on New Year's Day. Such bibbing, of course, is offensive to me, but I engage in it to be polite.

So no more today from your devoted admirer. How do you feel? And what has the Montgomery quack to say?

Yours,

M

Do you want any more magazines? The supply is endless. I dessay you are busy receiving the nobility and gentry. Suppose I send only the good ones?

Ah, that we 2 were maying!

¹Later canceled.

~

H. L. MENCKEN
1524 HOLLINS ST.
BALTIMORE

December 25th, 1924

Dear Sara:-

I have a feeling that there is something wrong with this story.[1] It somehow comes as an incredible surprise that Spann should steal the money. It is not sufficiently prepared for. Moreover, there are some spots where the narrative becomes difficult to follow, for example, on page 12. It appears there that Spann is the man invited to dinner, and by Scilla. On page 13 Scilla reproves her mother for inviting Cootie. The reader would get bogged here.

I note that you use the English spelling, as in honour and colour. Better use the American spelling, without the u.

The first part of "Career" is finished, and the rest is in the gal's hands. I should get it all in a few days. I'll send the two copies and the original MS. to you separately, and at different times, to guard against loss in the mails.

What of your temperature and how do you feel? Have you seen Laslie? Let me have some news.

My mother gave me a half gallon cocktail-shaker as a Christmas present. It will cost me a pile of gin! One round will be enough for a coroner's jury.

Ich kuss die Hand!

Yours,
M

[1] "Green Gold," never published.

H. L. MENCKEN
1524 HOLLINS ST.
BALTIMORE

December 29th, 1924

Dear Sara:-

Would you send coals to Newcastle! I refuse to let you burden Miss Thomas[1] with 22 loaded barges lying in the harbor, just in from the Bahamas.[2] Scotch is now so cheap in Baltimore that it is being used to bathe babies. A fact. I went to dinner at Paul Patterson's house last night, and got a dreadful overdose of it. But my people have been heavy drinkers for 200 generations, and so I bear such things very well. I am a bit drowsy today, but am otherwise up to normalcy.

A wild week impends—that is, for a man growing aged. Tomorrow morning at 7:30 my niece arrives per Schlafwagen from Pittsburgh for a three day session. Friday night, old Louise Pound[3] comes in to organize her new journal of American English, and I am giving her a dinner. Saturday Pearl[4] is dining (and wining) some Gelehrten from the Northern seminaries. Sunday I am going to Washington for lunch with the German ambassador,[5] who is returning home. By Monday I'll be ready for a monastery. God help us all.

Ich kuss die Hand!

Yours,

M

[1]Perhaps one of Sara's friends from Montgomery.

[2]Scotch and rum fleets were already a regular feature of those harbors that were dense enough to hide bootlegger launches to come and carry its liquor into the city. Boston, coastal New Jersey, and the lesser New England ports were infested with smugglers from the Bahamas and West Indies.

[3]Philogist and editor of *American Speech*.

[4]Professor of biology at Johns Hopkins University and French horn member of the Saturday Night Club.

[5]Ambassador Otto Wiedfelt, stationed in Washington, D.C., from 1922 to 1925.

1925

Throughout 1925 Sara stayed in Montgomery, recovering from tuberculosis. "She did very little writing," Mencken wrote, "but her eyes and ears were alert, and by the time she returned to Baltimore in the Spring of 1926 she was ready to get her observations down on paper." From afar, she watched as Mencken's popularity—and notoriety—grew, as he became involved in the celebrated Scopes Monkey Trial in Dayton, Tennessee, as well as the subject of two biographies.

H. L. MENCKEN
1524 HOLLINS ST.
BALTIMORE

January 1st, 1925

Dear Sara:-

The last of the MS.[1] went to you today. The registry office is closed, and so I took a chance. I hope it reaches you safely. You now have everything, in various packages: the fair copy, the carbon and your original. The labor of the stenog is my small tribute to your charm, beauty and Christian piety. As I wrote to you the other day, I believe it would be a good idea to tackle Little-Brown & Company with the MS. They are printing a good many novels, and seem to handle them effectively. Send the MS. express prepaid, with a label marked express collect for its return in case the Holy Saints are in their cups.

My niece has been here for three days. She leaves tonight, and I shall tackle a mountain of accumulated work tomorrow. I am glad to see her, but her presence is unfavorable to literary composition. I surely hope your nephew's[2] mumps are better. They at least have the merit of making the young silent.

I kiss your hand. How are you? Let me have a full report.

Yours,
HLM

[1]*Career.*
[2]Wickliffe, the son of Sara's younger sister, Ida.

H. L. MENCKEN
1524 HOLLINS ST.
BALTIMORE

January 6th, 1925

Dear Sara:-

Send the MS. to Little, Brown & Company first. If they refuse it, let me know, and we can discuss the Perkins business. Don't return the enclosed clipping.

I am in the midst of a dreadful week, trying to get through a pile of delayed writing in order to reach New York Monday morning. Then back to Baltimore for another session, and then to New York again on the 25th to tackle the new slave.[1] I hope he turns out well. If not, then out he goes. I have two substitutes on ice.

My book has again gone to pot. Perhaps it is God's will that I shall never write it. But if the slave pans out maybe I'll get a chance during the Spring. Despite all this infernal work I feel pretty vigorous. It is a miracle. But the hot blast of the crematory is not far off. Twenty-six years ago my father[2] died at my present age. He seemed old to me then.

Have you consulted Laslie? What does he say?

I miss you horribly. Ah, that we could sit at the amiable wop's, and get down his Bacardi! I kiss your hand.

Yours,
M

[1]As Nathan's duties diminished, the increased work began to wear Mencken down. Six to seven hundred manuscripts arrived at *The American Mercury* office each month. Charles Angoff, a recent graduate of Harvard, had been writing for an obscure Massachusetts newspaper before he applied for the position at the *Mercury*. He later became managing editor and, much later, editor, for eleven months (1934–1935).

[2]On December 31, 1898, August Burkhardt Mencken suffered an acute kidney infection. The end was painful: in a period of two weeks he lost twenty pounds, sank into a coma, and finally died on January 13, 1899. He was 44 years old.

ALS

THE AMERICAN MERCURY
730 FIFTH AVENUE
NEW YORK

January 10, 1925

Dear Sara:

This is garbage, but it may amuse you. The author is an old fellow named Stewart, a newspaper reporter of 40 years practice.[1] I must have shocked him. He seemed astonished that there were carpets on the floor of my house and paper on the wall.

Ich kuss die Hand.

Yrs.,
HLM

H. L. MENCKEN
1524 HOLLINS ST.
BALTIMORE

January 16th, 1925

Dear Sara:-

I have had a hell of a week in New York, getting a divorce from Nathan and making ready to put the slave into the office.[1] The whole business is naturally unpleasant, but I must go through with it, or end in a lunatic asylum. The slave comes to work on the 26th. If he turns out to be no good I shall can him and put in another. There is a long waiting list of gifted fellows. The magazine will be unchanged externally for six months. I shall make no announcement. A long battle over the stock of the publishing company is still ahead. I find, curiously enough, that I am still full of bounce in business, even at 44. It is God's mercy. But such dreadful combats are very depressing.

It is excellent news that your temperature is behaving. Spring is only a month away in Alabama: you will get plenty of exercise in a little while. I suspect and accuse you of neglecting your diet. You ought to stuff like an archbishop. But such recoveries as yours are anything but uncommon. Gradually all the symptoms wear off. You'll be fit for any work in the Fall, including work in a steam laundry.

Poor Sherman makes a worse ass of himself every day. Imagine calling me a proletarian! The cause of his Bookman yell was this: He wanted me to review his new book in his paper, and proposed that the review be printed alongside his review of my book. He sent Irita Van Doren[2] (a charming woman and a friend of mine, though his assistant) to me to negotiate. My reply, in brief, was that, while I'd probably review Sherman's book in the Mercury if, on reading it, I found it interesting, I could not enter upon any personal relations with the author himself, for his conduct during the war was that of a bounder. (He served on the Creel Press Bureau.)[3] This message, I daresay, offended him sorely.

Every day some new patriot comes in and wants to make peace. But I have a long blacklist of them. No man who was a press agent during the war will ever have the honor of shaking this lily-white hand. To hell with them all forevermore, and may they be doubly and triply damned. I have paid off a few so far (e.g., Cobb),[4] and shall pay off more.

Please present my regrets to Mrs. Paul Smith. I lament that I had to miss her soirée. If you happen upon any Americana in the Advertiser,[5] please let me have it. I'd like, especially, to get a few patriotic editorials. Or something on Christian work.

Thy hand is kissed.

Yours,

M

[1]The change from Nathan's coeditorship status to that of contributing editor would not be announced until the August 1925 issue of *The American Mercury*. His association for five years after 1925 only allowed him to save face, and in March 1930 he was fired.

[2]The wife of Carl Van Doren. She had been on the editorial staff of *The Nation* and was now working on the New York *Herald Tribune*.

[3]Stuart Pratt Sherman, an American critic, had written an article in the January issue of *The Bookman* magazine entitled "Mr. Brownell and Mr. Mencken," comparing *Prejudices: Fourth Series* with William Crary Brownell's *The Genius of Style,* as a confrontation of the literary proletariat with the literary aristocracy. In 1917 Sherman had charged Mencken with being unpatriotic and a defender of licentious literature, using Theodore Dreiser as a prime example. Mencken ridiculed Sherman and his sort in his article "The Dreiser Bugaboo," published in the *Seven Arts* magazine for August 1917, and Sherman responded with a negative review of *A Book of Prefaces* for *The Nation* in November 1917. Years later, Mencken would write Carl Van Doren that his objection to Sherman was not that he had denounced him as pro-German, but his denunciation of Dreiser. "Dreiser had written nothing about politics, and was hardly interested in the subject. The accusation that he was pro-German, was made without adequate evidence and had the obvious effect of greatly damaging him at a time when he surely had enough other troubles. It seemed to me that in the heat of controversy Sherman hit below the belt, and that's the reason I refused to have anything to do with him."

[4]Irvin Shrewsbury Cobb, journalist and humorist.

[5]The Montgomery *Advertiser,* edited by Grover Hall.

H. L. MENCKEN
1524 HOLLINS ST.
BALTIMORE

January 21st, 1925

Dear Sara:-

Your letter is vague. Has Little declined the MS.? If so, send it to Henry Holt & Co. Address it to Elliot Holt (note the spelling of Elliot) and tell him I advised it. The address is 12 west 44th street. Don't send anything to Liveright. As for Brandt, I don't think you need an agent.[1] G. P. Putnam & Sons, 2 west 45th street, would be as good as Holt. Shoot a nickel to decide between them.

I ascribe the floods along the Alabama river to the magic of the Pope. Here in Baltimore there are still piles of snow. I keep to my cell. On Friday Edgar Lee Masters will be here, and I shall have to exhume some jugs and fill him up. He is to lecture before the Poetry

Society on Saturday.[2] I hope to put him into the pulpit with a dreadful hangover.[3]

Well, Spring is not far off! Stuff away, and be patient! You are quite safe.

Where is the photographic view of you that I was to get?

I kiss your hand twice.

> Yours,
>
> M

[1]Carl S. Brandt.

[2]The Poetry Society of Maryland.

[3]Mencken and Edgar Lee Masters had been exchanging letters ever since 1916, but it was Theodore Dreiser who had been telling Masters about Mencken's "vitality," "erudition," "courage," and "forthrightness." This was their first meeting.

H. L. MENCKEN

1524 HOLLINS ST.

BALTIMORE

January 22nd, 1925

Dear Sara:-

I forgot to answer your question about La Newman's[1] book.[2] The fact is that I have not read it. I know the author; she is very amusing; but I doubt that her theories of the short story are worth hearing. La Saffold is new to me. Is she a novelist? Your account of her makes me suspect that she belongs to the league of American Pen Women. Or the Bookfellows.

I fear the divorce proceedings are about to become acrimonious. Twice, during the early negotiations, I avoided chances to hit below the belt. Now I am paying for it. It simply doesn't pay to attempt decency in such matters. But we shall see.

Masters is due here tomorrow. I shall take him to dinner with your rival, a beautiful creature of the stage, now playing here. She must be in her paint by 8 P.M. After that Edgar and I will commune at my house, with a jug on the hob. His privately printed works are very amusing. If you were 48 years old, and a grandma, I could show them to you.

You tell me too little about yourself. How do you feel? And how is your temperature running? I don't preach patience to you, but cynicism: it is the most comforting of philosophies. You will get over your present difficulties only to run into something worse, and so on until the last sad scene. Make up your mind to it—and then make the best of it. That is, do the best you can within the limits of your chance. If you can't write a book a year, then write one every two years. I believe that life is a constant oscillation between the sharp horns of dilemmas. I work like a dog, and accomplish nothing that interests me. Once I gave up all routine work and devoted myself to a book: I was sick of it in six months, and went back to answering letters and reading MSS. The slave does not deceive me: he will be twice as bad as his predecessor. Nevertheless, life remains livable. Biological necessities keep us going. It is the feeling of exerting effort that exhilarates us, as a grasshopper is exhilarated by jumping. A hard job, full of impediments, is thus more satisfying than an easy job. When I get letters from German Gelehrten,[3] complaining that they are having a hell of a time, I always congratulate them. They will do good work, and enjoy it. All the men at the Rockefeller Institute, with money to pay for everything they want, are unhappy; the place is full of intrigue. Moreover, they are accomplishing almost nothing.

But I run on a la Polonius. Please excuse poor pen. I kiss your hand.

Yours,

M

[1]Frances Newman. Her acerbic wit had attracted the attention of Mencken and James Branch Cabell, who encouraged her to give up her library post and write short stories and novels.

[2]*The Short Story: Mutations*.

[3]Scholars.

THE AMERICAN MERCURY
730 FIFTH AVENUE
NEW YORK

January 27, 1925

Dear Sara:

. . . Do you crave a photographic view of *me*? Good God, woman, where is your modesty? Can it be that jazz has you in its clutches?

Why don't you sit to a camera and send me a print? I formally petition for it.

. . . Ich kuss die Hand!

As ever,
HLM

H. L. MENCKEN
1524 HOLLINS ST.
BALTIMORE

January 30th, 1925

Dear Sara:-

I have just escaped from New York. The slave looks very promising. He fell upon his work instantly, and was running without bumping in 24 hours. He goes along for hours without saying a word. I begin to believe that he will relieve me of much wear and tear. But I'll have to go to New York oftener than usual until he has got through the round of at least two issues.

Marjorie Nicolson asks me by letter for permission to reprint "The Shrine of Mnemosyne" in Prejudices IV. It is a very sentimental piece. I have told her to go ahead. Knopf would ordinarily demand $3.65, but I have called him off. She is making a text-book.[1]

I went out to Mt. Vernon (N.Y.) by motor last night with Paul De Kruif,[2] and we came near perishing in a blizzard. But his amiable, industrious and beautiful wife[3] had a Stockes' Liniment cocktail ready for us, and we thawed out in ten minutes. At one time I feared that the wind would blow the machine into the Harlem river. Such are the perils of life in that great city.

At noon there was a vast literary lunch to Sherwood Anderson.[4] Had I known what a jam there was to be I should have come down with the ager and got off. (How is that for the subjunctive? Or is it?) All the vermin of N.Y. were there, from the Young Aesthetes to Sherman. I managed to evade them all, and to get at a table of eight which included but one Americano, and he was a parlor anarchist, Leonard Abbott, son to old Lyman[5] but a friend of Emma Goldman's[6]—once, perhaps, a better friend than he had ought to be. But enough of scandal. I picked up four dinner invitations. Four more hellish lies on my conscience when the time comes!

Anderson showed up wearing a navy blue shirt with a soft collar
and a flowing necktie to match. His tweeds, at least ¾ of an inch
thick, were yellow shot with brown. In his necktie he wore a ruby at
least an inch in diameter. He has lately married a new wife,[7] and is
not yet himself. Dreiser was invited, but didn't come. The ladies ran
to adiposity, but I saw 2 or 3 cuties. Probably stenographers. A dry
party.

God knows, I miss you. Your rival depressed me. I hope Dr. Slade
is better. Ich kuss die Hand.

Yours,
HLM

[1] *The Art of Description*, a textbook containing selections and commentary.

[2] American writer on science, who provided the scientific and medical background for Sinclair Lewis's *Arrowsmith*. His work, *Microbe Hunters*, published the following year, would become his first best-seller.

[3] Rhea Barbarin, who collaborated with de Kruif on several of his works.

[4] This was a large New York party given by B. W. Huebsch in honor of Sherwood Anderson. Stewart Sherman was also there, and he and Mencken came together for the first and only time. At the party, Carl Van Doren attempted to introduce Sherman to Mencken. Sherman consented and eagerly crossed the room to take Mencken's hand. Everyone assumed Mencken would readily forgive Sherman's attacks, but instead, he refused to acknowledge the outstretched hand of Sherman or even look at him, and later remarked: "I'd rather pass into heaven without the pleasure of his acquaintance. He is a dirty fighter." It was the only instance in which friends could recall Mencken's being unforgiving, but Mencken had found Sherman's charges without valid bases, and he knew that Sherman, in making up to Mencken, was trying to gain more personal recognition.

[5] American congregational clergyman, author, and editor of the *Illustrated Christian Weekly* and *The Outlook*. He distrusted radicalism in all forms and approved the suppression of wartime dissent. His son was editor of *The Christian Science Monitor*.

[6] International anarchist who conducted anarchist activities in the United States from 1890 to 1917. She served two years in prison for agitating against military conscription and U.S. involvement in World War I. *My Disillusionment in Russia* and *My Further Disillusionment in Russia* explained her antipathy for her homeland. Her controversial writings influenced many, including President William McKinley's assassin (Czolgosz), who claimed that Goldman inspired him to do the deed.

⁷Anderson's third wife, Elizabeth Prall, whom he had just married the year before. He would divorce her in 1929.

H. L. MENCKEN

1524 HOLLINS ST.

BALTIMORE

February 6th, 1925

Dear Sara:-

I suspect that you have been jazzing, if only psychically. In any case, don't let a small flare-up alarm you. You will note them as long as you keep a clinical thermometer in the house. Some day row out to the middle of the Alabama river and drop it overboard. I suspect that my own temperature ranges between 85 and 108. It is never over 92 on Sunday mornings, when the church bells ring.

Sloan was wise to avoid his pneumothorax. Kahn says the last plates showed your lungs to be quite clear. I suspect that you may have some small nose infection. If there is a good nose and throat man in Montgomery, have him take a look some day.

What did Little and Brown have to say? Did you send the MS. to Elliot Holt? When sober, he is a charming fellow. Don't be discouraged by a few rejections. "David Harum" was rejected 11 times.¹ Every publisher receives 40 times as many novels as he can print. He is thus apt to make slips.

"The Shrine of Mnemosyne" is too pianissimo. I should have presented more and better pictures of my purple past. But now I am a Christian.

And kiss your hand.

Yours,

M

¹*David Harum: A Story of American Life*, by Edward Noyes Westcott (1899).

~

H. L. MENCKEN
1524 HOLLINS ST.
BALTIMORE

February 14th, 1925

Dear Sara:-

The slave, by God's providence, seems to be extraordinarily competent. He has already rid me of half my daily mail, and is showing skill at weeding out MS., managing the stenog, and other such jobs. If he keeps on as he has begun I shall put his name on the flagstaff. Naturally enough, it appears that he is no Americano. In fact, he says he was born in Russia, though he is a Harvard man.[1] Harvard has had apparently only one effect on him: he is an excellent speller. He is 23 years old, and an immense, gnarled buck, with red hair—no beauty, God knows. But one handsome movie actor in the office is enough.

Getting rid of his predecessor promises to be a long and unpleasant business. His legal rights must be thought of, and he is hanging on very earnestly. But it is now too late for me to change my mind. No news of the business has got out so far. The flagstaff is to remain unchanged until July. After that there will be a sensation.

No news from you for nearly a week. How are you feeling? I hope you have not stopped all exercise. I believe that staying in bed so long did you far more harm than good. Get on your legs every day, if it is only for an hour. You have told me nothing about your short stories. Where did you send them? And what are you at work on?

If I can shake off a bit more of my routine work I hope to start my democracy book very soon. It will not take long, once it is begun. Then for Homo sapiens. I have an idea for yet another that is even better. In fact, it is so good that I am afraid to put it on paper. You must wait to hear it until we meet at the Epworth League convention.

I kiss your hand!

Yours,
HLM

[1]Charles Angoff had been born in Minsk, Russia, and brought to the United States when he was six years old. He became a naturalized citizen in 1923, the year he graduated from Harvard.

~

THE AMERICAN MERCURY
730 FIFTH AVENUE
NEW YORK

February 18th, 1925

Dear Sara:-

This story misses me. I detest the cracker dialect. Moreover, it seems to me to drag in the first part—a fatal defect. Put it off on La Mayfield[1] and go back to your own work!

Has it ever occurred to you that the white clergy of the South have never been done at length? Octavus Roy Cohen[2] and other such Rotarians have done the dark brethren, but the white ones remain untouched. What a chance! Imagine the struggle for appointments at a Methodist conference! Or a day in the life of a Baptist pastor! No plots are necessary: simply character sketches.

What is the news with you?

Thy hand is kissed.

Yours,
HLM

[1] Sara Mayfield.

[2] American novelist, short-story writer, and author of detective fiction. His tales about blacks were frequently read in *The Saturday Evening Post*. His character Florian Slappey, along with Irvin Cobb's J. Poindexter and Hugh Wiley's J. Vitus Marsden ("The Wildcat"), had become a household name, and all three were immediate antecedents for the "Amos n' Andy" radio show, which occurred later in the decade.

THE AMERICAN MERCURY
730 FIFTH AVENUE
NEW YORK

February 19th, 1925

Dear Sara:-

The announcement of prizes is superb. It goes into Americana at once. If you enter all of the competitions and win all of the prizes I figure that you will have $42.75.

You have my sympathy in the death of your Corona. I have to carry mine with me; no other typewriter is possible, not even another Corona. When mine is in dry-dock and I have to use my brother's, I moan and sob by the hour.

Brandt, I think, is a very good agent.[1] Of the stuff he sends to me not more than 80% is clearly impossible for the magazine. This is far above the average made by any other agent. Most of them flood me with stuff exactly suitable for the Christian Herald or Ladies' Home Journal.

The name of the new gent is Charles Angoff. I shall promote him to assistant editor anon, and maybe put his name on the flagstaff.

This is written from Baltimore. I am off to Washington in an hour to take a quiet snout at politics.

But pause to kiss your hand.

Yours,
HLM

ALS

THE AMERICAN MERCURY
730 FIFTH AVENUE
NEW YORK

February 25, 1925

My dear Sara:

What infernal bad luck! As soon as you feel like writing, let me know what happened. It must have been influenza. I am so sorry!

But such things pass. You will live to be the oldest woman in Alabama!

. . . Ich kuss die Hand!

Yrs.,
HLM

~

H. L. MENCKEN
1524 HOLLINS ST.
BALTIMORE

March 2nd, 1925

Dear Sara:-

You are devoid of the news instinct. Here I wonder how you are getting on, and not a line about your health in your letter! Has the temperature vanished? I take it that you picked up some influenza. It has been a pestilence of late in these parts. Only my bootlegger saved me from it. Let me have some news.

What of the novel? Have you heard from Holt? If he foozles it I suggest a new firm, Simon and Schuster, 37 west 57th street. They have made $100,000 publishing cross-words books, and are now ambitious to build up a good list. Send the MS. to M. Lincoln Schuster, and tell him that I suggested it. He is no Babbitt, but a very intelligent young fellow, and I believe that he will make a big success of his business.

The slave made a dreadful mess of the first make-up and I had to disentangle him by long distance telephone. But he will do better hereafter. Otherwise he is very good, and he has already cut down my routine correspondence, etc., by 50%. In fact, I begin to have hopes of starting my democracy book when the cold weather ends.

But first I must get together materials for a book about H.L.M. that Goldberg is to do, to be published by Schuster. G. plans an elaborate work, unlike anything ever heard of. It will take me several weeks to exhume the necessary early stuff. Needless to say, this tome will help me in my business. It will make, in particular, a powerful impression upon persons who do not read it. There are to be made illustrations—showing me in my confirmation suit, at the grave of Lafayette, sailing for Union Hill, N.J., etc. If it is ever finished you get a free copy, absolutely without expense.[1]

In a few days I hope to send you Lewis' "Arrowsmith." It is to be published March 5th. You will like it. It will not make the popular success that "Babbitt" and "Main Street" made, but there is good stuff in it, largely contributed by De Kruif, Lewis' collaborator.

The Johns Hopkins is in an uproar. After having spent millions establishing a refuge for morons, it now proposes to return to its old university status, and to cut out its undergraduate college.[2] Easier said than done. Years will pass before it lives down its present low reputation.

Send me some news! And hold out your hand to be kissed.

Yours,

M

[1]Mencken was in the process of typing out a 200-page manuscript consisting of notes, family history, and opinions to help Isaac Goldberg out with his book, *The Man Mencken, A Biographical and Critical Survey.* Goldberg later served as music critic of *The American Mercury.*

[2]Undergraduates were admitted to Johns Hopkins from the very beginning of instruction in October 1876. It had been the original plan of Daniel Colt Gilman, the first president, to admit only graduate students, but this was amended before classes began, owing in large part to lack of public support for the idea. The plan referred to by Mencken was known as the Goodnow Plan, after the president of the university who proposed it, Frank J. Goodnow. Despite the endorsement of the Academic Council, the plan was never put into effect, partly because of the public outcry which arose when details of the plan were first announced. Mencken wrote several columns castigating the university, and Hopkins, recognizing that it would lose the considerable support and goodwill of the community, and fearing the difficulty of getting enough students to transfer after two years at another college, abandoned its course.

H. L. MENCKEN
1524 HOLLINS ST.
BALTIMORE

March 4th, 1925

Dear Sara:-

Good news, indeed! It was, I take it, a bout with the flu. The damned disease is still epidemic. I escape it only by violating Art. XVIII. The medical journals are now full of reports on the hiccough pest I had three months ago. The symptoms were very curious and amusing: hiccoughs for three days and a fearful itching of the scalp. God has many tricks up His sleeve. I admire such humors.

I gave out no statement regarding the Mercury. Nathan very foolishly did so, with the result that he is now in an embarrassing position. But I can't do anything to help it. My announcement will be made in the July number, in three lines. We are still very far from a settlement.

It may come to rough stuff yet. Knopf, unfortunately, is an innocent bystander, and his interests must be thought of.

In the Borglum affair[1] I sympathize with the disciples of Jeff Davis. Borglum is a hog for money, and generally disreputable. During the war he made a great deal of money out of dubious airship contracts.

Twenty seven! You are just beginning to get your growth. A woman is at her most charming after 30, especially a brunette. You will be very handsome when you begin to oxidize. As for me, I begin to feel, at 44 ½, that the morticians have their eye on me. By the time you are that age I shall be 62. Think of it!

The article on the Southern lady is very good stuff.[2] Some polishing, perhaps, wouldn't hurt it, but I think it is saleable as it stands. Try it on the magazines I mentioned in my last. They all pay excellent honoraria. If they don't buy it, let me see it again. I think, with a few small changes, I can use it. But we are still paying less than the Century, Harper's etc. We closed our first year $2,200 ahead, but with no salaries paid to editors. What a world!

Isaac Goldberg now proposes to write a book about me, with illustrations. Inasmuch as he knows no more about me than Coolidge, I must dig up the materials myself. It turns out to be a frightful job. I have spent two whole days trying to discover and arrange the history of the Menckenii. When that is finished I must go through all my early newspaper stuff, and make selections from it. Then I must try to remember the details of my spiritual history—how I became a Christian, etc. If I had plenty of time it would be amusing, but I have very little. Goldberg will give a show, but he'll not make a book. That job is reserved for you. Title: "An American Patriot." I authorize you to publish it ten years after my lamentable exitus from these scenes.

Friend Sary, I miss you like hell. I have, in fact, transferred my eating from the Marconi to Max's place in Park avenue. If you were at hand I should probably risk your yells by trying to neck you. I have been practicing on a fat woman. When we meet you will see some technique. So beware again!

Ich kuss die Hand!

Yours,
HLM

~

[1]John Gutzon (de la Mothe) Borglum, sculptor of the colossal heads of Washington, Jefferson, Lincoln, and Theodore Roosevelt in the Mount Rushmore National Memorial in South Dakota, had begun working on a sculptural procession of Lee and his staff and soldiers marching in the Stone Mountain Memorial, in Georgia. Disputes with his patrons led Borglum to abandon his work, which was completed by others.

[2]"The Southern Lady Says Grace," later published in *The Reviewer*, October 1925.

H. L. MENCKEN

1524 HOLLINS ST.

BALTIMORE

March 11th, 1925

Dear Sara:-

This story puzzles me.[1] It contains, unquestionably, some of the best writing you have done, but I believe that it is too vague. At the end it simply stops. You may have a clear idea there, but it is not got on paper. Moreover, on page 3, you do not sufficiently explain Carrington's switch from Elia to Fredericka. But there is excellent stuff in the story. Try to straighten it out.

Send "Career" to Schuster, by all means. Tell him I suggested it. You are far too impatient. The other day, in preparation for the Goldberg book, I dug up an account book I kept in 1900, when I was writing and selling short stories. It showed that some of the stories were rejected 10 and even 15 times before they were accepted. This included some relatively good ones—that is, good for me. Every publisher who has seen "Career" has said something complimentary about it. What halts them is the question whether it will sell. I think it will.

Your ruling that I am not to hear about your health is utter damned nonsense. Let me have some news!

Enclosed is the short story article.[2] I thought I had sent it to you. Baker is an imbecile.

Ich kuss die Hand!

Yours,

M

I am hiring a stenog to help me with the Goldberg notes. There is a colossal mass of material.

¹"Trifles," never published.

²"Short Story Courses," which Mencken said did more harm than good, had appeared in the February 22 issue of the Chicago *Sunday Tribune*. (Mencken continued to write articles for the paper until 1928.) Baker, Sara's English teacher at Goucher College, had believed that such courses were helpful.

H. L. MENCKEN
1524 HOLLINS ST.
BALTIMORE

March 25th, 1925

Dear Sara:-

I suspect that Schuster will do "Career". . . . His partner, Simon, is a practical book drummer, formerly with Boni & Liveright. The success of the firm is the sensation of literate New York.

Oppenheimer and one Ginsberg are to operate under the name of the Viking Press. (The Nordic Blond complex!) Ginsberg is the heir to the Kleinert dress-shield, and has a lot of money. Oppenheimer was until lately with Knopf. These new enterprises interest me. I went aboard the Knopf barque at the start, and have never regretted it.

The Merkur business has got into an acrimonious state, and will probably end in a pitched battle, with lawsuits. But I must get clear at any cost. So far the facts have not got out. But I don't care if they do.

If I may say so politely, why in hell don't you send me some news about yourself? I repudiate your oaths. Let me have a bulletin, in detail. If you refuse I shall hire detectives.

Ich kuss die Hand zweimal!

Yours,
HLM

H. L. MENCKEN
1524 HOLLINS ST.
BALTIMORE

March 27th, 1925

Dear Sara:-

This, I believe, is the best story you have ever done.¹ A few suggestions:

1. There is some confusion in time in the next to the last paragraph on page 4. Surely Lee had not already got through medical school at the time of his father's death.

2. The "Ah, life!" refrain had better come out. It is apt to seem absurd.

3. The ending is rather vague. I don't think the place of the old lady's burial is important. Better finish her with something else—for example, a summary of life as she has found it.

If you agree, rework the story and let me see it again. I incline to print it. What has become of the Southern Lady article? Have you given it a tour? If not, why not?

Yours,
M

¹Sara kept few copies of her stories. This one, unfortunately, is missing.

H. L. MENCKEN
1524 HOLLINS ST.
BALTIMORE

April 1st, 1925

Dear Sara:-

Still not a line about how you are getting on. May God punish you for keeping me without news! I believe that a year in the West would be folly. After all, you surely don't want to live there permanently. If you get acclimatized to a high altitude, you may be very uncomfortable when you leave it. You can recover completely in Alabama. Altitude has nothing to do with it. The main business is to raise your immunity, and the way to do it is to keep your nourishment high. You busted by the simple process of living like an Armenian refugee, on fruit salads. More proteins! A perfectly fit, well nourished person is immune to bacteria.

The divorce (i.e. from Nathan) will end, I fear, in a row worse than the Stillman case.¹ The bride is hanging on desperately. But if I am to remain sane I must become completely free, and it will be worth a hundred rough fights to be so. The business is to be resumed in New York next week. If necessary, I shall shut down the magazine.

After all, it works me too hard, and I get very little out of it. I'd be better off writing books, and writing for some other magazine.

Send me some news. I miss you infernally. And kiss your hand.

Yours,

M

¹The divorce and legitimacy suit between banker James A. Stillman and his wife, Anne, had begun in 1920. He questioned the paternity of her unborn child (he said it was an Indian guide from Canada, where she had been on vacation); their son and daughter took sides; he became involved with another woman. After a series of suits and countersuits the couple were reconciled in 1926 and sailed to Europe.

H. L. MENCKEN

1524 HOLLINS ST.

BALTIMORE

April 4th, 1925

Dear Sara:-

I like this story very much. You are writing better all the time. But I have a feeling that the story about the old lady would be better for the Mercury. Have you finished revising it? If so, let me have it again. When you send it, please send "The Southern Lady" also.

I am off for New York. The other day Knight Dunlap sent me the MS. of his new book.¹ A great mass of platitudes. It is a sort of treatise on social psychology. He gives great importance to sex; what he says is what any intelligent Unitarian clergyman, after reading the *Literary Digest* for 15 years, might say. If this is the sort of stuff he teaches I congratulate you on your escape.

I have finished my notes for Goldberg: a tremendous job. What he will make of them God knows. He proposes that I read the MS. and insert footnotes, a la H.G.Wells. It is an idea. But I am full of doubts that he can get any sort of grip on me. We are too different. Nevertheless, even a bad book will be good for my business. There will be many illustrations, including a photograph of my palace at the above address, made yesterday.

Now for my own book. I'll tackle it as soon as I get back from New York.

Thy hand is kissed.

Yours,

M

Don't send me stamped envelopes! Ain't we friends?

M

¹*Social Psychology.*

H. L. MENCKEN

1524 HOLLINS ST.

BALTIMORE

April 11th, 1925

Dear Sara:-

I met La Kruif No. 1 but once.¹ She came to my office to ask me to induce her husband to come back to her. A dreadful woman, frowsy and foolish. Apparently much older than De K. She told me that his reading of Nietzsche had ruined their marriage. Looking at her, I found it hard to believe it. She later tried to stab him. He then escaped to Reno, and got a divorce there. He had to turn over a considerable property to her to keep her from appealing to the League of Nations. Whether or not he was accompanied to Nevada by the bride-elect I don't know. It is against my principles to speculate upon such matters. If he was, then I can only say that I envy him very sincerely, for she is a most charming gal. They seem to be happily married. She is good-looking, intelligent, tolerant of his occasional guzzling, and an excellent housekeeper. Dinner at their house is delightful, though probably somewhat hard on the kidneys.² Some time ago I took the two of them to Union Hill. We dined continously from 6:30 to midnight. De K is 6 ½ feet high and wears a No. 22 collar. A magnificent Dutchman. Once I took him to a party in New York. When the dancing women came in he grabbed one of them by the ankles and stood her on her head. Her yells terrified the host: he feared a raid by the Polizei. De K knows a great deal, and is a most amiable fellow.

Miss N,³ I think, had a just grievance against the Knopf office, which had neglected her letters. I had the whole transaction closed instantly and she now has her permission. Tom Beer,[4] it appears, was actually laid up. His health is not very good.

I never said that Lewis was a great artist. I said that he was a great technician—that he managed his novels superbly, especially "Babbitt." He is far more the scientist than the artist. Large parts of "Arrowsmith" were done by De Kruif—some of the best parts. I suspect that I must have been the grandpa of the book, or at least the midwife. It will not sell as well as "Babbitt." But Lewis and De K got $50,000 for the serial rights, and so they are happy. Lewis is now roving around Europe, stewed all the time. He has a pestiferous wife.[5] Life to him consists of an endless series of futile flights from her. She always overtakes and recaptures him. What a world!

I have just read the first novels of Mlles. Suckow and Winslow, in MSS. The former is "Career," but different greatly in detail. There is good stuff in it, but in general it is somewhat flabby.[6] The Winslow opus is the story of a girl who runs away from a small town, joins the chorus, and finally settles down to 100% respectability. It is full of amusing detail, but wanders all over the map.[7] I doubt that either will make much of an impression.

La Winslow waited on me last week, and I met La Suckow six or eight weeks ago. You remain the only beautiful lady novelist ever heard of. When "Career" comes out, and your portrait is circulated by the intelligent press-agent, you will make a sensation. I formally predict it.

God delivered into my hands, in New York this week, two cases of prime Moselle. I shall give a Maibowle party the first week of May. Ah, that thou wert here!

The divorce proceeds apace, with many sad scenes. What a world! But I have said so once before.

Ich kuss die Hand!

Yours,
HLM

[1]Refers to de Kruif's ex-wife, Mary.

[2]Rhea Barbarin often cooked German dinners for de Kruif and Mencken, and drank beer with them, seidel for seidel, without leaving the table before they had to. And "because Rhea was a small girl," de Kruif recalls, "this aroused Mencken's respect."

[3]Miss Nicolson.

[4]American writer from Iowa.

[5]Grace Livingstone Hegger, whom he divorced in 1928 to marry Dorothy Thompson.

[6]Ruth Suckow's *The Odyssey of a Nice Girl*.

[7]Thyra Samter Winslow's *Show Business*.

H. L. MENCKEN
1524 HOLLINS ST.
BALTIMORE

April 14th, 1925

Dear Sara:-

If there is no competent quack in Montgomery, then what of Atlanta? Could you go there conveniently? If so, let me know, and I'll find out who is the best man there. A thorough examination would not take more than two or three days. The most convenient way to have it would be to enter a hospital for that time. It involves nothing unpleasant.

If you talk of abandoning "Career" I shall get out a writ against you. The book will land soon or late. What is more, it will sell. Away with such gabble! There are at least 30 publishers in America. Not six have seen it.

I am having my usual troubles with touring acquaintances. Every week two or three show up, and I have a horrible time escaping them. They all seem to think that I come to Baltimore to loaf. But I really do all my work here.

I kiss your hand!

Yours,
M

H. L. MENCKEN
1524 HOLLINS ST.
BALTIMORE

April 18th, 1925

Dear Sara:-

On re-reading "Blood Will Tell" I was so won by its high merits that I am slapping it into type at once. Moral: never despair of an editor! The changes I suggested at first are *not* necessary; I was wrong. A proof will reach you anon, and a check by the beginning of week after next. I think the title is bad, and propose to change it to "A Mendelian Dominant." What do you say? The story may not get into the magazine until late in the Summer, but I'll announce it in June.[1] The May number is already on its way to you. Read "Mary Fisher's Philosophy": a very good piece of work.[2] . . .

I send you a Hegelian wave.

Yours,
M

[1]Published in the March 1926 issue of *The American Mercury*.

[2]A short story by Chester T. Crowell, the editorial writer for the New York *Evening Post*.

H. L. MENCKEN
1524 HOLLINS ST.
BALTIMORE

April 20th, 1925

Dear Sara:-

I incline to advise against going to Denver. You would be very lonely. Have you ever thought of trying Asheville? It is, at all events, in the East. If you decide for the West, I believe that Albuquerque would be better than Denver. You could live in the town, and there are agreeable people there. Harvey Fergusson lives there. Denver is a desert—half invalids and half Methodists.

. . . I surely hope you don't get into a despairist mood. It is very common for a patient to have two sessions in the sanitarium. My brother did, and he is perfectly well today, twenty years afterward. If you have any lesion at all, it is a small one. You will get well, and without difficulty. I think you need peace more than treatment.

Dreadful difficulties, but you will live to forget them. Have the x-ray made at once. The bronchitis won't affect it.

More when I hear from Cullen.[1]

Yours,
HLM

~

[1]Dr. Victor Cullen, a 1906 Johns Hopkins Medical School graduate, was the superintendent of the Maryland Tuberculosis Sanitorium and served there for 40 years, becoming responsible for its growth.

H. L. MENCKEN
1524 HOLLINS ST.
BALTIMORE

April 25th, 1925

Dear Sara:-

I enclose another letter from Ruhräh,[1] with two more names. I strongly advise you to see one of these men. A general internist would be far better than a specialist in the lungs. The latter always find something within the line of their speciality, if it is only the sound of a shirt sliding over a rib. I still believe that you have a focal infection somewhere or other, and that it is very mild. If you had any serious difficulty in the lungs it would have floored you at the start. Your history for a year and a half is surely a history of something or other that must be very mild. All the while you were at Sloan's your symptoms, save for the slight afternoon temperature, were trivial.

Please don't get any notion that you are alarmingly ill, or waste any thought on meeting the Twelve Apostles. You will recover completely, and ten years from now you may be a very stately gal, with a fine platform manner. But such things take a lot of patience. Between 1900 and 1906 I made up my mind at least 40 times to quit work, retire to the Blue Ridge Mountains, and prepare for God's bilious eye. Yet in 1910 I weighed 180 lbs., and in 1915 I was actually taking an anti-fat cure. My brother had two sessions in a sanitarium. Since then he has had dengue fever in Cuba and two bouts with influenza, and yet he is perfectly hearty. In his case, as in mind, I believe that it was nose surgery that finally finished the business. Hazlehurst[2] went at my nose with a hammer and chisel—not as bad as it sounds. I have never had a cold since.

The more I think of it, the more I am against the Maryland State Sanitarium. It is, I find, a sort of rolling mill. The pressure of patients is so heavy that the old ones are shoved out as soon as possible. Moreover, living among hundreds of invalids, many of them actively religious, must be very unpleasant. You haven't the humor for it. I could stand it and even enjoy it, but my troubles are different—mainly the stealthy approach of senility.

My assistant, Angoff, was immensely pleased with "A Mendelian Dominant." I shall announce it in June. Angoff is doing so well that I'll probably put his name on the flagstaff in August. He has cut down my routine work at least 60%. Unfortunately, the divorce proceedings have consumed all of the time thus gained. But they are near an end. It may be necessary to murder the defendant. If it be God's will, then so be it.

Ich kuss die Hand.

Yours,
HLM

[1]John Ruhräh, a Baltimore pediatrician.

[2]Dr. Franklin Hazelhurst, an eye, ear, nose, and throat specialist, had been a friend of Mencken's since boyhood. He was also a member of the Saturday Night Club.

H. L. MENCKEN
1524 HOLLINS ST.
BALTIMORE

May 8th, 1925

Dear Sara:-

This is excellent stuff and I want to print it.[1] A few suggestions:

1. The title should be simply "Alabama." Let "Here We Rest" be the first sub-title.

2. The quotations from the Advertiser is too long. I have suggested a few cuts on the MS. Others may be possible.

3. The fact should be mentioned that the South split on account of the Klan. It was the Underwood anti-Klan men, not the New York Catholics, who precipitated the Klan fight at the New York convention. Even many of the State delegations were split, for example, Georgia. If you are not familiar with the facts, omit the section altogether.

4. In the section on antiques mention should be made that hunting them has been practiced in the North for years, but is new in the South.

5. "A Certain Cast of Mind" should be developed. It would be the better for two incidents instead of one. Or even more.

6. "The Youth Movement" is rather solemn, and out of the key. Try to make the combat more exhilarating, or omit it altogether.

7. There should be a section on the physical charm of the State—the cotton fields, the woods, the wide rivers, the drowsy air. Here is your chance! It will placate the Confederates.

8. What of religion? Shouldn't there be a section on the evangelical clergy? And the Episcopalians, above the turmoil?

9. Also, what of the coons?

You have a very good article. Now perfect it! An easy job for a talented gal. I'll slap it into type at once.

Yours,
M

1"Alabama," printed in the September 1925 issue of *The American Mercury*.

H. L. MENCKEN
1524 HOLLINS ST.
BALTIMORE

May 14th, 1925

Dear Sara:-

. . . The Glasgow book seemed poor stuff to me.1 The old gal tried to write a novel about people she simply didn't know. In consequence, she had to fall back upon conventional melodrama—seductions, villains, etc. Compare her stuff to that of, say, Suckow. Suckow *knows* her yokels, and can feel with them. To La Glasgow they are simply animals in cages.

I am off to West Chester for a day with Hergesheimer. It will knock another chip off my kidneys. On Sunday we are going to Philadelphia to hear Stokowski's annual band concert. He organized this brass band as a lark, and gives a private concert once a year.2 Sunday night—New York and the treadmill.

"A Mendelian Dominant" made a short page 10. I have cut it into nine pages. The job has been done with magnificent skill. You will search for the cuts in vain. You have a very talented beau.

Here is a chance to find out, once and for all time, whether Goucher really teaches French. Ich kuss die Hand!

M

¹*Barren Ground.*

²Mencken raved about the concert and used it as a topic for an article for the Baltimore *Evening Sun*. Delighted, he wrote: "Here, at last, is a brass band that can play Bach!"

H. L. MENCKEN
1524 HOLLINS ST.
BALTIMORE

May 27th, 1925

Dear Sara:-

This Sloan letter naturally caresses me as a pathologist, but it makes me damn the whole faculty for not discovering the facts long ago. It is my opinion that you have never had any tuberculosis infection. The thing started plainly as a pneumonia abscess, and it should have been tackled with vaccines a year ago. I don't believe that climate has anything whatever to do with it. If the focus can be cleared up, you will be quite well anywhere.

You will probably not get much of a reaction until you reach the full dose. If the mixed vaccines do not accomplish the business, then try autogenous vaccines, or some vaccine containing more pneumococci. Let me hear in detail what happens after each injection, and I'll consult some men here who know a great deal about vaccines.

I'll write to you about the Alabama piece in a day or two. I have been swamped by work and visitors. Among other things, I have got myself involved in the Tennessee evolutionist trial, as a consulting Man of Vision to Darrow and Dudley Field Malone, both good friends of mine.¹ I incline to sympathize with the Christians. Malone was here yesterday, damning Bryan up hill and down dale. But I can't get rid of the feeling that good Jennings is on the side of the Twelve Disciples.

The Alabama article is all right, but obviously too long. I shall give it my eagle eye tonight.

I'll be 45 on September 12th, and begin to grow senile. Goodbye Hegel and the gay adventurousness of youth! I have applied for admission to a Trappist monastery.

Ich kuss die Hand.

Yours,
M

Saturday began with the temperature 98 and ended with 47 and a cold, wet wind. I came in off the sleeping-porch Sunday with lumbago in the right shoulder, and still have it. My potations made me sleep so soundly that I didn't notice the cold.

¹John Thomas Scopes, science teacher and athletic coach of Rhea County High School, had been arrested for teaching Darwin's theory of evolution, which denied the divine creation of man as taught in the Bible, thus violating the antievolution law that had been passed by the Tennessee legislature the previous March. Mencken helped enlist Clarence Darrow and Dudley Field Malone, perhaps the most outstanding lawyers of the time, as the leader of the team of defense attorneys for Scopes. William Jennings Bryan, a three-time presidential candidate and a Fundamentalist who believed that the antievolution code must be written into the federal Constitution itself, volunteered to join the prosecution.

H. L. MENCKEN

1524 HOLLINS ST.

BALTIMORE

May 31st, 1925

Dear Sara:-

My apologies for keeping this so long. I have been on the jump. In addition to my usual jobs, I have had to revise the four Prejudices books for a volume of selections to be printed in England, Germany and Italy,¹ and to plow through the first parts of Goldberg's book, and correct its more violent errors.

Your MS., as it stands, is obviously too long. I have indicated some cuts that will bring it into a more practicable length. Also I have made a few other changes. Go through it yourself, and give it a final polish. I note that you sometimes fall into banal phrases: a mere song, green with envy, pandemonium, waxed, ensconced, doomed to disappointment, etc. Avoid such things as you would a sin against the Holy Ghost. Never write a phrase that a newspaper editorial writer would use. If you can't think of a new one, change the construction of the sentence.

You may damn me all you please, but you now confront the job of making a fair copy of your MS., with no half-sheets pasted in. Such is military discipline. You are in the hands of the Prussian Guards. Do not yell, but go do it. Then return the MS. to me.

I kiss your hand!

Yours in Xt.,

M

¹*Prejudices*. In the text the changes were few, but it was a selection, not a revision. It was reissued as *Selected Prejudices* in London, in 1926, and a second series was published in 1927.

H. L. MENCKEN

1524 HOLLINS ST.

BALTIMORE

June 5th, 1925

Dear Sara:-

. . . . The Goldberg somehow makes me feel that I should soon retire. Perhaps I have Served God enough. The Republic, of course, remains ungrateful, as it was to John Wilkes Booth and Czolgosz. This morning, in New York, I saw Knopf off for Europe. While he is away I shall do some loafing.

You never send me any news. What was the effect of the mixed vaccines? And is there to be a course of autogenous vaccines? What of your temperature curve? Let me have a full account, or be accursed forever.

We are to do an annual volume of Americana, with notes by me.¹ There will be Study Helps, a Glossary, and a List of Books for Further Reading, including the works of Henry van Dyke, the editorials in the Washington *Star*, the state papers of Al Smith, etc. The Atlantic Monthly letter is priceless. It goes into type at once.

I kiss your hand.

Yours,

HLM

Keep "Career" moving. Your faint hopes enrage me.

~

¹*Americana*. A collection of selections that had appeared in the "Americana" column of *The American Mercury*. Another issue appeared in 1926.

H. L. MENCKEN
1524 HOLLINS ST.
BALTIMORE

June 11th, 1925

Dear Sara:-

. . . Last night the thermometer dropped from 95 to 59. I dreamed that you and I were cruising in the Mediterranean¹ on my 30,000 ton yacht, the Kaiser Wilhelm II, with an orchestra of 118 pieces to entertain us, and 1,000 kegs of beer in the hold. Today I mixed and laid concrete for four hours.

I am planning to print a volume of Americana, with notes—i.e., study helps, a bibliography of supplemental reading, and a glossary, all a la Prof. Balderdash. It goes to press July 15th. If you come upon any Alabama stuff during the next two weeks, please let me have it. The Alabama section is not as long as it should be. . . .

Ich kuss die Hand.

Yours,

M

¹"I dreamed that you and I were cruising in the Mediterranean," Mencken writes, half seriously here, never realizing that he and Sara would actually be cruising that sea nine years later, when they were married.

H. L. MENCKEN
1524 HOLLINS ST.
BALTIMORE

June 15th, 1925

Dear Sara:-

This is excellent stuff, and I think you can sell it readily. If I didn't have the other story and "Alabama" in type I'd take it myself. Send it to the Century, Harper's, Scribner's and the Woman's Home Companion, in order.

Two phrases had better come out: "she could ever more an' run" on p. 1, and "from the gravy he continually rode" on p. 6. They would probably puzzle most hereditary advocates of the Federal Union.

Yours,
M

H. L. MENCKEN
1524 HOLLINS ST.
BALTIMORE

June 17th, 1925

Dear Sara:-

When you get your proof of "Alabama" you will find that my bright young Harvard assistant cut out the point of your story about the Confederate heroes and the Klan. I have ordered him to restore it. I am sending proofs of the article to various persons, in the hope of getting similar treatises on other States.

Guth is the perfect model of the Christian cad. Why doesn't Marjorie land him one in the snout? Or throw his Bible at him?[1]

The Dayton business begins to look very unpleasant. I am informed that I am to be quartered with some Methodist deacon or other. The town hotel is to be monopolized by the lawyers. I think I'll sleep in Chattanooga, and clear out altogether as soon as possible. I must be in New York by the 16th.

You speak of dreams. In all that I have (after drinking coffee) I am kissing your hand.

Yours,
M

[1] Marjorie Nicolson had been offered a prestigious position in teaching, both at the University of Minnesota and at Smith College, and had been waiting for a reply from President Guth about her decision to leave Goucher. After much delay, he sent a brief telegram saying that she was under engagement to teach at Goucher. Apparently he declined to answer her other letters.

H. L. MENCKEN
1524 HOLLINS ST.
BALTIMORE

July 3rd, 1925

Dear Sara:-

My address at Chattanooga will be the Hotel Patten. I shall live there, and go out to Dayton every day. If you write to me here or in New York mark your letter "Personal," as heretofore. The refined and beautiful stenographer opens all letters not so marked.

A temperature of 99.2 is of significance only to medical men. I offer 10 to 1 that 99.2% of the people of Montgomery run it all Summer. If there were no clinical thermometers you'd never notice it. My suggestion is that you take your temperature but once a week, and then taper off to once a month. My sister-in-law ran 99.5 for six months. Then I induced her to throw away her thermometer and she got well at once.

My best thanks for the Stone Mountain half-dollar.[1] I shall cherish it in my archives. But Poet Barclay is quite wrong: the man with Lee is not Jackson, but Dr. Lyman Abbott. Moreover, Lee is not Lee, but Grant. There is a scandal here. I shall ventilate it at Dayton.

Mrs. Haldeman-Julius[2] is a niece of Jane Addams. Enough!

I wish Montgomery were next door to Chattanooga. But I am a slave, bought and paid for!

Who kisses your hand!

Yours,

M

[1] Commemorative coin issued in 1925.

[2] Marcet Haldeman had prefixed her fine family name to that of her husband, Emmanuel Julius. They coauthored various books and articles and were publishers of magazines and both the Little and Big Blue Books.

~

HOTEL PATTEN
CHATTANOOGA, TENN.

Sunday, July 8, 1925

Dear Sara:-

The show is five times better than I expected.[1] That such a place as Dayton exists is really staggering, and a superb testimony to the virtuosity and daring of God. I'll be writing about it for the next 10 years. Last night we were hauled to the top of Lookout Mountain for a bout with the Chattanooga noblesse. They have a magnificent country-club half a mile in the air, with a jazz orchestra and all the other trappings of a nigger dive in New York. The usual story in the Confederacy (and Nawth): the women were mainly very pretty and some of them were amusing, but the men were unanimously unspeakable. They are all rich here, but money has done them no good. I have met a number of charming younger fellows, educated beyond the Jordan. Their fathers are all like Rotarians in Bethlehem, Pa.

When I escape I shall write an elaborate treatise on Mountain cooking. It is quite incredible. I had 6 days of it, and then came down with a sort of cholera, with delusions of divine inspiration. The hotel here is excellent. But I must go back to Dayton in the morning.

I enclose my first two treatises—mild, preliminary stuff. The show has just begun.

Ich kuss die Hand!

Yours,

M.

I brought a proof of your Alabama with me, hoping to find a Tennesseean to do a similar article on his State. Ah, the vanity of human hopes!

[1]When Mencken and Darrow entered Dayton on the afternoon of July 8 they found the town decked out as though for a carnival. The road leading into Chattanooga had been lined with signs that read, "Sweethearts, Come to Jesus," "You Need God in Your Business," "Where Will You Spend Eternity?" and "Prepare to Meet Thy God." Across Main Street were strung colorful banners. Newly constructed hot dog, lemonade, and sandwich stands lined the sidewalks. Most of the sidewalks had comic posters depicting monkeys and coconuts; one circus man brought two chimpanzees to testify for the prosecution and set them up as a side show. "Two months ago the town was obscure and happy," Mencken wrote in the Baltimore *Evening Sun*. "Today it is a universal joke."

HOTEL PATTEN
CHATTANOOGA, TENN.

July 9th, 1925

Dear Sara:-

I am moving out to Dayton today. It turns out to be impracticable to cover the story from here. Dayton is 40 miles away, over a very hilly road, and it takes an hour and a half to get there, even at high speed. The trip out and in yesterday gave me the worst scare I have had since the battle of Chancellorsville. There are five grade crossings, all magnificently concealed. At every one there is a big sign giving the telephone number of a Chattanooga undertaker who has an ambulance. The local chauffeurs rush down the mountain at 40 miles an hour. Altogether, such riding is not for a man with a duty to Humanity. So the whole Baltimore Sun outfit moves to Dayton this morning. We have two rooms in the home of the Widow Person, a Christian woman. We hope to come in every few days to change our collars. Temperature: 100 degrees.

So no more this day from the eminent 100% American critic and publicist, Mencken, who kisses your hand.

Yours,
M

The Scopes Trial was about to begin, and Mencken was to send back to Baltimore some of the most brilliant dispatches in the history of journalism. His articles set the scene: "Try to imagine a trial going on in a town in which anyone is free to denounce the defendant's case publicly and no one is free to argue for it in the same way—a trial in a courthouse placarded with handbills set up by his opponents—a trial before a jury of men who have been roweled and hammered by those opponents for years, and have never heard a clear and fair statement of his answer." It was "astonishing," he wrote, and, in an average jurisdiction, "unthinkable." One evening, a few miles from Dayton, he attended a revivalist meeting of Brother Joe Furdew; when he returned to Dayton that evening he found a Seventh-Day Adventist arguing that Clarence Darrow was the beast with seven heads and the end of the world was at hand; an ancient who said no Catholic could be a Christian; and William Jennings Bryan, followed everywhere by a gaping crowd.

DAYTON, TENN.

July 14th, 1925

Dear Sara:-

Don't talk of heat! The temperature here must be 120 at least. The peasants pack themselves into the courtroom like sardines in a can, eager to see Darrow struck dead.[1] Yesterday afternoon the whole assemblage began to steam.[2] I have a window picked out, and shall jump 40 feet when God begins to run amuck.

Ah, that thou wert actually coming this way! I'd turn out of my elegant boarding house to make room for you, and sleep on the lawn. We have all begun to grow accustomed to the country food, and even to like it. I am actually gaining weight. But losing, I fear, my beauty.

When we'll get out I don't know. I must be in New York by Monday morning. I'll certainly not see the end. The lawyers are all set for a wrangle that may last a week. Holy Church is everywhere triumphant.

I have been sending you Baltimore Sun clippings because the Chattanooga paper makes a frightful hash of my stuff. The Sun, getting it by wire, prints it more or less accurately. The Chattanooga News, with plain typewritten copy, can't do it.

A good many Alabamans are here. They are all hot infidels. Thus the devil snares souls.

Ich kuss die Hand!

Yours,

M

[1]On July 13, the second day of the trial, Clarence Darrow had spoken at length, arguing that the statute against evolution violated the principles of freedom guaranteed by the Constitution of the state of Tennessee, concluding: "If today you can take a thing like Evolution and make it a crime to teach it in the public schools, tomorrow you can make it a crime to teach it in the private schools, and the next year you can make it a crime to teach it in the hustings or in the churches. At the next session you may ban it in books and in newspapers. Soon you may set Catholic against Protestant and Protestant against Protestant, and try to foist your own religion upon the minds of men. If you can do one you can do the other. Ignorance and fanaticism are ever busy and need feeding. Always they are feeding and gloating for more. Today it is the public school teachers, tomorrow the private. The next day the preachers and the lecturers,

the magazines, the books, the newspapers. After a while, your Honor, it is the setting of man against man and creed against creed until with flying banners and beating drums we are marching backward to the glorious ages of the sixteenth century when bigots lighted fagots to burn the men who dared to bring any intelligence and enlightenment and culture to the human mind."

But Mencken found that Darrow's eloquent appeal was wasted on ears that heeded only Bryan. "The net effect of Clarence Darrow's great speech yesterday seems to be precisely the same as if he had bawled it up a rainspout in the interior of Afghanistan," Mencken wrote in his article for the Baltimore *Evening Sun* of July 14. "You have but a dim notion of it who have only read it. It was not designed for reading, but for hearing. The clangtint of it was as important as the logic. It rose like a wind and ended like a flourish of bugles. The very judge on the bench, toward the end of it, began to look uneasy. But the morons in the audience, when it was over, simply hissed it."

Mencken warned his readers not to look upon the Scopes trial as "a colossal farce. . . . You probably laughed at the prohibitionists, say, back in 1914," he went on. "Well, don't make the same error twice.

"As I have said, Bryan understands these peasants, and they understand him. He is a bit mangey and flea-bitten, but by no means ready for his harp. He may last five years, ten years, or even longer. What he may accomplish in that time, seen here at close range, looms up immensely larger than it appears to a city man five hundred miles away. The fellow is full of such bitter, implacable hatreds that they radiate from him like heat from a stove. He hates the learning that he cannot grasp. He hates those who sneer at him. He hates, in general, all who stand apart. . . . And the yokels hate with him, some of them almost as bitterly as he does himself. They are willing and eager to follow him—and he has already given them a taste of blood.

"Darrow's peroration yesterday was interrupted by Judge Raulston, but the force of it got into the air nevertheless. This year it is a misdemeanor for a country school teacher. . . . Next year it will be felony. The year after that the net will be spread wider. Pedagogues, after all, are small game: there are larger birds to snare—larger and juicier. Bryan has his fishy eye on them. He will fetch them if his mind lasts, and the lamp holds out to burn. No man with a mouth like that ever lets go. Nor ever lacks followers."

²To make "the atmosphere of a blast furnace" even worse, there were no electric fans in the courthouse, except the one provided for Judge Raulston.

~

HOTEL PATTEN
CHATTANOOGA, TENN.

Friday, July 17, 1925

Dear Sara:-

I surely hope your sister hasn't really picked up typhoid. It is full of unpleasantness. I have had to drink the water in Dayton, and can only trust in God. I was once inoculated, but it was years ago. I took a swig of hookworm vaccine daily.

The trial has blown up.[1] I am now waiting for news from New York. The chances are that I'll have to leave tomorrow. The thing has been infernal, especially the weather. God help us all, say I.

Who kisses your hand.

Yours,

M

[1]Judge Raulston had already denounced Scopes's crime as a "high misdemeanor," and now it was only a matter of twenty-four hours before John Scopes would be declared guilty and fined $100. the Baltimore *Evening Sun* paid the fine for Scopes. In 1927 the Tennessee Supreme Court reversed Judge Raulston's decision on the technicality that he, not the jury, had fixed the amount of the fine. The *Evening Sun*'s money was refunded and Scopes was cleared.

July 19th, 1925

Dear Sara:-

The enclosed shows how near I came to perishing, a martyr to Truth and Justice![1] The whole episode was full of humors. I was solemnly summoned to appear before a committee (headed by the court clerk!) last Wednesday night. When I got to the scene only one member was present, and he was full of evasions. Meanwhile, the noble Lindsay Dennison, of the New York World, had organized a Battalion of Death, and it was in waiting two blocks away. The town bravos, getting wind of resistance, abandoned force majeure, and returned to mere glaring.

I wasted two weeks on the buffoonery, but I think there was some profit in it. For the first time in my life I was in daily contact with Christian people. I got to know dozens of them very well, and have enough material stored up to last me the rest of my life. The thing was downright fabulous. When Bryan began arguing that man was not a mammal I almost swooned. God help us all.

I got in this morning and must go to New York tomorrow morning. My mail reaches the ceiling, but I hope to sneak off this evening for dinner with 10 honest infidels. What a difference!

Please return this clipping. I want to send it to your rival, a rich widow in Union Hill, N.J.

Ich kuss die Hand!

M

¹Mencken's views of the Tennessee "yokels" had caused controversy in Dayton, and several had considered asking the editor to leave town or threatened to "take him into an alley." A. P. Haggard, chief commissioner of Dayton, prevailed upon them to leave Mencken alone.

Five days after the trial had ended, on July 26, William Jennings Bryan died of an apoplectic stroke while taking a nap. The following day, in one of his Monday articles, Mencken wrote: "It was plain to everyone, when Bryan came to Dayton, that his great days were behind him—that he was now definitely an old man, and headed at last for silence. . . . Hour by hour he grew more bitter. What the Christian Scientists call malicious animal magnetism seemed to radiate from him like heat from a stove. . . . His eyes fascinated me: I watched them all day long. They were blazing points of hatred. They glittered like occult and sinister gems. Now and then they wandered to me, and I got my share. It was like coming under fire.

"What was behind that consuming hatred? At first I thought it was mere evangelical passion. . . . One day it dawned on me that Bryan, after all, was an evangelical Christian only by sort of afterthought—that his career in this world, and the glories thereof, had actually come to an end before he ever began whooping for Genesis. So I came to this conclusion: that what really moved him was a lust for revenge. The men of the cities had destroyed him and made a mock of him; now he would lead the yokels against them. . . . The hatred in the old man's burning eyes was not for the enemies of God; it was for the enemies of Bryan. . . .

"It was hard to believe, watching him at Dayton, that he had traveled, that he had been received in civilized societies, that he had been a high officer of state. He seemed only a poor clod . . . . full of an almost pathological hatred of all learning, all human dignity, all beauty, all fine and noble things. . . .

"The job before democracy is to get rid of such canailles. *If it fails, they will devour it."*

H. L. MENCKEN
1524 HOLLINS ST.
BALTIMORE

July 27th, 1925

Dear Sara:-

. . . I fear the wealth of Sloan's bride is somewhat exaggerated.[1] The Wilms. firm is worth a great deal less than $2,000,000. But there is some mazuma there, and no doubt the sanitarium will now rise. I love to see worthy young men get on in the world.

Bryan's death fills me with sadness. He was full of the Holy Spirit. And today he has his harp and is trying his wings on the celestial flying-field.

I kiss your hand.

Yours,

M

[1] Julia Alice Williams. When she died she left an estate valued at $1,141,469, which was partly divided among the SPCA, the Woman's Board of the Hospital of Consumptives of Maryland, and the Presbyterian Church.

H. L. MENCKEN
1524 HOLLINS ST.
BALTIMORE

August 4th, 1925

Dear Sara:-

This is an excellent article, and I'd take it at once if it were not for the fact that the short story and Alabama are ahead of it.[1] The enclosed letter is quite sincere. Send it to Van Doren with the MS. I think you ought to try to widen your market at every opportunity. If Van Doren fails, then try Lee Foster Hartman, of Harper's, and send him a note quoting the first three sentences of my letter within. In case neither succumbs let me have the MS. again. It is very good stuff.

God knows you have my sympathy, working there in that infernal heat. It is hot enough up here, but there are intermissions. You seemed to think, some time ago, that I was arguing that you were not working hard enough. What nonsense! All I meant to say was that you were too quickly discouraged when stuff didn't sell. I marvel that you get so much done, ill and uncomfortable. But life on this mud-pie is always a mess. I sweat all day, and still find it impossible to get to my book. I shall get rid of the Chicago Tribune contract very soon. It has brought in some money, but it has also cost me something.[2]

Judging by the clippings that continue to flood in, the Dayton Bravos now let it be known that they actually ran me out of town. What a knightly outfit! They actually never even got up enough courage to call me names (that is, openly) until after I had left. The reason was simple: there were 50 or 60 newspaper men in the town. The episode had the usual accursed effect: it brought in a ton of mail, mainly from idiots, Christian and infidel.

My niece is due here tomorrow. I must get up early, and shave. Ich kuss die Hand!

Yours,

M

[1]On June 30 the Baltimore *Evening Sun* had published "The Youth Movement in the Cotton Belt." This may have been "The South Washes Its Hands," printed in the *Evening Sun* for August 19.

[2]Mencken would not discontinue writing for the Chicago *Sunday Tribune* until 1928.

H. L. MENCKEN

1524 HOLLINS ST.

BALTIMORE

August 10th, 1925

Dear Sara:-

Take warning by the experience of an aged man: let young Sara and her beau fight it out themselves.[1] In such battles, it is always the bystander that is killed. Tie them together and throw them overboard. Once I intervened in such a war, and was accused in the end of trying to steal the female. You should have seen her!

I went to Washington Saturday to see the Klan parade for The Sun. It turned out to be a very impressive procession. But now the Kluxers are damning me for saying that their women smelled of the wash-tub. Observe the enclosed.² Even Berlin is getting excited. Zu verprügeln means to cudgel. This is something new.

Hay fever has begun to kiss me. I have a sweet laryngitis and a low malaise. The weather was infernal in Washington, and I dam nigh gave out in the midst of my story. A noble swallow of rye saved me. Today I feel like one who has watched all night at Bryan's grave.

Did you notice, by the way, that his last act on earth was to catch flies?

Let me hear what happens to "The Flowerhood."³

I Kiss both your hands.

> Yours,
> M

¹Sara Mayfield had been married to John Allen Sellers since November 1924. They divorced in March 1927.

²On August 8 Mencken had covered the Klan parade in Washington, D.C. A few days later he received a communication from Little Rock. It came in the form of a resolution passed by the "Knights and Women of the Ku Klux Klan of Arkansas" and read: "Whereas one H. L. Mencken is the author of a scurrilous article recently published in the Baltimore *Sun* . . . in which he viciously slurs and insults the good women and patriotic men who marched in that parade to the number of more than 100,000 declaring that there was not an intelligent or comely face among them . . . and many other slanders and insults too vile and indecent to be repeated, therefore be it: Resolved, By the Knights of the Ku Klux Klan in Arkansas, a State which the said Mencken has in times past slandered as 'a land of morons,' that we condemn in the strongest possible language the vile mouthings of this prince of blackguards."

³It was published in the October 1926 issue of *The Virginia Quarterly Review*.

H. L. MENCKEN
1524 HOLLINS ST.
BALTIMORE

August 14th, 1925

Dear Sara:-

I am sending you a few books. Throw them away when you have finished with them. I have just finished a review of 29 volumes of poetry. It is mainly dull stuff. The poets all seem to be down with diabetes. Think of what they were doing ten or twelve years ago, and what they are doing now.

The Goldberg book is being set up; also the Boyd book. Two at once! They will get such a hammering as has never been seen. Especially the Goldberg book. It is full of stuff that has never got into any such tome before—a shameless affair. Worse, there are many pictures. The professors will take a week off to perform upon it.

Has "Career" ever been to Boni & Liveright? If not, let it go there.

Last night I had dinner with two clergymen. I am in a low state today. But kiss your hand.

> Yours,
> M

H. L. MENCKEN
1524 HOLLINS ST.
BALTIMORE

August 17th, 1925

Dear Sara:-

What is the New York job? That you are taking it is excellent news, first because it proves that you are much better, and secondly because we'll meet again. I am delighted. Downtown New York is a miserable place, but there is no reason why you should not live in it. Go up beyond 125th street and you will find plenty of charming neighborhoods, and quarters at reasonable rates. I hate the infernal town because I have to live south of 59th street, where the noise is frightful, day and night. I can sleep in a boiler-shop, and during my days as a war hero I once slept under shell-fire, but Manhattan is too much for me. Tell me all about what you have in mind.

The preliminary bout of hay fever is over, but I expect the main attack in a few days. No doubt it will hit me on the train Wednesday, going to New York. But it doesn't amount to much. I swear a great deal, but somehow my usual work gets itself done. Certainly a sinful man must expect a few prods from Omnipotence. I fear I neglect my church duties.

This has been a dreadful Summer. But hell will be worse.

Ich kuss die Hand.

> Yours,
> M

H. L. MENCKEN
1524 HOLLINS ST.
BALTIMORE

August 31st, 1925

Dear Sara:-

Catarrhus aestivus has me by the snout, and I am in a low and melancholy state. Meanwhile, my forty-fifth birthday is on me, and I prepare for senility. Prayer is unavailing. As soon as this hay-fever lightens I shall go to a beer-party. It is a sovereign balm. I have heard no decent music for three weeks.

Don't get impatient about your writing. You are doing it better month by month. The hard labor of the past years will come home to roost, so to speak, later on. At 35 my income from books was $200 a year. Now, if I had the time to write more, I could live on them.

So no more today from one who kisses your hand. The aestival depression is terrific. I am fit only for pious exercises.

Yours,

M

Boyd's book is certainly not bad. But he overlooked two things. First, the fact that my whole body of doctrine rests upon a belief in liberty. Second, that I am far more an artist than a metaphysician.

H. L. MENCKEN
1524 HOLLINS ST.
BALTIMORE

September 5th, 1925

Dear Sara:-

. . . Let me hear from you when you feel like writing. I sent you the new Sherwood Anderson book yesterday.[1] I think Anderson has at last got his formula by the tail. Certainly the book, in many ways, is the best he has done. I am working my way through the new Cather.[2] It seems pretty bad.

I can imagine the alarm when you went out! And the horrible discomfort. The world is run by an imbecile.

Ich kuss die Hand.

Yours,

M

¹*Dark Laughter.*
²*The Professor's House.*

H. L. MENCKEN
1524 HOLLINS ST.
BALTIMORE

October 3, 1925

Dear Sara:

God knows what is to be done with "The Fire"; now and then a story gets into such a vicious circle and it seems hopeless—but it is my experience that such stories usually sell in the end.¹ Something sold later on pulls them out of cold storage and not infrequently they are taken by one of the magazines that has already refused them. I once sold a story to the Red Book that had been refused twice by the same magazine. Have you ever, by the way, sent anything to the Red Book? It might be a good idea.

The autumn is in full blast here in Maryland with cold rains and windy nights. Barring rheumatism in both legs and a ringing in the ears, I am in very fair shape, considering my advanced age. I am off for New York to-morrow. Malone and Darrow are staging a burlesque of the Dayton trial and I am to play the part of Scopes. This buffoonery, I suspect, will be accompanied by libations.

Yours,
M

¹"The Fire" eventually appeared in the *Haldeman Julius Quarterly*, April–June, 1928.

H. L. MENCKEN
1524 HOLLINS ST.
BALTIMORE

October 5th, 1925

Dear Sara:-

The Century has a new editor, Hewitt H. Howland. Send him "All in the Family" and tell him that I suggested it and that you have a story in type for The American Mercury.

What is the news with you? Your letters have been telegraphic. My mother is ill here, and in much pain. Worse, it seems likely that nothing can be done about it. But the quacks continue their efforts. [1]
Ich kuss die Hand.

Yours,
HLM

[1]Anna Abhau Mencken had been suffering from arteriosclerosis for the past two years; there were times when she could not sew or hold a book to read. During the next few weeks she would be unable to sleep without the aid of drugs.

H. L. MENCKEN
1524 HOLLINS ST.
BALTIMORE

October 26th, 1925

Dear Sara:-

I believe La Welsh's advice is excellent, especially since her scheme offers a way to take it. The series ought to produce enough mazuma to carry you through to the Autumn of 1926. [1] Probably the best editor to tackle is Vance, of the Pictorial Review. He is intelligent and pays good prices. I enclose a letter that you may send to him. The part about the book rights is very sincere: Knopf will leap at the book. If Vance fails, try Barton W. Currie, of the Ladies' Home Journal. All the women's magazines pay high prices. The book, moreover, should be an excellent property.

If your temperature never goes beyond 99.4 you may well throw away your thermometer. Such rises are common: people never know they have them until some quack gets out his thermometer and begins to make trouble. As for your weight, it is very good indeed. Certainly you don't want to go much beyond 130. You will begin to waddle if you do. I weigh 180, and can no longer dance, skip rope or kneel to pray.

My mother is in less pain than she was, and is regaining the use of her hands. I surely hope the improvement keeps on. The underlying condition, of course, is incurable, but the quacks should be able to make her comfortable.

Ich kuss die Hand.

Yours,
M

¹Sara and Dr. Lillian Welsh of Goucher College were planning to coauthor a series of articles on women in science. They never did.

H. L. MENCKEN
1524 HOLLINS ST.
BALTIMORE

November 7th, 1925

Dear Sara:-

My best thanks for the clippings. Superb stuff! I am sending a portrait of Valentino to the Clio Study Club of Clayton. Such worthy women deserve encouragement.

My mother, thank God, is somewhat easier. She sleeps better and hasn't much pain, though her hands are still numb. I assume that a compensatory capillary circulation is starting up. Now comes my sister-in-law from Pittsburgh, ready for more surgery.¹ I fear she is in for a hard bout. The last time the butchery had to be halted to avoid killing her. She is now laid up at home, but will come to Baltimore anon.

This morning I had the melancholy pleasure of getting a lady out of jail.² She is one whose love knew no bounds, its object being a late friend of mine. When he passed to glory eternal she took to the wine-cup and last night the Polizei caged her. It cost me $6.45 to liberate her, and the cops gave me an inside professional rate at that. Consider her fate. It was curiosity, I daresay, that prompted her first false step. In the end she reached the hoosegow.

"On Democracy" is under way, but it certainly shows no sign of speed.³ Tomorrow I must abandon it to go to New York. But I begin to have hope that it will get itself on paper before Lady Day. The material is so vast that it staggers me. And the book must be short.

What is your news? Has Howland taken the story? And is the book ready for a start?

Ich kuss die Hand.

Yours,
M

¹Charles's wife, Mary.
²Helen, the wife of Carl Schon.
³Mencken had begun making notes for it in 1910. The actual writing was begun in 1923, resumed in 1925, and finished on June 3, 1926.

H. L. MENCKEN

1524 HOLLINS ST.

BALTIMORE

November 13th, 1925

Dear Sara:-

. . . I have heard no more from La Helen since the cops released her. Schon left her $10,000. Apparently it is all gone. On his death she made off with one of his workmen, an Italian, and they started a rival jewelry business. Now the business is closed and the wop has disappeared. Ah, love!

My book is moving with the speed of a lame snail. I have reached page 9 after 6 weeks' work. I am burdened by other work, and interrupted 40 times a morning. But prayer will carry me through.

Keep old Welsh prodded up. Find out where the material is; maybe you can dig up most of it yourself.

My sister-in-law seems to be better. When she is to come to Baltimore I don't know. My mother is still in discomfort, but it is very much less than it was.

Ich kuss die Hand.

Yours,
M

~

H. L. MENCKEN
1524 HOLLINS ST.
BALTIMORE

November 19th, 1925

Dear Sara:-

There is a special hell for such persons as La Welsh. My life has consisted very largely of warfare upon them. If all human beings were competent, and kept their engagements, then the work of the world could be done in half an hour a day. I was trying to figure out the other day how many members of The Sun staff really know their jobs. I found 6 out of about 100. It is a high score. If there were 12 the paper would be almost perfect.

My mother is still in great discomfort, but the more severe pains seem to have abated. She sleeps when she takes codeine, but not otherwise. Fortunately, it is harmless. She can go on taking it for years. There is some hope that her discomforts will diminish, as compensatory circulation sets up. But the underlying condition is incurable. She bears the thing very bravely.

"On Democracy" is surely not dead. I did 350 words on it this morning. It will get into type soon or late. I'll send you the Goldberg book as soon as I get a copy. It goes without saying that the publisher has sent me none. But I hear that it is out. After reading it, you will never speak to me again. Our beautiful, idealistic friendship thus perishes. I shall, on receipt of your passports, marry the Hoboken widow, and settle down in the Bismarck herring business. In the years to come, when you loll at Palm Beach with your Babbitt, surrounded by your lovely children, Gustav, Calvin and Mignonette, give me a sad thought now and then. It is the correct thing to do.

Howland's first number of the Century is full of garbage left to him by Frank.[1] But I think he will produce, after a while, a really good magazine. Keep at him with MSS. It would be an excellent thing for you to get into the magazine.

How are you feeling? You never send me any news.

Ich kuss die Hand.

Yours,

M

[1] Glenn Frank, previous editor of *Century* magazine.

H. L. MENCKEN
1524 HOLLINS ST.
BALTIMORE

December 11th, 1925

Dear Sara:-

My poor mother is laid up with a bad tonsillitis and has been very ill, with alarming temperatures. What a thing to have at her age! It has no connection with her arterial troubles, but the latter, of course, make it the more dangerous. And no nurse to be found! But one is coming in tomorrow, and I believe that she is already somewhat better. The thing is very painful, and after four days of high temperatures and no food she begins to look exhausted. But, as I say, she seems to be better, and if the infection doesn't spread she will get well.

I have not been sending you The Evening Sun clippings of late because the boy who used to leave extra copies of the paper here has quit, and I am still scouting for another. I'll find one anon. Several have promised to bring the paper, and then failed. The moron is an idiot, even at 10 years.

I shall get hold of Howland the next time I get to New York and whisper in his ear.

Ich kuss die Hand.

Yours,
M

H. L. MENCKEN
1524 HOLLINS ST.
BALTIMORE

December 11th, 1925

Dear Sara:-

My poor mother is very ill. We had to take her to hospital this afternoon. Her tonsillitis turned out to be streptococcal, and yesterday the glands of the neck became infected. A drainage operation has been done on one side; the other may have to be done tomorrow. At her age, 67, and considering her underlying condition, it is a serious business. But she is very cheerful, and faced the surgery bravely. More in a few days.

The news about the story is excellent.[1] Now keep Howland warm with more.

Ich kuss die Hand.

Yours,
M

[1]"All in the Family" appeared in the March 1926 issue of the *Century* magazine.

ALS

H. L. MENCKEN
1524 HOLLINS ST.
BALTIMORE

Sunday, December 13, 1925

Dear Sara:

My mother died at 6 o'clock tonight—very peacefully. It is the end of many things for me.

I'll write to you again in a few days.

Yrs.,
HLM

ALS

H. L. MENCKEN
1524 HOLLINS ST.
BALTIMORE

December 16, 1925

Dear Sara:

Thanks so much for your telegram. This is desolation indeed. My father's death was nothing, but now I am in the depths. How we are to go on here I don't know, but go on we shall. I am sending my sister to Pittsburgh (where my elder brother lives) on Sunday, and shall join her with my other brother on Xmas eve. Christmas here would have been awful . . . Somehow I always thought of her death as something far off. . . . Today we buried her.

I'll write again in a few days. Do what Orlson wants! He is an ass, but humor him.

Yrs.,
H

H. L. MENCKEN
1524 HOLLINS ST.
BALTIMORE

December 17th, 1925

Dear Sara:-

I wrote to you last night, but I have an uneasy feeling that the mail was not mailed—that it got lost with some others. It was a dreadful day, and I ended it in considerable confusion.

My mother died peacefully and in no pain. As you know, she had been failing for a year. There was a general arterio sclerosis, with very distressing symptoms. She had severe pains in the arms and her hands were cold and numb. Her blood-pressure was rising and her heart was getting into trouble. Nothing could be done for it. She had massage, but it gave her little relief. For three months she had not slept without codeine. We had tried to convince her that the thing was trivial and transient, but she was beginning to grasp the truth. There was the awful task ahead of telling her that she could no longer go out alone—that there was danger of a stroke. It was pathetic to see her come up the stairs: she had suddenly grown old. Up to 66 she was as vigorous and active as a woman of 50, and full of good spirits. Then, almost overnight, she began to go to pieces.

Last week, passing through her sitting room, I found her at her table, sitting idly (an unheard-of thing for her) and obviously ill. I took her temperature and found that it was nearly 103. She went to bed at once. The next day her fever continued and she showed signs of tonsillitis. But it seemed mild for two days. Then the infection spread to the glands of her neck, and she had to go to hospital to have them drained—a small operation. She went very bravely, and after it was over told me that her pain was gone and she felt much better. But there was no defensive mechanism left, and so the infection gradually spread. She simply drowsed off, glad that she could sleep. She died late Sunday afternoon.

It was, of course, a fortunate deliverance. The alternative was long helplessness and much pain. I think she had no notion that she was dying; the last time she spoke to me she was very cheerful. More, I think she was happy in her last years. Her children had grown up, they were all in good health, and she led a placid life, full of the duties that she liked. She will be missed indeed! We shall keep the house going, as she wished, but it seems hollow and forlorn today. God knows what is ahead.

Thanks so much for your telegram. It reached me when I needed it.

M

~
*Sara Powell Haardt in 1920, as
a graduate from Goucher College.*

*H. L. Mencken in his office at 1524 Hollins Street, editing
manuscripts.*

Sara at the Maple Heights Sanitarium, recovering from tuberculosis. Sparks, Maryland, 1924.

Cigar in hand, Mencken is led off to jail, moments after he sold a copy of the April 1926 issue of The American Mercury *to the Reverend J. Franklin Chase. Boston, April 1926.*

A jubilant Mencken, free and acquitted, waves the Maryland "Free State" flag among cheering students at Harvard Square. Mencken is at center, directly behind the flag. Boston, April 1926.

Mencken welcomes Joseph Hergesheimer to Hollywood with a grand gesture. Anita Loos holds the flag while Aileen Pringle presents him with a wreath of roses. Los Angeles, 1926.

The Sage of Baltimore shaking hands with Louis B. Mayer, the Mogul of MGM. Los Angeles, 1926.

*With Will Rogers and Amos G. Carter. The man at the far left is
the airplane pilot. Houston, 1928.*

Mighty Mencken Falls

"Bible Belt" Gives Bride To Mencken

Marriage, Like Hanging, Not So Bad as It Seems

ROMANCE MADE MENCKEN WISE

What Is This, Henry?

Oh, Henry!

A sample of the headlines which appeared in newspapers across the nation when the news broke that "America's foremost bachelor" was about to wed. News stories of the event filled seven and a half volumes of scrapbooks in Mencken's library.

~

Mencken and Sara used this Currier and Ives print as their marriage certificate, which the Reverend Herbert Parrish signed.

Outside the church, St. Michael the Martyr, the newlyweds are flanked by family and friends. To the left of Sara stands her nephew, Wick, with Ida, Venetia, John, and Paul Patterson. Directly behind her stands Hamilton Owens. To the right of Mencken stands his niece, Virginia, with Gertrude, August, Mary and Charles. Behind Charles stands the Reverend Herbert Parrish, who wed the couple. Baltimore, August 27, 1930. (Photo by the Baltimore News-American)

*The living room of Mr. and Mrs. Henry Louis Mencken, at 704
Cathedral Street, Baltimore.*

*Mencken playing a song for Sara at their new home. Baltimore,
1930. (Photo by Carl Van Vechten)*

~

Mencken and Sara during their two trips abroad: in the dining room of the Pasaje Hotel, Havana, Cuba. Mencken looks absolutely stuffed with food. Havana, January 1932.

At the pyramids in Cairo, Egypt, March 1934.

"Mrs. S. Mencken with the kind regards of her loving husband, Mr. H. Mencken, 1933. He scents a Christian."

Sara Powell Haardt. Baltimore, 1933. (Photo by A. Aubrey Bodine)

Mencken quaffs the first beer at the Rennert bar at 12:01 A.M. after the repeal of Prohibition, and pronounces it "Not bad at all. Fill it again." Grinning at the camera at the far right is Hamilton Owens. Baltimore, April 17, 1933. (Photo by Frank Miller, The Sunpapers)

*Mr. and Mrs.
Henry Louis Mencken.
Baltimore, 1933. (Photo
by A. Aubrey Bodine)*

Mencken on board the SS Bremen, on route to England, two weeks after Sara's death. June, 1935.

1926

In 1926 Sara divided her time between Baltimore and New York, gaining eminence on her own, publishing articles and stories in the Baltimore Evening Sun, The Virginia Quarterly Review, *and* The American Mercury. *Mencken, once again, was involved in more controversy. In April he risked imprisonment by fighting against censorship for his April edition of* The American Mercury, *which had contained a sketch about a small-town prostitute. It began a conflict that was for a short time nearly as widely reported as the Scopes Monkey Trial had been the year before. On October 14 Mencken went on a Grand Tour through the deep South, visiting, among other cities, Sara Haardt's hometown.*

H. L. MENCKEN
1524 HOLLINS ST.
BALTIMORE

January 2nd, 1926

Dear Sara:-

What is your news? Are you running any temperature? And what of your weight and the bronchitis? The freezing weather must have been a severe trial. Ah, this perfect climate! Let me have a full and accurate report, sworn to before a notary public.

My sister-in-law is here, getting herself elaborately x-rayed.[1] What ails her I don't know. Today the quacks devoted themselves to prospecting for gall stones. They will find them if they stick to the job long enough. I hope there is no more surgery ahead for her. Three years ago she was in hospital for ten weeks, and made a narrow escape from Paradise.

When she goes home there will be the problem of finding company for my sister when my brother and I are away. Solving it, I fear, will be very difficult. My sister, all her life, has been used to having my mother about. Of late they had slept in the same room. Now she will be immensely lonely. But I hope to find some one to give her company. All my female relatives, unfortunately, are either married or insane. Many are both.

My uncle's debacle has been giving me sad and expensive entertainment all week.[2] The old jackass let my mother in for a loss of nearly $1,000, and it will probably take as much more to clean up the wreckage. She died knowing nothing of all this. A lucky woman, even to the end! She left the house to my sister, with enough income to keep it in repair. So we hope to go on as heretofore. I begin to feel very old. My mother was only 22 years older than I.

Do you make your prophecy about "On Democracy" on your own responsibility? Or have you consulted the Montgomery sorcerers? I believe myself that I'll get back on the track very soon, and knock it out without much difficulty. But it will probably fall flat. The big show will come when I publish "Homo Sapiens."[3] I am steadily accumulating notes for it.

Don't bank on La Welsh. Collaborations are always curses. I have done four or five, and regret it every day.[4] Tackle your new novel: it will be easier than "Career."

Ich kuss die Hand!

Yours,
HLM

[1]Mary.

[2]John Henry Mencken ("Uncle Henry"), brother of Mencken's father and, according to Mencken, one of the world's worst businessmen.

[3]Never completed.

[4]By 1926 Mencken had already made four collaborations, three with George Jean Nathan, and one with Dr. Leonard Keene Hirshberg, *What You Ought to Know About Your Baby*.

H. L. MENCKEN
1524 HOLLINS ST.
BALTIMORE

January 7th, 1926

Dear Sara:-

Your news is excellent. Now is the time to be careful! Keep off those damned fruit salads and stick to honest hog and hominy. The afternoon temperature will pass off—if you get enough sleep. No hoofing with the Babbitts! Remember that you are a literary woman!

My uncle's low comedy affairs have kept me jumping, and so I have just got back to work. Such interruptions used to worry me, but no more. I have done enough for this glorious Republic. Until it shows some sign of gratitude I shall hold off coyly.

I hear from Mrs. Peterkin that she has had a fall and broken her knee-cap—a very serious accident.[1] It may leave her lame for life. Such news seems to come in flood. The other day I heard from London of the dreadful fate of a girl who used to work for me on The Sun, and later married one of the staff. She had cancer, it appears, a couple of years ago, with a breast operation. Now she has metathesis to the spine, and is coming home to die, helpless and in fearful pain. What a world! I marvel at the constant ingenuity of God.

Toward the end of the Summer I hope to get a holiday, my first in four years. Phil Goodman wants me to go to Constantinople with him, to breathe a few carboys of Christian-free air, but it will probably turn out to be too expensive. I hope your Summer job will be in the North. You will escape another boiling in Montgomery, and an unnamed admirer will enjoy the felicity of seeing you. If I go away it won't be until August. I have two books to finish, and Knopf is full of tremors.[2]

I shall print "A Mendelian Dominant" in March, God willing. A great deal of fiction stood ahead of it: hence the delay. Give your thoughts to the Mercury again. What ideas are entertaining you?

Ich kuss die Hand.

Yours,
M.

[1] Julia M. Peterkin, author and critic.
[2] *On Democracy, Prejudices V.*

H. L. MENCKEN
1524 HOLLINS ST.
BALTIMORE

January 23rd, 1926

Dear Sara:-

I'll be in attendance at the old ruined mill the whole last week in May. A genuine Old Home Week! Don't pay any heed to the current libel that I have gone on the water-wagon. My cellar is still full, and the wop has his instructions. What a gabble we'll have!

"A Mendelian Dominant" is in the forms for March. Thus you will have two stories that month in great moral organs.[1] Let the Confederates take notice.

Don't mourn for "On Democracy." It will get itself written yet. In such matters I put myself completely in the hands of God, yielding to His will. Don't forget the last words of the Martyr McKinley, foully murdered by the Bolshevik Czolgosz.[2]

Ich kuss die Hand.

Yours,

M

[1]"All in the Family" would also appear in the *Century* magazine, March 1926.
[2]The twenty-fifth president of the United States was six months into his second term when he was fatally shot by Leon F. Czolgosz on September 6, 1901. On September 14, as he lay dying, his last words were: "It is God's way. His will be done, not ours."

H. L. MENCKEN
1524 HOLLINS ST.
BALTIMORE

January 27th, 1926

Dear Sara:-

The enclosed is unimportant.[1] Nothing need be done about it. Every article we print brings in such corrections from pedants. Who gives a damn? I am certainly not trying to print a mathematically correct magazine. My aim is different: to promote the Kingdom of God.[2]

My legal troubles, I believe, near their end. My uncle now claims that I owe him money. He is really superb. Yesterday I put in two hours perfecting my will. I shall leave all my millions to Goucher.

Ah, that we two were Maying!

Yours,
M

[1]Probably an angry letter responding to "Alabama," Sara Haardt's article on her native state that was printed in the September 1925 issue of *The American Mercury*.

[2]*The American Mercury* had been banned from sale in sections of the rural South, and features such as "Americana" had led to frequent irate letters. To these Mencken sent his stock answer, printed on a card: "Dear ————: You're probably right."

H. L. MENCKEN

1524 HOLLINS ST.

BALTIMORE

February 5th, 1926

Dear Sara:-

Don't give yourself any concern about those few errors. I always insert a couple into my own compositions in order to give pedants a chance. If they challenge you in Alabama stick to your statement, and argue that the official history is a lie. In two days your crime will be forgotten, and the State historians will be flogging one another mercilessly.

A few more performances by Guth, and he will be ripe for an article. Why he should want to get rid of La N is unfathomable,[1] save it be that he dislikes intelligent teachers.[2] Probably he does. A joke for you: I have been offered the presidency of Miami University. A new go-getting seminary, founded by the realtors. It has an enormous endowment. Salary: $25,000 a year, a house, and a liquor license. I have refused. Say nothing of this. It is a shameful secret.

What does your chart show? Let me have some news of you. Boyd and I were overcome by the fumes in New York the other night, and had to be put to bed. Never again! I dislike such bouts. They leave me unhappy the next day. The ethyl is far too precious to be hogged. Ich kuss die Hand!

Yours,
M

[1]Marjorie Hope Nicolson left Goucher on her own accord to become a professor of English at Smith, where she later became dean (1929–1941).

[2]During World War I, when anti-German feeling ran high, Guth had demanded the resignation of Hans Froelicher, the professor of art history and one of the most respected and popular professors in the college. Of German-speaking Swiss origin, Froelicher had expressed sympathy for the German people while affirming his complete loyalty for the United States. President Woodrow Wilson (whose daughter, Jessie, was an alumna of the school) wrote a letter urging Guth to withdraw his demand. President Guth did so, and after his death, Froelicher became acting president of Goucher College.

H. L. MENCKEN
1524 HOLLINS ST.
BALTIMORE

March 3rd, 1926

Dear Sara:-

This article is very well done, and I believe that it should be readily saleable. The best markets, paying the most money, are the Century, Harper's and Scribner's. If they all fail, then try Vanity Fair. After that, if it is still unsold, let me see it again. I'll probably use it in the Mercury. But I want you to get a chance, first, at the larger honorarium. We are paying but 2 cents a word.

You do such things well. Now for another. Not a word from you about your bout with the thermometer. What is the issue?

Yours,
HLM

~

THE AMERICAN MERCURY
730 FIFTH AVENUE
NEW YORK

March 6th, 1926

Dear Sara:-

This is good stuff and I want to print it.[1] The picture of the fair young moron is full of color. But I think the ending is somewhat feeble. You ought to make it very clear that her deliverance has been a mere illusion—that life is still dreadful. It seems to me that you do it rather too briefly. The reader, remember, is also a moron.

Yours,

HLM

[1]"Commencement," published in the August 1926 issue of *The American Mercury*.

THE AMERICAN MERCURY
730 FIFTH AVENUE
NEW YORK

March 13th, 1926

Dear Sara:-

"Commencement" goes into type at once. It is an excellent story. Why don't you do a love story: such as a flapper and her beau? There ought to be irony in it, and yet sympathy. They are idiots, but their emotions are very real. Such a story wouldn't need much plot: simply the struggle against rivals, and then the two in each other's arms, dreaming the ancient, magnificent dream. There is too little simple sentiment in the magazines, and especially the above.

Yours,

HLM

~

H. L. MENCKEN
1524 HOLLINS ST.
BALTIMORE

March 26th, 1926

Dear Sara:-

I'll be delighted to show you the trick.[1] It is not difficult. Write to Freeman, saying that you are willing to try it, and asking him to suggest two or three books, to give you some range. Also, ask him how long the articles are to be. Don't mention the compensation: leave it to him.

When do we meet again? I suggest a session at the Grand Imperial Restaurant Schellhase on Tuesday at 9:45.

Yours,

M

[1]Acting on Mencken's suggestion, Donald Freeman, the managing editor of *Vanity Fair*, had written a letter to Sara asking her to do a series of book reviews.

H. L. MENCKEN
1524 HOLLINS ST.
BALTIMORE

March 28th, 1926

Dear Sara:-

. . . I refrained from waiting on you at Schellhase's last night because both Darrow and I were somewhat inflamed by the grape. I hope our loud roaring didn't deafen you. The old boy has been quietly at it since 1 P.M.

I'll look for you at Schellhase's at 9:45 P.M. tomorrow. I'll bring along some books for the Check List.[1]

Ich kuss die Hand.

Yours,

M

[1]Trusting Sara's good judgment, Mencken hired Sara to write some of the numerous one-paragraph reviews in his section "Check List of New Books," which appeared in the endpapers of *The American Mercury*.

H. L. MENCKEN
1524 HOLLINS ST.
BALTIMORE

April 2nd, 1926

Dear Sara:-

. . . By the time you get this I may be in jail. Last September we printed an article denouncing the Boston Comstock Society.[1] It now seeks revenge by barring the April Mercury from the Boston stands, on the absurd ground that the Asbury article is immoral.[2] I am going to Boston Sunday, and on Monday shall offer a copy of the magazine for sale, submit to arrest, and stand trial. If I am convicted, we are no worse off than we are now. If I am acquitted I shall start suits for damages against every director of the society, and push them vigorously. I have engaged Arthur Garfield Hays (of the Scopes trial) as counsel.[3]

More anon.

Yours,

M

[1]"Keeping the Puritans Pure," by A. L. S. Wood, an exposé of the Reverend J. Franklin Chase, secretary of the Watch and Ward Society of Boston. The society was named after Anthony Comstock, an American reformer and the society's secretary. Claiming to be a society for the suppression of vice, it conducted spectacular raids on publishers and vendors.

[2]Herbert Asbury, a reporter for the New York *Herald Tribune*, had written an article called "Hatrack," which attacked the clergy and described a small-town prostitute. Asbury's story was a chapter from his forthcoming book, *Up From Methodism*.

[3]Hays, who had been counsel for the defense to Clarence Darrow, was also the outstanding civil liberties attorney of the day.

Censors were well established in the 1920s. Over the years, Reverend Chase had been the terror of Boston and its nearby suburbs, sending booksellers, news vendors, district attorneys, and police captains scurrying to obey his orders if he indicated the slightest disapproval over material. He seldom went to court; he simply notified the Boston Bookseller's Committee or the Massachusetts Magazine Committee that he "believed" certain "passages" in a given work were illegal. Publishers and authors were never given a chance to be heard, and the newspapers didn't dare criticize the censor. The dilemma was this: Chase, unchecked, could go on to greater censorship, with other censors imitating Chase. Or, Mencken could defy Chase in open court and, assuming he won at some point in the judicial process, he could, as a citizen of Maryland, hope to appeal in federal court for relief against assault on his good name and property. Chase could probably name his own judge and win the first conviction, but Mencken stood an excellent chance of winning on appeal. If he lost, he could get two years in prison.

On April 5, Mencken and Hays were to meet at the Boston Commons and sell a copy of the banned April issue of The American Mercury *to Reverend Chase himself. In due time Chase appeared and paid his fifty cents, and Mencken, as if to test the coin, bit it. He was then seized by Captain Patterson, chief of the Boston vice squad, and a plainclothesman, and marched to a nearby police station. Since the evidence was possibly obscene, Judge James Parmenter declared that the trial on April 6 be conducted in a whisper. On April 7 Judge Parmenter declared that the Hatrack article was harmless, as was the rest of the issue, and that Mencken was free to go.*

THE AMERICAN MERCURY
730 FIFTH AVENUE
NEW YORK

April 8, 1926

Dear Sara:

Thanks very much for your telegram. The battle was superb and the victory was really riotous. The poor Comstocks are in full flight today. On Monday we begin suits against them in the federal court at Boston praying for a permanent injunction against them and heavy damages. Even if they win, the cost of defending these suits will ruin them.

I am tired out and hope to get back to Baltimore tomorrow morning to resume work upon my book. More anon.

Yours,
M

HLM:L

The injunction hearing was held on April 12. Two days later Judge James M. Morton granted the injunction and sustained the full $50,000 damage *claims, should* The American Mercury *choose to press it in the appropriate court of law. This was a blow to the Boston organization, which began to make Chase a scapegoat to avoid such a suit.*

H. L. MENCKEN

1524 HOLLINS ST.

BALTIMORE

April 11th, 1926

Dear Sara:

. . . The Boston case is in this state: I have been acquitted in a state court with honor. (The judge, in fact, praised The American Mercury highly.) I have entered suit in the federal court for $50,000 damages. I have asked for a permanent injunction, restraining the comstocks from molesting me further. If I win, they are ruined. If I lose, then the fact is at last established that they have a right, under American law, to persecute their opponents.

The magazine was barred from the mails retroactively and as a test. It had been passed by the Postoffice on March 15th and the mailing was complete. But the comstocks took another hack at me. I am going to Washington Thursday to begin proceedings there. If I win, I'll have another damage suit. If I lose, it will be established again that such swine may harass their enemies with impunity.

In other words, I am playing for final adjudications of all the points at issue, and shall print a complete record of the case, with comments. For years I have been advising other men to do the same. But now, for the first time, I have a chance to do it myself.

I kiss your hand.

Yours,

M

I am under 10 fathoms of letters and telegrams.

New problems had arisen. Even though Mencken had been acquitted in Boston, Chase, anticipating Judge Parmenter's decision, had arranged matters so that Horace J. Donnelly, solicitor to the postmaster general in Washington, D.C. would effectively ban the April issue from the mails.

H. L. MENCKEN
1524 HOLLINS ST.
BALTIMORE

April 19th, 1926

Dear Sara:-

Dreadful scandals rock this town: Montgomery has no monopoly in that direction. Yesterday an old friend called me up and told me that his marriage, ten days old, was already busted. Such are the evils of the times. He was an old bachelor, pathetically eager for progeny and the comforts of home. Now he is on the beach again. Fortunately, I don't know the bride.

It is good news that La Welsh[1] has begun work. The best place for you to work on the articles is Washington. The Library of Congress is superb, and the Surgeon General's Library is the best in the world in its line. I can get you a card for the latter. Moreover, I can introduce you to Lieut. Col. Garrison,[2] who knows more about medical and general scientific history than any other man in America. Moreover, I can come over and wait on you myself. You could, in fact, live in Baltimore and go to Washington as necessary. I hope you do it. The libraries in New York are hard to work in.

I am up to my ears in litigation. We are beginning mandamus proceedings against the Postoffice in the matter of the April issue. The whole business was outrageous. We were barred from the mails at the behest of the baffled comstocks two weeks after the Postoffice itself had passed the magazine and a week after the whole issue had actually gone to subscribers. Hays will make a great row about this in court. My damage suits against the wowsers must wait. One thing at a time. We have a year to act. So with libel suits against various Christian newspapers.[3]

My book lost two weeks, but I am resuming it tomorrow. It can wait. The present show is so good that I hate to miss any part of it.

The wop is instructed that you are on your way. He will do his damndest. And I kiss your hand!

Yours,
M

~

¹Lillian Welsh.

²Fielding H. Garrison, medical historian and assistant librarian at the surgeon general's office in Washington.

³The press coverage of the "Hatrack" case had described *The American Mercury* in lurid and unfair ways. Equally damaging was the effect the case was having on Mencken. He sent out a pamphlet, "To the Friends of the American Mercury," describing the case in order to convert a hostile press; he refused to reissue the April issue, which had become a collector's item, even though if he had he would have made a large profit (the case had cost *The American Mercury* $20,000); and he became sensitive about real and imagined abandonment by his friends. Despite the controversy, circulation of the magazine continued to climb.

THE AMERICAN MERCURY
730 FIFTH AVENUE
NEW YORK

April 28, 1926

Dear Sara:

. . . I know nothing of Miss Nicholson's [sic] doings except what was printed in the Baltimore Sun. I was naturally delighted that she had received one of the Guggenheim prizes. She is well rid of Guth and his abominations. The fellow is a jackass. He is so bad indeed that I marvel that he has not been promoted to the presidency of Johns Hopkins.

Yours,
M

HLM:L
More anon.

~

H. L. MENCKEN
1524 HOLLINS ST.
BALTIMORE

May 3rd, 1926

Dear Sara:-

When do you reach this great city? You say May, but mention no date. I'll be here for the next two weeks, hard at work on my book. Then I'll probably have to be in New York for a week. Then back to the book. I am hungry for a sight of you. You are, I hear, confidentially, handsomer than ever. As for me, you have a dreadful moment ahead of you. I am now visibly senile, and walk with two sticks.

The comstock business has kept me jumping. I have put in several days accumulating and arranging evidence. Our suit against the Post-master-General comes up in New York tomorrow, and our suit for false arrest is to be filed in Boston this week. We have refused to parley with the wowsers. If we lose in court, we lose. But the record will be there, and I shall print it in full, with moral comments, A book, indeed!

Yesterday, hard at work, I was hauled to Hagerstown, Md., 70 miles away, to bring home my brother, injured in an automobile accident.[1] His car was turned on its back, with the wheels in air, but he got out with only a few small injuries. I brought him home, and had him sewed up. He seems to be all right today. He is very lucky always. Once his car was completely smashed, and he escaped with only a bloody nose.

It is 84 degrees here today. But the workmen are at last out of my work-room[2] and I shall spit on my hands and fall upon the book in earnest tonight. Despite all the interruptions it is 2/3rds done. More, it is very good stuff. In fact, it is the damndest slating of democracy ever written. Your prayers saved it from wreck.

I kiss your hand.

Yours,
HLM

[1]August Mencken.
[2]Mencken was having his house repapered.

~

The government's appeal came up in New York before the circuit court of appeals, and the long fight would not be over until May 1927. The three-judge panel found for the Post Office. There was little use for an appeal to the U.S. Supreme Court, since no point of constitutionality was involved, and so Mencken lost on a technicality. Nonetheless, Mencken dealt the Comstock Society a blow from which it never fully recovered. Mencken's had been the first determined attack on censorship in Massachusetts; others followed. Everywhere Mencken's name became identified with tolerance and freedom of the press. Reverend J. F. Chase himself died on November 3, 1926.

H. L. MENCKEN
1524 HOLLINS ST.
BALTIMORE

May 5th, 1926

Dear Sara:-

I refuse absolutely to let you see me at 7:35 in the morning, especially a Sunday morning! You'd run like a deer. But by noontime, after the masseurs and barbers have done their work, I am presentable, in a sense. I therefore suggest that we have lunch together. Let me know where I am to call for you or meet you. I shall instruct the wop.

It is now two geological epochs since we met. Be warned: I have aged terribly. I'll keep the afternoon clear. Let us have a long palaver.

My democracy book is in its last stages. Despite the flood of mail and telephone calls I have been at work on it nearly every day.

Ich kuss die Hand!

Yours,
M

H. L. MENCKEN
1524 HOLLINS ST.
BALTIMORE

May 12th, 1926

Dear Sara:-

. . . Don't let the Book Chat article bother you.[1] Such storms always do good in the long run. Hall stood by you nobly.[2] But where is the article? I have not seen it.

Pro tempore, I kiss your hand.

Yours,
M

¹Sara's article, "Literary Life in the Cotton Belt," published in the May and June issue of *Brentano's Book Chat*, described the literary tastes in Montgomery. The result was an uproar.

²Grover Hall, editor of the Montgomery *Advertiser*, did indeed support Sara's view, as did the editors of *Brentano's Book Chat*, who, in their July and August issue, reprinted Hall's comments and called Haardt "easily one of the most promising of the younger writers in the South."

H. L. MENCKEN
1524 HOLLINS ST.
BALTIMORE

Friday, May 21, 1926

Dear Sara:-

What say'st thou to meeting the gifted critic, Mr. Mencken, at the wop's victualling rooms at 12.15 on Saturday? I hope it is convenient. If I don't hear from you I'll be there.

I got back from New York yesterday with a stye on my eye, and had to go to the wet banquet. Reed was superb, but the other orators dam nigh killed me.¹

Yours,

M

¹Senator James A. Reed of Missouri had come forth to turn the tide against Prohibitionists with "impeccable logic and devastating eloquence." He spoke against the fraud of Paternalism, of Uplift, of Service, and spoke in favor of reducing the functions of government to the barest essentials, and bringing the costs down. "The average Congressman," Mencken affirmed, "is a coward and a scoundrel. . . . It swarms with men who, in Senator Reed's phrase, think of their jobs first and their country second," but "Senator Reed is anything but usual. No man of greater forensic talents has been in Congress in our time, and no man of greater honesty and courage. . . . Reed has bitter enemies among the so-called Democratic party. The symbol of that party remains a jackass."

~

H. L. MENCKEN
1524 HOLLINS ST.
BALTIMORE

June 4th, 1926

Dear Sara:-

You are lucky to escape that pesthouse of a Goucher. If you pursued pedagogy for a few years more it would land you in a lunatic asylum. There is vastly more interest and charm in newspaper work, and I think you should have no difficulty whatever about landing on The Evening Sun. Have you seen Hamilton Owens?[1] If not, call him up and see him. He greatly admires you. What he has to offer I don't know, but there will be something soon or late. I'll see him myself when I get back.

Don't give any thought to going back to Montgomery. Or to spending the Summer at Saranac. This last would be very depressing. The Baltimore Summer is hot by day, but ordinarily bearable at night. It will seem very pleasant after Montgomery.

Let us discuss all this when we meet. I propose a session at the Southern on Saturday the 12th, beginning for the same at 12.15. I begin to tire of the wop's place.[2]

Yours,
M

[1] Editor of the Baltimore *Evening Sun* since 1922. Hamilton Owens had also been responsible for organizing a staff of special correspondents covering the United States, especially the south.

[2] And with reason. He and Sara were meeting there regularly, more than once a week.

H. L. MENCKEN
1524 HOLLINS ST.
BALTIMORE

June 6th, 1926

Dear Sara:-

I think this is charming stuff, and I see absolutely no reason why you shouldn't sell it. A good agent could place it in ten days, but I know of no good agent. They are all demoralized by movie rights, and pay no attention to short stories.

I have Goodman on my hands today, and tomorrow I am off for New York with him. Knopf sails on Wednesday, and I'll be in session with him almost continuously until then. The American Mercury case, thank God, is to take a Summer holiday. I have got enough of it to last me a lifetime, but it must be carried on to a finish.

I hope you see Owens during the week.

Ich kuss die Hand.

Yours,
HLM

H. L. MENCKEN

1524 HOLLINS ST.

BALTIMORE

June 15th, 1926

Dear Sara:-

The MS. has reached me from Brentano's,[1] and I'll read it the first time I get a clear two hours. Maybe that will be Saturday, on the train. I have got stuck in my book reviews for August, and am making very heavy weather. Prejudices V remains untouched. But I'll be at it before the end of the week. Two hours of heavy exercise today, sawing logs! I feel weak but refreshed.

Ich kuss die Hand.

Yours,
M

When Murphy[2] gets back, next week, Owens will try to find a suitable place for you. I think he will manage it.

---

[1]"Literary Life in the Cotton Belt."
[2]Managing editor of the Baltimore *Evening Sun*.

H. L. MENCKEN

1524 HOLLINS ST.

BALTIMORE

June 18th, 1926

Dear Sara:-

Somehow, this leaves me in a certain doubt. I have a feeling that the approach may be too serious for a newspaper. But on that point

Owens' opinion would be better than mine. Let him see the stuff. It is very well done.

I'll get to Career next week. I am off for West Chester.[1]

Yours,

M

[1]Mencken was on his way to visit Joseph and Dorothy Hergesheimer, who were living in Dower House in West Chester, Pennsylvania. Here, he would meet the actress Aileen Pringle, who had been delegated to pick him up at the railroad station. She found the Sage of Baltimore holding gladstone bags, loaded down with the terrapin he was bringing for dinner.

H. L. MENCKEN

1524 HOLLINS ST.

BALTIMORE

June 21st, 1926

Dear Sara:-

I dare you to victual with me next Saturday. Or any other day after Wednesday. Name the time and the place. I suggest that we try the wop's victuals again. He has better stuff than the Southern.

Hergy's party was very strenuous. I cleaned out the starboard hold of his cellar.

But kiss your hand.

Yours,

M

H. L. MENCKEN

1524 HOLLINS ST.

BALTIMORE

June 27th, 1926

Dear Sara:-

I am holding two of Lee's poems, and have written to him.[1] I don't want to choose definitely between them until I see all of the Alabama stuff.[2] I may be able to take both of them. They are "The Tigress" and "The Singing Hills." I think they are very good. So is the Joseph piece, but I hesitate to print Biblical verse.

I am off in an hour for New York. What a girl you are! I kiss your hand!

Yours,

M

¹Lawrence Lee, from Montgomery, Alabama, was a graduate of the University of Virginia and a magazine editor in New York.

²Mencken was putting together a collection of poems by Alabama poets, and he commissioned Sara to collect them.

H. L. MENCKEN

1524 HOLLINS ST.

BALTIMORE

July 8th, 1926

Dear Sara:-

Let me know what your plans are as soon as you make them. I'll be in New York by Monday, July 19th. What of lunch on that day, or on Tuesday or Wednesday? We can victual at the Algonquin, where my cellar is available. Will you bring Miss Greil along?¹

My malaise is passing off, but the infernal weather still makes work difficult. However, I shall tackle the remainder of Prejudices V head-on this afternoon. It must be completed by the end of next week.

You are far too nice to be real. I kiss your hand.

Yours,

M

¹Anne Louise Greil, with whom Sara was living on 130 East 40th Street, in New York City.

H. L. MENCKEN

1524 HOLLINS ST.

BALTIMORE

July 13th, 1926

Dear Sara:-

It is too damned bad that we are not to meet before you go to the Adirondacks.¹ But I think you are wise to get out of New York. Later on I shall certainly come up to Saranac if it is at all possible. I think the trip can be made very conveniently from New York. I hope to finish Prejudices this week. It will leave me a wreck.

The weather here is still infernal, despite the drop in temperature. The humidity remains high, and work is very difficult.

More anon. I am rushing this off to reach you before you leave New York.

And kiss your hand!

Yours,
M

[1]Sara was to describe "The Little New York of the Adirondacks" for the Baltimore *Evening Sun* of August 13.

H. L. MENCKEN
1524 HOLLINS ST.
BALTIMORE

July 17th, 1926

Dear Sara:-

God knows, I wish I could come up to see you, but at the moment there are impediments. The proofs of two books are flowing through, and they turn out to be very dirty, and so need a lot of work.[1] Worse, I am involved in various other business. But maybe I'll be able to run up in two weeks. I hope so.

The Alabama stuff promises to be very interesting. In a short while you will receive the vast sum of $25 to pay your expenses in this great literary enterprise. My best thanks you already have, and my prayers.

I am delighted to hear that you find Saranac so lovely. Stick it out for a month or so, but don't stay too long. I believe it is dangerous to get acclimated to such high altitudes. But you will be coming back, of course, as the temperature on the coast falls. It has been almost wintry here all week, but now the heat is coming back.

Ich kuss die Hand!

Yours,
M

[1]*Notes on Democracy* and *Americana 1926.*

H. L. MENCKEN

1524 HOLLINS ST.

BALTIMORE

July 27th, 1926

Dear Sara:-

. . . Paul Patterson, of the Sun,[1] wants me to make a brief dip into the South with him in October: a sort of prospecting tour, to get into contact with the more civilized editors. I'll do it if I have the time. I don't know what the route is to be precisely, but he plans to go as far as Texas. More of this anon.

I begin to grow cool about the Constantinople trip. It would take at least two months, and I begin to conclude that foreign travel is a nuisance. The passport matter alone would drive me crazy.

I am cleaning up a lot of long-delayed routine work, and reading the proofs of the books—a horrible job. The Postoffice has just appealed our injunction, so we'll have two separate law cases in the higher courts this Fall. Another reason for staying in the United States. Knopf and Hays will be back by September 15th.

Ich kuss die Hand. When are you coming back?

Yours,

M

[1]President and publisher of the Baltimore *Sunpapers*.

H. L. MENCKEN

1524 HOLLINS ST.

BALTIMORE

July 29th, 1926

Dear Sara:-

I was wrong about the time of publication of Alabama Poets. It will be run in October, not in November. I have enough stuff now, but if any masterpieces come in I can add them. Half of the authors have been paid; the rest will get their checks this week. My best thanks for your noble aid.

I have been harassed all week by literary visitors. They have been on my hands every day, and as a result I have got very little work done. Now The Sun asks me to go to Chicago to cover the Dempsey fight, whenever it is, and I'll have to do it, for the paper has not asked me to do any such thing since the Scopes trial, and my contract requires me to do a certain amount of it.[1]

Knopf's sales manager was here last night. He tells me that "Notes on Democracy" has a large advance sale. Such are God's wheezes.[2] The book, in proof, seems dreadful stuff, but it will probably sell. I'll probably do "Prejudices VI" for next year. "Prejudices V" is now on the linotypes.

Guy Holt, late of the Robert M. McBride Company, was here yesterday. He has just started business for himself under the name of the John Day Company, 25 west 45th street. Will you please tell Weil to send him "Career," and to mention the fact that it is the book I told him of? He is the man who rescued Cabell and brought him out decently.

The MacLean MS. is returned.

And your hand is kissed twice.

Yours,

M

[1]The heavyweight champion since 1919, Jack Dempsey was to take on Gene Tunney on September 23, but in Philadelphia, not Chicago. He would lose to the marine yet again a year later in Chicago, trying to win his title back. Mencken had first seen Dempsey fight against Carpentier in July 1921.

[2]Most of the notices, Mencken wrote, had been "furiously hostile." There was a second printing in November 1926, and after that sales tapered off.

H. L. MENCKEN

1524 HOLLINS ST.

BALTIMORE

August 2nd, 1926

Dear Sara:-

God knows I'd like to run up for a day, but I begin to believe it will be impossible. Of this, however, more anon. I expect to get to New York by Sunday. The temperature down here is infernal. I sit in my B.V.D.'s, trying to work, but it is almost impossible. Tonight I must write an editorial for the Mercury. I'd rather be polite to an archibishop. You'd be insane to leave that cool climate while this heat goes on. But I begin to believe that the last time I set eyes on you was during the Eocene.

The Alabama Poets are now all in type. Today comes a letter from one Ada H. Hedges protesting that she announced that she would be represented, and that my rejection of her masterpiece now embarrasses her. I shall send her a Bible, and advise her to pray. The two pieces from the Advertiser are superb, and I am putting them into type at once. The heading is "Literary orgies in grand old Montgomery."

God help us one and all. First mopping my brow delicately, I kiss your hand.

Yours,
M

H. L. MENCKEN
1524 HOLLINS ST.
BALTIMORE

August 5th, 1926

Dear Sara:-

. . . I spent Tuesday and yesterday at Joe Hergesheimer's place in Pennsylvania. It was so hot that Joe anointed me with stearate of zinc. It turned out to be perfumed and I still smell like a chorus girl. We wrote a one act movie, and played it on the lawn. Very rough stuff, with touches of the salacious. He has a movie machine.[1]

I'll be in New York but probably stuck again. The elder Knopf[2] has got me into a negotiation for the sale of a magazine. It is business, and hence horrible, but it may yield some mazuma.

Dying of the heat, I kiss your hand!

Yours,
M

Don't return the enclosed.

[1]Once again, both Aileen Pringle and Mencken were guests at the Hergesheimer's. Mencken reported to a friend that the movie was very thrilling and Aileen "very amusing."
[2]Samuel Knopf, Alfred A. Knopf's father.

H. L. MENCKEN
1524 HOLLINS ST.
BALTIMORE

August 19th, 1926

Dear Sara:-

Yesterday was a red letter day. I rolled in at 2:30 the night before, after a Sun dinner that lasted 8 solid hours, and early in the morning was awakened by my sister. She was in horrible pain—an occasional consequence of an old appendicitis operation. All day the house swarmed with quacks. It was not until evening until she got any relief. Today she is quite well, though weak. The thing is dreadful while it lasts, but it is only spasmodic, and so is over soon.

This morning I had an engagement at St. Agnes hospital, to have four small moles chopped off. They have now gone the way of McKinley and Harding. One was on my left cheek—an old-timer, constantly getting itself cut by my razor. In its place there will be only a superb Schläger scar: it will get me respect the next time I am in Germany. This single defacement was all that kept me from challenging Valentino on his own ground. He will be jealous of me now.

The temperature here has dropped suddenly from 100 to 65. What a relief! I have been snoozing all afternoon, comfortable for the first time since July 1. Three cheers for the Twelve Apostles!

Who kisses your hand.

Yours,
HLM

H. L. MENCKEN
1524 HOLLINS ST.
BALTIMORE

August 21st, 1926

Dear Sara:-

Sending me a MS., you run a risk of having it mutilated. I have exercised my evil art upon the enclosed. The changes are slight, but I believe they are worth making. You use too many terminal dashes and periods. Hold them down.

I don't believe I can take the story, as much as I like it.[1] Using only one piece of fiction a month I am horribly crowded. But I believe that La Weil can certainly sell it as it stands. Curse me a little, and then recopy it and let her try. Tell her I suggest Scribners, and then the Century. . . .

My sister got well in 24 hours. She celebrated her recovery by getting her hair bobbed. I tremble for the safety of my gin.

But kiss your hand.

Yours,

M

¹"The First Wild Oat."

H. L. MENCKEN

1524 HOLLINS ST.

BALTIMORE

August 24th, 1926

Dear Sara:-

My poetical parts run out. The facts become too sad for sweet strophes. I can only point to the Song of Solomon II, 5. But it is contradicted by Proverbs XV, 17. Who shall decide when even Jahveh wobbles?

I hope you didn't get drowned on the journey to Whiteface. It has been raining here for eight days. Did I say no? At least I get a respite from catarrhus aestivus. But all the damned symptoms save the snuffling are on me, especially the infernal depression. I feel like a Presbyterian on the eve of the Judgment Day.

But my plasters come off Saturday. This morning I got a glimpse of what is under them. The sight really made me uneasy. I begin to fear that, once all the stitches are out, I'll be one of the prettiest fellows of modern times. Valentino, to be sure, was a handsome dog, but he lacked my perfect manners.¹

When do you get back to New York? Don't forget that we have an engagement there.

Yours,

M

¹The Italian-born screen idol, Rudolph Valentino, had been taken ill at a friend's apartment on August 14 and had died on Sunday, August 23. Through

his friend, Aileen Pringle, Mencken had met Valentino one evening in New York a week or so before he had become ill, and had taken a great liking to him. He wrote one of his most moving tributes to the actor for the Baltimore *Evening Sun* on August 30; it would appear again in *Prejudices: Sixth Series*.

H. L. MENCKEN
1524 HOLLINS ST.
BALTIMORE

August 26th, 1926

Dear Sara:-

. . . The wet weather has given me a reprieve from hay fever, but I feel it coming on. My blood pressure must be down to 100. I am as weak as a kitten. But that is surely better than arterio sclerosis. There is an undertaker at the corner of my block. Every time he sees me he darts into his garage and spits on his hands.

I have received an invitation to the Valentino funeral orgies, and shall go on Monday. He was a great artist, unappreciated by a Philistine world. I never saw him on the screen, thank God.[1]

When do you return to New York?

Yours,
M

[1]One hundred thousand people filed past Valentino's open casket in the Gold Room at Campbell's funeral chapel in Manhattan, but Mencken was not able to attend.

H. L. MENCKEN
1524 HOLLINS ST.
BALTIMORE

September 18th, 1926

Dear Sara:-

I am 146 years old today, my typewriter is jammed and it is Sunday and I can't get a repair man, I have an infernal hay-fever cough and my eyes burn, and in an hour I must grab a Pennsylvania D Zug and sweat and curse my way to New York. Three cheers for the Twelve Apostles! And a tiger! Knopf has the same birthday, but his hay-fever comes in the Spring. We shall celebrate tonight by devoting six hours to uninterrupted business, mainly legal and unpleasant. A hoch for the Holy Ghost!

I shall buy a pair of pajamas with your $5 note. I have just discovered that my only silk pair is split down the back. The maid at the Algonquin will lose respect for me. Maybe she will even go to the length of refusing to sneak a daily drink out of my jug. Ten thousand banzais for the whole hierarchy of Heaven!

But we meet soon!

Yours,
HLM

H. L. MENCKEN
1524 HOLLINS ST.
BALTIMORE

October 9th, 1926

Dear Sara:-

My best thanks for the lovely set of highball glasses! They are charming indeed. . . .

Barring some great convulsion or cataclysm of Nature, involving at least 1,000,000 deaths, I'll be in attendance at the Marconi souphouse on Monday at twelve sharp. If I am to suggest alcoholic refreshments to Mlle. Parmenter[1] give me a wink. If not, keep your eye wunk for five minutes.

You were superb scenery on the train. All the bucks in the car were gaping at you.

Yours,
M

[1] Mary Parmenter, Sara's good friend from Goucher College, had submitted a short story to Mencken, who returned it, saying he had "a prejudice against stories of sad loves."

~

H. L. MENCKEN
1524 HOLLINS ST.
BALTIMORE

October 13th, 1926

Dear Sara:-

You and your sister will be rewarded by the bon Doo. I am now all set to leap off. I figure that I'll average four hours sleep a night the first five days. That includes three nights on sleepers. But I shall take a long nap, I hope, in Atlanta on Sunday, while the pastors rant and roar.

You are infinitely nice! But I have told you that. And now another geological epoch!

Yours,
M

RALSTON HOTEL
COLUMBUS, GEORGIA[1]

October 19th, 1926

Dear Sara:-

The Confederates have outdone themselves. I have had scarcely any sleep for four days. But now we are off for Montgomery (sacred spot!), and tomorrow we'll be in New Orleans.

More anon. I shall alarm your fair sister with a bottle of Burgundy. For each hand 200 kisses.

Yours,
M

[1] In Columbus, Mencken visited Mr. and Mrs. Julian Harris, editors of the Columbus *News Dispatch*. Mencken presented Mrs. Harris with the flag of the Maryland Free State for her fight in behalf of religious freedom and racial tolerance.

THE ROOSEVELT
NEW ORLEANS

October 22nd, 1926

Dear Sara:-

It has taken two days to recover from Montgomery. Hall staged a superb party, and sent us aboard the sleeper in a semi-liquid state.[1]

Your lovely sister[2] was at the hotel, and had a noble flask of Alabama Schnapps under her coat. At dinner I sat beside your brother.[3] What a handsome dog! I was tempted to take him along to Hollywood.[4]

We came here to rest, but have run into the usual strenuous life. Patterson is returning to Baltimore Saturday, and I'll probably pull out for Texas on Sunday afternoon. I hope to get some sleep on the train.[5]

More anon.

Yours,

M

[1]The dinner party was held at the Exchange Hotel, where Grover Hall engaged the bridal suite for the occasion. Hall wrote to Sara: "Patterson sent up an enormous basket of beautiful roses which Mencken, upon seeing, immediately exclaimed: 'My Gawd! Who's dead?'. . . . Mencken swept up everything before him, as was anticipated by all of us. He kept his congregation in an uproar, and joy unconfined. . . . There were no more *misters* by the end of the services. I was 'Hall,' Rice was 'quack,' Patterson was 'Uncle Paul' (John named him), Mencken was 'doc,' Zuber was 'professor,' and so on . . . early in the evening all coats were shucked and thrown on the bed." About Mencken, Hall wrote Sara: "You instantly feel his dynamic force. His ready adaptability puts everyone at ease; he would be at home in the house of a white tenant farmer, and probably could eat pot liquor and greens with a relish, if he had to. The visit excited a great deal of interest in town, and I have been asked many questions. Everybody is curious about Mencken's person, and people are pleased that he came to Montgomery."

[2]Ida.

[3]John.

[4]Mencken had decided to take an extra two weeks to visit Los Angeles and San Francisco for a brief vacation. It had been four years since he had had so much as three days off.

[5]Once he arrived in New Orleans, Marshall Ballard, Sanford Jarrell, and others from the *Item-Tribune* took Mencken around the French Quarter. The fire chiefs of Louisiana, Arkansas, Kansas, and Missouri, meeting at a convention at the Roosevelt Hotel, made Mencken an honorary member and presented him with a white fire helmet.

~

THE AMBASSADOR
LOS ANGELES

October 30th, 1926

Dear Sara:-

This place is fit only for Christians. Its first gift to me was a nasty bronchitis. Every visitor, I hear, gets it, on account of the dry, idiotic climate. I shall clear out for San Francisco as soon as Joe Hergesheimer arrives, three days hence.

The Confederacy dam nigh finished me. It is a literal fact that I was never completely sober from the Potomac bridge to a point in New Mexico, 400 miles west of El Paso. The climax was a dreadful dinner in Juarez, over the Mexican line. But now I am restored to normalcy.

Los Angeles is even worse than I suspected. The architecture would make you yell. The noblesse of Spotted Cow, Idaho, come here, erect gaudy Spanish palaces, and then fill them with Grand Rapids furniture. The effect is really kolossal.

I am to dine with La Gish tomorrow.[1] Maybe you will now respect me. One of your other Far Western rivals met me at the train, heavily veiled, and the next day the papers were full of a mysterious woman story. The common theory is that the gal was Aimee McPherson.[2] Well, maybe she was.

I give you a smack.

Yours,

M

[1]Lillian Gish was being seen in two films that were released that year: *La Boheme* and *The Scarlet Letter*.

[2]The evangelist Aimee McPherson of the Angelus Temple of the Foursquare Gospel had caused a sensation earlier that year by disappearing with Kenneth G. Ormiston, her radio operator. McPherson, believed to have drowned in the Pacific Ocean, miraculously reappeared in the Mexican desert. Her statement, that she had been kidnapped, was challenged by those who claimed that she had been hiding with Ormiston. The ensuing court battle was far from over by the time Mencken visited Los Angeles.

~

THE AMBASSADOR

LOS ANGELES

October 31st, 1926

Dear Sara:-

Anita Loos[1] and John Emerson[2] get in today and Joe Hergesheimer is due on Wednesday. I shall have a busy week. The climate, I find, is infernal. I picked up a slight bronchitis on the desert, and it still entertains me. I hear confidentially that every newcomer gets it. I am to dine with La Gish tonight. This afternoon I am to see Aimee McPherson, that lovely wench. She is said to radiate a colossal Sex Appeal. I only hope I can resist it.[3]

The visit to Montgomery was really lovely. I stole Rice's hat as a souvenir. Patterson and I went to bed on the train in our clothes, and had to be blasted out in the morning. I begin to scoff at the news that the South is dry.

I have done no work save read a few MSS. and correct a few proofs.[4] A vast delayed mail is now catching up to me. I am tempted to hire a beautiful blonde secretary, Miss Dolores Ginzborough. But of this more anon.

I'll see all the movie gals when Hergy gets in.[5]

And offer you a buss now.

Yours,

M

[1]American humorous screenwriter, best known for *Gentlemen Prefer Blondes*.

[2]Writer and director of early Douglas Fairbanks films, including over twenty-five plays on Broadway, and husband of Anita Loos since 1919.

[3]On this sunny Sunday afternoon Mencken made tracks to hear "the town's most distinguished citizen" but slipped away before he could be baptized.

[4]While passing through Atlanta, the Southern novelist Frances Newman had given Mencken, on his insistence, the proof for her manuscript, *The Hard-Boiled Virgin*.

[5]Joseph Hergesheimer was due to arrive on the Southern Pacific on November 3. With the help of his friend, Walter Wanger, producer of Famous Players–Lasky studio, Mencken managed to stage an extravaganza. An hour before Hergesheimer's arrival, Mencken had the platform surrounded with motion picture cameras (without film), a white open touring car with a chauffeur, and a squadron of motorcycles mounted by actual police, waiting to provide escort. With Mencken and James Quirk, editor of *Photoplay*, the leading Hollywood magazine, were

Anita Loos, John Emerson, and Aileen Pringle to form the official welcoming committee. Once the baffled Hergesheimer arrived, he was decked in a garland of roses, and then the company rode conspicuously to the Ambassador Hotel. Hollywood reporters mistook Mencken, and not Hergesheimer, for the dupe. "They're making the old boy like it," they wrote. "This is the sort of thing he harpoons all the time and they're giving him a double dose."

THE AMBASSADOR
LOS ANGELES

November 5th, 1926

Dear Sara:-

This place is a genuine horror. If I described it literally I'd be set down as the damndest liar ever heard of. Architecturally it is inconceivable, and the people all seem to be imbeciles. The movie folk, by comparison, are enlightened and civilized.

Hergesheimer is here, and we have been gadding about, seeing the objects of interest. This morning, motoring, we ran into what seemed to be the whole German Army. It was a herd of 1,000 movie actors, making a war film. I hoched for the Kaiser, and felt at home.

The climate is infernal. I am sleepy all the time. One drink of gin makes me drunk. I had a bronchitis for a week. Now it is gone, but I still feel hay-feverish. Hergy and I have been photographed at least 50 times. A camera man is behind every tree.

I find that the movie queens save their money, and so I have cast an eye on several of the least scandalous of them. They live in superb Venetian palaces, with $3,000 radio sets. More of this anon.

Whether you yell or not, I send you a buss.

Yours,
M

THE AMBASSADOR
LOS ANGELES

November 11th, 1926

Dear Sara:-

Did I send you the enclosed?¹ It has brought me some charming social contacts with the more refined colored people of this great city. Yesterday I had lunch with a dark-skinned lady with immense gold teeth. A fact. But the Caucasians are even more amiable. In the afternoon I had the honor of taking tea with Mrs. Jack Dempsey,[2] Mary Pickford,[3] Mrs. Leslie Carter,[4] Kathleen Norris[5] and Jack Himself.[6] Another fact, though you won't believe it. Norma Talmadge was the hostess, and her sister Constance[7] served as barmaid, all done out in a white cap and a long apron. The tea ran to 65 % alcohol by volume.

I am off for San Francisco tomorrow for a very short stay. George Sterling[8] is on a grand drunk, and has been long distancing me. A week hence Hergy and I start homeward. We are making up a large party and shall probably take a whole car. Anita Loos is here with her husband, and plans to return with us.

I yearn for a sight of you!

Yours,

M

[1]The Los Angeles *Negro Paper* had printed a story about Mencken's visit to Los Angeles in its November 5 edition, celebrating "his sterling honesty and a genuine sincerity that he has always maintained in his splendid crusades for mankind's rights and the same square justice for the downtrodden ones."

[2]Estelle Taylor, an actress. Her film, *Don Juan*, with John Barrymore, had been released that year.

[3]Canadian actress and "America's Sweetheart," the D. W. Griffith discovery became cofounder of United Artists Films and one of America's richest women. By this time she was already married to actor Douglas Fairbanks, who was also a good friend of Jack Dempsey.

[4]The well known American stage actress had made her debut on Broadway in 1890. In 1926 she had been touring as Mother Goddam in *The Shanghai Gesture*. She would be remembered as Lady Catherine in Somerset Maugham's play *The Circle*. Her film appearances were rare.

[5]The American novelist.

[6]Jack Dempsey had just lost his title of heavyweight champion to Gene Tunney in Philadelphia on September 23.

[7]The Talmadge sisters were considered the sex symbols of their generation. They were both silent heroines; Norma specialized in emotional roles, while Constance became a comedienne.

[8]The poet George Sterling had begun preparing for Mencken's visit by laying in a stock of liquor and fixing a banquet for him at the Bohemian Club. Mencken had published two articles and a poem by Sterling in various issues of *The American Mercury* for 1926 and would continue doing so in 1927.

HOTEL ST. FRANCIS
SAN FRANCISCO

November 16th, 1926

Dear Sara:-

My visit here is spoiled. George Sterling accumulated a stock of bootleg poisons to entertain me, and then foolishly tried some samples. He went down and out and is now laid up. I saw him yesterday: a terrible spectacle. I really fear for his life.[1]

I shall return to the Christian Inferno tomorrow or next day, and on Saturday I shall start for home with Hergesheimer. I plan to stop off in Kansas City and Chicago. But I should be back in Baltimore a few days after Thanksgiving. I feel very good, and begin to be eager for work.

The tale I have to tell will make your eyes pop. I offer you a respectful hug.

Yours,
M

[1]Mencken had visited George Sterling at his room at the Bohemian Club, accompanied by his friend G. B. Lal, a Hindu science writer. Sterling had greeted them with effort but, unable to get out of bed, had assured them he would be on hand for the banquet. On the same day that Mencken wrote this letter to Sara he had called Sterling several times and wrote him a note saying he would see him again the next day. Shortly before his fifty-seventh birthday, on November 17, Sterling killed himself. The causes of his suicide were complicated, among them being failing powers as a writer and as a man, and his hopeless struggle with alcoholism.

THE AMBASSADOR
LOS ANGELES

November 18th, 1926

Dear Sara:-

George Sterling's suicide threw me out of San Francisco. A very dramatic business, to be whispered into your ear the first time we visit Schellhase. Hergy and I are leaving day after tomorrow. I'll be in-

Chicago by Thanksgiving, and home by the Monday following. What a relief!

And what a joy to see you again!

>Yours,
>M

H. L. MENCKEN
1524 HOLLINS ST.
BALTIMORE

December 17th, 1926

Dear Sara:-

Back from Babylon! By this mail I am sending you a box of cigarettes.[1] It is NOT a Christmas present. I abhor and abominate all the Christian holidays, including even Good Friday.

I have a scandalous and amazing tale to tell you, concerning certain eminent literati. It will shock you that great men should be so idiotic. What of meeting at the Schellhase palace on Sunday evening? I'll call you up tomorrow to make sure.

>Yours,
>M

[1]Mencken always bought gold-tipped cigarettes for his secretaries, Blanche Knopf, and friends. The brown wooden box they came in looked smart on the table at dinner. It was a form of flattery; cigarettes were new for women, and Mencken gave them as a sign that he thought they were sophisticated and up to date.

H. L. MENCKEN
1524 HOLLINS ST.
BALTIMORE

December 20th, 1926

Dear Sara:-

Keep this in reserve. The mood for work will return, and then you will find easier going. I hope you fall upon the Southern article at once. You can do it better than anyone else.[1]

It is 11 A.M. and the first mail is not yet in. The letter-carrier, a moron, is later every day. I have been reading MSS. In a little while he will come in, and swamp me. What a life!

I kiss your hand.

Yours,
M

How lovely you were last night!

---

¹"Govenor Brandon Accepts an Invitation," published in the Baltimore *Evening Sun* on December 31.

[TELEGRAM]

DEC 24 1926 10:55 PM

HOLIDAY GREETING

WESTERN UNION

EAST LIBERTY, PENN.

ALL THE USUAL INSINCERE FELICITATIONS ON THE WORST OF ALL CHRISTIAN HOLIDAYS   THIS IS A SWELL TOWN   HAVING A SWELL TIME   EVERYBODY IS TREATING ME SWELL   I HOPE THE TEMPERATURE HAS GONE

MENCKEN.

George Sterling's suicide had put Mencken "in a horribly low state of mind," making him feel "200 years old." The anniversary of his mother's death was also upon him. "A hundred times a day I find myself planning to tell her something, or ask her for this or that. It is a curious thing: the human incapacity to imagine finality," Mencken would write to Theodore Dreiser. To Sara, Mencken wrote: "I wish I could get drunk at this damned season, and wake up in the middle of May."

1927

Mencken's sixth and last series of Prejudices *appeared in* 1927, *as did a separate volume,* Selected Prejudices. *Throughout the autumn of* 1927 *Sara lived in Los Angeles, working on screenplays for Hollywood's Famous Players–Lasky Paramount Studio. Sara found Hollywood to be "the loneliest place in the world." As each day passed, Mencken worried about her from afar. "Baltimore is a desert without you," he telegraphed.*

H. L. MENCKEN

1524 HOLLINS ST.

BALTIMORE

January 11, 1927

Dear Sara:-

Obviously the Judge[1] was a noble old fellow. May I be permitted to drop a tear upon his bier! I am sorry that I never met him.

I incline to think you'd be happier with Miss Mayfield than alone.[2] True enough her presence would interfere to some extent with your work but what you need at the moment is not more leisure for work but more recreation for the hours when you can't work. After all, it is impossible to bang away at the typewriter for more than five or six hours a day. Even under the best conditions. The great curse of authors is loneliness.

If you fail to show up at noon on Thursday I shall spread the report that you are a colored woman. I have got a private room and shall lay in a few superb jugs. Hergesheimer tells me that he is on the water-wagon. So much the better!

Yours,
HLM

¹Sara Mayfield's father, Judge James Jefferson Mayfield, had died on New Year's day.
²Sara Mayfield shared Sara's apartment for a few short months.

H. L. MENCKEN
1524 HOLLINS ST.
BALTIMORE

January 12th, 1927

Dear Sara:-

The revised MS. is here, and I shall fall upon it today. I'll look for you tomorrow at noon. Your instructions are to fall upon Hergy with your roughest, wildest stuff.¹ Don't try anything subtle. He is best fetched with fire-axe and shovel. Nancy Hoyt² has the same instructions. She is of the sporting type, and able to jump over two bales of hay. You are refined. Between the two of you the fellow is doomed.

Yours in Xt.,
M

¹Sara was to help research Joseph Hergesheimer's book, *Swords and Roses*.
²The writer Elinor Wylie's sister.

H. L. MENCKEN
1524 HOLLINS ST.
BALTIMORE

January 30th, 1927

Dear Sara:-

Knopf was butchered by Hazlehurst this morning and is making very heavy weather of it tonight. But he should be all right by tomorrow. I shall see him in the morning, and present myself at the wop's at 12:15, as arranged.[1]

Yours,

M

[1]Dr. Frank Hazlehurst removed Alfred Knopf's tonsils at St. Agnes Hospital that morning. The previous evening the doctor had been host to the Saturday Night Club, supplying enough bottled home brew to fill a bathtub. As the evening advanced and the drinking continued, one member after another came up and spoke words of reassurance to Knopf: "Don't worry about Frank, the more he drinks the steadier his hand will be in the morning." It was Mencken who finally broke up the party, and Mencken who accompanied Alfred to the hospital the next morning. As Knopf remembers it: "When a sister turned up soon after I had been put to bed to ask why a tonsillectomy had to be done on the Sabbath, I recall Henry's telling her in his sweetest and most disarming manner something that made it sound as if Sunday were the only day on which any operation could ever be performed on me. And then he advised me that if priests came to talk with me after the operation, as they undoubtedly would, I had only to point to my throat, nod my head from side to side, and say nothing."

H. L. MENCKEN

1524 HOLLINS ST.

BALTIMORE

January 31st, 1927

Dear Sara:-

That you should be laid up for two days without a doctor is utterly damned scandalous and inexcusable. Why didn't you let me know that you were ill? Do you need anything—money, say, or anything else?

I am in somewhat of a sweat. Knopf is laid up here after tonsillectomy and a submucous, and his father threatens to come down from New York.[1] I haven't done a stroke of work since I got home. Now Jim Quirk[2] telegraphs that he is coming in tonight. I shall hire a pastor to pray for me.

I hope you are better at once.

Yours,

M

¹Samuel Knopf, who served as business manager.
²James Quirk, a Bostonian who lived in New York, was editor of *Photoplay*.

H. L. MENCKEN
1524 HOLLINS ST.
BALTIMORE

February 25th, 1927

Dear Sara:-

I'll send you some more books in a day or two.¹ In the case of a book whose price you can't determine, simply put down a question mark in place of it: the office will find out. Be as tart as you please, especially with the learned. In case you find a book that is beyond you, don't return, but let me have a memorandum of it. Two volume books are to be listed thus:

7 1/2 × 5 3/4; 2 vols.; 563 + 524 pp.

Be sure to mention bibliographies, and to call attention to it when a book should have an index, and hasn't.

Ich kuss die Hand.

Yours,
M

¹For the section "Check List of New Books," which appeared in the endpapers of *The American Mercury*.

H. L. MENCKEN
1524 HOLLINS ST.
BALTIMORE

February 26th, 1927

Dear Sara:-

The questions of the charming Mayfield are delicate and encouraging. Let them start when I wink my left eye. I also suggest:

1. Does the magazine business offer any good openings to bright and worthy young girls?

2. How is a young lady writer to support herself while she is learning her trade and making her way?

3. Do authors, as a class, make good livings?

Yours,

M

H. L. MENCKEN

1524 HOLLINS ST.

BALTIMORE

February 28th, 1927

Dear Sara:-

You are prompt and admirable. In fact, your notices shame the others in the Check List. Don't take too much trouble with them. And, in general, try to keep them within eight or nine lines of your typing. More books will reach you from time to time. And within is a check for the five delivered.

I am spending the day in prayer. I hope our Heavenly Father inspires me tomorrow night. Pearl[1] will be in attendance at the beer-house at 10 P.M., with a table waiting and Mitzi[2] primed for action.

Yours,

M

[1]Raymond Pearl.

[2]Probably the waitress, and perhaps even a fictional name. Sara often gave nicknames to people; "Modish Mitzi" was a popular regular cartoon feature of the Baltimore *Evening Sun* that showed the fashions of the day, with Mitzi as its star.

H. L. MENCKEN

1524 HOLLINS ST.

BALTIMORE

March 3rd, 1927

Dear Sara:-

Thanks very much. The reviews are excellent, and go into type at once. The office will send you a check in about a week. I have written to Weisberger, of the Peabody Book Shop,[1] suggesting that he open negotiations with you. He says that he needs books. Make him pay cash on the nail.

I am struggling to clear up my necessary writing before going to New York on Sunday. Tomorrow night is the Free State Association dinner to Lawrence Henderson,[2] and on Saturday I have the music club here. What a life. But my house is cleared of workmen at last, and needs only cleaning to be habitable again.

What of a session at the end of next week? I suggest lunch on Saturday.

You made all the other gals look like scarecrows.

Yours,
M

[1]Hugo Weisberger, a 1912 emigré from Austria, had set up shop as a bookseller in 1922. His brother Siegfried lent him $1000 to start it and joined him three years later. The bookshop would become an institution.

[2]Professor of biological chemistry at Harvard.

H. L. MENCKEN

1524 HOLLINS ST.

BALTIMORE

March 16th, 1927

Dear Sara:-

I propose that we meet at the wop's on Saturday at 12:15. The Fitzgeralds are in Washington and I am asking them to come along, but I am not sure that they can.[1] If they do so, you and Zelda can have a session on the latest crimes of the Montgomerians. If not, you and I can commune.

I suspect that you are finding the clipping job tedious.[2] If so, simply drop it for a while. In a few days I'll send you some bibliographical questions.

Yours,
M

[1]Scott and Zelda Fitzgerald were staying at the Ritz Hotel in Washington, D.C. Fitzgerald had written Mencken that if he invited them to lunch one day they would promise to go home "immediately after," and that they had been

hearing "soft whisperings from that debonnaire Aileen [Pringle]." In an attempt to clarify matters, Mencken brought Sara.

²Sara was collecting salient specimens of anti-Mencken invective for *Menckeniana: A Schimpflexikon*, published by Knopf in 1928.

H. L. MENCKEN

1524 HOLLINS ST.

BALTIMORE

April 1, 1927

Dear Sara:

I am trying to establish the fact that men closely resembling primitive man are still to be encountered in modern societies. I believe that some material to that end is to be found in a book by H. J. Fleure called "Anthropological Types in Wales" and also in an article by the same man entitled "Some early Neanthropic Types in Europe and Their Modern Representatives," in the Journal of the Royal Anthropological Institute, Volume L, 1920.

When you get the time, will you please look up these references?¹ If you can find anything else to the same effect by Fleure or anyone else, I'll be delighted to have it. What I want is a few paragraphs in point, with the page, volume, year and so on accurately noted. In brief, I want to establish the fact that Neanderthal man is still alive and flourishing.

Yours,

M

¹Along with her work for *Schimpflexikon*, Mencken was paying Sara $100 a month to research and collect material for his book *Homo Sapiens*, which he later abandoned.

～

ALS

THE AMERICAN MERCURY
730 FIFTH AVENUE
NEW YORK

April 27, 1927

Dear Sara:

Will you please keep Sunday evening clear, after 9 o'clock? A movie man[1] wants to see you, and may be in Baltimore then. I'll call you up Friday.

Yrs.,

M

[1]Herman "Mank" Mankiewicz, American screenwriter, respected journalist, and brother of screenwriter, director, and producer Joseph Mankiewicz. At this time (1927), Mankiewicz had just become head of Famous Players—Lasky Paramount scenario department and the West Coast representative of the Author's Council. The meeting was later canceled.

H. L. MENCKEN
1524 HOLLINS ST.
BALTIMORE

May 5th, 1927

Dear Sara:-

I am off for North Carolina, immunized against hookworm, but still a bit uneasy.[1] I hear that yellow fever is raging down there.

Will you have lunch with me on Wednesday? La Sutherland will be present.[2] I trust to you to handle her: God will reward you. I suggest that we meet at the Marconi at 12:15.

Yours,

M

A letter from Mankiewicz says of you "Her stuff seems to be just what we are looking for. I am sorry I didn't see her, but I don't think it will make any difference in making a deal with her." Hooray!

[1]Mencken was on his way to visit Dr. Fred Hanes and his wife, Betty, who had a summer home in Roaring Gap, North Carolina. Mencken often spent part of each summer with the Hanes family.

²Perhaps the British author, Joan Sutherland, who had published several novels by 1927 and who also spent some time living in the United States.

H. L. MENCKEN
1524 HOLLINS ST.
BALTIMORE

May 10th, 1927

Dear Sara:-

This is an excellent story indeed: the best thing you have ever done.¹ It is very well designed and even better written. It deserves at least one shot at the grand money: try it on the Red Book. If it fails there let me know.

You first call the Jew Max and then Isidore.² Again, the wagon of the undertaker would not have been a hearse. A hearse is used only for actual burials. His closed covered wagon is called a dead-wagon. He uses it to fetch customers from hospitals.

Yours,

M

¹"Licked," published in the September 1927 issue of *The American Mercury*.
²His name would be changed to Isidore Kaplan.

H. L. MENCKEN
1524 HOLLINS ST.
BALTIMORE

June 3rd, 1927

Dear Sara:-

Instead of sending you another book of clippings I have at you with this:

I want to find out when, so far as is known, the various domestic animals were domesticated, and where. Also, when and where were such things as wheat first cultivated. Probably no one knows, but maybe there are some references in the literature. I have, in fact, a few myself, but they are unsatisfactory. I'd like to get half a dozen concrete quotations from authorities, even if they are only speculative, with page, name and date. Take your time with this.

My sister-in-law was to go home tomorrow, but began to run a temperature yesterday, and is now in bed, with 103. If it doesn't go down, Bloodgood will have to get at the sinus with the knife—a somewhat serious business. I have 40 engagements in New York the coming week. If I am held up Sunday, I'll have to spend 2 hours telegraphing.

Yours,
M

H. L. MENCKEN
1524 HOLLINS ST.
BALTIMORE

June 13th, 1927

Dear Sara:-

Bravo! My prediction is that you will go to Hollywood as a literary gal, and remain as a screen star. When they see you there will be a riot. Meanwhile, get together some ideas. We can discuss them before you sail.[1]

A sweet note from La Mayfield arrived this morning. Please kiss her hand for me. Tell her she has another bottle of gin coming to her.

My sister-in-law resumes her old place on the table tomorrow morning. More anon.

Yours,
M

[1]Mankiewicz had written Sara a letter only a few days before, offering her a job through the autumn of 1927 as a screenwriter at a salary of $250 a week, with travel expenses paid both ways and a bonus of $3750 if a story of hers was produced.

H. L. MENCKEN
1524 HOLLINS ST.
BALTIMORE

June 21st, 1927

Dear Sara:-

By God's omnipotent will, I wrote the last word of Prejudices VI at nine o'clock tonight, just as the clock was striking the hour. Soli Deo gloria! It is mainly bilge, but there are some moments.

I have the Latinist on my hands tomorrow night and old Dr. Joseph Jastrow, the patriot-psychologist Friday.[1] What of Thursday? Will you be free at 9:45? If so I suggest that we take a look at the Southern Hotel roof. I'll meet you in the lobby on the instant. If it is too cold up there we can proceed to the Grand Café Schellhase.[2] I'll bring along some gin.

Yours,
M

[1]The first student of Johns Hopkins to graduate with a Ph.D. in philosophy with psychology as a special field, Jastrow had walked in his academic procession with Woodrow Wilson. His syndicated articles, "Keeping Mentally Fit," were being circulated at this time.

[2]Schellhase's, on 302 W. Franklin St., run by Otto Schellhase and his wife, Minna Schulz.

H. L. MENCKEN

1524 HOLLINS ST.

BALTIMORE

July 9th, 1927

Dear Sara:-

I note your new address.[1] Let us meet at the wop's on Monday at 12:15. I am up to my neck in the Cabell pamphlet.[2] It will be short, but very high in tone.

Ich kuss die Hand.

Yours,
M

[1]2305 North Charles Street, a summer apartment that Sara was renting "dirt cheap" until October 1 from Mrs. de Roode, her friend Polly's mother. "You know the usual story," she wrote Mayfield. "Mrs. de Roode is going to have to be away for a couple of months with a sister who is ill and wanted a womanly woman . . . next to Polly. So I was elected."

[2]*James Branch Cabell* (New York: McBride). In 1928 this pamphlet was reissued in hard cover.

~

H. L. MENCKEN
1524 HOLLINS ST.
BALTIMORE

July 17th, 1927

Dear Sara:-

I am off for New York. Do we meet on Friday? If so, I suggest that we try old Schellhase again. Maybe his beer is better than it has been: the ways of God are mysterious. I suggest that we meet there at 9:45. Or would you rather go to the Southern? Let me have a note in New York.

It occurs to me that the beautiful Mayfield may sprain her knee dancing in Chicago, or dislocate her shoulder-blade necking, and so stand in need of some rubbing alcohol. So I enclose a card to Parshley. He is Prof. Dr. H.M. Parshley, Dept. of Zoology, University of Chicago.[1] He belongs to Schmidt College,[2] but is teaching in the Chicago Summer School. I am sending him a note.

Yours,
M

[1]One of the many science writers Mencken was cultivating for *The American Mercury*.

[2]Smith College.

H. L. MENCKEN
1524 HOLLINS ST.
BALTIMORE

July 22nd, 1927

Dear Sara:-

. . . You are far too nice to be real!

Yours,
M

~

ALS

ROARING GAP
NORTH CAROLINA

August 1, 1927

Dear Sara:

Patterson has been laid up with a fever ever since we landed.[1] He will have to stay here 2 or 3 days. But I am off to Cincinnati this afternoon.[2]

What scenery!

Yrs.,

M

[1]Mencken and Paul Patterson were staying at the home of Dr. Fred and Betty Hanes. Patterson developed a bronchial pneumonia but recovered shortly thereafter.

[2]Mencken was traveling to St. Louis, via Cincinnati, to settle a libel suit against *The American Mercury*. Marquis Childs had written "The Home of Mark Twain" for the September 1926 issue of *The American Mercury* and said that the Tom Sawyer cave was dangerous to enter. The owner of the cave, fearing the outcome would harm his profitable tourist attraction, was suing for libel. Mencken saw him in St. Louis, paid him $600, and the matter was dropped. In Cincinnati, it turns out, another libel suit was being prepared, this time against Arthur J. Cramp's article "Therapeutic Thaumaturgy," which had appeared in the December 1924 issue of *The American Mercury*.

H. L. MENCKEN
1524 HOLLINS ST.
BALTIMORE

September 22nd, 1927

Dear Sara:-

This, I think, is really a picture.[1] It moves from the start and is nine-tenths pure action. Obviously, it would be very expensive. I suggest that you offer some slighter ones first, and then hand it in. Maybe you will make some changes after you get to Hollywood, but probably not many. But I think the chances it offers ought to stir up any movie man. He will probably suggest some flag-waving at the end.

Yours,

M

[1]*Way Down South* (later changed to *The Promised Land*), Sara's epic screenplay based on historical fact. After the American Civil War, Don Pedro, the emperor of Brazil, sent an invitation to all those Confederates who were dissatisfied with the outcome of the war to come to Brazil, where he virtually offered them acres of land if they would come take possession of it. Five thousand white Southerners and 10,000 former slaves took advantage of this offer. (Slavery was not abolished in Brazil until 1888.) Two of the main towns were named Americana and Santa Barbara in the state of São Paulo. The towns exist to this day; their graveyards show tombstones with crossed Confederate and Brazilian flags.

H. L. MENCKEN

1524 HOLLINS ST.

BALTIMORE

Friday, September 29, 1927

Dear Sara:-

If I seemed idiotic yesterday, blame it upon the fact that it had suddenly dawned upon me that I'd not see you for weeks. Worse, my sister-in-law's infernal troubles had upset me. But I'm glad to these things after all: left to myself, and full of normalcy, I might have bust into sobs.

I surely hope the trip was comfortable, and that you have good quarters. Don't forget to let me hear of it by wire when you move. I have written to Tully again, telling him that you are to be treated as visiting royalty.[1]

Embalmers surround me. I am to be a pallbearer for the old lady next door tomorrow, and now I hear that my old aunt,[2] living a few blocks away, has just died. Such things run in threes. I only hope the next is not Rebecca West.[3]

It is hot here, and very uncomfortable. The carpenter is banging away. And you are making off at 60 miles an hour. What a world!

Yours,

M

[1]Jim Tully, a former boxer and hobo, wrote critical reviews of film personalities and was also a frequent contributor to *The American Mercury*. Mencken had written to Tully that Sara was brought up in Montgomery, Alabama, and was still "extremely shy," and that "the life of Hollywood will probably shock her half to death."

[2]Aunt Pauline, who lived three blocks away on Fayette Street.

[3]The English critic and novelist had criticized *Notes on Democracy* in 1926, saying no English author would ever have produced a book as shallow or as empty as Mencken's.

H. L. MENCKEN

1524 HOLLINS ST.

BALTIMORE

September 30th, 1927

Dear Sara:-

. . . My Aunt Pauline has passed away, by God's inscrutable will. She lacked the gift of intellect, but was not bad. When I was a boy she used to keep a wash-boiler full of doughnuts for my brother and me. She made my grandfather's collars until his lamentable decease: he could never wear the boughten ones. I shall depart in ten minutes to view her clay. . . .

Ich kuss die Hand.

Yours,

M

[TELEGRAM]

SEP 30 1927

WESTERN UNION

BALTIMORE

MISS SARA HAARDT

   SANTA FE TRAIN NUMBER 19 WESTBOUND DUE ELEVEN AM

   SATURDAY EMPORIA KANS

   REMEMBER YOUR SOUTHERN MANNERS   YOU ARE PASSING THRU

THE HOME CITY OF WILLIAM ALLEN WHITE[1]   HOPE THE JOURNEY IS

COOL AND COMFORTABLE   GIVE YOUR EYES TO THE MAGNIFICENT
SCENERY OF KANSAS   YOU ARE DREADFULLY MISSED

M.

¹Known as the "Sage of Emporia," the American journalist whose 1896 editorial "What's the matter with Kansas?" was credited with helping elect William McKinley as president over William Jennings Bryan.

ALS

THE AMERICAN MERCURY
730 FIFTH AVENUE
NEW YORK

October 4, 1927

Dear Sara:

Why not suggest to the magnates that they do Gulliver's Travels? The book would be impossible on the stage, but the movie photographers have tricks that would make the giants and pigmies easy. The answer will be made, of course, that there is no love story. But why not have a *comic* love story, with Gulliver pursued to the end by a Lilliputian hussy 16 inches high, and a Brabdignagian [sic] wench weighing 500 pounds? At the finish he turns into a horse, and gallops away. Go read the book: it is really fine stuff.

I am sweating away here, clearing off accumulated work. Angoff is on vacation. Ah, that thou wert here!

Yrs.,
M

THE AMERICAN MERCURY
730 FIFTH AVENUE
NEW YORK

October 5th, 1927

Dear Sara:

I am having dinner tonight with your supreme master, Walter Wanger,¹ and, if the chance offers, I shall certainly track him into a corner and inflame him with the notion that in catching you he has caught a wow. Unfortunately, he drinks freely and what I tell him tonight may be erased from the tablets of his memory by the dawn.

That Kansas wept as you went through is really too bad. But there is never any rain in New Mexico and so I assume that you had a charming day on Sunday.

Let me hear how you find the Mark Twain Hotel. If the cockroaches are unduly aggressive, don't hesitate to call up Marcia Heath[2] and ask her for advice. She'll be delighted to see you. If by any chance you cannot get into communication with her, call up Tully.

The weather here has fallen to normalcy at last and I am beginning to breathe again. Last night I went to dinner with old Samuel Knopf. It will take me four days and five nights to digest the cargo of delicacies that I took aboard.

Yours,

M

[1]Production chief of Famous Players—Lasky Paramount studio, later vice president of Columbia Pictures and an independent producer.

[2]Wife of Edwin James "Percy" Heath. Heath had begun his career in 1902 on the *Sun* and had met Mencken not long afterwards. Mencken had known Marcia around the same time.

H. L. MENCKEN

1524 HOLLINS ST.

BALTIMORE

October 6th, 1927

Dear Sara:-

So I lose my $5000! But let God have His way! You must be in Hollywood by now, and up to your eyes in gin. I hope you are comfortably settled in the hotel, and in pleasant contact with the great artists of the films.

Last night I had dinner in New York with your boss, Walter Wanger, and his wife. I told him that you were to be treated with the utmost politeness, and he made a note of it. But no doubt he will forget to wire to his office. All movie magnates lie fluently: moreover, he was somewhat in his cups. His wife is Justine Johnson, once a star herself, but now a contented housewife, with horn-rimmed spectacles.[1]

My sister-in-law, by the divine will, has gone home. She is to come down every two weeks. Soon or late, the quacks will intern her here for a couple of months. So I live in some trembling.

The weather continues infernal. Let me have news of you!

Yours,

M

[1]Justine Johnson had been a chorus girl in the Ziegfeld Follies. It turned out that she was greatly interested in medicine and later received her college and medical degrees and began publishing articles in the medical journals.

The Hollywood that greeted Sara was still a relatively peaceful, pastoral town, surrounded by bean fields and orange and lemon groves, palms, and eucalyptus trees. Houses and apartments were only beginning to sprout, new tracts were being surveyed, and streets were being laid out. From her window at the Mark Twain Hotel Sara could look out and see the glowing night lights of Hollywood, the huge searchlights sweeping the arc of the sky, and the shoplights of the windows along the avenues. In another moment, she would be catapulting past them toward the twinkling lights farther up the mountain that was Beverly Hills and residence of many of her friends. "But somehow," she would write, "for all their glamour, I shall wish I were speeding through a Maryland night, and that the outlines of those mountains, now mercifully shrouded, were the soft contours of Maryland hills. . . ."

H. L. MENCKEN

1524 HOLLINS ST.

BALTIMORE

October 8th, 1927

Dear Sara:-

The Western Union is taking to efficiency! It delivered 100% of my two telegrams. I shall have to spread the fact on the records.

That maid was only the first of them.[1] You will find that the door-opener once worked for Louis B. Mayer,[2] and that the night clerk is a decayed Ronald Colemayer.[3] Behind the Ambassador Hotel, in Los Angeles, stands a swell apartment house full of movie gals. The commissionaire under the front marquee, a Swede eight feet high, is Hor Horsen.[4] Whenever a giant is needed he gets a part.

Let me hear about the eminent movie dignitaries that you meet. I am enjoying an attack of lumbago in the right shoulder. I fear to take anything for it. What follows it will probably be worse.

Ich kuss die Hand.

Yours,

M

[1]Sara's maid at the Mark Twain Hotel was an Englishwoman who had traveled from London to be in the movies. She had gotten as far as the costume room when she was laid off.

[2]Head of Metro-Goldwyn-Mayer and soon the most powerful Hollywood executive in Hollywood, Mayer had discovered Greta Garbo, Rudolph Valentino, Joan Crawford, and later, Clark Gable. The movie *Ben Hur*, released the year before, gained MGM the reputation for high-quality films. Mencken had met him on his own visit to Hollywood.

[3]Mencken probably means Ronald Colman. Colman would later play the doctor-hero in the movie version of Sinclair Lewis's *Arrowsmith* in 1931.

[4]Here again, Mencken probably means Lars Hanson, the Swedish actor. At the New York City opening of *Flesh and the Devil* in January 1927, Hanson appeared alongside John Gilbert and Greta Garbo.

H. L. MENCKEN

1524 HOLLINS ST.

BALTIMORE

October 10th, 1927

Dear Sara:-

I suspect and fear the worst! In a week you will actually like it! Well, I warned you. There is a horrible fascination about such things. Take Mankiewicz's advice: do it the way they want it, get the money, and then depart, as Ring Lardner would say, laughingly. I am glad that you have met Percy Heath and like him. And Stallings—a wild fellow, but with a head on him.[1] Tully writes that he and Mrs. Tully[2] will be delighted to see you. He is one of the solid characters of those wilds.

I have just got in from New York, and must dress anon and go to the Babbitts' banquet to Van Lear Black.[3] I went to New York yesterday afternoon with The Sun committee of welcome. There was a dinner there last night. Only one man drunk—and that was not your humble admirer. He brought his two Dutch aviators with him—very charming young Edam cheeses.[4] I promised to take them out into the country tomorrow and have a nigger lynched for them. The banquet tonight will be a horror, but Pearl is to be there, and he and I will escape to Schellhase's by 11 o'clock. But Schellhase's magnificent establishment ain't the same no more, since you have went away. Old Anna, the waitress, will be asking for you.

My old friend Herman Scheffauer,[5] has just killed himself in Berlin. First he murdered his secretary—a blonde lady, somewhat large— with a butcher knife. Then he cut his own throat and jumped out of a window. He was my German agent, and his recent peculiarities were responsible for most of my troubles about the translation of "Notes on Democracy." Now it appears that he was dotty. I have written to the widow, offering to pay her for his services, such as they were. The old rule holds: anyone who bothers me dies.[6] Warn Jack Gilbert.[7]

We came down from New York in Daniel Willard's private car.[8] At Mt. Royal Station a band was playing and Ritchie leaped forward.[9] He will be toast-master at the banquet tonight. Sixty Babbitts have put up $200 each—$12,000 in all. It should be a gaudy affair.

Tully's last letter would delight you. I warned him that you were no movie wench, but a Confederate Lady, and to be handled very tenderly. He writes: "We'll both treat Miss Haardt O.K. *I know Alabama.*" Obviously, he has heard of the Klan.

Ich kuss die Hand.

Yours,

M

[1]Lawrence Stallings, a captain in the Marine Corps, had lost a leg during the war but the infirmity did little to slow him down. He was brought to the attention of Hollywood for his honest and factual war play, *What Price Glory?* In 1925 he achieved success for his story *The Big Parade*, which established him as a good story writer, Irving Thalberg as a production genius, and King Vidor as one of the top directors.

[2]Marna (Margaret Rider Myers).

[3]Van-Lear Black was not only chairman of the *Sunpapers* board and a financier of legend but also a devoted sportsman and pilot. In 1927 Van-Lear Black had

chartered a plane from the Royal Dutch Airways and in it toured Europe. Later, he purchased a Fokker (named the "Maryland Free State," a term coined by Hamilton Owens, editor of the Baltimore *Evening Sun*) and began a series of long distance flights which made him known all over the world. On June 15 Van-Lear Black had made an air trip to the Dutch East Indies by way of the Mediterranean, Asia Minor, and India. The round trip of 20,000 miles was made in 183½ flying hours. The exploit attracted wide attention, and Van-Lear Black was greeted with enthusiasm, in Holland as well as in the United States.

[4]G. J. Geysendorffer and J. B. Scholte, two Dutch pilots employed by Van-Lear Black who accompanied him on his travels.

[5]Herman George Scheffauer, German author, had interested himself in promoting Mencken's work, his most recent being a June 7, 1927, translation of an article of Mencken's that had appeared in the Baltimore *Evening Sun*.

[6]One of Mencken's superstitions was that anyone who tried to injure him invariably died, all suddenly and unexpectedly. Among them were Stuart Sherman, William Jennings Bryan, and J. Frank Chase.

[7]John Gilbert, leading man of the 1920s who worked his way from bit parts to romantic leads, playing opposite Lillian Gish and Greta Garbo. After Rudolph Valentino's death he had inherited the title of "The Great Lover." Sound revealed his voice to be less dashing than his looks.

[8]President, B&O Railroad.

[9]Albert C. Ritchie, governor of Maryland.

H. L. MENCKEN

1524 HOLLINS ST.

BALTIMORE

October 11th, 1927

Dear Sara:-

The Scheffauer business was really appalling, and I can't keep it out of my mind. He first slaughtered his secretary with a butcher-knife, and then stood in front of an open window, hacked his own throat, and jumped out, while a crowd watched. He landed on his head and died on the way to a hospital. What his poor wife will do I don't know.[1] She has a daughter about 11 years old. She is an Englishwoman, and a poet of some skill. Scheffauer married her in London, where he had been living for years, in 1914. Just before the U.S. entered the war he moved to Berlin, and I saw him there in 1917. He became a violent 100% German, though American born, and wrote a number of books on the U.S., in German.[2] He had been handling my translations in Germany since 1919, and had had perhaps 60 of my articles translated and published. Of late he got me into a snarl over "Notes on Democracy." Obviously, his mind was beginning to fail. Now that he is dead, the book will probably go forward.

The banquet last night was a horror. The last speech ended at 12.05. The food was miserable, and there were no drinks after the cocktails. The Babbitts spent $3500 on the decorations, and incidently [sic] they cut off all air from the hall. When I got home I couldn't sleep. The rich Americano is really almost fabulous. Imagine entertaining the two Dutch pilots in such a way! Cold and tasteless food, and nothing to drink. For the same money they might have given a charming dinner, with good wines. Tonight I must go to a dance given by The Sun staff! But I shall get there late and leave early. This afternoon there is a beer party in a brewery for the two pilots. It will be a fairly decent affair, but I must work. Mayor John Smith, of Detroit, is coming in Thursday. Saturday night I entertain the club. Sunday there is a Free State dinner at the Maryland Club. And I am a week behind in my writing!

The speeches last night passed the bounds of the conceivable. Hoover made the worst. He is the most miserable-looking man in America, save only Cal. Imagine Jim Reed set beside him![3] I met every swine in Baltimore, and actually had to shake hands with Soper, the Federal judge.[4] There were 500 head of Babbitts. A few decent people were there, for example, Franklin D. Roosevelt.[5] He gave me a couple of noble winks. Pearl was on hand, bawling for a drink and cursing God.

Have you met the Tullys? I refuse to enter the wop's or Schellhase's until you return.

Yours,

M

[1]Ethel Talbot Scheffauer.

[2]One of them, *Das Land Gottes, das Gesicht des Neuen Amerika*, published in 1923, discussed H. L. Mencken as being the fearless exponent of American political life.

[3]Senator James Reed of Missouri.

[4]Morris Ames Soper.

[5]Then the vice president of Fidelity & Deposit Company and a member of the law firm Roosevelt & O'Connor, Roosevelt was also a close friend of Van-Lear Black.

Every day, after Sara had returned from the enormous and impressive Spanish stucco Paramount Pictures studio, the British maid at the Mark Twain Hotel would ask her whom she had seen. To Sara, watching the maid move across the room, "the tragedy lay in the fact that for her the glamour of this incomparable show had not worn off. She had seen the movie business inside and out, all its cheap tinsel and hardship and hokum and cruelty, and yet she could still dream her dream. She could still thrill at recognizing Gloria Swanson in a crowd on Sunset Boulevard. She could thrill at talking to me because I had that day seen Clara Bow and Ruth Taylor and stood on the same set with Charles Rogers. It is the same with the newsboy on the corner, the amazingly handsome drug clerk at the fountain grill a block away, the flat-footed waitress in the sandwich shop across the avenue. To a visitor they are smiling and urbane; they make conversation easily and charmingly—and yet there is always a sense of tragedy, a sense of heartache beneath the surface. . . . This, in essence, is the spirit of Hollywood—this inescapable loneliness at the heart of things . . . it floats, a wistful something, on the movie lot itself where lovely ladies waft past your windows in billowy tulle dresses and cowboys romp and tall gentlemen in frock coats shrug their shoulders superciliously. About everything in Hollywood is this air of carnival, this air of impermanence. . . ." By the end of Sara's stay a building would have been knocked down next door to her hotel, a new one would be started up across the street, and still another would have loomed up on the corner. "Who could ever feel at home in the midst of such a hub-bub?" she asked.

H. L. MENCKEN
1524 HOLLINS ST.
BALTIMORE

October 13th, 1927

Dear Sara:-

Don't say you hate it! I refuse to listen to such blasphemies! It will bring in enough money to let you do what you want. Praise God from Whom all blessings flow!

Adams, of The Sun, died this morning. I have spent the afternoon writing an editorial on him, and an article for the morning Sun.[1] He suffered the horrors of arthritis for 12 years; finally his heart fetched him. I am to be a pallbearer on Saturday.

I feel like hell. Age! Age!
But kiss thy hand.

Yours,

M

¹John Haslup Adams, editor of the Baltimore *Sun*.

H. L. MENCKEN
1524 HOLLINS ST.
BALTIMORE

October 14th, 1927

Dear Sara:-

What an industrious gal! I marvel that you got the Jellybean script done so quickly. On the heels of it try out Mankiewicz on the honeymoon *a trois* idea, and then introduce delicately the subject of Gulliver. Gulliver would not be expensive: it would be very cheap. All the effects would be achieved by trick photography. The settings would cost practically nothing, and there would be only three parts needing expensive hams: Gulliver and the two women who pursue him. The rest would all be extras, and not many would be needed. Punch and Judy would make another capital picture.

Don't laugh at the fillums while you are in their house. Try to find out what the trick is, and then do it. It must be easy. Nor is it necessary, in the long run, to do trashy stuff. Soon or late the Jews will have to try something better. If you are in on the ground floor, you will have a gaudy time of it. I think doing Gulliver would be immensely interesting—quite as interesting as writing a book. Listen to the wiseacres, and then draw your own conclusions. You are immensely more intelligent than any of the master-minds. The thing to do is to take their measure, and then operate on them.

So speaks Polonius. I am off to another funeral.

Yours,

M

~

H. L. MENCKEN
1524 HOLLINS ST.
BALTIMORE

October 15th, 1927

Dear Sara:-

Adams is duly planted according to the Christian rite. A somewhat formidable affair, with Ritchie, Senator Bruce[1] and other dignitaries present. I found myself, at the grave, beside Judge Soper! We passed the time of day amicably. My editorial and article seem to have satisfied The Sun men, but I tremble to think of the widow.[2] She is somewhat acidulous, and used to hate me fervently. But in late years she has been milder. Life is full of strange quirks, as the judicious have hitherto observed. In 1920 Adams swore that he would resign from The Sun unless I was canned. It took Patterson a month to smooth him down. The row was over Woodrow: I had called him a liar.

Various spies send me reports of you. One says that you are mashed on Mankiewicz; another that you have succumbed to Ronald Cole-mayer. Beware of these handsome men! You say nothing of the climate. How is it using you? I have warned Tully that he must find some sound gin for you.

Emily Clark writes that she will be here on Wednesday. She is in an uproar about her book—Knopf is not advertising it enough, etc.[3] I have advised her to shut up, lest he boot her out.

Ich kuss die Hand zwei hundert Tausend mal![4]

Yours,
M

[1]William Cabell Bruce, lawyer, author, and U.S. senator from Maryland.
[2]Lillian Craigen, a newspaperwoman, was a member of the staff of the *Sunpapers* from 1910 to 1916; she died on August 20, 1928.
[3]*Stuffed Peacocks.*
[4]"I kiss your hand two hundred thousand times!"

~

[POSTCARD]

THE SOUTHERN HOTEL
LIGHT AND REDWOOD STREETS   BALTIMORE, MARYLAND

THE SOUTHERN HOTEL

October 15, 1927

A swell place, especially the roof. But now somewhat lonely.

An Admirer

H. L. MENCKEN
1524 HOLLINS ST.
BALTIMORE

October 17th, 1927

Dear Sara:-

I am glad you like Tully.[1] You are quite right: the fellow is in-credible, but wholly genuine. I'd rather play with him than with any of the gaudy vacuums who infest Hollywood. You have yet to meet the worst: they are the great stars of the screen. If you can manage it, get yourself invited to a soiree at the Talmadges'. There you will see the real swells.

Play along with Mankiewicz and try your damndest to unload a scenario or two on him. I shall remind his boss, Walter Wanger, that you are to be treated with very special politeness. Wanger has probably wired to him before this.

The weather here has grown damp and cold, with cloudy skies. But the best is just ahead. November is one of the few really good months in these parts.

I have done nothing on the book:[2] life has been too jammed with troubles and nuisances. But it is not forgotten.

Emily Clark writes that she will be here Wednesday, and craves a session at Schellhase's. It will be amusing to see the shocked look of old Anna, the waitress. I have not been there since you left.

Your paw is gnawed!

Yours,

M

[1]Forty-eight hours after Sara had arrived in Hollywood she met Jim Tully, who greeted her: "Don't get too lonely, kid. This is pretty damned bad"—he waved an arm toward the boulevard—"but it isn't half as bad as being on the bum in Alabama!" Sara was later to write an article about him for *The American Mercury*, May 1928.

[2]*Homo Sapiens.*

~

FAMOUS PLAYERS - LASKY CORPORATION
PARAMOUNT PICTURES
WEST COAST STUDIOS
HOLLYWOOD, CALIFORNIA

October the eighteenth, 1927

Dear Henry,

Jim Tully brought two of Ernest Booth's[1] letters around for me to see last night. They were masterpieces. In one of them he says that the prison authorities have forbidden the publication of any more prison articles. His wife has the manuscript of his book, or as much as he has written of it—some 80,000 words, I believe. Booth seemed to think that you could intervene in getting this ban on the articles removed. Jim Tully doesn't seem to think that much can be done for him.

The prison authorities are stirring up such a rumpus, there is a possibility that, if Tasker's book incites any comment, it will delay his pardon.[2] Jim Tully says he is having the time of his life as it is, and getting a tremendous kick out of his martyrdom.

Without the Tullys I would have been extinct by now. This whole business is simply impossible and these Jews insufferable. I am rapidly developing a Nordic complex that is mounting to a phobia. Mankiewicz is still in a morose stupor. I handed in two scripts to him over a week ago and they are still lying around his office. I doubt if he ever reads them. I shall finish the two I am working on, and knock off.

My devotions!
Sara

[1]Ernest Booth, serving a life sentence in Folsom Prison for armed robbery, had written several stories and articles which Mencken published in *The American Mercury*. "We Rob a Bank" was one; "Ladies of the Mob" would appear in the December 1927 issue.

[2]Robert J. Tasker was serving a five-year sentence at San Quentin for robbery. His book, *Grimhaven*, described prison life and was published by Knopf in 1928.

～

FAMOUS PLAYERS - LASKY CORPORATION
PARAMOUNT PICTURES
WEST COAST STUDIOS
HOLLYWOOD, CALIFORNIA

October the nineteenth, 1927

Dear Henry,

I stayed with the Garretts[1] last night at their place near the beach. Laurence Stallings was there, and he proceeded to advise Oliver Garrett and me according to his lights. He said, in the first place, we shouldn't hand in too many scripts or appear too prolific. And furthermore that it was better to talk the thing than for the Jews to see it in cold print. I am positive he is right. Mankiewicz has had my stuff nearly two weeks and has done absolutely nothing about it. Moreover, Mankiewicz is scared to death of his own job right now and won't press anything with Fineman and Schulberg,[2] who say what goes and what doesn't. Oliver Garrett and Laurence Stallings both say that I am up a blind alley with Mankiewicz, and that my one chance is to get Fineman and Schulberg, or better still Wanger, and sell them my idea. Just how I am to maneuver the thing I don't know. I can't go over Mankiewicz's head without making him furious, and yet I know that his own job is so shaky than he hasn't an ounce of power and would be afraid to recommend anything. I have an appointment with him this afternoon, and I'll see how far I get. Both Laurence Stallings and Oliver Garrett say that I absolutely shouldn't hand in another word. I know they are right. Everything I have heard that has gone over big here has been talked in a grand abstract manner at white heat, and then written after an apparent soul-struggle, giving the Jews the effect that it is art inspired. They cherish the notion that one of these so-called scripts consumes five or six weeks, and so are prepared to accept it when an artist goes through all the agonies. Stallings has pulled the gag with every one of his.

Oliver Garrett came out with a letter from some New York Jews to Schulberg, and got an immediate hearing. I believe he is going to sell them his New York cop story. But I've got nowhere with Mankiewicz. He has dallied around with me, advising me in a lofty manner, and shelving the stuff I've handed in to him. So I'm resolved to hand in nothing else and try to get at one of these other magnates without antagonizing him. Mankiewicz is writing titles—so you can imagine the authority he has.[3] They have taken this author's council away from him, and as Oliver Garrett and I happen to be the last ones on it we are stuck with him. Only Oliver has his drag with Schulberg.

You would have delighted to hear Laurence Stallings on the race war last night. I am treasuring his best stories for you. I am going out to the Garretts again for the week-end. They are just across the cliff from the Stallings, and we'll be camping at both places.

It is marvelous the way Laurence Stallings has the Jews jumping. All of them hate him, but are scared to death of him. He simply shouts them down. He vows he is leaving within the next few weeks. And that's distinctly that. Your prayers!

As ever,

Sara

[1]Oliver H. P. Garrett, American screenwriter, and his wife, Louise.

[2]B. P. "Ben" Schulberg, American executive and former publicist, was then the general manager of Paramount.

[3]In silent films the only words that existed were flashed on the screen as titles, a sentence or two that explained the plot or helped characterizations. Producers wanted titles that could "hit the back wall," that could turn a dull film into a hit. Writing titles was actually difficult, and Mankiewicz was a virtuoso at them, referred to as "The Titular Bishop of Hollywood." At this time he was working in a quasi-literary capacity and would soon progress to screenplays with the coming of sound. One of his biographers has written, however, that as the years passed, Herman Mankiewicz "lived with the knowledge that his intellectual life was irrelevant." His obsession with alcohol and gambling continued and he died in 1953, convinced that he had wasted his talent in Hollywood.

H. L. MENCKEN

1524 HOLLINS ST.

BALTIMORE

October 20th, 1927

Dear Sara:-

What stuff you are gathering! Have you ever thought of doing an article on Tully? I think it would be excellent. If it falls in with your ideas, now is the chance to get the facts. His adventures have been curious, and probably to some extent imaginary. But what a fellow!

Do what the movie brethren want in the way of scenarios, and try to unload a couple of them. You will then be set to write your novel at your leisure. That is the way to manage the Literary Life! When you do hack work, make them pay big prices. The common error is to do it too cheaply.

I am putting "A California Afternoon" into type.[1] It is a superb piece of work. Tully is to do another on Folsom.[2]

The beautiful Emily is here, and we had a session last night. She is in a sweat about her book, which has just come out. I fear it won't sell very well. I am off for New York on Sunday. Mrs. Hanes, of North Carolina, is there, and I am to take her to dinner on Monday. Paul Patterson will probably be in the party.

Yours,
M

[1] "A California Holiday," by Jim Tully, appeared in the January 1928 issue of *The American Mercury.*

[2] "Two Time Losers," *The American Mercury*, March 1928.

H. L. MENCKEN
1524 HOLLINS ST.
BALTIMORE

October 21st, 1927

Dear Sara:

This is charming stuff indeed.[1] But I believe that it would be unwise to print it as it stands. In the first place it is rather too short for an article, and in the second place it gives away certain stuff that you ought to keep for longer articles later on. A piece for the Sun, I think, ought to run to four pages of typewriting. There is very good writing here. If you expand it, I suggest putting in several small episodes in illustration of the thesis.

I suspect that Tully has succumbed to your slick Southern ways and oily smile.[2] Beware of Marna! It is the custom in Hollywood to shoot to kill.

Yours,
Mencken

[1] "Heart of Hollywood," never published.

[2] Tully had written Mencken a letter, praising Sara for her writing in "Licked"

and her plans for her contemplated novel. "She is too genuine to be impressed by the infamies out here," Tully concluded. "There is no need to worry about her."

HOTEL MARK TWAIN
HOLLYWOOD, CALIFORNIA
October the twentieth, 1927

Dear Henry,

Yesterday I was supposed to have an appointment with Mankiewicz for him to advise me concerning the scripts. I waited in his office for an hour and a half: finally his secretary[1] suggested that he must have forgotten the appointment, and started calling around for him. After another half hour she located him, and he informed her that yes he had forgotten the appointment and would I call at the studio this morning at eleven. I leave you to imagine my state of mind. Yesterday the temperature in this place was 98. Besides being on the verge of swooning, I was seeing fire.

I gathered my dignity together somehow and asked the girl politely to please call me if Mr. Mankiewicz found he was unable to keep the appointment in the morning. This morning, just as I was making off, she did—and informed me that Mr. Mankiewicz would be glad to see me next Monday morning, if I would come over.

I know you'll never forgive me if I don't sell these Jews something, but you can't imagine—I know the stuff I've cooked up is better than the stuff I hear talked around the studio, but there's a bare chance in a thousand that I can put it over. Louise Long, the chief woman scenarist on the lot, told me yesterday that they brought Dixie Willson the circus gal out here, paid her three hundred and fifty a week for nine months, and simply forgot she was on the place. She turned out some good stuff, at least good movie stuff, but it is doubtful if they read it.

Schulberg has departed for some convention and I'd rather not tackle Fineman, so I see nothing to do but wait until Wanger returns. I have three scenarios done, and I believe it is futile to work up any more.

Tonight I am having dinner with the Tullys in their new house. It is the first time they have had any guests in. Tomorrow night I go out to the Garretts to spend the night. The Stallings are coming in for dinner, and Laurence is bringing some champagne.

I loathe this climate. It was 98 yesterday and 99 today. I've had a mild bronchitis or something ever since I landed. What a country! And you a million miles away—

Yours,
Sara

¹Katherine Michel, later replaced by Rachel Linden.

HOTEL MARK TWAIN
HOLLYWOOD, CALIFORNIA

October twenty-first, 1927

Dear Henry,

This morning, as a stroke of diplomacy, I went over to the studio and said I wanted the two manuscripts I had handed in. Mankiewicz came blowing in with his hair standing on end. He wanted to know what I wanted with them, and wouldn't I talk to him about them first. In brief he was on his ear for fear I was up to something with them. I was very sweet and serene, and said I had a new line on them that I *knew* would cinch them. He got wilder and wilder, and I got calmer and calmer, and allowed that it was ridiculous for him to think I could write a movie in five weeks. I needed more time, and indeed I didn't care to talk to him about them until I could put more time on this big idea I had in mind. You have never seen anything as funny as the way he carried on. He said he wanted me to see Walter Wanger and could I arrange to stay two weeks longer—until he arrived. I said I *might* be able to arrange it.

Jim Tully put me up to the whole thing. Laurence Stallings gave me precisely the same advice, but not as specifically. I am so eternally tired of playing politics. I can't tell Jim that I talk to Laurence and I wouldn't breathe to Laurence that I talk to Jim because they hate each other. But both of them told me precisely the same thing. Only I would trust Jim, and somehow I am a little wary of Laurence.

I know this WAY DOWN SOUTH script will sell somewhere from the stuff I've picked up. But I am not going to turn it in until Walter Wanger returns. Don't you think I ought to stay until I get a shot at him? He is the only man on the place who has the power to do anything. In the meantime I am going to lay low and keep them jumping after me. It is absolutely the only game to play. I told Mankiewicz I didn't want to see him Monday, and he insisted that I come in. But I am not going to take a scrap of anything with me. I shall talk vaguely and magnificently, and keep him standing on his ear.

Have you ever talked THE BARBAROUS BRADLEY plot to any-body?[1] Mankiewicz fell for it like a ton of bricks, but I have an idea he recognizes it from something he said. I just touched upon it lightly in our conversation this morning, but if he asks me about it I am going to say that you told me I could use it. These Jews!

If you don't hate me for entering into this skin game—I hate myself. What do you think about my staying on? I know I can stall around and make them extend my contract, but I hate staying. On the other hand, my one chance is to get at Wanger. I'm sure I could put over WAY DOWN SOUTH with him, and maybe another one.

You simply can't imagine what a help Jim Tully has been. I am going out to the Cruzes[2] with him and Marna on Sunday. I wish I could tell you Jim Cruze's affair with Laurence Stallings and Lasky,[3] but it is too long to write. Somehow I have a feeling that I'll like them a lot. Betty Compson[4] asked Marna to bring me out because she read "Licked" and wept over it. It seems half of her family have died of T. B. Tonight I spend with the Garretts and the Stallings, and of course won't dare mention the fact that I ever heard of the Cruzes.

Please write me what angle to take on this contract scheme. Do you think I should wait to see Wanger?

Your brow is kissed!

As ever,
Sara

[1]H. L. Mencken's story in *The Smart Set*, November 1914. Mencken sent her a telegram and a formal letter giving her permission to use the story.

[2]James Cruze, a Danish-American silent screen actor, had turned to direction and became one of the top directors of Hollywood. During the 1920s directors had definite box-office standing (their prominence had declined somewhat during the 1930s, 1940s, and early 1950s), and *The Covered Wagon*, the first real Western epic, made in 1923, had put Cruze into the forefront.

[3]Jesse Lasky, American pioneer who had formed his first production company in 1914. He gained control of the Famous Players in 1916 and later became a producer for Fox, Warner Brothers, and RKO.

⁴Wife of James Cruze and American leading lady of the 1920s whose career would last well into the 1940s. The following year she would be in the much acclaimed *Docks of New York*, directed by Josef Von Sternberg.

[POSTCARD]

LEXINGTON MARKET, BALTIMORE, MD.   70919

LEXINGTON MARKET
BALTIMORE, MD

October 22, 1927

Just a reminder of the swellest, most progressive town North of Roanoke. Oysters are coming in, and terrapin and duck are not far off. But Schellhase's near-beer is as bad as ever.

A Friend

[TELEGRAM]

OCT 24 1927 4:08 PM

WESTERN UNION
NEW YORK NY

IF YOU RECEIVE A LETTER FROM MRS BOYD DELAY YOUR ANSWER UNTIL YOU HEAR FROM ME BY MAIL¹

H.L.M.

¹Madeleine Boyd, wife of Ernest Boyd, was also a literary agent and, according to Emily Clark, a nonstop talker. Mencken had met with her and she had suggested she handle Sara's novel, whereupon Mencken said he had "foolishly" given Madeleine Sara's address.

HOTEL MARK TWAIN
HOLLYWOOD, CALIFORNIA
October the twenty-fifth, 1927

Dear Henry,

Thank you very much for your telegram. I hope you are not going to any trouble for anything for me. Please don't! You've been much too nice as it is.

Everything here is at a standstill. Mankiewicz insisted that I come over to the studio yesterday for an appointment. I appeared, but he was nowhere about the place and his secretary had no idea when he would be in. I positively refuse to participate in any more such nonsense. Wanger is due here three days after my contract is up. I think it would be inadvisable for me to seek an audience with him. At any rate I don't propose to do it.

The authorities advise me to send these three scenarios to you by registered mail before I submit them to *anybody*. If I hear nothing from Paramount before I leave, I shall try to unload them somewhere else. The WAY DOWN SOUTH one is absolutely marketable.

I had a perfect time at Jim Cruze's Sunday. I'm going out there to dinner tonight. In the meantime I'm getting a marvelous article out of Jim Tully.

As ever,
S

[TELEGRAM]

OCT 26 1927 12:51 AM

WESTERN UNION
LOS ANGELES CALIF
H L MENCKEN

HOTEL ALGONQUIN NEW YORK NY
CRUZE HAS OFFERED A TENTATIVE TWENTY THOUSAND FOR WAY DOWN SOUTH BUT HE SAYS IMPERATIVE TO PROTECT IDEAS WITH WILL

HAYS[1] AT ONCE   WILL YOU CALL HAYS UPON RECEIPT OF THIS AND
REGISTER TITLE IDEA AND STORY AS YOU REMEMBER IT   THERE IS
DANGER OF OUR LOSING IT ALTOGETHER   IF YOU FAIL TO GET HIM
IMMEDIATELY REGISTER TITLE WAY DOWN SOUTH AND THE PROMISED
LAND   CRUZE URGES YOU GET HAYS OVER TELEPHONE OR ANY WAY
AND GET IDEA ACROSS TO HIM   LETTER AND REGISTERED SCRIPT
FOLLOW TO BALTIMORE   PLEASE WIRE ME

S.H.

[1]The "Czar of the Movies," Will H. Hays, the postmaster general in Harding's
cabinet, had been approached to become the president of the Motion Picture
Producers and Distributors of America. The Hays Office was responsible for
establishing rigid adherence to Production Code rules.

[TELEGRAM]

OCT 26 8:12 AM

WESTERN UNION
NEW YORK NY
MISS SARA HAARDT

MARK TWAIN HOTEL
   HAYS OFFICES SAYS IT DOES NOT REGISTER SCRIPTS FOR AUTHORS
IT CAN ACCEPT SCRIPT FOR REGISTRATION ONLY FROM PRODUCER AND
AFTER CONTRACT IS SIGNED

H. L. MENCKEN.

October the twenty sixth, 1927

Dear Henry,
   I hope the telegram didn't get you up at dawn, but I had just come
in from Jim Cruze's and he was insistent that I get in touch with you
at once. I told him the idea of WAY DOWN SOUTH because Jim
Tully told me I could trust him, and because I couldn't lose on it
anyway as Paramount has done nothing. Of course Jim Cruze was
absolutely sworn to secrecy, and I'm sure he can be trusted. He fell
for the idea at once—well you can imagine if he offered twenty thousand for it. If I handed it in to Paramount under this contract, the
most I can get for it is five thousand.

As usual there are a dozen angles to the thing. In the first place I've handed in the script to Mankiewicz but I'm sure he didn't read it. You see I talked to him that day at lunch and told him the idea in the abstract with the title so it is imperative that Hays protect it for me. Otherwise the thing is lost—even if I sell to Paramount. The point is they simply lift ideas and Jim Cruze says this one could be grabbed with no trouble at all. All they would have to know is the incident of the Confederates going to Brazil.

I propose to hand in one of the lesser scripts to Paramount under the five thousand contract if Jim Cruze takes it. On the way home Jim Tully warned me that Cruze was dilatory himself, but that he was certain the idea had knocked him cold else he wouldn't have offered twenty thousand for it. It is all a gamble anyway. Even if you can't get it protected and Cruze doesn't take it, he would be willing for me to say to Paramount that he had offered me twenty thousand for it, and I could use that as a wedge with them. Anyway I won't hand it in to Paramount again unless I lose out with Cruze. I am going to change the title on the script from WAY DOWN SOUTH to THE PROMISED LAND and shift WAY DOWN SOUTH to the jellybean story. The jellybean story I'll hand in to Paramount. Jim Cruze likes THE PROMISED LAND better.

I don't see you approving of this but it is absolutely the only way out. As long as I am in this game I am going to gamble for big stakes, and get out once and forever. Jim Cruze said tonight, if he does the picture and does it big I can put over whatever else I may have.

I am protecting the script every way I know how. I am mailing you a copy sealed and registered and I am mailing one to myself. In the meantime I shall say nothing to Mankiewicz and keep away from the studio until Wanger returns. Then I shall talk to him, and with the idea protected by Hays, offer it to him for twenty-five thousand. Both schemes may fall through, but at least it's a shot.

Thank you so much for all your trouble! Your brow is kissed. . . .

Yours,

Sara

I may add that Jim Cruze hates Wanger and Wanger hates Cruze, and they are apt to push the price up between them. Moreover Cruze says it could be made the biggest picture since THE BIRTH OF A NATION[1] or THE COVERED WAGON. I am safe in playing Mankiewicz until Wanger returns. He knows nothing about pictures. 3 a.m.! I am dead. . . .

The way Cruze would do the WAY DOWN SOUTH piece would change it into a completely new picture. He would change the title, stress the promised land idea rather than the Southern and leave out all the Negro stuff. In addition he would change the love story and *begin* with Sherman's March to the Sea! It would be a marvelous thing, as such things go. Also he'd omit a lot of the Brazilian part, especially the politics.

I am going to pull the stall at Paramount that I've never hinted it before. If Mankiewicz has anything to say about WAY DOWN SOUTH I can say he was drunk which he was and out of his mind. The only thing he could steal would be the idea of the Confederates going to Brazil. Cruze says he is terribly crooked and a stool pigeon for Wanger in the organization. That much is certainly obvious. I am sure he hasn't read the stuff I've handed in and he has avoided seeing me, mainly because he's been so drunk.

It is a dastardly game. And I'm sick to death of it.

The whole thing is a gamble. Jim Tully warned me against believing too strongly in Cruze. He is trustworthy, but dilatory in such matters. He says however that if Cruze doesn't take the thing he would be glad enough for me to say he had offered twenty thousand for it to Wanger.

Cruze said last night that anybody ought to snap at the idea. He was terribly keen about it.

Jim Tully is too amusing. He is so afraid somebody is going to steal it from me he is frantic. He wants me to get George Palmer Putnam to handle it. He says he is sure he could get more money out of Wanger. He has warned me on pain of death not to say anything to Wanger until I can get the idea protected and not to say anything to Cruze about Wanger.

This letter is insane, but I am so tired I can't think.

¹D. W. Griffith's epic of 1914.

October the twenty-sixth, 1927

Dear Henry,

You probably think I am mad. Thank you so much for the telegrams. Jim Cruze, as you know, has left Lasky and gone with de Mille,¹ but he is staying with him for only one more picture. I couldn't sign up with him and protect the idea with Hays; anyway I still have this Paramount contract. I am convinced, after talking with Cruze, that I could get twenty thousand out of WAY DOWN SOUTH if I worked it right.

I think I shall wait until Wanger returns and play him. The trouble is that it is heresy to talk an idea or let it out until it is protected in some way or other. Cruze and Jim Tully and Laurence Stallings and everybody I've talked to say not even to hand in anything to Lasky on this contract until I've mailed it to a lawyer or somebody who could be depended upon for evidence.

What do you advise? Cruze is having me meet his scenario writer this week to talk over the possibilities in WAY DOWN SOUTH. I am sure I can trust him. He was absolutely frank and downright. And it is obvious he wants the idea because it is his stuff. He would want to change the title to THE PROMISED LAND and I would have to strengthen the love story for him, probably bring the Yankee boy over earlier and link him up with the Southern beauty in Rio de Janeiro.

I am preparing to hand in THE JELLYBEAN to Paramount under the title WAY DOWN SOUTH. In the meantime I am dead I am so tired. You simply can't imagine what this thing is like. At this minute I can't see the importance of trying to do anything.

The script goes forward to you in this mail. I am told you are not supposed to open it.

Yours,

S

'Cecil B. De Mille, one of Hollywood's pioneers and autocrats, had gone into partnership with Jesse Lasky and Sam Goldwyn, but later broke with the Famous Players-Lasky Co. and bought Ince studios in 1925. He did much to establish the pattern of feature-length films.

~

ALS

HOTEL ALGONQUIN
NEW YORK

Tuesday, October 26, 1927

Dear Sara:

I shall see Wanger tomorrow, and try to stir him up. Why not ask Garrett to introduce you to Schulberg? Schulberg, to be sure, is an ass, but it may have a useful effect on Mankiewicz. But God knows what is to be done about the general situation. Stick it out as long as you can. And don't pay too much attention to Stallings. He is apt to be extravagant in his ideas.

I have a fear that you returned the $200 too soon. If you did, it remains at your disposal.

I am in my usual whirl here. Yesterday I had Thomas Mann's son and daughter on my hands,[1] and today I have another German—and a Norwegian professor. Tomorrow, the Boyds.

I kiss your hand.

Yrs.,

M

[1] Probably Klaus Heinrich and Erika Mann. Klaus became editor of *Decision* magazine and sought Mencken's contributions; Erika was to marry the poet W. H. Auden.

October the twenty-seventh, 1927

Dear Henry,

Thank you so much for your telegram. I am holding Jim Cruze off. I know he wants the thing, but of course he'll try to get it as cheaply as he can. He tried to get me to talk to his scenario writer, but I refused. Cruze himself has called me a half dozen times since I saw him.

I know positively that the people who have come out here on this Author's Council have got nowhere. It is common talk around the studio that they beat Ben Hecht.[1] Mankiewicz's secretary has confided a lot of stuff to me that it would have taken me years to find out. She says I would have gained absolutely nothing by just filing my script with them. They have excellent stuff they've got from people. They'll keep it for a certain length of time, and one of their scenario writers on the lot will work it over.

Yesterday I had lunch with Mal St. Clair who directed GENTLE-MEN PREFER BLONDES.[2] Under the influence of the worst cocktails I have ever tasted, he divulged his all. At the moment he is the biggest director on the lot, and the most sought after, but the tale he told would have raised your hair. I know all these people are lying—all except Jim Tully—but I know too some of the motives back of their gilded stuff and I've heard enough to know what hitches together.

Oliver H. P Garrett is a knock-out. I like his wife almost as well. The rest of the ones who have paid their respects to me—Well, Jim Tully is the only big person in the landscape. But what a lot of stuff I've gathered!

I've started feeling low, and I'll probably have to stay in for the next day or so. You can't imagine the strain in this business. I am simply dead.

Yours,
Sara

[1] American writer and critic with screenplay credits. Much later he would write the screenplay for *Wuthering Heights* (1939).

[2] In 1926 Malcolm St. Clair was at the peak of his career, a top director of comedies, working with such stars as Florence Vidor and Pola Negri. After *Gentlemen Prefer Blondes* he essayed different genres and never again had a big success.

H. L. MENCKEN
1524 HOLLINS ST.
BALTIMORE

October 27th, 1927

Dear Sara:-

Wanger and his wife had dinner with me in New York last night, and we gabbled all evening. Wanger was much interested in you, and told me he had received good reports of you from the front. I told him that you had to be handled with great care—no standing around.

He said he would see you as soon as he got to Hollywood. He is leaving New York tomorrow, but will stop in Chicago for a few days. I believe that you should wait for him by all means. I enclose a note to him.

The Cruze business presents obvious difficulties. By your contract with the Famous Players you are bound to show Mankiewicz everything you do. But you are certainly not bound to show him what you have NOT done. Thus all you have to do is to deliver nothing to Cruze until you are through with the Famous Players, and clear of your obligation. They certainly have no claim on what you do after you are out of their clutches. It is always possible, of course, that it may seem advisable, when Wanger gets to Hollywood, to let him have "Way Down South" instead of Cruze, who is with De Mille. But don't cross that bridge until you come to it. Cruze is likely to do a big spectacle better than the Famous outfit. He is a reasonable man, and Tully can influence him. When he sees your predicament he will not press you. I suggest asking him to make you an offer in writing conditioned on your liberation from the Famous Players. He can't deal with you while your contract runs, save by violating the managers' agreement.

As I wired to you, the Hays office does not register scripts for authors, but only for its own manager-members. What Cruze may think, this is the case. I got it direct from the Hays office, and was also told that it was true by Jim Quirk and various others.

The prospect of $20,000 is immense. I offer 10 to 1 that your head is swimming. Well, it only shows how much money can be got out of those Old Testament heroes, once you get your hand in. Stick it out until there is some action.

I am distressed to hear of the bronchitis. I hope it is only trifling. I had it all the while I was in Los Angeles. But you must be very, very careful. If it bothers you, go to see Dr. Fishpaugh, in Los Angeles. He is a Johns Hopkins man, and the only good doctor out there. If he is not on hand, call up Mrs. Slemons,[1] wife of Dr. Morris Slemons,[2] and tell her you are a friend of mine. Or see Slemons himself. He is an obstetrician, but can advise you about other medical men. He is an Eastern Shoreman and a Johns Hopkins man. I have known him for 25 years.

I hope my telegrams reached you promptly. The news of the possible

$20,000 made my own head swim a bit. You will end lending money to Emily Clark.

The register script is not yet here. I'll hold it at your orders.

Yours,

M

[1]Anne Goodsill.

[2]A native of Salisbury, Maryland, Josiah Morris Slemons, the nationally known obstetrician and gynecologist, had moved to Los Angeles in 1920.

H. L. MENCKEN
1524 HOLLINS ST.
BALTIMORE

October 28th, 1927

Dear Sara:-

Another word from you about being beaten, and I'll swear out some sort of writ, and have you incarcerated. Be patient. Great and rich corporations, consecrated to the beautiful arts, do not move quickly. If you were dealing with the Pennsylvania Railroad it would be just as bad. The Government would be worse. I wrote to the Postmaster General 17 days ago and have yet to receive a reply.

Stick it out a while, and see what happens. At the worst, the $250 a week are safe. And you may pick up something to stagger you. That Cruze offer is superb. Play along with him.

This as an appendix to my air mail note.

I kiss both your hands frequently.

Yours,

M

HOTEL MARK TWAIN
HOLLYWOOD, CALIFORNIA

October the twenty-ninth, 1927

Dear Henry,

Thank you so much for your letter. I am holding off on everything until my contract with Famous Players is up. I shall submit one story to them, and then talk with Wanger about this other idea. I should be able to get more for it than I would by handing it in for $3750. I know Jim Cruze wants it, and wants it badly. Jim Tully is advising me on every move. He has played this game himself, and knows it through and through, and I am convinced I can trust him.

I know positively that Mankiewicz did not read my stuff. He told Oliver Garrett he hadn't and his secretary tells me the same thing. Apparently he is getting nervous now, and assures me he wants me to talk to Mr. Wanger. Aside from that, he was perfectly willing to let me slide and slide out. I know that he could have turned me over to people who would have been immensely helpful, and he has done absolutely nothing. Oliver Garrett saw Schulberg and is putting over his story, and Nunnally Johnson[1] came in yesterday and has talked with any number of people. As far as Mankiewicz knows I haven't talked with one other person on the lot. If I had just played with him I would have been completely out of it. I talked to Jim Cruze because I saw nothing else ahead. Curiously enough, it now turns out that it has been lucky for me that Mankiewicz has been so remiss.

I wouldn't talk anything to Laurence Stallings. He is absolutely not to be trusted. He has dealt out some abstract advice that has been helpful, but it has been mainly through Oliver Garrett that I have got it, and Oliver doesn't trust him any farther than he can see him.

I haven't heard from Madeleine Boyd, but I shall put her off if she writes. Marna Tully is leaving today for New York to attend to some business for Jim. She may come down to Baltimore, and if she does I am having Margaret de Roode put her up and Mayfield look out for her. She is a nice child and highly intelligent, and she and Jim have been lovely to me. I hope that you can arrange to see her. She is Jewish, is she not? It appears that her family is now High Episcopalian.

If I survive this business I have amassed an untold amount of material that I'll have at some day. I have made it my job to delve into it from every angle. I hope, of course, to get enough out of it to enable me to go on with my novel. But I hope too to preserve what shred of dignity I have left to me. It seems to me, even in this precarious moment, that that is about the only thing that could ever matter. . . .

As ever,
Sara

¹The Georgia native had began his career as a newspaperman at the New York *Herald Tribune*, the *Post*, and other papers, then went on to writing humorous short stories for *The Saturday Evening Post*. In more than 35 years of film work he would go on to write the scripts for such films as *The Grapes of Wrath* and *The Three Faces of Eve*.

HOTEL MARK TWAIN

HOLLYWOOD, CALIFORNIA

Monday, November the first, 1927

Dear Henry,

I am holding off on everything until Wanger arrives and calls me. Of course he was lying to you in New York. He has had no good reports of me for the simple reason that nobody on the Paramount lot knows what I have been doing. Mankiewicz hasn't read any of my stuff, and I have had no talk with him that amounted to anything. He hasn't even told me what type of thing they needed most—or given me an inkling.

As for Schulberg, it is a fact that he is Wanger's rival and knows much more about pictures than Wanger does. Undoubtedly he is Wanger's most formidable second, and it will be only a question of time until he is eliminated. As a check on Schulberg Wanger has planted Fineman to cross and harass him. I think I wrote you some time ago that I couldn't dope out Fineman's job. Well, I now know that he is supposed to act as a check on Schulberg. Mankiewicz is Wanger's spy, and as far as I can discover, has no other office on the place.

This morning Mankiewicz called me to bring in my script, but I told him it wasn't ready. I am signed up in the office for GOOD INTENTIONS, and GOOD INTENTIONS it will be. I shall finish it within the next few days and get it in to him. That will terminate my contract.

At present I am debating whether to play Wanger for longer time and a better contract, or crash down with WAY DOWN SOUTH. It seems to me now that it might be better to shoot the whole works and have the thing decided one way or another. Despite my effort to keep my temperature down I am in a constant fever and desperately tired. To have a second break as a result of a parley with movie bandits would be almost too ignominious.

Yours,

S

H. L. MENCKEN

1524 HOLLINS ST.

BALTIMORE

October 29th, 1927

Dear Sara:-

Your two letters are here. Don't get excited. "The Promised Land" is protected quite as well as 1,000 Hayses could protect it. I read it six weeks ago, and, as you say, a copy of the script is now on its way to me by mail, with the postmarks showing. If the Famous Players tried to lift the idea without paying you I could raise such hell that they wouldn't dare to go on. Simply let it be known that I read the story six weeks ago, and am familiar with it. That will be enough notice to Mankiewicz and company. In any case, Wanger would not stand for any robbery.

The main difficulty is to get the story loose from the Famous Players so that you may sell it to Cruze. I suggest coming to terms with him at once, but with the condition that the contract is not to go into effect until you are clear of the Famous Players contract. Cruze is a wise one. Sherman's march would greatly help the picture. Don't let Tully's alarms worry you. He believes that all movie men are thieves. This is true in general, but they are sometimes honest. I don't think either Wanger or Mankiewicz would care to get into a row in which I was interested. They know I have access to too many means of publicity.

Take things easily! You are fretting too damned much. Take a couple of days off, and go to Santa Monica, to the Miramar, to rest. Or go to San Francisco for a week. If you still have any bronchitis the fogs there will stop it. Mankiewicz will give you the time off. Tell him you want to write away from the lot.

Wanger should reach Hollywood in a week. I have already sent you a note for him. See him as soon as you can. I have impressed on him that you must be treated politely—that is, as politeness is understood in Hollywood.

You have made more progress in two weeks than any other writer has ever made in two months. Instead of being dissatisfied you ought to be thanking God on bended knee. Joe Hergesheimer fiddled with Vidor for four weeks, and then got nothing.[1] But here you already have one of the best directors in America intensely interested, and offering you money.

The Hays organization does NOT register scripts for authors. No such registration is necessary if you have witnesses. You can't copyright plots, but only words. It is sufficient, in the case of "The Promised Land," that Tully and I know what is in the script.

I kiss your hand 222 times.

Yours,
M

[1]By the end of 1925 Hergesheimer had been closely involved in six films.

ALS

HOTEL MARK TWAIN
HOLLYWOOD, CALIFORNIA

November the first, 1927

Dear Henry,

. . . You are quite right. I have yelled to you unmercifully. I'm terribly sorry! . . .

Yours,
S.

H. L. MENCKEN
1524 HOLLINS ST.
BALTIMORE

October 31st, 1927

Dear Sara:-

The MS. of "The Promised Land" is here. I opened it, but have preserved the envelope and noted the time of receipt on the MS.

Take things slowly, and be very careful about your health. . . .

The gossip you will hear on the lot is mainly buncombe. Every soul out there believes that he is a mixture of Charlie Chaplin[1] and Louis B. Mayer. But listen to it politely, and draw your own conclusions. I think you can be frank with Wanger. Tell him you want to deal with some one who keeps engagements.

You have got further in a few weeks than anyone else ever heard of. It is due to your high talent for being nice. They have never seen anything like you. You will descend into legend in those wilds.

Tell Mankiewicz you want to see Wanger, and have a letter from me to him.

I kiss your hand.

Yours,
M

[1] The comedian Charlie Chaplin had by this time already formed United Artists with Mary Pickford and D. W. Griffith.

H. L. MENCKEN

1524 HOLLINS ST.

BALTIMORE

November 1, 1927

Dear Sara:

I believe that it is of the utmost importance that you wait in Hollywood until Wanger shows up. Try to get Mankiewicz to keep you on the payroll until that time. I see no reason why your salary should stop so long as you are at work on Famous Players business. The chances are that Wanger will fire Mankiewicz when he gets to the front. Present my letter to him and tell him the whole truth at once. If he does business promptly, keep on with him, even although it may be at some preliminary sacrifice. If he delays like Mankiewicz or shows any reluctance otherwise, tell him that you feel that you are clear of your contract and then go to Cruze. I think that Tully probably will be able to hold off Cruze until the time is ready.

I am very fond of Marna and shall be delighted to see her in Baltimore. I am writing to her at the Algonquin at once and when she comes here I shall give a party for her and invite Miss de Roode and

Mayfield. That Marna is Jewish is news to me. I always took her for an Irish girl.

Don't be too touchy. Take the thing as a comedy, not as tragedy. After all, the Jews have been polite enough and I see no violation of your dignity in what has been going on. A drunken man is simply a drunken man. Once you get a fire built under Mankiewicz, he will jump quickly enough.

Yours,
M

HOTEL MARK TWAIN
HOLLYWOOD, CALIFORNIA
November the second, 1927

Henry dear,

Thank you so much for your letter about "The Promised Land." Jim Cruze called me this morning, and said we could come to terms as soon as I am free of the Famous Players contract. Jim Tully insists that he will try to get it for no less than twenty thousand, but if he does [not] I'll offer it to Wanger and United Artists. I know Cruze is terribly eager for it.

I hear that Wanger returned today. I'll probably see him on Monday.

In the meantime I called your Mrs. Slemons about a physician, and she is sending Dr. Mason in to see me tonight.[1] I am beginning to feel strangely wobbly and I thought I'd better see somebody. I know I have fretted and fumed and driven you half mad, but it has been pretty ghastly. You've been a dear and I'll love you forever for it.

Sara

[1]Dr. Mason went over her lungs and found nothing, but he advised her that the climate was "the worst in the world" for TB patients and not to stay there long. Sara's contract had been extended a week so that Wanger and Mankiewicz could read what she had brought in.

~

H. L. MENCKEN
1524 HOLLINS ST.
BALTIMORE

November 3rd, 1927

Dear Sara:-

I am sorry indeed to hear that you are running a temperature. Why not see Fishpaugh at once? I think a week of rest would restore you to normal. Why not ask for a week and go to San Francisco? The climate there is much more comfortable, and there is no dryness.

At this distance, advising you is very difficult. But I hope you don't give up the ship simply because there is intrigue on the lot. . . .

But above all, be careful about your health. You run temperatures easily. I think a few days at the Miramar, at Santa Monica, would help a lot. If you feel incapacitated, see Fishpaugh or Slemons.

I am beset by all sorts of visitors, and making heavy weather. Clarence Darrow and Lincoln Steffens are due in an hour.[1] Next week my sister is to have some house guests, and I am clearing out for New York.

Yours,

M

[1]After reportorial and editorial work on the New York *Evening Post* and the New York *Commercial Advertiser*, Steffens found his metier in *McClure's* magazine as a writer of muckraking articles exposing civic corruption, with Clarence Darrow helping him on numerous occasions. Steffens was author of *The Struggle for Self Government* and *Upbuilders*.

[TELEGRAM]

NOV 5 1927 12:03 AM

WESTERN UNION
HOLLYWOOD CALIF
12 NITE DO NOT DELR BEFORE 8:30 AM
H L MENCKEN

1524 HOLLINS ST BALTIMORE MD
WANGER APPARENTLY SOLD ON JELLYBEAN STORY   HOLDING OFF ON THE PROMISED LAND

S.H.

[TELEGRAM]

NOV 5 1927 9:41 PM

WESTERN UNION
BALTIMORE MD
MISS SARA HAARDT

HOTEL MARK TWAIN HOLLYWOOD CALIF
    WANGER NEWS EXCELLENT   CONGRATULATIONS   HOLD OFF THE
PROMISED LAND   ONE THING AT A TIME   IN CASE CRUZE NEGOTIA-
TIONS FAIL YOU CAN ALWAYS SUBMIT IT TO WANGER   NO NEWS OF
MARNA TULLY   CANNOT LOCATE HER IN NEW YORK   GOING THERE
MONDAY   MISS YOU TREMENDOUSLY

M.

[TELEGRAM]

NOV 6 1927 8:39 PM

WESTERN UNION
BALTIMORE MD
MISS SARA HAARDT

HOTEL MARK TWAIN HOLLYWOOD CALIF
    WANGER TELEGRAPHS AS FOLLOWS   HAVE HEARD SARA HAARDT'S
STORY WHICH IS EXCELLENT   SHE ALSO IS IN GOOD HEALTH   END
WANGER   THIS NEWS GREATLY RELIEVES ME   IF YOU RUN TEMPER-
ATURE BE SURE TO TAKE A WEEK OFF IN SAN FRANCISCO OR SANTA
MONICA   MY CHAPLAIN IS ON HIS KNEES

M.

H. L. MENCKEN
1524 HOLLINS ST.
BALTIMORE

November 5th, 1927

Dear Sara:-
    I am delighted to hear that Wanger has arrived, and that he is
interested in The Jelly-Bean. I knew he would stir things up. As for
The Promised Land, I counsel caution. Let the Cruze negotiations ride
until you find precisely how you stand with the Famous Players. It

may turn out to be advisable to let Wanger see the story, even at the cost of selling it for less than Cruze would pay. The Famous Players will probably long outlast the Cruze organization, and they use a greater variety of scenarios. I suggest saying nothing until you find out more. Remember that you can always submit The Promised Land to Wanger after you leave. Or resume business with Cruze after your Famous Players contract expires. Just how long it runs I don't know. If you are in doubt, you can see a lawyer when you get back here.

I think you can trust Wanger. Don't proceed on the theory that he is trying to rook you. Give him your confidence until he shows some sign of not deserving it. Don't forget that the Jews are naturally suspicious. And with good reason. Everyone they encounter is trying to get money out of them. . . .

Yours,
M

HOTEL MARK TWAIN
HOLLYWOOD, CALIFORNIA

November the sixth, 1927

Dear Henry,

It looks very much as if Wagner were sold on the jellybean story. Paramount wants such a piece to star Ruth Taylor[1] in, as a follow-up to GENTLEMEN PREFER BLONDES. She is made for the part of the girl uplifter. Wanger spoke of having Mal St. Clair direct it. If he does, and Ruth Taylor or Clara Bow[2] play the lead, it will be about as excellent a thing as the Art permits. When I told Wanger that the script had been in Mankiewicz's office for a week, without his reading it, he almost passed out.

I shall hold off on THE PROMISED LAND until this business is off. I am to have supper at the Cruzes tonight. Jim Cruze tells me that the treasurer of his corporation is coming on from New York this week, and he wants to put this picture in the budget for next year. Whether he will still want to pay me twenty thousand for it, I don't know. But I do know that he is terribly eager for it, and he would hate to see me sell it to Paramount or to Clarence Brown.[3]

This afternoon I am riding up the mountain to see Lorna Moon.[4] You perhaps know about her. She is dying of tuberculosis, and every morning Irving Thalberg[5] sends a secretary over for her to dictate a story for John Gilbert. She has wealth, beauty, and I think a very real talent for writing. I remember some very lovely things she did for the CENTURY.

I had dinner with the Stallings the other night, and Eleanor Boardman[6] and King Vidor were present.[7] Eleanor Boardman is rather charming; Helen Stallings tells me that she is her closest friend out here. But on the whole they seemed to me dull and ordinary. Still, all picture people, no matter what their pretenses, strike me the same way. The most amusing thing in this world is the high-brow complex running through the movies. The synthetic ladies boasting of their conquests among the literati; the gag writer, on the Paramount lot, who tells me that her favorite writer is Elinor Wylie;[8] poor little Jackie Logan, an ambitious movie star, trying to read Joyce and Gertrude Stein because she fears she must not only appear a lady, but an intellectual!; the Jews seizing upon the smallest crumb the critics have tossed them and tricking it out as sales talk. Perhaps I am all wrong. This may be a great Art I am engaged in; there may exist a lady in Hollywood I have never heard of—or perhaps a gentleman, but I am disposed to doubt it. The whole business, from end to end, is cheap and pretentious: a golden vacuum made in the image of a Joseph Hergesheimer on a week-end carousal.

Afterwards, we held a memorial service to the Confederacy. Laurence Stallings dreams of rebuilding his ancestral house in Caswell County, North Carolina, and there spending endless days.[9] I dream of spending one more Spring on the Meriwether plantation before I die.[10] The truth is that I confess to something like homesickness; for the South, or something of the South. As a Southerner you must have felt it too. At any rate, I like to think that you did. . . .

~

[1]One of the first to play "Lorelei Lee" in Anita Loos's film.

[2]American leading lady and the "It" girl of the 1920s, Clara Bow depicted the gay young flapper generation, and her wide-eyed vivacity was tremendously popular. *Mantrap*, one of Clara Bow's finest vehicles, had been released during 1927.

[3]The son of a cotton manufacturer, Clarence Brown had grown up in the South and graduated from the University of Tennessee at age nineteen with two degrees in engineering. His films became elaborate star vehicles for Greta Garbo, Rudolph Valentino, and Joan Crawford, but in later years he was underrated as a director.

[4]The Scottish short story writer (and author of *Dark Star*) had started as a scenarist for Cecil B. De Mille. She died of TB on May 1, 1930.

[5]Immortalized as Monroe Stahr in F. Scott Fitzgerald's *The Last Tycoon*. Everything that came out of MGM from 1924 to 1933 passed under Thalberg's eye. He carefully promoted the career of Greta Garbo and was later responsible for *The Barretts of Wimpole Street, Mutiny on the Bounty, The Good Earth*, and *Camille*. During 1927 Thalberg had married the actress Norma Shearer.

[6]American leading lady who married the American director King Vidor on September 8, 1926.

[7]Vidor's *The Big Parade*, made in 1925 but released in 1927, was the first important film depicting World War I.

[8]American poet and novelist. Her popularity was enhanced by poems of satire or fantasy appearing in *The Saturday Review of Literature*.

[9]Laurence Stallings had attended Wake Forest College at Wake Forest, North Carolina. He later settled only briefly in North Carolina, traveling and living in New York and using the "Forest Home" for the summer.

[10]Approximately 15 miles east of Montgomery, the plantation of the Meriwether family, which had settled the Mathews community. Sara had often gone there as a child.

[TELEGRAM]

NOV 8 1927 12:40 AM

WESTERN UNION
HOLLYWOOD CALIF
H L MENCKEN

HOTEL ALGONQUIN NEW YORK NY

CRUZE MEANS BUSINESS   PLANNING MILLION DOLLAR PRODUC-
TION   DO YOU ADVISE SUBMITTING STORY TO WANGER BEFORE CLO-
SING   TULLY SAYS HE WOULD SURELY OFFER MORE   CONTRACT UP

SATURDAY WIRE ME BEFORE TEN MARNA AT HOTEL ANSONIA YOUR TELEGRAMS RECEIVED MY DEVOTIONS

S.

[TELEGRAM]

NOV 8 1927 7:16 AM

WESTERN UNION
NEW YORK NY
MISS SARA HAARDT

HOTEL MARK TWAIN HOLLYWOOD CALIF
    STICK TO YOUR CONTRACT   TELL WANGER THE TRUTH   LUNCH-ING WITH MRS TULLY TODAY.

M.

[TELEGRAM]

NOV 8 1927 10:04 AM

POSTAL TELEGRAPH-COMMERCIAL CABLES
NEW YORK NY
MISS SARA HAARDT

HOTEL MARK TWAIN HOLLYWOOD CALIF
    ON MATURE REFLECTION STRONGLY ADVISE BEING COMPLETELY FRANK WITH WANGER   IF HE CAN'T USE STORY HIMSELF HE WILL LET YOU SELL IT TO CRUZE

M.

HOTEL MARK TWAIN
HOLLYWOOD, CALIFORNIA
November the eighth, 1927

Dear Henry,

Thank you so much for your telegrams. I shall talk frankly with Wanger the day my contract expires, and if he doesn't want the story I'll sell to Cruze. Cruze is getting impatient to close, for the reason that he wants to start production in February and I'll have to deal with him promptly if I am to deal with him at all. He is simply mad over the idea, and I think he would make a splendid picture. Betty Compson told me Sunday that he has talked of nothing else. He even has his cast picked.

I am glad that you are seeing Marna Tully. Jim has been priceless. Last night he brought Joe Bertucci around to call on me. Joe grew up in an orphanage, ran away and was a hobo for years. He is a typical bum with the most ingratiating manner I have ever seen. He and Jim fell to talking about their adventures on the road, and I sat down in the lobby for three hours listening to them. You have never heard anything so entertaining in your life.

I hope to run up to San Francisco, if I ever get through here. I have a conference with Schulberg today about the jellybean story. I am trying to rest as much as I can, but you can see the situation. In addition, a dozen Confederates have been at the Ambassador, calling me every minute, and in a weak moment I let Helen Stallings rope me in for three dinner parties she is giving this week.

My devotions always . . .
Sara

HOTEL MARK TWAIN
HOLLYWOOD, CALIFORNIA

November the ninth, 1927

Dear Henry,

I am making absolutely no headway with Walter Wanger and Paramount. He liked the jellybean story, as he wired you, and in the course of two days Schulberg called me. I went in to talk to him and Wanger hadn't even told him what it was about. I had to rehearse the whole thing again. He told me he liked it, and would I call at Mankiewicz's office this afternoon about staying on for a longer time. He would not say that he liked it well enough to pay me three thousand for it now, and he wouldn't guarantee that he would pay it after I had stayed this indefinite time.

Accordingly, I went to Mankiewicz's office this afternoon. He was out, as usual, and after waiting an hour he sauntered in and said he could tell me nothing. He hadn't seen Schulberg, he hadn't seen Wanger—and that being that I reminded him that my contract was up on Saturday and departed.

They mean, of course, to hold off and keep from paying for the story as long as possible; in the meantime I am unable to make any other connections, and it is very probable that they may not buy the story but use anything they please out of it. Regardless of what you feel about Walter Wanger's honesty, these are the facts. Oliver Garrett's story is in continuity, and he cannot get a penny out of them. They are even hedging around and saying that they are not sure they will take it.

Under the circumstances I shall certainly not consult with Wanger about THE PROMISED LAND. If Cruze wants to buy it, as he apparently does, I shall close with him and the deal can be kept secret until after I leave here. If he decides not to take it, I shall turn the whole business over to George Palmer Putnam[1] upon leaving here.

This is positively the last account I shall write you of this miserable business. It is futile to try to make you understand the conditions here; that Wanger, for all his deference to you, is no different from any other executive in the movie industry. His highbrow complex is a little more pronounced, he has definite social ambitions and a flair for Christian women not too unsightly. You can see the road I have travelled. If you still think I should be "frank" with him and offer THE PROMISED LAND to him after you receive this, please telegraph me. I hate to appear to be going against your advice, but these are the facts.

As ever,
Sara

[1] Agent, later publisher.

H. L. MENCKEN
1524 HOLLINS ST.
BALTIMORE

November 11th, 1927

Dear Sara:-

. . . Don't pay too much attention to Stallings. He professes a great contempt for the Jews, but is actually as hard a money-grubber as they are. That he is making any sacrifice by working for them I doubt. It is not probable that he could do much better work anywhere else than he is doing now. It is the fashion in Hollywood to denounce everyone as a moron. This is only partly true. There are some shrewd dogs hidden in the crowd. When the time comes to civilize the movies my guess is that Wanger will have more to do with the business than Stallings. He has some schemes, in fact, already.

It is capital news that you are homesick for the South. You ought to try a couple of weeks in the Middle West! They would make you burst into sobs at the sight of an Alabama country ham. California is not the worst. Some day you must take a look at New England.

I am in my usual low state, thank you.

Yours,
M

Will you let me hear of it when Eleanor Boardman achieves her destiny? I want to send her my blessings.[1]

M

[1]Eleanor Boardman was expecting a baby in a few weeks.

H. L. MENCKEN
1524 HOLLINS ST.
BALTIMORE

November 12th, 1927

Dear Sara:-

Beware of social relaxation in those wilds! Anon the tabloids will be reporting you engaged to some actor. It is the local notion of good publicity. Before he lets you leave town Wanger will inveigle you into the photograph gallery at the studio, and have you embalmed for the fans.

La Tully is somewhat vague about coming to Baltimore. If she pops up during the coming week I'll give her a party to split her head. She seems to be somewhat suspicious of Cruze. I am in communication with Misses Mayfield and de Roode. The day news reaches me that you have signed for "The Jellybean" I shall order them out, and fall upon a couple of bottles of Moselle.

At the end of the week I am going to Easton, Md., for the annual stag party of the learned. Then, on Sunday, I'll probably go up to Wilmington, and thence to West Chester.[1] I saw Joe in New York night before last, with his new flame, a tall lady named Carter nee Brekenridge, of Kentucky. He was all smiles. I suspect that Marjory Hathaway, the tenor's lady,[2] has given him the air.

It seems 10,000 years since I saw you.

Yours,
M

[1]Aileen Pringle had telephoned Joseph Hergesheimer and said she felt divided between the pleasures of being in West Chester and having Mencken meet her. "We think you ought to be here then and suggest that you find out from Aileen her plans and make your own, where we are altogether concerned, accordingly," Hergesheimer wrote to Mencken.

[2]Mrs. Charles Hathaway.

[TELEGRAM]

NOV 12 1927 9:43 AM

WESTERN UNION
HOLLYWOOD CALIF
H L MENCKEN

1524 HOLLINS ST
   WANGER HAS REFUSED JELLYBEAN STORY   TRYING TO CLOSE WITH CRUZE   IF I FAIL TULLY ADVISES GOING TO NEW YORK AND GIVING THE PROMISED LAND TO GEORGE PALMER PUTNAM   I FEAR IF I TELL WANGER STORY HE MAY DELAY ACTION FOR MONTHS AND KILL SALE WITH CRUZE WHAT DO YOU ADVISE

S.

[TELEGRAM]

NOV 13 1927 8:01 AM

WESTERN UNION
BALTIMORE MD
MISS SARA HAARDT

HOTEL MARK TWAIN   HOLLYWOOD CALIF
   ADVISE TRYING TO CLOSE WITH CRUZE   HAVE YOU ANOTHER STORY FOR WANGER   IF NOT TERMINATE YOUR CONTRACT AND COME HOME

M.

H. L. MENCKEN
1524 HOLLINS ST.
BALTIMORE

Sunday November 13, 1927

Dear Sara:-

Your letter describing your session with Schulberg and your night letter saying that Wagner has refused "The Jelly-Bean" came in this morning, and I sent you the enclosed telegram at once.

My fear is that Cruze is not too reliable, but if Wanger and his outfit have become impossible it is obviously best to give Cruze a chance. If you have nothing else to offer Wanger, notify him that you are terminating your contract. If he wants to go on with it, and discuss another story, I believe it would be well to stay a bit longer, even at the cost of stalling off Cruze some more. After all, if Cruze wants "The Promised Land" he will wait. But if the Wanger business looks hopeless, close with Cruze at once.

I am sorry indeed that there have been so many delays. But I think you are wrong to set them down to mere indifference and imbecility. After all, it takes some time to work out the possibilities of a picture—the casting, cost, direction, etc.—and many men have to be consulted. That the Famous Players, after buying a picture, would refuse to pay for it is sheer nonsense, Garrett to the contrary notwithstanding. But the delays are very exasperating, and I don't blame you for being tired of them.

I'll be here until Friday. On Saturday, Nov. 19th, my telegraphic address will be in care of Daniel M. Henry, Easton, Md. On Sunday and Monday, the 20th and 21st, it will be in care of Joe Hergesheimer, West Chester, Pa. Then I'll be back here for at least a week. When you head for home let me know exactly when you will arrive, and I'll meet you at the station.

I know nothing about Putnam. Is he an agent? If so, it may be well to take him on. You have learned the requirements of the Jews, and he may be able to sell an occasional scenario for you. Don't put down the trip to loss, even if you sell nothing at once. You have at least learned something about the business, and got paid for learning.

I only hope you are feeling better. A day or two at Santa Monica would do you a lot of good, and it is not far away. You say nothing about this.

I am in my usual whirligig. Willie Woollcott has come down with a duodenal ulcer, and will be in hospital for a couple of months. It is a distressing business: he has four children. But I think he'll get out safely. Louis Hamburger has him in charge.

God knows, I am eager for a sight of you.

Yours,

M

[TELEGRAM]

NOV 14 1927 6:00 AM

WESTERN UNION
HOLLYWOOD CALIF
H L MENCKEN

1524 HOLLINS ST   BALTIMORE MD
    SIGNING CONTRACT WITH CRUZE TOMORROW   HE WILL PAY TWENTY THOUSAND BY MARCH FIRST WHEN HE STARTS PRODUCTION   JIM TULLY HAS BEEN MARVELOUS AND BECAUSE OF YOU   I COULD NEVER HAVE SWUNG IT WITHOUT HIM   THE UNITED DAUGHTERS OF THE CONFEDERACY UNANIMOUSLY KISS YOUR BROW

S.

[TELEGRAM]

NOV 14 1927 7:17 AM

WESTERN UNION
BALTIMORE MD
MISS SARA HAARDT

HOTEL MARK TWAIN   HOLLYWOOD CALIF
    FELICITATIONS   CRUZE SHOULD MAKE PAYMENT ON ACCOUNT AT ONCE   INSIST ON IT   SHOW THIS TO TULLY

MENCKEN

~

HOTEL MARK TWAIN
HOLLYWOOD, CALIFORNIA

November the fourteenth, 1927

Dear Henry,

I can't imagine how you managed to achieve any confidence in Walter Wanger. He has been rude, inefficient and negligent with me. I would certainly have lost the deal with Cruze, if I had played with him. As it is Cruze has made a payment on the twenty thousand, the rest to be paid in by February 11th. There is not the slightest doubt that he is sincere. He plans a million and a half dollar production, and is already trying out for the cast and making other preparations. I must say that of all people I have met in this business, he is the most honest and fair.

I had a conference with Wanger this morning and told him that I had sold a story to another corporation for twenty-five thousand. He changed his tactics at once, called Schulberg in, and made me the magnanimous offer of staying on here at two fifty a week for another four weeks and working on another story for them. I told him I would give him my answer tomorrow.

As for Stallings, he certainly is no better than anybody else in the industry. I wouldn't trust him any more than I would trust Wanger or Schulberg. The fact that he is in pictures at all has to be explained. Or rather, the fact that he remains in pictures when he has had a chance to get out with as much money as he has made certainly puts him in the same class with the Jews and the other fakirs. That is, if he thinks he has any literary talent. As a matter of fact he is done in pictures. He is writing revisions of Ben Ames Williams' stories, if you please.

Despite the line Walter Wanger has shot you about civilizing the movies, the atrocities go on just the same, and he is as much responsible for them as anybody else. But more of this anon, if we ever meet.

THE PROMISED LAND promises to be one of the biggest pictures of the year, but after all it is a picture and a picture is distinctly a picture—and no more. I am delighted, of course, that Cruze is so enthusiastic about it. He has planned some beautiful and costly stuff—as pictures go—but it will come no more to being a work of art than a story in TRUE CONFESSIONS is a work of art by your standards. Such is my belief in this highly organized skin game, and such is my belief of every person who has stuck in it for whatever reason.

You have been a dear to see me through it all. I am desperately tired, now that the strain is over. If I can, I'll probably run off somewhere before I decide anything.

As ever,

S

[TELEGRAM]

NOV 16 1927 11:30 PM

WESTERN UNION
BALTIMORE
MISS SARA HAARDT

HOTEL MARK TWAIN   HOLLYWOOD CALIF
WANGER WIRES QUOTE AM TRYING TO KEEP MISS HAARDT LONGER END QUOTE DOES THIS MEAN ANYTHING   SURELY HOPE YOU INDUCE CRUZE TO MAKE A PAYMENT DOWN   LET ME KNOW BRIEFLY BY NIGHTLETTER WHAT THE SITUATION IS   LEAVE HERE FRIDAY FOR EASTERN SHORE AT HERGESHEIMER'S HOUSE SUNDAY NIGHT

M.

[TELEGRAM]

NOV 16 1927 11:36 PM

WESTERN UNION
HOLLYWOOD CALIF
H L MENCKEN

1524 HOLLINS ST   BALTIMORE MD
CRUZE HAS MADE PAYMENT ON THE PROMISED LAND   IS ALREADY PREPARING MILLION AND HALF DOLLAR PRODUCTION   I CLOSED DEAL WITH HIM AFTER CONTRACT WITH PARAMOUNT EXPIRED   WANGER ASKED ME TO RENEW CONTRACT FOR FOUR WEEKS   I SIGNED WITH

HIM YESTERDAY   MY BEST THANKS FOR YOUR TELEGRAM AND LET-
TERS   I HOPE YOU HAVE A LOVELY TIME AT WESTCHESTER
S.H.

H. L. MENCKEN
1524 HOLLINS ST.
BALTIMORE

November 18th, 1927

Dear Sara:-

You are both right about Wanger and wrong. He is highly intelligent, and knows what is wrong with the movies, but his attitude
toward them is the usual one: he is getting what he can while the
going is good. Discourtesy goes with the business. It was organized
by bounders, and is still mainly run by them. I am delighted that you
let him have a hint of the Cruze business. Its immediate effect was to
get you $1,000. And he will probably buy a story from you.

I think you are too pessimistic. Where is your sense of humor? You
go out a stranger, tackle the Jews in their lair, and get enough money
to enable you to defy the world for four or five years. Is the thing, in
its details, unpleasant? Well, so would working on a newspaper be
unpleasant, or teaching in a college. Most money is got unpleasantly.
But it is a useful thing to have.

I see nothing infra dig about doing a movie or two. Joseph Conrad
was quite willing to do it.[1] Shaw has been haggling with the Jews for
years.[2] True enough, the permanent literati of Hollywood are swine,
but you are not among them. You have accomplished more than
Hergesheimer accomplished on his last attempt. I think you deserve
three cheers.

You say nothing about your health. How are you feeling? I surely
hope you go to San Francisco. It will rest you, and it is worth seeing.

Poor Willie Woollcott is in a desperate state.[3] He had a horrible
stomach hemorrhage yesterday morning, and if another comes on he
will probably die. But there is still a chance that he may get through.
His poor wife is distracted. Pearl and I are going to the Eastern Shore
this afternoon, but the party is spoiled, for Woollcott was to go along.
If he is still alive Sunday I shall proceed to West Chester. He is too
ill to be visited.

I am quitting the Tribune as of January 1st, and have arranged with the Evening Sun to skip articles when I don't feel like writing them. During the past two months I have more than earned my retainer in various other ways. Thus the way begins to clear for Homo sapiens.

I am glad you are dragging the additional $1000 out of Wanger, but it begins to seem a ghastly time since I last saw you. When I get back I shall organize a party with Miss Mayfield and Miss de Roode, and we can gabble about you.

Yours,
M

[1]*Victory* (Paramount-Artcraft, 1919), *Lord Jim* (Paramount, 1925), *The Silver Treasure* (from *Nostromo*, Fox Film Corp., 1926), and *The Road to Romance* (MGM, 1927) had all been made into films, with 10 more to follow.

[2]Shaw was an ardent filmgoer since the flickering Charlie Chaplin talkies. His first English talkie, *How He Lied to Her Husband*, adapted from a play he wrote in 1904, came out in 1929. It was followed in later years by *Caesar and Cleopatra*, with Vivien Leigh, *Pygmalion*, with Leslie Howard, *Major Barbara*, and others.

[3]William "Willie" Woollcott, Saturday night club composer and brother to the author and journalist Alexander Woollcott.

H. L. MENCKEN
1524 HOLLINS ST.
BALTIMORE

Sunday, November 18, 1927

Dear Sara:-

I surely hope you don't think the trip to Hollywood was wasted. After all, the show was worth seeing, despite the exasperations. You have had a journey across the Continent at the Jews' expense, enough money to live on, and a chance to meet some interesting people. Such experiences are always worth while. You'll be dredging material out of this one for years.

The muck and fraud won't look so bad a year hence. A novelist must take an occasional header into the muck. I think you needed it especially, for you have been leading a very quiet life. So no matter how it comes out, chalk it up to profit. So speaks Polonius.

I hope the Cruze business goes through, but I am distrustful of Cruze. He is a hard trader, a genuine peasant.

As for Wanger, I don't think you owe him anything. Don't think you have to be polite to him on account of me. As the account stands between us, he is in my debt. If he is too incompetent to get anything out of you, then it is his own fault.

I am crazy to see you again.

Yours,
M

Marcia Heath's mother, aged 77, is in hospital. Before you leave will you call up Marcia and ask about the old lady?

HOTEL MARK TWAIN
HOLLYWOOD, CALIFORNIA

November the eighteenth, 1927

Dear Henry,

Thank you so much for your letters. I needed them more than I can ever tell you. This business has been fiendish. Paramount did not notify me until the last hour on last Saturday that they would do "The Jellybean." Walter Wanger assigned the job to Mankiewicz, and he handed me a pink slip signed by Schulberg saying that it was satisfactory for me to return to New York. In brief, I was out. Walter Wanger, during all this time, hadn't called me and I would have left Hollywood without another word with him, as far as he was concerned.

As you can imagine, I was in the depths. I called Jim Tully and we debated whether to play Cruze here or wait until I got to New York. Finally I was so tired and desperate I told Jim it would be worth twenty thousand to have the thing decided one way or another. I left him in the lobby and came up here and called Jim Cruze and told him I was leaving town Monday: if he wanted to see me again he would have to come in—that is, if he was still interested in THE PROMISED LAND. He said he would send in for me Sunday afternoon, and he would settle it then.

Remember, all this time Cruze has never had a word on paper from me. I took Jim Tully with me, and we arrived before all of Hollywood that congregates there on Sunday. Jim Cruze took me in the back of the house, and we fought for one solid hour. He undoubtedly is mad for the story, but he wanted an option from now until the first of March for $1,000. I said no, if he really wanted it as badly as he said he did he could pay me $1,500 and the rest on Feb. 11th. Well, he finally gave in. It doesn't sound like anything to you, but you simply can't imagine what a victory it meant over him. I fought and hedged and lied until I hated myself and could have wept; and all the while registering a sweet aloofness that admitted nothing. When he agreed to my terms, and I agreed to meet his treasurer at the Metropolitan Studio at nine the next morning—believe it or not, he came over and kissed my hand! I might add that, peasant or no, he essayed it in the grand manner.

As a matter of fact, he is the most honest and by all odds the most attractive and competent man I have met in this art. He invited me to come on his set the next morning—he is directing "The Red Mark"—and his work is like nothing seen on the Paramount lot. Moreover, the man has a strange dignity. I confess to a liking for him, which is natural enough when you consider that, for all his hardness, he has been fair and downright with me. The minute he knew he had the story, he told it all over the place. He brought three movie stars up and asked me if they would do for several parts. He says that this picture will be just as big as he makes it, and he means to put everything he has into it, in addition to over a million dollars. I am aware of the fact that he lies and exaggerates too, else he wouldn't be in pictures, but I have a feeling that if he does it, it will be as big as such things go.

He will undoubtedly do it—unless Famous Players contest it. Jim Tully was amazed that he gave in to my terms. He says he has never been as eager for a picture before, and he has never paid more than five thousand dollars for one.

The minute I signed the contract with him I got in a taxi and rode over to the Paramount lot. There I managed to see Walter Wanger and told him I had just sold an idea for twenty five thousand dollars. He was simply aghast. As a matter of fact, he thought I came in to bid him a sweet good-bye and started explaining about the other story—a lot of alibis that let him out of the blame. When he had finished I quietly announced that I had just sold this idea, and I felt sorry that I hadn't had any closer cooperation on his lot.

In a flash, all his ingratiating and decorative manner fell away from him. He was simply an excited, grasping Jew who had in some way been outwitted. He took down the telephone and yelled into it, and in two minutes Schulberg was there and they were trying to get me to stay on. If I did they promised me this and that, all the cooperation I wanted, everything on the lot. I told them I would let them know in the morning. In the meantime, Wanger sent you that telegram. He never in the world would have asked me to stay, or put himself out to be courteous, if I hadn't faced him with the other sale. Then, immediately, he turns it to account with you.

I agreed to stay on the next day solely because you had advised me to in previous letters. He did not offer me more than two hundred and fifty a week, which is rather scandalous under the circumstances. I confess that I have treated him with more politeness than I would have dreamed of, because you did seem to have such confidence in him. If I have an illusion left in this world, it seems to be trusting your judgements completely and implicitly. But in this instance, I can't help feeling you are—deceived in him.

He tried by every wile to get me to tell him what company I had sold, and then tried to worm the idea out of me. I told him it was an idea I had projected for a novel, and that it had been in your possession before I came to Hollywood. I live in mortal terror of their claiming it belongs to them, and stopping Cruze from going on with it.

All this happened over a week ago. Since then, I have heard nothing from nobody on the Paramount lot. Nobody has called me about any ideas I may have and I haven't seen a sign of the close cooperation I was to have had. I'll probably leave without seeing a sign of it too.

I am dead tired. Within the next day or two I shall certainly call Mrs. Heath for you, and inquire about her mother. I wrote her a note when I came here, and forwarded your letter, but I have heard nothing from her. It isn't the sweetest situation in the world, but for you, I fear, I'd commit worse than that . . .

I hope you've had a lovely time in West Chester!

As ever,

Sara

~

HOTEL MARK TWAIN
HOLLYWOOD, CALIFORNIA
November the nineteenth, 1927

Dear Henry,

I enclose a letter from our Marjorie[1] for your perusal. I insist that there is no one quite like her. The picture she gives of Virginia's future alma mater is instructive, to say the least.[2] Please tear it up when you have read it.

Jim Tully tells me that Marna is due to arrive in the morning. He assumes a vast indifference, but the truth is he has been very lonely without her.

Your predictions are all awry. What social relaxation I have found has been quite outside the bounds of Hollywood. And not even Walter Wanger, I fear, could inveigle me into being photographed on a movie lot. I did have dinner with Clarence Brown the other night, and discovered that he directed a picture in Montgomery ten years ago. He talks now of going up to Folsom and seeing Ernest Booth about the rights of "We Rob a Bank." He says it would make a beautiful movie. I know that Wanger plans to send Oliver Garrett up about "Ladies of the Mob," but I believe Brown would do a better job.

I dread these next three weeks. I have written Margaret de Roode to rent my rooms in the apartment until the first of January. My contract is up here the middle of December.

But enough of my miseries! What of *Homo Sapiens?* Who is doing the Check List? And what good stuff have you bought for the *Mercury* lately?

I sat for William van Dresser an hour today while he sketched me in charcoal—a last tribute to my waning pulchritude. Tonight I have an engagement to dance at the Roosevelt with his engaging young son.

I am having tea with Mrs. Slemons on Tuesday. She is a most charming person, and has been awfully nice. I tried to get Mrs. Heath over the telephone today, but she was out. I shall try again within the next day or two, and inquire about her mother.

Your brow is kissed!

As ever,
Sara

¹Marjorie Nicolson, dean of Smith College.

²Virginia went on to attend Sweet Briar College. Mencken helped pay for her four years.

HOTEL MARK TWAIN

HOLLYWOOD, CALIFORNIA

November the twenty-second, 1927

Dear Henry,

Walter Wanger called me today in a great hurry, and asked me to come to the studio within the hour. When I arrived there he wanted to know what I was working on. I told him a youth movement story for Ruth Taylor, featuring the same color and character as "The Jellybean." He then told me to stop work on it, and start something for Pola Negri.¹ I am supposed to evolve an idea overnight and report to him tomorrow at twelve. It is rather a large order, and I am terribly tired—too tired, I fear, for a great inspiration even for the movies; but I dredged up something tonight, after four hours, and I'll manage to get it to him somehow.

I had tea with Louise Garrett this afternoon, and she tells me that Laurence Stallings is furious over the idea of my having written a story dealing with South America. It seems that he was at Jim Cruze's yesterday and Cruze was outlining his plans for THE PROMISED LAND to him. Laurence races away, swearing to everybody that he is working on a novel dealing with South America and that my picture will ruin the movie rights to it. He even told the Garretts that he had told me the plot of the novel, and that I had doublecrossed him. Can you imagine it! I give you my word he has never discussed his novel with me. He did tell me the plot of a picture he was doing, but it doesn't touch upon my story in the slightest.

I hate to drag you into such a mess, but I am sticking to the story that you saw the outline of THE PROMISED LAND before I came to Hollywood, and that I was planning to do a novel on it. The whole thing is wearying me to death. The truth is that, coming at this time, the amount I received for the story is almost sensational. All the studios are cutting the prices they pay for stories in half. I doubt if Wanger would have offered me more than ten thousand for it, if I had given him a chance at it. Laurence Stallings himself only got twenty-five thousand for WHAT PRICE GLORY. Wanger offered him twenty thousand for it. When you consider that I have had no real success to trade on here, that my name is worth nothing in publicity, it is astounding. Katharine Michel—Mankiewicz's secretary—told me that the critics on the Paramount lot were staggered, and many of them are holding that I didn't make the sale. Mankiewicz refused to believe it until Wanger told him he thought it was true. Wanger believes that I sold it to Metro-Goldwyn.

I think I promised that I wouldn't burden you with another recitation of woe, but the temptation is too great. What a relief to share my miseries with you!

Yours,
Sara

'During the mid 1920s the new dominance of the female star emerged. Pola Negri, the earthy and tempestuous Polish-born Apollonia Chalupek, had been a leading lady on the German stage before she arrived at Paramount in 1923.

[TELEGRAM]

NOV 27 1927 12:16 AM

WESTERN UNION
THANKSGIVING GREETING
BALTIMORE MD
MISS SARA HAARDT

HOTEL MARK TWAIN HOLLYWOOD CALIF
   GET RID OF YOUR COMPLEXES AND GIVE THANKS TO GOD   YOU HAVE DONE BETTER THAN ANYONE ELSE EVER HEARD OF AND THE END IS NOT YET   STICK IT OUT FOR THE TWO WEEKS REMAINING AND THEN COME HOME AND LAUGH   WHAT A NOVEL LIES IN YOUR HANDS

MAYFIELD AND
MENCKEN.

H. L. MENCKEN
1524 HOLLINS ST.
BALTIMORE

November 24th, 1927

Dear Sara:-

Miss Mayfield and I telegraphed to you last night, protesting against your gloom. You have really got further than any other writer who ever went to Hollywood, and we are proud of you. . . .

Miss Mayfield says you talk of coming back to Baltimore by way of Montgomery. Is this your plan? If so, when do you leave, when do you get to Montgomery, and when do you reach Baltimore? I now begin to feel that it was during the Early Mesozoic that I saw you roll out of Union Station.

This is Thanksgiving Day—and the usual horror. My sister is in bed with violent pains. She has had them at 2 year intervals. Ketzke has just left. He thinks they are probably due to a kidney stone, or something of the sort. When she gets out of bed he and Hamburger will give her a complete examination. She is ordinarily very healthy, but these pains have come on now and then since an appendectomy, ten or twelve years ago. They knock her out completely.

My niece demands a diamond ring for Christmas—at twelve! What a gold-digger! I am suggesting to her delicately that such gauds do not befit her tender years.

I am in my usual low state.

Yours,

M

La M and I had a session in your praise at Schellhase's. We shall resume it at the wop's. Schellhase, his wife and old Anna asked after you tenderly, and wanted to know why they saw me so seldom.

HW

HOTEL MARK TWAIN
HOLLYWOOD, CALIFORNIA

November the twenty-fifth, 1927

Dear Henry,

It was so nice to have your telegram yesterday. I hope you and Mayfield drank a julep in my memory.

I had a very lovely time with the Slemons. Dr. Slemons, it turns out, is a nephew of Josiah Morris[1] who was a celebrated figure in Montgomery in the olden days and one of my grandfather's closest friends. He was president of the Josiah Morris Bank that failed so sensationally, and carried most of the fortunes in Montgomery down with it. None of us ever knew just how much my grandfather lost, but it was close to fifty thousand—a fortune in those days.

What a world!

I am off to dine with the Tully's in another moment. My devotions!

Sara

[1]A native of Maryland, Josiah Morris arrived in Montgomery in 1852 and opened a private banking house, which from its commencement was a huge success. His financial assistance made possible the founding of Birmingham, Alabama. There is no written record of the bank's failing.

HOTEL MARK TWAIN
HOLLYWOOD, CALIFORNIA

November the twenty-third, 1927

Dear Henry,

. . . The news that you are dropping the *Tribune* contract is excellent. How you have accomplished all the work in connection with it these past two years, together with all your other work, is a marvel. I hope you let the *Sun* business slide too, if it harasses you. I begrudge the time you have given to them as it is. Heaven knows you have earned a vacation from everything that proves of the slightest interference with Homo sapiens.

I have had three conferences with Wanger in the last two days. He poured out his life story and life ambition to me today, and concluded by reading his *American Mercury* article aloud. I do appreciate his intelligence. He is quick and shrewd, and he knows how to use people. I cooked up a Negri story for him last night, and he says he likes it immensely. What will come of it I don't know, but I am to whip it in shape and then work on it with Lloyd Sheldon.[1]

Don't bother to call Mayfield and Polly de Roode. You couldn't stand them for a whole evening. I have written nothing about my affairs here to anybody but you. Goucher is beginning to get alarmed over my staying on. I hear from one or the other of the faculty every day. They imagine, with their usual naivete, that I am having a thrilling time of it, and that I'll wind up in a mansion on Beverly Hills.

I doubt that I'll get up to San Francisco, now that this Negri business is on. I tire very easily here in this ghastly climate, but I can stick it out if I am careful.

The literati are staging a huge celebration Thanksgiving night, but I am ducking it and having dinner with the Slemons. I haven't seen Marna Tully since her return, and I begin to fear for Jim. He has been in a very low state the past two weeks. I'll let you hear how he is.

I continue to bore and irritate you with recitations of the atrocities here, and you continue to accuse me of having lost my presence and sense of humor. Well, you have been a dear—and I love you a lot for it.

Yours,
SH

¹By 1917 Sheldon had contributed 150 short stories, novelettes, and articles to national magazines and 48 feature films by various companies. He was an associate producer at Paramount until 1936.

H. L. MENCKEN
1524 HOLLINS ST.
BALTIMORE

November 23, 1927

Dear Sara,

My most sincere and hearty congratulations. You did a superb job with Cruze and I am delighted to hear of it. You greatly under-estimate your talents as a business woman. After all, you managed to knock off Cruze for a superb contract and to get twice as much out of Wanger as you expected to get when you reached Hollywood. My prediction is that he will yet come back for "The Jelly Bean." Joe Hergesheimer told me yesterday that he had lately met Jesse Lasky and told him (Lasky) that if his organization failed to get a scenario out of you it would go down to eternal infamy as a band of imbeciles. Joe, as you know, was immensely impressed by "Licked." He has mentioned it every time I have met him.

When does your second contract expire, and when do you expect to reach Baltimore? Let me know of it as far in advance as possible so that I may be on hand to greet you. Some time before the end of the week Miss Mayfield and I hope to have lunch together. I needn't assure you that we will drink your health.[1]

Six weeks after you get back to Baltimore you'll be roaring over your experiences. Completely aside from the cash revenue that they have brought you, they'll be worth thousands of dollars to you.

Sincerely,

M

[1] Mencken was meeting Sara Mayfield often so he could talk about Sara Haardt. During that lunch Mencken said they came to the conclusion that Sara was not only "the most beautiful" writer they knew but also "the most charming" and the "luckiest."

H. L. MENCKEN

1524 HOLLINS ST.

BALTIMORE

November 25, 1927

Dear Sara,

. . . Don't tell me that you are having a lonely time in Hollywood. My spies report that you are not only a success in the literary sphere but also a grand success socially. There are broad hints indeed that no less than seven head of handsome actors have got mashed on you. I have put another spy to work and expect the details shortly.

The letter of the lovely Marjorie is charming. She points the way to a superb story, scenario or even novel. Imagine what could be made of the demoralization wrought by a few rich gals! Some time ago I was told that my old friend, Edgar Speyer, had sent his daughter $1500.00 as spending money between the end of September and Christmas of last year. This must have bought a gigantic stock of lip sticks, cream puffs and gin. There have been plenty of college films, but I don't recall any dealing with a women's college. . . .

I am off to New York on Sunday for a round of dizzy social gaiety. That is to say, I am doomed to eat a solemn dinner at the Knopf's, to spend another evening listening to Madeleine Boyd, and to put in most of the rest of my time in the society of homely lady literati, each of them with something to sell. But on one glorious evening I shall dine with Phil Goodman and his wife, and then go down on one of the German steamers for a session in the bar.

Yours,
M

FAMOUS PLAYERS - LASKY CORPORATION
PARAMOUNT PICTURES
WEST COAST STUDIOS
HOLLYWOOD, CALIFORNIA

November the twenty-sixth, 1927

Henry dear,

. . . I had dinner with the Cruzes last night, and Jim Cruze told me that Laurence Stallings said THE PROMISED LAND had killed the picture rights of the novel he is writing. He told the Garretts he couldn't understand why I hadn't told him the idea for the picture, or at least told him I was working on it. The truth is that he is money mad and he resents Cruze making a road-show of it. He has told a number of people that he was going to call me about it, but he hasn't done it.

The whole thing is upsetting, but it is just another phase of the business. The rivalry and jealousy among the socalled writers here is unimaginable. Laurence actually resents my selling a story that he missed out on, for no other reason than he didn't know the stuff. Cruze has been trying to get an epic out of him for months. He knows the plot of Laurence's novel, and he says it doesn't compare with THE PROMISED LAND for pictures.

It is very probable that Cruze will do it as his next picture. He is full of plans and preparations, and already has the scenario in its first treatment. He has asked me to join his staff during the while he shoots the thing. He says he could teach me everything I would ever want to know about pictures in that time—all the technicalities and the tricks that Laurence talks so much of. But I am truly not interested.

It is a trickster's art and a trickster's business, and for my part I'd
rather come back to Baltimore and finish my novel.

My devotions!

Sara

H. L. MENCKEN

1524 HOLLINS ST.

BALTIMORE

November 25th, 1927

Dear Sara:-

In God's name don't be so full of alarms and sensitive to atrocities.
The report about Stallings seems incredible. Certainly he is not insane.
You are quite free to write all the South American novels and scenarios
you please, regardless of what he is doing. If it turns out that he
actually suspects you of taking a suggestion from him show him this
letter. I remember that you told me the whole story of The Promised
Land in September, immediately after our lunch with Dr. Williams,
and that you showed me the complete scenario at least two weeks
before you went to Hollywood. The whole business is absolutely clear
in my mind. I remember many details of the story. Tell Cruze and
Stallings that I am willing to make affidavit to all this, and to come
out to Hollywood and testify to it in court until the very judge drops
dead. Stallings is not an idiot. He certainly knows that your story is
not his, and that you are perfectly free to write it and sell it. Never
believe what Hollywood gossips tell you. It is possible that Stallings
may have got tight, and deplored the fact that your story invaded the
field that he thought he had to himself. But if he ever claimed a
monopoly on that field, I'd be delighted to come out and butcher him
legally.

I think you are far too sensitive to the natural difficulties of your
job. First you complain because Wanger doesn't see you, and then
because he sends for you. In one letter you say you are going to a
dance, and in the very next you say you are tired. Play the game
according to the local rules, and laugh at its follies. Whatever Wanger
may say, he certainly doesn't expect you to complete a whole movie
in 24 hours. If you want a rest, tell him you can't work in Hollywood,
and go to Santa Monica or to San Francisco for a week. You say yourself

that the amount you got from The Promised Land was sensational, and yet you act as if your whole trip were a failure. I think you ought to view the situation more reasonably, and with more humor. You have done immensely well, and gathered in a great deal of new and valuable experience. What if the place is full of fraud and pretense? So is New York. Between the two, in fact, Hollywood has the better of it.

Yours,

M

Tully probably has Asiatic cholera. Give him my love.

November the twenty-eighth, 1927

Dear Henry,

My contract is up here either the tenth or the seventeenth of December. If Wanger takes this story I am working on he'll probably want me to stay until the seventeenth. In that case I would be arriving in the East a few days before Christmas, and knowing that you would probably be in Pittsburgh or West Chester for the holidays, I have been thinking that it would be pleasanter if I stopped off in Montgomery until the first of January. The memory of last Christmas is too fresh for me to contemplate coming to Baltimore if you would be away for any length of time after I arrived. And you usually are away during the holidays. What are your plans? Now that my time here is getting short, I am impatient to see you. I have missed you more than I ever dare tell you.

I had lunch with the Garretts today, and Oliver tells me that Laurence Stallings is very outraged with me. He insinuates that I have broken every law of decency by not having told him that I was working upon THE PROMISED LAND, and he still claims that he told me the idea of his novel. He told Oliver that he had called here three times and left messages for me to call him, but I have never received a notice of them from the office. It is certainly an unpleasant situation, but I truly don't know what can be done about it.

You are a dear for saying such nice things about my adventures here. If I have accomplished anything, it has been due to your own counsel and confidence!

As ever,

Sara

HOTEL MARK TWAIN
HOLLYWOOD, CALIFORNIA

November the twenty-ninth, 1927

Dear Henry,

. . . You are perfectly right when you call me insane, humorless, unreasonable, unaccountable, delirious. In addition, I miss you most terribly.

Yours,
SH

ALS

HOTEL ALGONQUIN
NEW YORK

November 29, 1927

Dearest Sara:

You are now among the most talented photographers in Christendom. If you come home without a noble likeness of yourself for your humble slave he will feel himself justified in raising hell.

As ever,
M

THE AMERICAN MERCURY
730 FIFTH AVENUE
NEW YORK

November 29th, 1927

Dear Sara:

Nathan believes that it would be extremely unwise to put yourself into the hands of Putnam. He says that a far better agent is Richard J. Madden of the American Play Company. Madden handles only the work of established authors, but with a film or two behind you and the interest of Nathan, he'd certainly be glad to take over anything you do hereafter. I therefore suggest that you make no contract, or even contact, with Putnam until you get back to the East.

Yours,
M

ALS

THE AMERICAN MERCURY
730 FIFTH AVENUE
NEW YORK

November 29, 1927

Dear Sara:

May I ask, with all due respect, when in Hell are you coming back to Baltimore? It begins to seem centuries and centuries since you left. La Mayfield and I sat mourning for 2 hours the other day. The Schellhase's want to know what has become of you, and old Anna refuses to believe, as I tell her, that you have become a movie star.

I am clearing off accumulated debris, and shall begin work Jan. 1st.

M

HOTEL MARK TWAIN
HOLLYWOOD, CALIFORNIA

December the first, 1927

Dear Henry,

Eleanor Boardman has a daughter, born last Friday. But perhaps you have already heard.

I had a conference with Wanger yesterday. He assumes that my contract is up the seventeenth of December, but he likes the story I am doing for Negri very much, and spoke of my staying on several weeks longer and working with a scenarist on the script. He made some excellent suggestions about the story himself. I haven't fully made up my mind about it.

I spent the day in Pasadena with Mrs. Slemons. Her friends are very charming, and I had a lovely time.

I am sending you a little ivory figure that I found on a shopping tour with Marna. It isn't a Christmas present, or any kind of a present,—so don't fuss at me for sending it; it's just rather nice, and belongs in your collection.

Yours,
S

H. L. MENCKEN
1524 HOLLINS ST.
BALTIMORE

December 1st, 1927

Dear Sara:-

Don't let the enclosed worry you.[1] Obviously, the thing was given out by the arch-ass, Baker. I was in New York on Monday, and so heard nothing of it. If I had been here, I'd have prohibited it, of course. But don't let it annoy you too much. Such things are bound to get into print. I only hope that Cruze has made a payment down. Has he? You send me no news. And how is the Negri business going?

I have sent Mary Parmenter a note that she will undoubtedly show to Baker. It denounces him as the champion imbecile of the Western World.

As for the portrait, Bachrach is a scoundrel.[2] You are at least 7,000 times more lovely. I order, command and beseech you to sit to one of the Hollywood artists, that I may pin a print to my chest when I am hanged, a la Whittemore.

I am delighted to hear that you found the Slemonses so pleasant. Slemons himself is a capital fellow, and a very good surgeon. Don't bother about the Heaths. I suppose that the old lady has died, or is dying. She is close to 80.

Yours,

M

[1]Sara Haardt had written a note to Harry Baker, in answer to a question he had asked, saying that her success with James Cruze was probably due to the English instruction she had received from Goucher. Baker then informed the Baltimore *Evening Sun*, which published a long story on November 29 under the headline "Goucher Graduate Sells Moving Picture Scenario. Miss Sara Haardt, Member of Class of 1920, Receives $25,000." The article went on to say that the first news of her success had been received by Harry Baker, who was quoted as saying that Sara had thanked him for his courses on literature that she took at Goucher College in 1919.

[2]Photograph that accompanied article.

~

H. L. MENCKEN
1524 HOLLINS ST.
BALTIMORE

December 2, 1927

Dear Sara:

Stallings is a cheap and vain fellow. If he gives you any trouble, show him my telegram and also show it to Cruze. It would be a great pleasure to get into action against him. He has been bellowing around Hollywood for a year past about the great sacrifices he has made by working for the Jews. The plain fact is that there is very little probability that, even if he were released, he could do writing of any serious value. His lust for money and his inconceivable vanity have combined to make him ridiculous. . . .

Don't let the Baker indiscretion bother you. Publicity is never objectionable to film magnates. I am only sorry that I was not in Baltimore at the time. If I had heard of the story I'd certainly have had it killed instantly. The photograph that appeared with it was a gross libel. I renew my respectful suggestion that you posture while you are on the Coast for one of the artists there resident. They really are capital photographers.

Yours,
M

HOTEL MARK TWAIN
HOLLYWOOD, CALIFORNIA

December the fifth, 1927

Dear Henry,

I have almost had a relapse over that dreadful story Harry Baker gave to the SUN. As I feared, practically every paper in Alabama copied it; letters and telegrams are pouring in, and altogether I feel like heaven's prize fool. Nothing can be done about it, I suppose, but if you ever have the opportunity I hope you tell him what an embarrassing situation he has created. Whether it has been published out here or not, I don't know, but I certainly hope it doesn't get to Cruze. He has made no announcement as yet, and of course it is his business to do so.

I thought I wrote you that Cruze has made a payment of $1500. I banked it in a savings account, where it is now reposing. If he ever pays the other $18,500 I shall want you to tell me what to do with it.

I shall probably be able to write you more definitely about my plans after Wednesday, when I am to see Wanger again about the Negri story. I have rewritten it on the basis of his suggestions. He may propose that I remain here for some weeks longer and work with a scenarist. If you aren't going to be in Baltimore for Christmas, I won't return for it. On the other hand, if you are going to be in Havana until the first of February, I'll either stay on out here or remain in Montgomery until you return to Baltimore.

I am enclosing a letter that came in today from George Palmer Putnam. Jim Tully had written to him before I heard from you about Madden. Jim insists that Putnam is the best agent for pictures to be had. He himself had Madden for a while, with no success. He says that Madden takes on a great many more people than Putnam, and takes a great deal less trouble for them. I know nothing about the business, one way or the other, and shall do what you advise about it. I have the jellybean story and one other that I shall want to place as soon as I finish this Negri picture.

I can't tell you how nice it is to have you advising and consoling me in these emergencies. I may have had phenomenal luck out here, as you and Mayfield remarked, but it has been so mingled with unpleasant incidents like the Stallings and Baker business, and so many uncertainties, that I have scarcely had a chance to enjoy it. In addition, what started out to be a five weeks holiday has lengthened into an interminable exile. I begin to think that I shall never see you again.

Yours,
Sara

H. L. MENCKEN
1524 HOLLINS ST.
BALTIMORE

December 3rd, 1927

Dear Sara:-

Mary Parmenter tells me that the arch-ass, Baker, was urged not to give out that story, but that he insisted upon doing so. But don't let it annoy you too much. It would have come out soon or late. I have thrown a scare into Baker by sending word to him that his imprudence will cost you a great deal of money. He deserves to be scared a bit.

I am to have lunch with La Parmenter during the week. I have not seen her since our session together.

It seems likely that I'll have to go to Pittsburgh for Xmas, though I am still trying to get out of it. I take it that if you go to Montgomery you will be here before New Year's Day. I surely hope so, and petition God to that end. You will see a man who has greatly aged. And who feels horribly lonesome without you.

Don't forget the photograph. I must have it for Xmas. Remember that you are forbidden to give me any Xmas present, now or hereafter, but I accept the photograph.

I am leaving for Havana on January 11, but shall be gone only 10 days. Then I'll be here until June. The two conventions will probably be in Detroit and Cleveland.[1] San Francisco has been eliminated.

Ich kuss die Hand.

Yours,

M

[1]The national Republican and Democratic conventions were held in June 1928 in Kansas City, Missouri, and Houston, Texas. It was the first time since 1860 that the Democratic party's nominating convention had been conducted in a Southern city.

[TELEGRAM]

DEC 5 1927 6:35 PM

WESTERN UNION
BALTIMORE MD
MISS SARA HAARDT

HOTEL MARK TWAIN HOLLYWOOD CALIF.

    BELIEVE IT WOULD BE WISE TO CALL UP STALLINGS AND FIND OUT EXACTLY WHAT HE COMPLAINS OF   STORIES YOU HEAR AT SECOND HAND PROBABLY GREATLY EXAGGERATED   SHOW HIM MY TELEGRAM

OF LAST WEEK   IF HE ACTS BADLY LET ME HEAR OF IT BY WIRE   MISS YOU DREADFULLY.

M.

H. L. MENCKEN

1524 HOLLINS ST.

BALTIMORE

December 5th, 1927

Dear Sara:-

. . . When are you coming back? You don't say in any of your letters. Schellhase bursts into tears every time he sees me. And I do some snuffling myself. Old Anna told me the other night that you were the most beautiful woman ever seen in the place. I think that was a high compliment.

Yours,

M

ALS

HOTEL MARK TWAIN

HOLLYWOOD, CALIFORNIA

December the sixth, 1927

Henry dear,

I have heard nothing from Lawrence Stallings in the last few days or from Cruze about the *Sun* story. I am seeing the Garretts tonight though, and if they report that he is still raving, I shall call him.

Tomorrow I see Wanger about the Negri picture. I shall write you what he proposes.

You are so thoughtful and so reassuring. And I love you for it.

Yours

Sara

~

H. L. MENCKEN
1524 HOLLINS ST.
BALTIMORE

December 6th, 1927

Dear Sara:-

As I wired to you this morning, I think it would be foolish to leave too soon, with Wanger in a favorable mood. You have stuck it out nobly so far, and you can stand it for a few weeks longer. Wanger himself plans to be back in New York by Christmas, so I assume that it will be possible to return at the same time. But in any case don't do anything to imperil the business. You are still getting $250 a week!

If everything turns out well, all your uneasiness will be at an end. You'll be able to put in all the time you want on your novel, and without any worries. At once you will discover that when you don't need money it will come flowing. I believe that this adventure is and will be of immense value to you. It is giving you both money and experience. Give thanks to le bong Doo!

I hope you have seen Stallings and settled him. If he shows any nastiness, let me hear of it, and I shall start operations against him. It would be easy to make him look a cheap bounder. I begin to suspect that he may be. But I don't think he will venture to say flatly that you lifted anything of his. The accusation would be too preposterous.

God will punish you for sending me that ivory. But it is very lovely of you. I am waiting for it eagerly. When you get back to these parts there will be a reception to stagger humanity.

Has Cruze made any payment down? If so, how much? You send me no news. And how are you feeling? Let me hear. I was horribly worried three weeks ago. I hope you are much better. The climate is infernal, but its effects pass off as soon as one leaves it. I am delighted that you spent a day in Pasadena with Mrs. Slemons. Loaf all you can!

Yours,

M

~

H. L. MENCKEN
1524 HOLLINS ST.
BALTIMORE

December 7th, 1927

Dear Sara:-

The Kaiser has sent me a large, elegant, grand photograph of himself as a Christmas present, and in recognition of my fidelity to his Lost Cause.[1] It is actually tinted! What a proud boy I am! When you get back to your apartment I'll lend it to you for as much as a week at a time.

I am off for Washington to see Nick Longworth[2] and try to put in some licks for San Francisco as the scene of the Republican National Convention. The thrifty statesmen object to the heavy cost of the long trip, and Detroit seems to be favored. The Native Sons of S.F. are deluging me with appeals for help. If Nick is sober, I may be able to do something. But probably not.

Boyd is to be here on Sunday. He announces that he will have his thirst with him, and maybe a fair companion. Who she is, I don't know—probably some one he knew here. I am petitioning La Mayfield to come along. Ah, that thou wert here! Fred Hanes, of N. Carolina, will be here Sunday afternoon. I shall give him a lunch party at the Rennert, with six men. Then for Boyd. My poor gizzard!

Ich kuss die Hand.

Yours,

M

[1] Kaiser Wilhelm II was a big fan of Mencken. When he read the German translation of *Notes on Democracy* (*Demokratenspiegel*) in 1930 he sent Mencken two more photographs, this time autographed.

[2] The husband of Alice Lee Roosevelt, the daughter of President Theodore Roosevelt. The Ohio congressman had also been the floor leader of the House of Representatives until 1925.

~

HOTEL MARK TWAIN
HOLLYWOOD, CALIFORNIA

December the eighth, 1927

Henry dear,

After I sent you that telegram last night I almost repented. How I am going to stick here much longer without seeing you, I don't know. It is too ghastly. I keep busy, and heaven knows I see enough people, but they just aren't capable of making up to me for what I miss in you.

I had a talk with Wanger yesterday, and he asked me to put the Negri story in writing. I saw Mankiewicz later and he was in high spirits over the fact that they have given the author's council back to him. That is, he is now empowered to bring authors out from the east in droves of ten and twelve on the same contract Oliver Garrett and I are on. He said quite frankly that he used my case and Oliver's as his argument in getting it through. It is a beautiful piece of irony. Katharine Michel told me that he actually used the act of my having sold a story to Cruze as his chief card. Only he still thinks I sold to Metro-Goldwyn. And this after the strange way he received me. Katharine Michel was so amused over the letter he wrote you, and the line he strung about Wanger and Schulberg being out of town when I arrived that she came by here to tell me.

Mankiewicz says he is going by Baltimore to see you for you to suggest other candidates. On the strength of it he has almost fallen over backwards being nice to me the last few days. It is all very amusing, for I know he will treat these new people in precisely the same manner he treated me. Furthermore, they'll be told to copy all the cheap successes Paramount has perpetrated in the last ten years. You won't believe it but that is what has happened to the story I am writing with Wanger. I started out with a fairly original idea, within the bounds of the requirement, but he has gradually made it over into an imitation of Negri's first picture, "Passion," the story of Du Barry.[1] I had Negri cast as a French peasant girl, who was kidnapped off the streets of Paris and chained with six other prostitutes and brought to New Orleans by the officers of the king to populate his colony. It was a marvelous role for Negri, because she is a peasant and acts it. But no, Wanger must have her a mistress of Louis XV, with a lot of meritricious, suggestive stuff that actually lessens the dramatic values of the story. I don't care, of course; I would have made her a sunflower or a dandelion if he wanted her so, but it ruins a possible story. And that's all the uplift in the movies amounts to.

The Tullys are giving a very elaborate party on Saturday night.[2] Marna had tea with Mrs. Slemons and me this afternoon. Afterwards I talked with her here for a while. Jim has been in the depths lately, and she has been very worried about him. She has none of the martyr complex, but the strain is beginning to get on her nerves. After all, she is only twenty four, and I think a remarkable child for her age.

Let me hear how Dorothy Hergesheimer[3] progresses. I am writing to Joseph.

On Monday I sit for a picture for you. And I may add, darling, that it is positive proof of my devotion!

Yours,
Sara

[1]*Madame DuBarry*, retitled *Passion*, had been shown with enormous success in the United States in 1922, and Paramount invited Pola Negri to America, making her the first of the European actresses to be wooed by Hollywood.

[2]A few days after the party Jim Tully sent a letter to George Jean Nathan describing Sara and the event: "Sara's poise has been bothering me. I had a young fellow begin on O'Neill, then shift to you and Mencken. Her poise was 240 percent until he rapped you guys. Then you should have heard her say—Heah! Heah!! Gawd, did she come to the rescue. I haven't told her she was framed yet."

[3]Dorothy Hergesheimer was having an appendix operation.

H. L. MENCKEN
1524 HOLLINS ST.
BALTIMORE

December 9th, 1927

Dear Sara:-

Before you close with any agent, ask Wanger what he thinks of them. He may be prejudiced, but at all events his prejudice must be considered. Nathan tells me that Putnam is not the best man, but his opinion is not worth a great deal. Inquire among movie people. What you want is an agent who has their ears.

I am delighted to hear that Cruze has paid the $1500. Why in hell, may I inquire with all due respect, didn't you tell me? Don't let the Baker imbecility bother you. Cruze has now paid in his money, and will not be scared off. Baker takes the pie as the damndest ass in Christendom. . . .

I'll be here up to December 23rd, and again at any time between December 26th and January 11th that you arrive. I can arrange my trip to New York to fit your own movements.

I have quit the Chicago Tribune as of January 1st. They protest politely, but I am standing pat. I am also in treaty with the Evening Sun for less work. The book must, will and shall get itself written. But how can I do it while you are lolling on the Coast, with handsome movie actors buzzing all around you? Marna Tully sends me news that 18 head of them are mashed on you.

You have stuck it out very nobly. I am proud of you.

Yours,
M

H. L. MENCKEN

1524 HOLLINS ST.

BALTIMORE

December 8th, 1927

Dear Sara:-

I hope you stick it out until the Negri business is finished. That is, provided the climate is not endangering your health. What does the doctor say? If you are uneasy in that department, come home, Wanger or no Wanger!

. . . I was in a taxi smash in Washington yesterday, but escaped with a bruise across the right gluteus maximus, or ham. A lady who appeared to be in her cups drove her car into the taxi head-on. The driver was stunned and the taxi was demolished. But God preserved me. I am being kept for death on the gallows.

I went over to see Nick Longworth, and we had a pleasant session. Later I had dinner with two widows and a grass-widow. A Christian day. The Republican National Committee has decided to hold the convention in Kansas City, not in San Francisco. This is a disappointment, but with a silver lining. Logan Clendening[1] lives in Kansas City, and so does Jim Reed.

I'd swap Schellhase, his kaif, old Anna and 20 barrels of beer for a glimpse of you.

> Yours,
> M

[1]Logan Clendening, a physician and author from Kansas City, had established a friendship with Alfred Knopf through Mencken. *The Human Body*, a textbook conceived by Mencken, written by Clendening, and published by Knopf, had become a standard work since its publication in 1927.

H. L. MENCKEN
1524 HOLLINS ST.
BALTIMORE

Thursday, December 8, 1927

Dear Sara:-

The Montgomery Advertiser has been sold to Frank Glass, and for a while it looked as if Grover Hall would be turned out. But now he reports that he and Glass have come to terms, and that he will continue blazing away along the old lines. I am writing to him today, and have put out some feelers in the hope of getting him the Pulitzer Prize.[1]

How long! How long!

> Yours,
> M

[1]Grover Hall won the Pulitzer Prize in journalism in 1928 for the best editorial series in 1927 lambasting Ku Klux Klan violence.

H. L. MENCKEN
1524 HOLLINS ST.
BALTIMORE

December 9th, 1927

Dear Sara:-

The ivory came in this morning. A charming piece! My very best thanks! You are immensely nice to me. My collection grows beautifully. Some day it will be one of the glories of the Baltimore Museum of Art.

I am having lunch with Mary Parmenter tomorrow, and shall fill her with stuff to alarm Baker. His utter damned foolishness is really sublime. On Sunday Boyd is to be here, and says that he will have some mysterious lady on his hands at dinner—NOT the lovely and amiable Madeleine. I am asking Sara Mayfield to come along. But it ought to be your job.

No news from Dorothy Hergesheimer. I assume that all is going well. I'll call up Joe tomorrow.

Let me hear of it by wire as soon as you find out when you'll leave Hollywood, and when you'll get back to Baltimore.

I kiss both your hands.

> Yours,
> M

ALS

HOTEL MARK TWAIN
HOLLYWOOD, CALIFORNIA

December the ninth, 1927

Henry dear,

The package I am getting off to you tomorrow is not a Christmas present. Please don't fuss about them;—you simply had to have them.

> Yours,
> Sara

H. L. MENCKEN
1524 HOLLINS ST.
BALTIMORE

December 19th, 1927

Dear Sara:-

By air mail this day I am sending you a small bauble. It is NOT a Christmas present. I simply saw it and began to think how nice it would look in your hands. So it is on its way, provided Lindbergh doesn't fall.[1]

I had lunch today with Mary Parmenter. Despite all her waspishness she admires you tremendously, and has a great affection for you. Her own situation is disquieting. God knows what she ought to do. I think she is wasting her time studying Middle English rubbish with Malone, and idiotic Restoration political doggerel with Greenlaw.[2] After lunch we walked out to the hospital and called on Woollcott. He seems to be better, but the question as to what sort of tumor he has remains to be settled. His poor wife is a wreck.

Let me have a wire as soon as you find out when you'll leave. A letter from Mankiewicz this morning apologizes for your first difficulties, and says that you are now in Wanger's hands, and that everyone in the office likes the Negri thing. He apparently believes that it is sure to be accepted.

I am off to the club.[3] We play Richard Strauss' "Don Juan" tonight, with Pearl operating the cow-horn. Then for a bath of malt.

I wish it were at Schellhase's.

Yours,
M

[1]In May 1927 Charles A. Lindbergh flew across 3600 miles of the Atlantic from New York to Paris in a record time of 33 hours and 29 minutes. In December Lindbergh was planning to fly to Havana, Cuba, via Mexico. The "Flyin' Fool" had previously been an airmail pilot.

[2]Edwin Greenlaw, professor of English at Johns Hopkins University from 1925 until his death in 1931. His specialities were linguistics and Spenser.

[3]Saturday Night Club.

H. L. MENCKEN
1524 HOLLINS ST.
BALTIMORE

December 12th, 1927

Dear Sara:-

The news of the photograph revives me! You say you are sitting on Monday, which is today. My prayers are with you and the artist. It must be a masterpiece. Don't let Tully choose the best negative! I'd rather trust Slemons, or even Wanger.

To hell with Mankiewicz. He is a poor worm, and afraid for his job. Give him the high hat. I shall answer him sardonically, and have a session on him with Wanger when Wanger gets back. It would be charming if he dropped off in Baltimore after your return. I suggest that we ask him to meet us somewhere in Highlandtown, and then not go.[1]

Don't let the Negri business worry you. It is comedy, not tragedy. The main thing is to get the money of the Old Testament brethren, and then laugh at the world. If all your nets come in you'll be independent, and can write what you please. Don't forget that the interest on $30,000 is $1500 a year, or $30 a week. And even $5,000 NOT invested, will last three and a half years at that rate.

Moreover, you know the way of the world. The instant you can laugh at money it will begin to roll in.

When? The second millennium begins.

Yours,
M

[1]One of Baltimore's oldest neighborhoods, and perhaps one of its most closely knit communities. During the 1920s many Germans resided in Highlandtown, the majority of them Roman Catholics.

THE AMERICAN MERCURY
730 FIFTH AVENUE
NEW YORK

December 13, 1927

Dear Sara:

The enclosed letter from Hall came in today.[1] As you will note, he seems to be safe under the new administration. In fact, he seems to be better off than he was under Hanson.[2] It goes without saying that I am delighted to hear it.

Yours,
M

[1]Grover Hall had written Mencken a note thanking Mencken for his concern, adding: "Mr. Glass is a thoroughbred. He is without editorial fear, is as wet as a baby diaper, and seems disposed to be extremely considerate of me. Greater virtues no publisher of The Advertiser could have."

[2]Victor H. Hanson, chief owner of the Birmingham *News*, had just sold the Montgomery *Advertiser* to Frank P. Glass.

H. L. MENCKEN
1524 HOLLINS ST.
BALTIMORE

December 14th, 1927

Dear Sara:-

God will punish you for sending me a Christmas present, however cunning your effort to disguise the fact. It has not yet come in. I am telegraphing to Harry New[1] to hold it up, but he will probably refuse. If there were ice in Hollywood you would fall on it and break your leg. But you are immensely nice.

When are you leaving Sodom? My sister-in-law is here today, insisting that we must come to Pittsburgh for Christmas. I'll probably have to succumb. But I'll keep on fighting.

I have had at least 40 visitors this week. They are driving me frantic. My work is weeks behind. But after January 1st I'll be relatively free. Then for the book. You will be just in time to see the agonies.

Yours,
M

[1]The ex-United States Senator, reporter, and publisher was now serving as postmaster general.

H. L. MENCKEN
1524 HOLLINS ST.
BALTIMORE

December 15th, 1927

Dear Sara:-

If the chance offers, sound out Wanger on the "Gullivers Travels" idea. You could do it after you got back to Baltimore; I have some notions for it. I believe it is technically feasible. Wanger will know whether it is or not. The main problem is to get Gulliver and the Lilliputians on the film together. The story is full of possibilities, and I believe it would make a very successful film.

Yours,
M

H. L. MENCKEN
1524 HOLLINS ST.
BALTIMORE

Thursday, December 15, 1927

Dear Sara:-

It is good news that you are tackling Stallings. Obviously, he ought to be shut up. If he shows the slightest sign of hostility, let me know at once and I'll have at him. What ails him is mainly vanity. He is one of the most swollen of men. But I doubt that anyone in Hollywood takes him seriously.

I hope you can close business with Wanger and get to Montgomery in time for Christmas. But if he wants you to stay, I advise you to do it. Now that you have gone so far you ought to go all the way. Is he still paying you salary? I seem to be doomed to go to Pittsburgh for Christmas, but I am still trying to get out of it.

I told old Anna last night that you would be home soon after Christmas. She almost hugged me. Obviously you have left a deep impression on that faithful heart.

I am saving up gin for your return. And assembling a brass band.

Yours,
M

H. L. MENCKEN
1524 HOLLINS ST.
BALTIMORE

December 17th, 1927

Dear Sara:-

If I find "Varina Howell" in New York I'll send it to you at once.[1] It is not here. But I fear it will be at least ten days getting to you. The mails are horribly congested.

The San Francisco business blew up. The Republicans decided for Kansas City. I shall have to guard my gizzard there. Both Senator Reed and Dr. Logan Clendening will be in town during the convention. I believe that the Democrats will go to Detroit. Another dangerous place for my kidneys.

Let me have a wire as soon as you find out when you will get to

Baltimore. I think I have got out of the Pittsburgh journey at Christmas. I'll be here steadily until about January 7th.

If you think you'll escape being hugged when you get home you are far off the facts.

Yours,

M

I met Beardsley today, and told him that I would take a stall between two cows at the next Timonium Fair[2] and exhibit Baker as the champion jackass of the Atlantic Seaboard.

[1]*Varina Howell: Wife of Jefferson Davis*, a two-volume work by Eron Rowland, would not appear until 1928. Sara reviewed the first volume in the New York *Herald Tribune Books* on February 8, 1928, and the second volume in 1931.

[2]The first state fair was held in 1878, but the Northern Central Railway forced it to move to its present site in Timonium, adjacent to Timonium Mansion. The fair attracts produce and cattle exhibitors, but in addition to the exhibition barns there is also a race track.

At last Sara's contract with Famous Players-Lasky had expired, and she was ready to come home. With the $1500 advance she had received from Cruze and the $2000 she had saved from her salary at Famous Players, she was, Mencken noted, "richer than she had been for years."

H. L. MENCKEN
1524 HOLLINS ST.
BALTIMORE

Thursday, December 22, 1927

Dear Sara:-

It is superb news that you are bound home at last. I think you have done a capital job, and ought to be very proud of it. Whatever the imbecilities of the magnates, you have at least got a substantial amount of money out of them, and can thus fall upon your novel with an easy mind. Let us continue in session from day to day until I have heard all of it. Three months! It seems at least five years. You will see a much aged and broken man.

I stopped off in West Chester this afternoon to see Dorothy. She is in fine condition and drank her first cocktail with me. Joe is to slip off the wagon on Christmas Day. Both of them think you are perfect, and Dorothy wants you to come to West Chester in January. I gave her your address. The operation turned out very well. She had little pain and is making an excellent recovery. I am spreading the story in New York that she had no appendicitis at all, but a son and heir.

I am fagged out, and there is a stack of mail 20 feet high. I shall tackle it in the morning.

A happy Christmas at home![1]

Yours,
M

[1]Sara spent Christmas in Montgomery, Alabama.

[TELEGRAM]

DEC 22 1927 7:24 PM

WESTERN UNION
BALTIMORE MD
MISS SARA HAARDT

SANTA FE SUNSET LIMITED EASTBOUND DUE 9:20 AM FRIDAY EL PASO TEX

DON'T DALLY TOO LONG IN MONTGOMERY   THE DAYS SEEM ENDLESS

H.L.M.

H. L. MENCKEN
1524 HOLLINS ST.
BALTIMORE

Friday, December 23, 1927

Dear Sara:-

The news that you are coming back at last is glorious. I have missed you horribly. Now you'll be just in time to shove me into the book. If I don't do it in 1928, then it will never be done.

Let me know, as soon as you can, precisely when you'll reach Baltimore. I'll be clear all of New Year's Eve until late in the evening, and I can get out of that if you are coming in. On New Year's Day I'll be waiting all day. I won't return to New York until the 7th or 8th. There is trouble about the Havana bookings. We planned to leave on the 14th, but can't get reservations. The 12th and 13th—thank God!—are also booked up.[1] So we may have to leave on the 11th. The American Mercury annual meeting is in New York on the 10th. Thus I may have to cut corners sharply.

Both your hands are kissed 275 times.

Yours,
M

[1]Mencken could never get rid of certain superstitions and suspected that there must be some logical basis for them. One of them was about the number thirteen: both his father and mother had died on the thirteenth.

[TELEGRAM]

DEC 23 1927 4:01 PM

WESTERN UNION
BALTIMORE MD
MISS SARA HAARDT

SANTA FE SUNSET LIMITED EASTBOUND DUE 9:15 AM SATURDAY HOUSTON TEX.

IT IS CHARMING TO THINK THAT YOU ARE A THOUSAND MILES NEARER

M.

H. L. MENCKEN
1524 HOLLINS ST.
BALTIMORE

December 24th, 1927

Dear Sara:-

Those beer seidels are really too lovely! Did you notice that one is from the Hofbräuhaus at Munich? In other words, that it comes from the Holy Sepulchre Itself? I shall make a special brew to start it off in life as an Americano. It will be a double-brew, with at least 8% alcohol. If I swoon you must take the blame. The little Santa Clas with the feather is on my desk—a very warm and friendly fellow. I shall call him Schellhase.

I have got out of going to Pittsburgh, and shall spend the day here, mainly working. In the afternoon I shall wait upon Willie Woollcott, who has been let out of the hospital for Christmas. It will be a gaudy day in his house, and his four daughters will be happy.

Next week will seem a year long. Don't forget to wire me the exact time of your arrival, and as soon as possible.

Yours,
M

[TELEGRAM]

DEC 26 1927 11:21 AM

WESTERN UNION
BALTIMORE MD
MISS SARA HAARDT

CARE JOHN HAARDT MAGNOLIA CURVE CLOVERDALE MONTGOMERY ALA

CERTAINLY I'LL MEET YOU AT SEVEN THIRTY OR AT FOUR THIRTY WIRE ME THE EXACT TIME

H. L. MENCKEN.

H. L. MENCKEN
1524 HOLLINS ST.
BALTIMORE

December 26th, 1927

Dear Sara:-

What talk! Certainly I'll meet you at the train, no matter when it gets in. Let us have breakfast together in the station, or at the Belvedere.[1] And then for the first canto of the Hollywoodiad. I am wild to hear it. The next day I'll introduce you to the best firm of investment bankers in Baltimore. A rich woman should have advisers.

I am hurrying this off, and shall read the story before the day is out. Let me hear by wire exactly when you arrive. You are apt to be hugged in public, with all of the red caps gaping.

Yours,

M

'The turn-of-the-century hotel at Charles and Chase Streets was for over seventy years host to Baltimore society and world-famous personalities (Queen Marie of Romania, the Fitzgeralds, Edward VIII and his duchess, Wallis Warfield Simpson, Sara Bernhardt, and John F. Kennedy).

H. L. MENCKEN

1524 HOLLINS ST.

BALTIMORE

Tuesday, December 27, 1927

Dear Sara:-

The only thing that can keep me from Union Station Saturday morning is the failure of all the alarm clocks in the house. I'll be there with the other red caps, ready to tote your baggage. In addition, I shall claim the high privilege of giving you a hug. It will be glorious to see you back.

There is no meeting of the club Saturday night, but I have promised Hemberger' to come to his house late in the evening. However, there will be plenty of time for dinner.

Miss Mayfield called me up yesterday, and almost had hysterics when I told her you were on your way back. I was a bit lighted up myself!

Yours,

M

'Theodore Hemberger, violinist, composer, conductor, and director of the Zion Church choir, one of the oldest German choirs in the United States. Hemberger was first violin member of the Saturday Night Club.

Sara's film, The Promised Land, *was never produced. For the next two years Jim Tully would try to persuade Cruze to make it into a film and thereby obtain Sara's remaining $18,500 for her, without any success. In the 1930s Sara's novel* The Making of a Lady *attracted the attention of Hollywood, and for a brief period a letter or two appeared, expressing interest in making the story into a movie. Sara did not pursue it.*

1928

1928 saw Mencken more often away from Baltimore than in it. In January he covered the sixth Pan American Conference in Havana; in June, the Republican national convention in Kansas City and the Democratic national convention in Houston; and in October he followed Al Smith's campaign tour. During the sporadic weeks Mencken was in Baltimore, however, he constantly asked Sara to be by his side whenever he had to play host. Sara wrote her friend Sara Mayfield, traveling abroad, to buy her some perfumes ("whatever is poisonous") and finished the year by telling her: "Henry is his usual thoughtful self."

ALS

PLAZA HOTEL
HAVANA, CUBA
Tuesday, January 17, 1928

Dear Sara:

I surely hope you have seen Hamburger[1] and that he has stopped that cough. Let me have some news of you. The weather here is muggy by day, but cool enough at night. I'll probably be stuck for 2 weeks. It is the usual dull imbecility. I got an overdose of stimulants last night with Will Rogers,[2] but now I am on beer and shall stay there. I have met at least 25 old acquaintances. But the only recreation here is guzzling. There is no decent entertainment of any sort—only cabarets and saloons, with a few movies. The town is a dreadful burlesque of both Spanish and American towns, with the worst characters of both.

Don't forget your elderly slave! I crave more of you.

Yrs.,

HLM

¹Dr. Louis Hamburger, one of the top internists in Baltimore.
²The American humorist and motion picture actor was also a writer of a syndicated newspaper column that was famous for its homespun humor and for its good-natured but sharp criticism of contemporary men and affairs.

"Nations get on with one another, not by telling the truth, but by lying gracefully," Mencken wrote of the twenty-one nations represented at the Sixth Pan American Conference being held that year in Havana, Cuba. Havana, Mencken found, was full of rumors of governmental oppressions, with allegations that free assemblage was prohibited, that the surviving press was bribed into acquiescence, and that persons who were opposed to the Cuban administration had been assassinated. "They celebrated the arrival of Mr. Secretary Kellogg by jailing two Bolsheviks," observed Mencken. "It was a delicate attention, and I believe it was appreciated."

With Will Rogers, Paul Patterson, and others, Mencken toured the city and found "the aping of the abominable Janqui" visible throughout. Havana now had golf clubs, press agents, and all the other "ineffable flowers of American Kultur," including a Rotary Club (indeed, the sign of its executive secretary hung in plain sight of Mencken's room at the Plaza Hotel). At the University of Havana there was a baseball diamond, and in all of the saloons were portraits of Coolidge, Lindbergh, Tunney, "and the rest of the Yanqui hierarchy." Douglas Fairbanks movies packed the largest theaters; Camel cigarettes crowded out native brands. But it was in the bars that Americanization went furthest. Eleven years ago, Mencken noted, they had been cafés—now they were simply saloons of the United States, with "the same brass rails, the same gaudy ranks of bottles behind the bar, and the same free lunches of olives, pickled onions, crackers, and rat-trap cheese. Some of them even have Irish bartenders." One evening he went to the Casino, where he came "very near" the borderline of intoxication and gambled for the first time since 1908. "No woman winked at me all evening, though I was in full evening dress and wore all my orders. Worse, I was not tempted to wink at any of the women, despite the fact, as I have hinted, that I was moderately inflamed by wine. The ride ended with a long ride back to Havana, along the glorious sea," driven by a taxi driver whose belief was that the Yanqui was there to be looted. "Well, I don't blame the Havanese," Mencken concluded. "Their season is very short. . . . They are not as prosperous as they ought to be. Havana, with its flags flying, looks very gay, but the price of sugar is down below the cost of production, and Cuba as a whole is suffering from very hard times. Some friends of a Bolshevik kidney offered to take me out and show me how the poor were living."

H. L. MENCKEN
1524 HOLLINS ST.
BALTIMORE
Wednesday, February 15, 1928

Dear Sara:-

In New York last week Nathan gave me a copy of his new book to bring to you.[1] I brought it home, and then clear forgot it. It is going to you by first-class mail tonight. Will you please write to Nathan at once, saying that you have been out of the city, or something of the sort? His address is The Royalton, 44 street, New York City.

I'll be in attendance at the Hauptbahnhof at 6:10 P.M. tomorrow.

Yours,
M

[1]*Art of the Night.*

H. L. MENCKEN
1524 HOLLINS ST.
BALTIMORE
Wednesday, February 22, 1928

Dear Sara:-

I have a severe lumbago, and can scarcely move. It is a damned nuisance, but not serious.

The chiropractors spent a couple of hours Monday examining my throat. The result: there is no sign of anything alarming. In the old tonsil crypt on the left side lymphoid tissue has collected, and there is an infection in it. Apparently I caught cold early in January—my first cold in ten years. The treatment is local, and my naso-pharynx and teeth are being examined. If the discomfort persists the lymphoid tissue will be taken out. But that is not likely, and in any case it is a small matter.

I am planning a dinner at the Rennert for Friday of next week. Will you and Miss Mayfield come? I surely hope so. Dan Henry is to bring terrapin from Easton, and there will be these other guests: Pearl and his wife,[1] the Owenses[2] and the Paul De Kruifs. Will you keep the evening open, and ask Miss Mayfield? I am going to N.Y. on Sunday, but shall be back by Thursday.

I hope you let me see you before I go—that is, if my lumbago permits me to navigate. What of lunch Saturday, at Baum's?[3]

Yours,

M

[1] Raymond Pearl and his wife, Maud De Witt.
[2] Hamilton and Olga (von Hartz) Owens.
[3] Baum's restaurant, at 320 W. Saratoga Street.

H. L. MENCKEN

1524 HOLLINS ST.

BALTIMORE

March 3rd, 1928

Dear Sara:-

For office reasons I think it will be best for me to accept your very generous offer to give The American Mercury the Tully article for Alabama April.[1] May God forgive me! I'll make it up to you the next time you have an article.

I'll call you up on Tuesday. The bloody brothers say that the business Monday will be trivial.

Yours,

M

What a party! I feel far-away today!

¹"Jungle Justice" (April 1928 *Mercury*) replaced Sara's article "Alabama April" which had been in galley proof. "Alabama April" was never published.

H. L. MENCKEN
1524 HOLLINS ST.
BALTIMORE

Tuesday, March 6, 1928

Dear Sara:-

I am back home, have just got down 18 raw oysters for dinner, and hope to spend the evening reading MSS. Such are God's wonders. The tonsil muck was clawed out yesterday morning, and the two little moles were cut out this morning. All the tissue removed turned out to be absolutely benign. So that's that!

I shall call you up Thursday. By that time I should be able to talk by telephone. At the moment my tongue is swollen.

The Check List MSS. is here. My best thanks.

Yours,
M

H. L. MENCKEN
1524 HOLLINS ST.
BALTIMORE

Friday, March 23, 1928

Dear Sara:-

I am dreadfully sorry about tonight, but this Sun business has me jumping.¹ I was engaged on it all week in New York, and scarcely saw my own office. Tomorrow I must go to Washington, and tonight I must see various men to prepare for it. I'll tell you about it when it is over.

I feel very fit. In New York yesterday there was a heavy squall and I got soaked, but nothing happened. My throat is practically normal. All this I ascribe to the intervention of SS. Anheuser and Busch.

From one who kisses your hand.

Yours,
M

'For the past eighteen years the Baltimore *Evening Sun* had been trying to become a member of the Associated Press. The Baltimore *Sun* was already an Associated Press paper, as was the *News American*. The admission of a new member was subject to veto by existing members in its city; of the fifteen directors of Associated Press, fourteen were in favor of admitting the Baltimore *Evening Sun* to membership; only the *News American*, then owned by William Randolph Hearst, continued to maintain its veto, and when the proposal was put to a vote before the directors, the necessary four-fifths majority was not obtained. In 1928 negotiations were opened with Colonel Frank Knox, then general manager of all the Hearst newspapers, and on his recommendation Hearst finally waived the veto, and the Baltimore *Evening Sun* became a member of the Associated Press on March 31, 1928.

[POSTCARD]

Boston, Massachusetts
April 24, 1928

This morning I called on the police lieutenant' who arrested me 2 years ago, and he gave me a very polite reception. They believe here that criminals may be reformed.

M

'Captain George W. Patterson, chief of the Boston vice squad.

~

BUNKER HILL MONUMENT, 221 FEET IN HEIGHT, CHARLESTOWN, MASS.

H. L. MENCKEN
1524 HOLLINS ST.
BALTIMORE

Wednesday, May 9, 1928

Dear Sara:-

I'll be in New York until the first mail next Thursday. If you finish either of the Ladies' Home Journal articles by Wednesday, let me have the MS. there, marked Personal, and I'll read it on the train coming down. If you do any of the Check List stuff, send it in the same way. Anything mailed before noon of Wednesday will reach me in time.

You were very lovely last night. But you always are.

Yours,
M

[POSTCARD]

May 12, 1928

Having a swell time. The music is very swell. At the last minute they lacked a man to sing Pontias [sic] Pilate in the B minor mass, and I volunteered.

M

ALS

H. L. MENCKEN
1524 HOLLINS ST.
BALTIMORE

June 8, 1928

Dear Sara:

I am off! It will seem years until I get back.[1]

Yrs.,

M

[1]Mencken was on his way to report on the Republican national convention being held that year in Kansas City.

The presidential campaign of 1928 placed two candidates before the voters who had long been familiar public faces: commerce secretary Herbert Clark Hoover of California as the Republican candidate versus Alfred Emanuel Smith, the Democratic governor of New York. The campaign opened the door to rumors and bigotry. Doubts were raised about Hoover's loyalty to the Republican party (he had entered the 1920 presidential primary as a Democrat), and about the fact that Smith would be the first Roman Catholic president if he was elected. These issues, plus the familiar one of Prohibition (the Republicans were in favor of it, the Democrats for repeal) gave Mencken added copy for his dispatches to the Baltimore Evening Sun. *Hoover and Al, Mencken found, were "as far apart as Pilsner and Coca-Cola," and he did not hesitate to proclaim his sympathies for Al. "It is difficult to make out how any native Marylander, brought up in the tradition of this ancient Commonwealth, can fail to have a friendly feeling for Al Smith in the present campaign," Mencken would write in one of his Monday articles. "He represents as a man almost everything that Maryland represents as a State. . . . He is enlightened, he is high-minded, he is upright and trustworthy. What Frederick the Great said of his officers might well be said of him: he will not lie, and he cannot be bought. Not much more could be said of any man. The contrast he makes with his opponent is really appalling. Hoover stands at the opposite pole. He is a man of sharp intelligence, well schooled and familiar with the ways of the world, and more than once, in difficult situations, he has shown a shrewd competence, but where his character ought to be there is almost a blank. . . . His principles are so vague that even his intimates seem unable to put*

them into words." If the country could elect Al Smith, Mencken wrote a friend,
"it will be the greatest event in history of the Republic since the hanging of
John Brown."

ALS

HOTEL MUEHLEBACH

KANSAS CITY, MO.

June 11, 1928

Dear Sara:

This is the usual dull imbecility. There are roars all day, and yells all night. But I get a lot of fun out of it.

Yesterday I had a palaver with two high-toned coons of Alabama. They seemed like Goethes, compared to the white politicians.[1] Knopf is here visiting Clendening, but I shall see little of either of them. Yesterday afternoon Clendening took me to a tea-party of the local lady literati. They were pretty awful, yet I got out alive.

Don't forget to send me a few sweet lines!

Yrs.,

M

[1] After spending hours listening to the "burbling" of "vacuums," Mencken took a long ride into Kansas City to investigate the black bloc of the convention. He met with A. F. Holsey, secretary of the Tuskegee Institute, and Claude A. Barnett, director of the Associated Negro Press. "They showed good humor, good manners, and sound sense," Mencken wrote in one of his dispatches to the Baltimore *Evening Sun*. "It was a pleasure to meet them after suffering for hours among the white morons. They remain the most intelligent men I have encountered among persons officially attached to the convention, one United States senator and five bootleggers excepted."

RICE HOTEL

HOUSTON, TEXAS

Friday, June 22, 1928

Dear Sara:-

The Tully business leaves me wondering what it was all about.[1] I have heard nothing from him save a telegram saying that the reports were "exaggerated." All I did in the matter was to send him an abusive night letter.

The trip through the wilds of Missouri, Arkansas and Oklahoma was horrible. The dust almost finished me, and I arrived at Fort Worth with a violent hay fever. But it has passed off, and Houston seems very comfortable. I have a quiet room on the 11th floor, with a fine breeze, and expect to get through the orgies safely.[2] The entertainment at Fort Worth was of the 1000 horse-power Texas variety. They did everything from giving us all 10 gallon hats to photographing us with lovely cowgirls. These photographs will now pursue me for months, like the picture made in New Orleans, with the fireman's hat.[3]

I surely hope you are quite well. When I got no word from you at Kansas City I was greatly worried. The Check List stuff is not yet here, but no doubt it will come in today. I found the usual pile of MSS. when I got in this morning.

I made three speeches in Fort Worth, one for the radio and all of them bad.[4]

We should be home by Monday a week.

Yours,
M

[1]The Associated Press had printed a story on June 12 that Jim Tully and his wife, Marna (Margaret R. Myers), were to be divorced. After a brief reconciliation, the couple were finally divorced in 1930.

[2]The Democratic national convention was about to begin. Nominated on the first ballot, by Franklin D. Roosevelt, was the Catholic governor of New York, Alfred Emanuel Smith.

[3]The hospitality at Fort Worth had been "terrific," Mencken wrote to Sara. Within a scarce ten minutes after Mencken had arrived in town he had been outfitted with one of those hats, photographed with the girls, and taken to a club. "It is all very charming," he confided, "but also somewhat terrifying."

[4]As soon as Mencken entered the Fort Worth Club he apologized to the press, "Please excuse my appearance; that damned dust in Arkansas and Oklahoma has given me the hay fever," and then proceeded to denounce Prohibition and praise Al Smith and Governor Ritchie. As he spoke he spotted a young woman making a charcoal sketch of him. "Please don't make me look so fat," he cautioned her. "They say if you put a bay window around me, I look like Hoover."

RICE HOTEL
HOUSTON, TEXAS

Tuesday, June 23, 1928

Dear Sara:-

The ivory has just come in. God will reward you throughout eternity! It is lovely, and I shall keep it for my death-bed jug. Your hand will be kissed magnificently when we meet.

Life down here is somewhat strenuous. My room was shot up by a wild Texan yesterday, and the town cops raised an awful uproar. The fellow was trying to show me a hospitable attention, but there were balls in his cartridges, and so he caused a panic in the hotel across the street.[1]

Unless these Christians grow really savage tomorrow, we ought to be out of here by Friday night and back in Baltimore by Monday. We shall travel by way of New Orleans, and lie over there half a day.

The weather is infernal.

Yours,
M

[1]"Texas exuberance takes forms that are sometimes rather disquieting to the visitor from the decadent cities of the East," Mencken wrote a few days later in one of his dispatches to the Baltimore *Evening Sun*. "During the afternoon, while I was engaged in literary endeavor in my hotel room, a distinguished Texan [Amos G. Carter] waited upon me to inquire if I was being treated right. I told him that I was, but he apparently thought I lacked entertainment, for he presently pulled out a six-shooter and fired four shots out of the window. The flashes and the noise brought a huge crowd to the street, eleven stories below. In another hotel room across the street there were signs of a panic. The Texan, with the big gallery thus assembled, stepped to the window and fired a fifth shot.

"Five minutes later ten panting policemen, led by the Chief of Police, were in my room, violently demanding that I give up the criminal. With them was a civilian who acted as a complainant, and it quickly appeared that he was one of the local judges. The whole party, unable to get into the crowded elevators, had climbed the eleven stories to my room.

"The essence of the complaint, it developed, was not that the Texan had discharged his artillery, but that his cartridges were loaded with balls. He denied it, and there was a long wrangle. Everyone admitted that firing blank cartridges was no more than harmless pleasantry, but the cops insisted that five bullets had hit the hotel across the street and badly scared the non-Texan guests. The artillerist, however, refused to admit anything and in the end the cops were placated and departed with him. It is difficult for an Easterner, with such sports going on around him, to concentrate his mind upon the highly complicated and difficult problems of politics. But, like the rest of the journalists here assembled, I do my best."

RICE HOTEL

HOUSTON, TEXAS

Saturday, June 28, 1928

Dear Sara:-

The Tully business appears to have been low comedy. Instead of stopping over in Ohio Tully went direct to Hollywood, and there accused Marna of playing about with Marshall Neilan, the movie director, in his absence.[1] Neilan had actually taken her to dinner and to a dance, but that was apparently as far as it went. But Tully insisted that infamy was afoot, and went to the length of arranging a telephone conversation between Marna and Neilan and listening in. He then demanded that Marna sign a confession, and alleged that his enemies among the movie clowns were trying to strike at him through his home. Marna refused to sign, fled the house, and served him with divorce papers. They are now reconciled, but Tully insists that there is a plot afoot to ruin him, and even butcher him. It sounds like nonsense to me. I had a letter from him just before I left home saying that he was receiving threatening letters. I told him that I used to get 50 a week, and that nothing ever followed. The movie mountebanks would never dare to molest him. Even Neilan, who is a former taxi driver, is plainly afraid of him.[2] All this news comes from La Pringle. She dislikes Tully and hence probably exaggerates, but the main facts sound probable. I wired her for the inside stuff. Tully's statement that I helped to reconcile him to Marna is piffle. All I did was to send him a telegram, denouncing him as an ass.

The weather here is infernal, but there is a cool breeze at night. Today I drank some capital beer. The hotel is really first-rate, and there is a superb dining-room on the roof, with very good food. The hall, I suppose, will be hot, but not unbearably. Some ass of a newspaper reporter today printed an interview with me in which I am made to say immensely embarrassing things about Jim Reed.[3] I have asked his editor to send a man to see Reed, and square me. If the old man were offended I'd be desolate. His chances here seem to be slim, but I have admired him for years, and we have been on good terms for a long while.⁴ I had a session with him last night, before the imbecile's interview appeared.

The Christians are preparing for a rough battle. Whether the Smith men will be able to knock them out remains to be seen. I am in some doubt about it. If the fight goes to any length, the party will be wrecked.

Ah, for Baltimore again! And thou!⁵

> Yours,
>
> M

¹Marshall "Mickey" Neilan typified the flamboyant silent film director. With seemingly inexhaustible energy, he would work all day and hold parties in the evening. When the orchestra at the Coconut Grove finished for the night, he would invite them and the guests to his home and keep the party going until dawn.

²Neilan had worked as a chauffeur for D. W. Griffith before becoming a film editor and later a director.

³Houston *Post-Dispatch*, June 22, 1928: "Mencken Stumped for Words for Painful Ordeal with Reed."

⁴During the Hatrack case of 1926, Senator Reed had authored one of the bills to change the censorship powers of the post office and had offered his services as counsel to Mencken without charge. (Mencken declined his offer.)

⁵"The Duke of Palmolive" was due in town on Monday, July 2, and, Sara wrote to Mayfield, "no doubt he will contribute to my instruction on the political dirt of the day."

THE AMERICAN MERCURY
730 FIFTH AVENUE
NEW YORK

July 7th, 1928

Dear Sara:-

Poor Tully! His troubles are very real, and he only makes them worse. It is up to you, as a Christian woman, to write him a nice letter. I suspect that Marna was very foolish. At all events, Hollywood believes that she gave her marriage vows a severe strain. What damned fools people the world!

I am off to Gomorrah.

Yours,

M

H. L. MENCKEN

1524 HOLLINS ST.

BALTIMORE

July 26th, 1928

Dear Sara:-

This looks very good.[1] I believe that it might be well to write to Bigelow, adding Mrs. Cabell.[2] Richmond is not far away, and Emily Clark could give you a lot of stuff—most of it, of course, unusable, but good enough to fix the landmarks. Mrs. Rogers[3] is in California, and out of reach. But maybe she will be coming East. Marna is spoiled by the divorce story. Let us discuss some others when we meet.[4]

Be very polite to Bigelow!

Yours,

M

[1]Sara had submitted two interviews she had with Zelda Fitzgerald and Dorothy Hergesheimer to W. F. Bigelow, editor of *Good Housekeeping* magazine, along with an outline for a series of interviews with other women married to famous husbands: Mrs. Edison, Mrs. Rockefeller, and Mrs. Ford. The series finally developed into interviews with wives of famous authors.

[2]Priscilla Bradley Shepherd Cabell.

[3]Betty Blake, wife of Will Rogers.

[4]Mrs. Joseph Hergesheimer and Mrs. Ring Lardner were also included.

H. L. MENCKEN

1524 HOLLINS ST.

BALTIMORE

Monday, August 19, 1928

Dear Sara:-

. . . Don't forget to send me that photograph! I am mailing mine by this mail. It is swell. The baby picture will follow.

Did the log of wood reach you? The cedar sticks will follow. They are far down the wood-pile, and I must wait until some of the top wood is consumed.[2]

Yours,

M

[1]Mencken had a pile of sawed-up railroad ties, each weighing thirty pounds. He sent one of them, covered with postage stamps, which the mail carrier, grunting and groaning, delivered to Sara.

ALS

THE AMERICAN MERCURY

730 FIFTH AVENUE

NEW YORK

August 29, 1928

Dear Sara:

Mayfield writes very well indeed.[1] Tell her I must see all the stuff she is doing.

Hay fever has me by the ear, but it is not bad. The weather here is infernal.

I hope and pray to God that we meet Friday. I'll call you up in the morning.

Red Lewis is here with his new wife.[2] A hearty gal with red cheeks.

Yrs.,

M

[1]Sara had given Mencken excerpts of Sara Mayfield's letters to read. Sara Mayfield and her brother were traveling throughout Europe, and her letters entertained Sara Haardt "for hours."

[2]Dorothy Thompson, whom Sinclair Lewis had married in May, one month after his divorce from Grace Hegger.

~

H. L. MENCKEN
1524 HOLLINS ST.
BALTIMORE

September 14th, 1928

Dear Sara:-

The handkerchiefs are far too lovely. I think they are completely and absolutely swell. And so are you. You did an excellent job with the initials. But it is absolutely prohibited for you to give me such lavish presents. First those ivories, then the Chinese carving, and now these beautiful handkerchiefs. God will both reward and punish you. My very best thanks.

If your sister[1] comes in tonight or tomorrow, call me up, and we can have lunch together tomorrow. I'll be here all evening, and all tomorrow morning.

Yours,

M

[1]Ida and her husband, Charles Wickliffe Stevenson, had moved to Ruxton, where they could put Wickliffe in school.

H. L. MENCKEN
1524 HOLLINS ST.
BALTIMORE

September 14th, 1928

Dear Sara:-

Patterson and his wife will be on deck at 7:15 next Sunday. I have written to Mrs. Hamilton, but so far have no news from her. If she and Hamilton can't come what shall I do? Invite the Duffys?[1] Let me have your prayerful counsel at the office. Perhaps it would be better to postpone the dinner.

I am off to N.Y.

Yours,

M

[1]Anne Rector and Edmund Duffy. Anne was one of Sara's closest friends; Edmund was a political cartoonist for the Baltimore *Evening Sun* and had accompanied Mencken to the Scopes trial.

ALS

THE AMERICAN MERCURY
730 FIFTH AVENUE
NEW YORK

September 20, 1928

Dear Sara:

Tell Miss Glasgow that I am sorry indeed that I didn't see her in N.Y. She is a very charming woman.

All is set for Sunday. I'll call you up on Friday.

Hay fever subsides!

Yrs.,

M

H. L. MENCKEN
1524 HOLLINS ST.
BALTIMORE

Wednesday, September 26, 1928

Dear Sara:

. . . I hope you are having a swell time in Richmond.[1] If you find any graves of the Federal hordes, desecrate them in my name.

It is cold here.

Yours,

M

[1]Sara was visiting the Cabells and interviewing Mrs. James Branch Cabell for her series for *Good Housekeeping*. On this visit, Mrs. Cabell and Ellen Glasgow gave her a lunch party.

~

ALS

H. L. MENCKEN

1524 HOLLINS ST.

BALTIMORE

October 5, 1928

Dear Sara:

I'll drop in tomorrow (Saturday) at about 7:30. Today I was so upset[1] I forgot to bring you a bottle of sherry. But *don't stay in*. If you are out I'll leave it at your door, safely tied up.

Yrs.,

M

[1]Mencken had discovered that Sara was suffering from a cyst and appendicitis and would have to undergo surgery.

[TELEGRAM]

OCT 8 1928 7:06 PM

POSTAL TELEGRAPH - COMMERCIAL CABLES

NEW YORK NY

MISS SARA HAARDT

16 WEST READ ST BALTIMORE MD

PLEASE DON'T BE ALARMED   RICHARDSON AND HAMBURGER WILL FIND A WAY OUT RETURNING TUESDAY

M.

[TELEGRAM]

OCT 12 1928 8:08 PM

WESTERN UNION

NASHVILLE TENN

MISS SARA HAARDT

16 WEST READ ST BALTIMORE MD

PLEASE SEND ME NIGHTLETTER IN CARE SMITH TRAIN LOUISVILLE TELLING ME WHAT HAMBURGER SAYS AND WHAT HIS PROGRAM IS

MENCKEN.[1]

[1]Distressed that he had to leave Sara for two weeks, Mencken telegraphed this while on the first leg of Al Smith's campaign tour.

Nashville, Friday night, October 12, 1928

Dear Sara:-

I am dreadfully sorry that there must be surgery, but if Hamburger advises it then certainly you must go through with it.[1] He will see that it is made safe: you can trust him completely. And Richardson as a surgeon.[2] Whatever his caution, he will make a good job of it, and you get rid of all that long agony at last. You should be back at work in a month, and able to work far better than you have ever been in the past.

How long this nonsensical trip will last I don't know.[3] According to the present plan Smith will speak in Chicago toward the end of next week. As soon as he does so I shall come home. That should bring me in by the 22nd.

It is infernally hot here, and the train is filthy. But I hope to clean up in Louisville tomorrow. We shall lie on a siding half of tonight.

I have seen 100,000 morons in two days, and they all look alike. What a country!

But this afternoon we dipped into Alabama, and the country was lovely.

I know you will be as brave as you always are.

Yours,

M

[1] Sara's operation was to take place on October 23.

[2] Dr. Edward Richardson, a leading gynecologist.

[3] The campaign tour would end in New York on October 30. During Al's campaign tour through the South, Mencken concluded in his article for October 12 that campaign tours were not only inane but futile. Few people were ever close enough to hear what the candidate was saying, and there was never time enough for local politicians or editors to get a chance even to "whisper to him." After one particularly "banal" ceremony in Raleigh, North Carolina, Mencken reported, the entourage made its next stop at a suburban station called Method, only here, "the Smith automobile got there twenty minutes before the special train was backed out from the city and the candidate spent the time standing up in the car, autographing handkerchiefs, slips out of memorandum books, the backs of envelopes and hatbands. A crowd of two or three hundred people surged about him, thrusting up such things, hoofing over one another, and bawling idiotically. Finally he tired of this uproar, shoved his brown derby over his ears and refused to write his name any more.

"When the train came in at last it stopped with the private car a block or two away. Mrs. Smith and the other ladies of the party had to stagger down the track, their high-heeled shoes battered at every step by the rough ballast. No police were visible, but four or five militia officers in uniform appeared from somewhere and gave the ladies aid. It was a grotesque picture. There stood the celebrated $1,000,000 campaign train, its long line of Pullmans glittering, and there the candidate laboriously trudged the ties, his wife and daughters trailing after him.

"But campaigning, of course, has its discomforts, even when it is done in Pullmans. The question is whether such barnstorming accomplishes anything. Do the morons, by simply gaping at the candidate, acquire a mad, irrational passion to vote for him? Is one brief glimpse of him, at an average distance of fifty yards, sufficient to make him forget the endless harangues of their pastors, the natural instincts of Christians and patriots and the awful letter of Holy Writ? It seems improbable. More, it seems silly. Yet all that has been done on this expedition so far is to let hordes of half-wits see the brown derby. Not a single politician, as far as I can determine, has said a word worth hearing or got a piece of news worth knowing."

H. L. MENCKEN
1524 HOLLINS ST.
BALTIMORE

Monday, October 22, 1928

Dear Sara:-

Good luck! And don't let them alarm you. You will be very comfortable, and in a week you'll be feeling (as Ma Smith says) fine and dandy.

Hyde and I have both come down with a mild flu, apparently as a result of broken rest and irregular meals. I am on my legs, but somewhat wobbly. It seems to be precisely what I had last Winter. Then it lasted three days.

Obviously, God has some objection to my waiting on you. But I'll come up to see you at the very first chance, maybe tomorrow.[1]

I trust to your courage.

Yours,

M

[1] Sara was in Room 428 of Union Hospital, surrounded by flowers. Her friend Mary Parmenter visited Sara at the hospital and found her "a badly broken blossom

. . . nothing but big black eyes." Mencken arrived later that afternoon, with a suitcase full of beverages and a pack of Methodist and Baptist newspapers. "His idea of an uproarious afternoon, said Mary Parmenter, was, apparently, to read what the hardshells were saying about Al Smith."

H. L. MENCKEN

1524 HOLLINS ST.

BALTIMORE

Monday, October 29, 1928

Dear Sara:-

The effects of prayer begin to show themselves. My malaise has gone and my nose begins to feel more normal. I shall wait on you tomorrow afternoon. How well you looked last night! My guess is that this surgery will make you a handsomer gal than ever.

Al's agent called me up an hour ago and asked me to dinner, but I had to decline. Whether or not I go to the great outpouring tonight[1] will depend upon the inspiration of the moment. I have written about all I want to say about Al.

Yours,

M

[1]Al Smith was scheduled to speak at the Baltimore Armory that evening at 9:00 P.M. He opened his speech by stating that the Ku Klux Klan and the Anti-Saloon League were participating in the Republican campaign, and then he proceeded to declare that common decency should be the treatment of Latin America. In the end, Mencken did attend and wrote: "The thing took courage. With the South wobbling and the Middle West wriggling there was surely plenty of excuse, at least by the code that politicians follow, for weasel words. But Al sailed into all the gods of Moronia in the fashion of a longshoreman cleaning out a saloon. First the Anti Saloon League was stretched in the sawdust, and then the political parsons, and then the Klan. 'When I get on a subject of this kind,' he explained, 'I get heated up a bit.' The heat transferred itself to the crowd. It was an old-time meeting and it was a grand success. Twice Al had to appeal to the galleries to let him go on. He might have spun out his speech to two hours, and there would have been whoops and applause to the end. . . . The speech at New York Saturday night should be worth going miles to hear—and see. Plain hearing, as by the radio, is not enough."

~

H. L. MENCKEN
1524 HOLLINS ST.
BALTIMORE

Tuesday, October 30, 1928

Dear Sara:-

Hamburger told me the whole story today, and I'll pass it on to you on Thursday, in simple and refined language. You ran in considerable luck. The cyst was completely benign, but it might have multiplied and given you much trouble. Now it is safely gone, and there will be no more heard from it. All the other troubles should go with it. Richardson apparently made a very good job. Give yourself no concern. You bore the business splendidly, and are a tougher gal than you look.

It turned out that I had no fever. I am to lie low, use some ephidrin in the nose, and employ rye whiskey freely. It doesn't sound bad. I feel very rocky, but such things always vanish as suddenly as they come on. I may be quite well by tomorrow or next day. In any case I shall wait upon you on Thursday.

I have begged off going to New York to cover Al. Last night was enough.

Yours,
M

H. L. MENCKEN
1524 HOLLINS ST.
BALTIMORE

November 3rd, 1928

Dear Sara:-

Blame my senility! I clean forgot the whiskey. The bottle stands on my table, rebuking me. I'll bring it Monday. Meanwhile, if there is a competent bartender in the hospital the sherry will serve almost as well.

You looked splendid today. The butchery will make you bloom. I shall see Woollcott tonight, and find out when he is to be anatomized. Probably next Wednesday. He wants to vote for Al first.[1]

Yours,
M

¹Election day was Tuesday, November 6.

H. L. MENCKEN
1524 HOLLINS ST.
BALTIMORE

November 6, 1928

Dear Sara:

I saw old Anna last night and found her in a sorely dilapidated state. She has been ill for a week with what she describes as "pleurisy of the heart." What this may be God knows. She said that she was feeling better and hoped to come to work tonight. I'll probably see her after I leave the *Sun* office. I told her that you had been greatly disturbed that she had been barred from your room and she said that she would come to see you again. A note to her would probably please her immensely. Unfortunately, I don't know her last name.¹

I shall grind away all day, put in the evening at the office and then leave for New York in the morning. You looked splendid yesterday and I am sure that the leeches will let you out by the end of the week. Don't let the persistence of the pain alarm you. It usually goes on for some time, but it steadily diminishes.

I hope to wait on you next Sunday evening.

Yours,

M

¹Anna Oberleitner.

~

ALS

H. L. MENCKEN
1524 HOLLINS ST.
BALTIMORE

November 7, 1928

Dear Sara:

I am off to console Al. What a débâcle! But Alabama stood firm.
Now for four years of the Anti-Saloon League and good hunting.

Yours,
M

Hoover had won the election, receiving 444 electoral votes of 40 states; Al Smith received only 87 electoral votes in 8 states—surprisingly, 6 of them Southern. He failed to carry Virginia, Florida, North Carolina, Tennessee, and Texas, though he did win more popular votes throughout the nation than had any previous Democratic presidential candidate.

H. L. MENCKEN
1524 HOLLINS ST.
BALTIMORE

November 16th, 1928

Freind Sara:-[1]

You sure looked swell when I seen you Wed. Being sick ain't done you no harm. All I hope is that you get well and be yourself again. I hate to see anybody sick, especially when I hold them in personal regards. Keep off the booze, Sara. Let this be a lesson to you, and don't let it floor you again. I hear Willie Woollcott has went on the wagon. Well, it was time he done it. Of course I ain't no Prohibitionist, but there is such a thing as knowing when to let it alone. I try to drink it and let it alone. Also, I think that coke is dangerous stuff. If it was good, then all the doctors would be drinking it, but you don't see none of them drinking it.

Well, Sara, I must go to the Eastern Shore on business, and so I must close. Give my kind regards to Dr. Hamburger and the other boys. When I get back I'll give you a ring.

Kindest personal regards.

Yours,
M

¹Every now and then, Mencken wrote in "pure American."

[POSTCARD]

1120 The Jail, Talbot County, Easton, Md.

November 17, 1928

This is a swell place. Having a swell time. One and all treating us swell. Kindest personal regards.

M

~

[CARD]

Mr. H. L. Mencken

1928

A less miserable Christmas than usual!

M

1929

1929 *was the year of the great stock market crash. For most of the year Americans were blissfully unaware of the impending disaster; life went on, and there was much optimism in the air. Even after the event the nation did not know quite what had happened, and it was not until months later that they awoke to the fact that they were in the midst of a Depression. Mencken chose not to write an editorial on the Depression in* The American Mercury *until 1932. He believed, as did many others, that the business crisis was only temporary.*

During the first half of 1929 Sara decided she would escape the "vile" weather of Baltimore and get away to Europe for the summer, but in the spring she became seriously ill and had to spend most of the summer at Union Hospital, where her tubercular kidney was removed. As usual, Mencken visited Sara and paid her a great deal of attention. Their friend Paul de Kruif wrote to Sara: "Don't listen too much to Henry, who is so damned fond of hospitals that he'll try to keep you there indefinitely just to be able to talk to you about your experiences in them."

If Sara's health was on the decline, so too was Mencken's popularity. Nonetheless, when Mencken was about to set sail for Europe in December, he and Sara had already become engaged to be married the following year.

H. L. MENCKEN
1524 HOLLINS ST.
BALTIMORE

January 14th, 1929

Dear Sara:-

A few unimportant changes would make the Glasgow sketch[1] fit into The American Mercury perfectly. But I believe Bridges will like it as it stands, and so I think he ought to be given a chance at it. It would be excellent politics for you to get into Scribner's. It would do you more good than six appearances in The American Mercury. So I am sending him the MS. But if he doesn't take it I want it back.

I think it would be a good idea for you to go to see Perkins, and tell him that you think his criticism of your novel was sound, and that you are preparing to rewrite it.[2] He will ask to see it again, and I think he will take it in its new form. It doesn't need many changes. What it needs mainly is copy-reading. This you can get free of charge from the Old Professor.

Baltimore is empty without you. Last night I caught myself going to the telephone to call you up and beg you to share my sufferings at Schellhase's. Old Anna will not see me until you get back. I hope to be in New York by next Sunday night. Will you be there then?

Yours,

M

[1]"Ellen Glasgow and the South" was finally published in *The Bookman*, April 1929.

[2]F. Scott Fitzgerald had recommended *The Making of a Lady* to Maxwell Perkins.

H. L. MENCKEN
1524 HOLLINS ST.
BALTIMORE

January 15th, 1929

Dear Sara:-

Give Lardner,[1] Phelps[2] and Cobb[3] my kindest personal regards— or, at all events, Lardner and Phelps. Cobb dislikes me, and with sound reason. The wives I don't know, save Mrs. Lardner.[4] She looks 25, and has children nearly grown. The selections are not bad.

I expect to get to New York Sunday. I have a dinner engagement for Sunday night, but I might be able to escape by 10 or 10:30. If you are going to Emily's house I'll join you there.[5] Monday I am dining with the Goodmans.[6] If you are free, why not come along? I'll ask Mrs. Goodman to call you up. She'll be delighted.

It is good luck that your sister is in New Haven.[7] The trip will be very much pleasanter than going alone.

Let me hear about Sunday and Monday.

I hear that Anna is pining away.

Yours,

M

[1] Ring Lardner.

[2] William Lyon Phelps, essayist, and Professor of English at Yale.

[3] Irvin Shrewsbury Cobb, American journalist and humorist, a man, Mencken believed, "who was born dead," had been one of the several "corpses" exhibited in Mencken's writing.

[4] Ellis Abbott. One of their children is the screenwriter Ring Lardner, Jr.

[5] After the death of her husband, Emily Clark Balch had moved to New York and opened up a salon (or "saloon," as Sara Haardt liked to call it).

[6] Phil and Ruth Goodman.

[7] Ida.

H. L. MENCKEN
1524 HOLLINS ST.
BALTIMORE

Saturday, February 9, 1929

Dear Sara:-

Two valentines reached me today from anonymous sources. Obviously, two more handsome and romantic gals have got stuck on me. Tomorrow I am off for New York to loll among the blondes, brunettes and red-haired. It is a hard life for an ageing man. But Jack Gilbert and I must bear it. It is our Art.

I wish you were in N.Y. this week.

Yours,

M

H. L. MENCKEN
1524 HOLLINS ST.
BALTIMORE

February 23rd, 1929

Dear Sara:-

"The Etiquette of Slavery" is well.[1] I am sending it to the printer at once, and the usual check will reach you in about a week. My best thanks. I shall fall on the Glasgow treatise tomorrow morning.

What of bringing another gal Monday to make it four? Have you any in mind? If so, I hope you ask her. Or as you please.

Yours,
M

[1]"The Etiquette of Slavery," published in *The American Mercury*, May 1929.

ALS

THE AMERICAN MERCURY
730 FIFTH AVENUE
NEW YORK

March 5, 1929

Dear Sara:

I met Crawford[1] here yesterday and made an engagement with him to meet at the Marconi *next Tuesday* at 12:15. He says he wants to see you, so I hope you can come along. I'll be back by Friday evening and shall call you up as soon as I get in.

It rained on Hoover! After all, God has a certain decency.[2]

Yours,
M

[1]Nelson Antrim Crawford, editor of *Household* magazine. He would publish many of Sara Haardt's stories and articles in the 1930s.

[2]The Baltimore *Evening Sun* wanted Mencken to cover Herbert Hoover's inauguration on March 4. Mencken had written to Marion Bloom that he wished it would rain and Hoover would get soaked. His wish was granted.

ALS

THE AMERICAN MERCURY
730 FIFTH AVENUE
NEW YORK

March 6, 1929

Dear Sara:

Bigelow is a swine.[1] Tell him that Zelda is a 100% Christian woman.
I can find you 50 perjurers to substantiate it.

Yours,

HLM

---

[1]Sara had written an article about Zelda Fitzgerald, but after hearing several pejorative rumors about Zelda from various informants (including his art editor), W. F. Bigelow was hesitant about publishing any article that dealt with the wife of F. Scott Fitzgerald.

H. L. MENCKEN
1524 HOLLINS ST.
BALTIMORE

March 14th, 1929

Dear Sara:-

Tell the ass that, so far as you know, it is a complete calumny. Tell him that Mrs. F. may, of course, take a drink occasionally, but that you have known her for years, and know most of her friends, and none of them think she drinks too much. Tell him that Fitz, in the past, occasionally got a bit boisterous, and that probably the doings of the two were confused.[1]

This Bigelow is an almost fabulous swine. It was for such that Christ died on the Cross!

Yours,

M

---

[1]In the end, Bigelow decided not to use Sara's interviews with Zelda Fitzgerald or any of the other interviews with wives of famous authors. As Mencken explained: "When she [Sara] delivered the manuscripts to Bigelow he told her that he had observed that she was a contributor to *The American Mercury* and warned

her solemnly against succumbing to my influence. Bigelow was a poor fellow and regarded me as an anarchist. Sara did not tell him, of course, that she and I were then engaged." When the news of their eventual wedding reached Bigelow, "he pigeon-holed the manuscripts," and although they had been paid for, neglected to print them.

H. L. MENCKEN

1524 HOLLINS ST.

BALTIMORE

April 30th, 1929

Friend Sara:-

No matter what you say, you will be the queen of the party. Them other girls are all right, but don't think I ain't got eyes in my head. I only hope nobody gets no edge on, and don't start no rough stuff. It was swell of you to fix things up.

I get a letter from Jim Tully, saying Marna will be here between May 10 and May 15. That will be just the time I am in Bethlehem and N.Y.

Well, Sara, I guess I will now close. Don't be late on Thursday. You know how I hate to be kept waiting for my victuals.

Yours,

M

At last Sara had recovered from her ills, "though I knock on wood," as she wrote to Sara Mayfield. Suddenly, she took a turn for the worse.

H. L. MENCKEN

1524 HOLLINS ST.

BALTIMORE

Sunday, May 26, 1929

Dear Sara:-

Don't forget to ask the professors (a) if ginger-beer is a prudent drink for you, and (b) if you can have a stick of rye in milk at night. You looked superb today, and are plainly very much better. I think all the treatment should be over in ten days. And you will be back to normal weight. I ascribe all this to the power of the Holy Spirit, working in answer to prayer by Mayfield and me.

Yours,

M

Sara had developed an infection in her kidney and was eventually admitted to Union Memorial Hospital. Mencken had been keeping Sara Mayfield informed of her progress; soon afterwards he asked her to come up from Tuscaloosa to watch after Sara during the few days he had to be in New York. "It is distressing to leave," Mencken wrote to Mayfield.

H. L. MENCKEN

1524 HOLLINS ST.

BALTIMORE

May 31st, 1929

Dear Sara:-

Curiously enough, I have neither Java Head nor The Three Black Pennys.[1] Some government spy must have broken into my house and carried them off.

Hamburger told me that you were making excellent progress, and that he hoped to clear up the infection very soon.[2]

I'll wait on you on the Sabbath.

Yours,

M

[1] *Java Head*, and *The Three Black Pennys*, both novels by Joseph Hergesheimer. Sara had been helping Hergesheimer gather material for *Swords and Roses*.

[2] The doctors and Sara still believed there was only a small, local infection.

~

H. L. MENCKEN
1524 HOLLINS ST.
BALTIMORE

June 28th, 1929

Dear Sara:-

God willing, I shall wait upon you tomorrow (Saturday) in the afternoon. I am very eager to hear what Walker has to say.[1] He knows more about urology than any of them, and is a very good fellow. Tell him he is NOT to hurt you. I can't bear to see you in pain. It must be stopped.

Yours,

M

[1] A team of doctors examined Sara the next morning and found that she had a secondary bladder infection and that her right kidney was clear. The left kidney was to be examined the next day. A decision to perform surgery was to be reached on July 15. Mencken advised Sara Mayfield not to alarm Sara's family unduly until the question of an operation was definitely settled.

H. L. MENCKEN
1524 HOLLINS ST.
BALTIMORE

July 2nd, 1929

Dear Sara:-

There is absolutely no reason to be uneasy. Walker tells me that the right lead is found at last, and that a cure will follow promptly and will be complete. I have very great confidence in him, as you know. Some small studies remain to be made, but the horrible examinations are over. You have been immensely brave and now you will get your reward. I marvel how you have gone through all the tortures of the last months.

I am to see the dentist again tomorrow, and shall wait upon you after he turns me loose. If I looked a bit silly yesterday it was because part of my lip was still anesthetized and I felt lame.

Yours,

M

Throughout Sara's illness Mencken tried to hide the reason for his concern. The date of her operation was suddenly advanced from July 15 to July 6, and her left kidney was removed. Soon afterwards, George Walker informed Mencken that Sara's infection was tubercular and that she had, at most, only three more years to live.

H. L. MENCKEN
1524 HOLLINS ST.
BALTIMORE

August 14th, 1929

Dear Sara-

The enclosed is from the Birmingham News. Who wrote it I don't know—probably Gladys Baker.[1]

How swell it was to see you navigating again, and looking so well! It has been a long pull, but now the end is in sight. You are a game gal!

Yours,
M

[1]Gladys Baker had written a lavish article, praising Sara Haardt's writing.

[TELEGRAM]

AUG 29 1929 7:03 PM

WESTERN UNION
BALTIMORE MD
MISS SARA HAARDT

UNION MEMORIAL HOSPITAL

PLEASE DO NOT BE UNEASY[1]   WALKER IS A NATURAL PESSIMIST YOU WILL GET WELL AND COMPLETELY   I'LL SEE YOU SOON

H.L.M.

[1]While visiting Sara, Anne Duffy, recently back from Europe, inadvertently broke the news to Sara that Sara's tubercular kidney had been removed. The

doctors were withholding this information from Sara until she had made more of a recovery. Most likely, Mencken's telegram followed after Sara had had a conference with Dr. Walker.

H. L. MENCKEN
1524 HOLLINS ST.
BALTIMORE

Thursday, September 20, 1929

Dear Sara:-

I hope you are very much better.[1] Tomorrow I shall call you up. Maybe you will let me see you in the afternoon or on Saturday. The cold weather has pretty well finished hay-fever, though I am still poisoned by it.

Here is a slip that Paul de Kruif sent to me for you, to paste in your copy of his new book.[2]

Yours,
M

[1]For the first time in months Sara was able to sleep through the night.

[2]Paul de Kruif had sent her *Seven Iron Men*, with a slip on which he had written the inscription "To Sara Haardt—With my best regards and sincerest wishes for her well-being till 80+, from Paul and Rhea."

ALS

HOTEL ALGONQUIN
NEW YORK

Monday, October 14, 1929

Dear Sara:

A letter came in from Tully today, reciting what he told you the other day.[1] He says the money looks sure. Good news! The Irish are like cross-eyed mules: they bring luck—but not to themselves.

Paul Patterson is here and the Haneses of N. C. I will see them before the end of the evening. Ah, that thou wert here too!

My office desk is the usual chaos. But I'll get through it by Friday morning, with God's help.

Tomorrow I go to the solemn dinner to Tom Beer.[2] My inclination is to show up in my cups.

Yours,

H.[3]

[1]Jim Tully was trying to get money from James Cruze for Sara's film, *Way Down South*, which she had sold to Cruze in 1927.

[2]His biography of Stephen Crane did much to establish Crane's fame. His book *The Mauve Decade*, an interpretation of American life during the last part of the nineteenth century, was similar in theme to *Hanna*, a study of the American businessman and politician Mark Hanna, which had come out that year.

[3]By this time Mencken and Sara had already become engaged.

H. L. MENCKEN
1524 HOLLINS ST.
BALTIMORE

October 28th, 1929

Dear Sara:-

The rug goes to you by parcel-post this morning. It was my fault that it was forgotten.[1]

You were lovely as always, and won the family all over again.[2] What a gal!

I am stuck tonight and tomorrow by Sun business, but hope to tear loose by Wednesday. What of a session at the Grand Café Schellhase Wednesday evening?

Yours,

M

[1]On her return to Tuscaloosa Sara Mayfield had taken back some of the furniture she had been loaning Sara, with the consequence that the apartment now looked like a "barn." The year before, in an effort to make the apartment more cosy, Mencken had wanted to give Sara some fabric to hang up on her wall. "God knows where he gets such ideas of interior decoration," Sara had written to Mayfield. This time Mencken sent her a rug.

²Sara Haardt and Jim Tully had been invited to spend Sunday dinner at the Menckens the day before. For the time being Mencken and Sara's engagement was kept secret; Mencken would not tell his brothers or sister of his intentions to marry Sara until April 26, 1930.

[TELEGRAM]

NOV 29 1929 10:06 PM

WESTERN UNION

BALTIMORE

MISS SARAH HAARDT

16 WEST READ ST BALTIMORE MD

THE BOOK WAS FINISHED AT NINE FIFTEEN TONIGHT[1] GLORY HALLELUJAH   I WILL BE READY TO CELEBRATE SUNDAY   YOUR PRAYERS MUST GET THE CREDIT

HLM

¹On Thanksgiving night Mencken finished writing *Treatise on the Gods*. It was to remain one of his favorite books and would go into nine printings.

H. L. MENCKEN

1524 HOLLINS ST.

BALTIMORE

December 18, 1929

Dear Sara:

When I was in New York two weeks ago I had Gladys Baker to lunch to meet La Suckow and her husband.¹ Miss Baker works for the Birmingham *News* and wanted to do an article about them. At lunch she gave me a message for you and I clean forgot it. It was that she had lately met a highly intelligent Hungarian woman, a great admirer of Thomas Mann, who told her that she thought "Licked" was a better story than Mann's "The Magic Mountain." I promised to convey this to you, but I forgot it. Here it is.

Yours,

M

[On March 11 Ruth Suckow had married Ferner Nuhn, of Cedar Falls, Iowa.

HOTEL ALGONQUIN
NEW YORK

December 27, 1929

Dearest Sara:

I am tempted to tear up my ticket and start back to Baltimore at once.[1] How lovely you are, and how I'll miss you! You will never know how much I think of you, and depend on you, and love you.

Yours ever,

H

[1]Months before Mencken had decided he had earned a vacation. Now, on Sara's insistence, he embarked on the S.S. *Columbus* and spent six weeks in central Europe, taking two weeks off to report on the naval conference being held in London.

[TELEGRAM]

DEC 30 1929 5:35 PM
DELR 31ST

HOLIDAY GREETING
WESTERN UNION
RADIO VIA SS COLUMBUS CD CHATHAM
SARA HAARDT
16 WEST READ BALTIMORE (MD)
    HAPPY NEW YEAR   LOVE

H.

HW

ALS

December the thirty-first, 1929

Darling,

It was so sweet to have your New Year's message. I came in from Ruxton last night, tired and cold, and it reassured me and made me all warm again. You seem so far away, and it was only a week ago that we last met. . . .

The Duffys are having a party tonight, and also the Hamiltons, but I'm staying in to work. I remember you're to have a party—New Year's at sea!—I hope you have a lovely time, darling. I miss you and love you so . . .

As ever,
Sara

H. L. Mencken, Esq.,
704 Cathedral street
Baltimore, Maryland

MEMORANDUM

FROM

MRS. H. L. MENCKEN

To

Mr. H. L. MENCKEN

1934

I LOVE YOU

LOVE YOU

LOVE YOU

LOVE YOU

THE
Marriage Years

1930 — 1935

1930

In 1930 Mencken went to Europe and reported on the naval conference being held in London: "an orgy," he wrote, "of hollow oratory, much of it in bad English." Both Mencken and Sara came out with books: Mencken's Treatise on the Gods to controversy and acclaim; Sara's The Making of a Lady to mixed reviews. Their relationship continued with more intensity than before. To Sara, Mencken wrote: "I love you more and more and more." Before he set sail for Europe Mencken called Sara from the dock in New York and sounded, she told her friends, "quite doleful. I'll miss him terribly." In a few months they would become man and wife.

NORDDEUTSCHER LLOYD BREMEN
AN BORD DES D. "COLUMBUS"

January 1st, 1930

Dearest Sara:-

Your letter was lovely, as you are, and always will be. I am horribly homesick for you. But the next time you will be aboard, and everything will be perfect. I love you!

The voyage has been very quiet. There has been some rolling and some fog, but now the sea is calm and the sun is shining, and it is almost summery. Dudley Field Malone[1] is aboard; also a gorgeous young Swedish gal.[2] They are to be married in London next week. It will be Dudley's third venture. He is an old friend, and we have been having a pleasant time together. He, the Swede, a New York banker and I eat together. But the fair one has missed two meals out of three: evidently the Viking blood begins to run thin.

Last night there was a mild New Year's eve party in the smoke-room. We drank the usual German toast with Fritz Kreisler[3] and his wife and a few others, but there was no general uproar. Most of the people aboard look very uninteresting. I put in the first two days sleeping, and am doing a lot of it yet. Today I got up at noon. I feel rested and hearty, and hope to floor Goodman when we tackle the Pilsner together. There is plenty of it aboard and it is excellent. Goodman is to meet me at Cherbourg on Saturday.

The Norddeutscher-Lloyd has done very well by me.[4] I have a huge room with a private bath. It has all sorts of luxuries—a desk, two chintz-covered chairs, two windows, electric heaters, a fan, reading lights, and so on. There is one washstand in the room and another in the bathroom. I use one for shaving and the other for washing off the lather. The Queen of Sheba herself lived no more luxuriously. Yesterday morning I went to the barber-shop and let the professor perform all of his masterpieces on me. It took an hour and cost $1.50, but it was swell.

I have no plans until January 25th. How long Goodman will be able to stay in Europe I don't know—probably no more than a week. His last letter said he had a lawsuit in New York January 20th, and would have to get home for it. I gather that his wife and daughter will remain in Paris. If he leaves in a week I'll probably go to Germany. I hear aboard that the south of France and Italy are cold and gloomy at this season. In Germany the cold is frankly admitted, and the houses are built to make it bearable. I may go to the Black Forest for a week, or to St. Moritz. I don't know. There will be no need for me to get to London until toward the end of the month.

I surely hope Richardson liberates you at once, and that you go south. It would do you a lot of good. And the sooner you go the sooner you will be coming back! Will you let me have a cable at 40 Fleet street (Baltimore Sun office) as soon as you know your plans?[5] I'll be in contact with Fleming,[6] the correspondent, soon after I land.

This is a lazy life. I have read five or six books, and begin to tire of reading. Malone and I sit by the hour, gabbling about nothing.

We have been swapping reminiscences of the Scopes trial, and talking of doing a joint record of it. Certainly such a record ought to be made. There are four or five books on the trial, but all of them are full of nonsense. The real facts of history are always lost. Only balderdash survives.

I am now a week nearer to seeing you! And thinking of you all the time. I love you.

H

[1]Mencken's old friend from the Scopes Monkey Trial.

[2]Malone's third wife, Edna Louise Johnson.

[3]American violinist, born in Vienna, and composer of classical music for violin and the operetta *Apple Blossoms*.

[4]By 1930 the German Norddeutscher Lloyd *Bremen* was one of the fastest and largest vessels afloat. Nicknaming it the "Queen of the Seas" in one of his Monday articles, Mencken commended the ship not only for its speed, beauty, and food, but for the small additional luxuries, such as "footrests to facilitate the lacing of shoes." To Mencken, a man who had never learned to tie his laces well, this last detail would have been a special delight. The *Bremen* continued to be a favorite with the traveling public until it was destroyed in 1939 during an air raid on Bremen.

[5]The *Sun* headquarters, at 40 Fleet Street, were right next door to *The Manchester Guardian*. The Baltimore *Evening Sun* and the *Guardian* shared a close alliance, under which the *Evening Sun* had rights to all the special correspondence and other material published in the *Guardian,* and vice versa.

[6]Dewey L. Fleming, the London correspondent for the Baltimore *Evening Sun*.

HOTEL LA TREMOILLE
CHAMPS ELYSEES
PARIS

January 5th, 1930

Dearest Sara:-

I am having a lovely time with the Goodmans.[1] The victualling here is really colossal, and every third place has German beer on draft. In fact, Paris has gone beer crazy. There are actually brews on tap that I never encountered in Germany. Today Phil and I spent six hours walking about. My legs feel like lead, but otherwise I am in grand condition. In fact, I already begin to feel like work. The town is almost bare of Americans. A man told me today that at the very fashionable Hotel Meurice, which is usually full of them, only 29 are registered. This saddens the poor French, but is pleasant otherwise.

The Goodmans must return home on Friday, so I am going to Vienna on Saturday. How long I'll stay there I don't know—probably about ten days. Then I'll work my way to London. I should reach there by the 27th. The Sun brethren will get in on the 17th.

God knows, I wish you were here! How lovely it would be to rove around the town with you! But you must give some study and prayer to the local dialect. It is quite beyond me, as it is beyond Goodman. He and I depend on his daughter Ruth, who speaks it very well. Last night she took us to a low cabaret to hear some songs. The music was charming, but we missed most of the words. Worse, she couldn't translate them, for they seemed to run beyond the exchanges proper between a young gal and two elderly men.

I am going to Vienna because I have never been there, and must certainly see Beethoven's grave before I come home. I'll probably not stop in Germany, but shall proceed direct to London. My telephone is working as usual, as the enclosed clippings indicate. Today I got an invitation to call on Gertrude Stein![2]

There was no letter from you at the American Express office. Apparently I beat it to Paris. I shall go back for it tomorrow. I'll feel much easier when I hear from you. Have you moved into the new apartment? And is Richardson letting you go home? Let me have FULL news of you in London.

I miss you dreadfully, and love you completely.

Yours,

M

[1] Throughout their stay the Goodmans watched in amazement as Mencken consumed beer after beer, disappeared into phone booths, organized friends, grabbed the check, and overtipped. They reported that Mencken was amused by the astonishing resemblance of the maitre d'hotel to Al Smith. (Naturally, "Al" was overtipped.)

[2] The American writer was living at 27 rue de Fleurus. Mencken, whose view of "Miss Stein's genius" was "somewhat low," did not meet her.

~

ALS

SARA HAARDT

January the eight, 1930

Henry dear,

It will probably be another week or two before your letters begin to arrive. I'm quite, quite desolate without them. Are you thoroughly rested, darling? And are you having a very marvellous time? I hope so. You've had such a dreadful year.[1]

I'm supposed to go to the Bary concert with the Woollcotts Friday night, but I fear I'll have to decline. Richardson is trying out a new scheme and I have to stay close. He thinks I should go away for a while, not to Montgomery particularly, where there are mainly tomb-stones, but further South, or to Bermuda. It's quite impossible of course. I only know I shouldn't be in this state of mind. I'm working though, every day and every night.

All my love
S.

[1]Although the stock market crash had not affected Mencken directly, he nonetheless lost money.

HOTEL LA TREMOILLE
CHAMPS ELYSEES
PARIS

January 10th, 1930

Dearest Sara:-

The Goodmans left for Cherbourg this morning and I shall shove off for Vienna tomorrow. How long I'll stay there I don't know—probably not long. It has been a very quiet and pleasant week. Good-man is back in his old form, and we got down some dinners of the first calibre. Last night he and his wife and daughter and I closed the semester with a Pilsner evening. We sat until 3 o'clock.

No letter from you at the American Express. I surely hope it is on its way. And that you are well. I miss you every minute. Never again without you! You would have been delighted by the week here, despite

the gorging. The weather is almost Spring-like and the town is very
beautiful.

Yesterday I went to see old Emma Goldman, the anarchist, who is
living here, finishing her autobiography.[1] The U.S. took away her
citizenship and threw her out. So she went to Canada, married a
convenient Canuck,[2] became a British subject, and is now here with
a British passport, unmolested. Considering her years and adventures
she looks very vigorous. We drank tea together! It sounds incredible,
but it is a fact. If I find the time I may do an article about her for
the Evening Sun. But first I must frame a report on the way that Paris
has gone beer crazy. German signs are all over the place.

Today I am to see my French translator, Michaud,[3] and tomorrow
I am to have lunch with Dr. Thomas Buckler,[4] an old Baltimorean,
who has been living here for 10 years. Then I'll pack and start for
Vienna. The train goes through Munich, but I shall not stop off. After
that it proceeds into Austria via Salzburg, by daylight. It should be
a magnificent trip. I know all that country pretty well on the German
side, but not on the Austrian side. If Vienna turns out to be too cold
I'll move back into Germany, and so work my way toward London.[5]
The Sun outfit sailed yesterday and should be in London by the 17th.[5]
This morning I had a telegram inviting me to a farewell lunch in
London to Van-Lear Black, but I can't make it. Apparently he is
preparing to begin his air trip to South Africa.[6]

My dear, I love you beyond everything. I am horribly homesick for
you.

Yours,

M

---

[1]The Russian socialist, anarchist, feminist, and author had given Mencken
her manuscript, *Living My Life*, for him to read. Mencken's admiration for
Goldman—and hers for him—was mutual. Responding to the opinion of her
friend Alexander Berkman that Mencken was a "superficial clown," she would
write in a letter of 1933: "Nor is it true that Mencken is a clown. More than
any other American, Mencken has pleaded for libertarian ideas. And he has stood
his ground when others of the intelligentsia had failed. . . . [The deterioration
of his popularity] does not lessen his contribution and inspiration of young
writers."

[2]The Welsh miner James Colton.

[3]Régis Michaud, who had also been a professor of French at the University of California and at Illinois, was the translator of *Prejudices*.

[4]Thomas Hepburn Buckler, a general practitioner from Baltimore, had been living in Paris. He would return to live in Baltimore in 1935.

[5]Along with Mencken, those reporters covering the 1930 naval conference would be Paul Patterson, John Lowens, Drew Patterson, and D. L. Fleming.

[6]The commander in chief of the *Sunpapers* and an enthusiastic aviator and yachtsman, Van-Lear Black, had already completed several long-distance flights which made him known all over the world. This particular trip would take him from London to South Africa to Tokyo and then back again to Baltimore. The farewell party would be a premonition of sorts: Van-Lear Black died eight months later, on August 18, when he fell overboard from his yacht during a heavy storm off the coast of New Jersey.

HOTEL LA TREMOILLE

CHAMPS ELYSEES

PARIS

January 10th, 1930

Dearest Sara:-

Your two letters came in today. How lovely you always are! They make me horribly homesick. And now I am putting another thousand miles between us! But in a week I'll be turning back, and then it will be nearer all the time. You are infinitely dear. . . .

I doubt that I could stand Paris for long. The worst difficulty is the language. I find I can understand a lot of it, but speaking it is impossible. So I feel strange when I am on my own. Vienna will be easier. I have laid on a pocket dictionary and a phrase-book and shall brush up on the train.

Another job for tomorrow: to see a French interviewer. Fortunately, my translator, Michaud, will be along. He went out to the U.S. 20 years ago, married an American woman, and tried to settle down. But in the end he had to give it up. He told me today that Methodism had fetched him in the end. He is making much less money here than he made in America, but he is half busting with happiness. No wonder! Paris is charming enough to an Americano. To a Frenchman it must be heaven.

I feel very good, and begin to be eager for work again. But I'll probably have no time tomorrow to do an article. Maybe I'll tackle it on the train. Certainly the beer flood here deserves a few lines.

I'll love you forever.

Yours,
M

HOTEL BRISTOL

WIEN

January 13th, 1930.

Dearest Sara:-

I reached here before dinner yesterday and have put in the day plodding around. The town looks a bit forlorn after Paris, but it is still very interesting. Beethoven's grave really astonished me. There is a simple stone with only the briefest of inscriptions, but within 100 feet are the graves of Mozart, Gluck, Schubert, Brahms and Hugo Wolf, to say nothing of Johann Strauss. What a guard of honor! King George himself will never have the like.

The music on tap here is really colossal. Tonight I am going to the opera to hear an early work of Mozart's, and tomorrow there is a grand Schubert-Strauss concert, with the Wiener Gesangverein (all men) *singing* two of the Strauss waltzes. It will be a gaudy debauch of beauty.

The few people I know here don't know I am in town, so I expect to put in a very quiet week, looking about. The food and drink are almost as good as in Paris, and I feel much more at home, for my German is sufficient for everyday purposes. In Paris I had to depend on Ruth Goodman. At the last minute I discovered that Ludwig Lewisohn was there, and so I had to call on him.[1] I found him in a downright luxurious apartment, with a French butler. His new wife (they seem to be married at last) has put on weight, and looks considerably overdone. But compared to the first one she seems like Venus.[2]

I have been wandering around all day, wishing you were here. Some day we must do Vienna together. I'll put you in training a year ahead, so that the walking won't floor you! I think only of how lovely you are, and how every passing day means I'm that nearer seeing you. I'll cut the London business as short as possible. It is already plain that the conference will be the usual flop.

I love you.

Yours,

H

[1]American educator, editor, critic, and novelist.
[2]Thelma Spear.

HOTEL BRISTOL

WIEN

January 16th, 1930

Dearest Sara:-

A fair creature serving the Chicago Tribune here waited on me yesterday, and now I am up to my ears in Austrian and Hungarian literati. It appears that she roves the hotel searching for Americans, who are scarce in Winter. So I am clearing out day after tomorrow for Budapest, and shall probably go direct from there to London. The literati are very amiable but seeing them seriatim makes far from a peaceful holiday.

The town itself is pleasant, but somewhat shabby in Winter. There is a café every thirty feet, most of them pretty good. The victualling is excellent, though not as good as in Paris. I could stand it for ten days if I were free to wander about the streets, but seeing people every hour is most uncomfortable, especially since all of them want to talk shop. My Hungarian translator and his wife are here—the most amusing of the lot. Tomorrow I am taking on a lady Ph.D. for lunch: she has done some of my articles into German. The newspaper outfit, as usual, is mainly third rate. It is always marvellous to see what dubs represent the great American papers in foreign parts. They lead easy and lordly lives, learning nothing and forgetting nothing.

I should reach London by January 22nd, nearly a week ahead of my schedule. The secret of this haste is that I am crazy to get home as soon as possible. It now seems that we parted in 1861, when I left for the Civil War. You will receive such a hug when I reach Baltimore that you'll yell for the police. My one hope is that there will be a couple of letters from you in London, and that they will say you are well, and out of Richardson's hands at last. What a long siege it has been! And how brave you have been! I am very proud of you.

And love you more and more.

> Yours,
> H

ALS

U N I T I

GRAND HOTEL

HUNGARIA

BUDAPEST

January 19, 1930

Dearest Sara:

This town is really astounding. It is by far the most beautiful that I have ever seen. I came expecting to see a somewhat dingy copy of Vienna but it makes Vienna look like a village. There is something thoroughly *royal* about it. Everything is on a large scale, and the detail is magnificent. The Parliament House, inside and out, is to the Capitol at Washington as the Capitol is to the filling station at Charles St. and North Ave. The Danube is under my window, and across the river, on a range of hills, lies a long series of truly superb palaces. What will become of all this grandeur, now that Hungary is sacrificed to the Czechs, Serbs and Romanians, God alone knows. It must take millions to keep it up.

I shall return to Vienna tomorrow and begin the long journey to London the next day. I am horribly lonely. This afternoon I was reduced to hiring a Jew to show me around. He had no English, but we got on very well in good German. I miss you every minute. If there are no letters from you in London I shall bombard you by cable. Every day you seem lovelier.

> As ever,
> H.

~

UNITI
GRAND HOTEL
HUNGARIA
BUDAPEST

January 20th, 1930

Dearest Sara:-

I am going back to Vienna and shall mail this there. Budapest is really colossal, but the weather is cold and I am tired of walking about. I begin to fear that I am growing too old for such travel. I used to enjoy it, but that was in my infancy. The trip down from Vienna was very tiresome, though I had a compartment to myself. Hungary seems to be one long succession of farms. The soil is black and so they look rich, but looking at them for hour after hour is a dreadful chore. The villages, compared to those of Austria and Germany, seem shabby. The roads seem to be appalling—simply black sloughs. How even oxen get through them I can't make out.

Budapest is magnificent, but it looks like an empty ballroom.[1] Hungary lost ⅔ of its territory and people by the war, and is barely able to exist. There are traffic cops every street corner, magnificently turned out in trench coats and swords, but there is no traffic to regulate. The Hungarian cuisine, however, seems to hold up. Last night I had a Székely gulyás (made of pork, saurkraut and paprika) that was a dream, and the night before a superb paprika chicken. The first cost 30 cents and the second 50 cents. The local beer seems to be good, but I don't like the Tokay wine—it is too sweet.

In three days I'll be in London, and that much nearer home. I miss you every minute. What a folly to come so far away. But the next time we'll be together. I am expecting full reports from you in London. I hope everything is going well, and that you'll be able to get home. When my job will be done I don't know, but I'll surely make it as short as possible. I love you.

Yrs.,
H.

[1] At the outbreak of World War I Budapest had a population of eighteen million; in 1920 the situation was radically changed when, as a result of the Treaty of Trianon, which created new nation-states from the former territories

of Austria and Hungary, Budapest found itself the overly large capital of a country with a population of eight million. The city suffered severe damage during World War II.

SAVOY HOTEL
LONDON

January 25th, 1930

Dearest Sara:-

. . . The Naval Conference turns out to be the usual tedious horror. The frauds meet all morning, and then issue idiotic statements, meaning nothing. The French always upset the apple-cart by telling the simple truth. It shocks the British beyond endurance. As for the Americans, they sit around vacantly, learning to drink tea.

The usual telephone calls and letters entertain me. At the end of the week, along with Patterson and Owens, I am going to Manchester to visit the Guardian brethren. Next week I'll probably go to Oxford for a day to see old Robert Bridges.[1] Beyond that I shall stick to London. It seems silly to waste cable tolls on so dull a show. I'll write very little.

When I got here I was greeted by the news of poor Reynolds' death.[2] A charming fellow. He had angina pectoris, and his last year was very uncomfortable. . . .

I miss you frightfully, and you are always in my thoughts. In three weeks I'll be back! You are doomed to be hugged severely!

My love forever.

Yours,

H

[1]The English poet laureate interested Mencken for his philological studies. In 1913 Robert Seymour Bridges had founded the Society for Pure English, which examined the correspondence between written and spoken words.

[2]Stanley M. Reynolds, a graduate of Johns Hopkins University, began his career in journalism as editor of the Johns Hopkins *News-Letter*. He subsequently worked for several newspapers, including a job as a Washington correspondent for the Baltimore *Evening Sun*, before becoming managing editor of the *Evening Sun* in 1922. An enthusiastic man of miraculous energy, he was a perfectionist

who found no detail too small for his attention. Consequently he burned himself out, and illness kept him away from his desk until his death on January 19, 1930.

For nearly fifteen years between World War I and II, the major naval powers voluntarily agreed to certain limitations on their navies. Mencken concluded that the real aim of the conference, under what he thought to be false pretenses, was to restore the old balance of power. After several agonizing weeks, the First London Naval Conference drew to an end. The fourth and final naval limitation conference met again in London in 1935. In 1936 the United States, Britain, and France signed a treaty giving recognition to the general principles of limitation, but it contained so many "escalator clauses" to meet outside rivalry that it really marked the end of the fifteen-year effort, and, as Mencken predicted, the United States and Europe once again entered into war.

[TELEGRAM]

JAN 23 1930

POSTAL TELEGRAPH
SAVOY HOTEL LONDON
HAARDT

16 WEST READ BALTIMORE MD
    NO LETTERS   HOPE YOU ARE WELL   LOVE

H

SAVOY HOTEL
LONDON

January 30th, 1930

Dearest Sara:-

I hope Richardson's attack on the wound is over, and that you are feeling very much better.[1] What a nuisance it has been to you, and how bravely you have faced it! On the whole, it will probably be better for you to go home after the weather is better. Take your time with the novel. Whenever it begins to bother you, lay it aside, and do some articles or a short story. A book is a dreadful thing. It always outwears its welcome. . . .

Boyd[2] is here with Herman Oelrichs.[3] Boyd says he is going to Dublin to stay six months, but I doubt it. He is doing no work. What is to become of him God knows. Oelrichs tells me that Madeleine is harassing him at long distance. She probably has good reason.

The Conference is dull and I dislike the job. I am writing very little. Everything has to be skeletonized, with all articles and prepositions omitted. I am wondering that sort of job the copyreaders are making of clawing it back into English.

I think of you every minute.

Yours,
H

[1]The wound from Sara's 1929 operation had been giving her much pain, and Richardson was visiting her daily to dress it.

[2]Mencken had met the Dubliner in 1913, when Boyd was posted to Baltimore as British vice-consul. The two enjoyed a long lasting friendship: Mencken often reviwed his books, and, when the chips were down, lent him money. Boyd wrote the biography of Mencken in 1925.

[3]Son of Hermann Oelrichs, the shipping merchant and agent for the North German Lloyd Steamship Company. In 1916 Oelrichs had gone into the diplomatic service, serving as attaché of the American Embassy in Berlin before World War I. But the venture which attracted the most attention was in 1929, when he wrote to the *World* offering a prize of $200 for a suitable valedictory to be delivered by him on the occasion of his mounting the scaffold to pay the ultimate price for taking a drink. The letter was an attack on Prohibition, of course, but he became swamped by what he called "blizzards of mail," and in the end he had to call the whole thing off, explaining it was only a joke.

SAVOY HOTEL
LONDON

February 6th, 1930

Dearest Sara:-

By the time this reaches you I'll be aboard the Bremen and on my way home. Hooray! . . .

I surely hope that the business of the wound is over, and that it is well at last. Don't give any thought to the scar. It will disappear in a few years. The main thing is to get it healed.

The Conference is hopeless, at least for me. All its good stories are morning paper stories. I am reduced to the same futilities that kept me groaning at Havana. This is the last such job that I'll ever undertake. There is enough to do in the United States. . . .

I went to Oxford yesterday to see old Bridges. He is now 86 and a sad wreck. For an hour or so he is lively, but then he suddenly goes to pieces and has to rest. Nevertheless, I had a very pleasant palaver with him. His wife, who must be at least 68, seems young beside him.[1] She watches over him as if he were a baby. He had two Oxford dons to lunch, and solemnly told me that they were to carry on his philological business after his death. I'll probably never see him again.[2]

The weather here is warm, but very damp and depressing. The view from my room, up and down the Thames, is lovely, especially in the mornings. There is always a mist on the river, and the tugs and their tows go through it like ghosts. The hotel is quiet, and if there were no visitors I could work comfortably. But people are always coming in and out. . . .

I have seen too many people, and begin to feel tired. But the five days at sea will pick me up. The victualling here is a ghastly comedown after Paris. Nietzsche was right: the English are next door to cannibals. Worse, the native beer is bad. But I have found an Hungarian restaurant that has excellent goulashes and perfect Pilsner.[3]

I miss you dreadfully!

Yours,
H

[1] Mary Monica Waterhouse.

[2] Mencken was right; Bridges died later that year.

[3] England revisited, Mencken found, was a "damp, soggy land" whose people served boiled food and ate it in a "resigned, medicinal manner." After spending several cold evenings in "chattering conversation" and eating "depressing vegetables" ("I'd as lief eat stewed hay"), Mencken looked anew at the members of the naval conference and commented: "If American admirals have to eat many more English dinners the weaker will begin to crack. Some are already taking four ounces of bicarbonate daily."

In April Sara took the Crescent *back to Montgomery to tell her mother and family that she had become engaged to Mencken.*

ALS

SARA HAARDT

April the twentieth, 1930

Blacksbury, South Carolina

Darling,

This morning I awoke in the deep South, and despite my lamentations, I confess that I was strangely excited. There was no mistaking the perfume of kiss-me-at-the-gate. It is a late Spring but a full one: the cemeteries are bright with all the Easter flowers. On the outskirts of Charlotte there was a row of one story houses flaunting a tarnished golden sign SOUTHERN APTS, and on the ramshackle veranda rocked the colored gentry in their Easter best. Certainly there is nothing in this landscape to dazzle the tourist but to the native it has a curious poisonous charm. Even these red hills and straggling growths of vines and scrub pine . . .

I am as comfortable as it is possible to be, and you are infinitely dear to have arranged it. I felt an unnamable panic when the lights of Baltimore faded out last night. You've been so precious, and I love you . . . love you . . . beyond everything.

Sara

ALS

H. L. MENCKEN

1524 HOLLINS ST.

BALTIMORE

Sunday, April 20, 1930

Dearest Sara:

The Easter card was lovely. I return every smack with a loud buss, and give three cheers that you exist. It is now 6 PM and you are on the borders of Alabama. I surely hope you find your mother much better, and that it is a pleasant visit altogether—and not too long! I am horribly homesick for you already. By the middle of the week I'll be mooning like a lost calf.

My niece goes home tomorrow, and I'll resume my labors. The damned preface for De Chantntaneria Eruditorum must get itself written somehow, and in short order.[1] Then for the book![2] But by that time, you'll be back—and I'll put you to work. You will be a very hard-worked gal.

Have you ever heard that I love you? Well, here is the news. You are perfect!

As ever
H

[1]*The Charlatanry of the Learned*, by Johann Burkhard Mencke. Francis E. Litz translated the Latin and Mencken's "Preface" was a history of the celebrated eighteenth-century mockery of fake erudition, plus a brief genealogy of the Mencken family. Knopf published it in 1937.

[2]*Treatise on Right and Wrong*.

ALS

SARA HAARDT

April the twenty-first, 1930

Henry dear,

Thank you so much for your telegram. I arrived last night—on time—and found my mother slightly improved. But she is obviously very ill. I shall see Dr. Pollard[1] within the next few days, but nothing can be done. I am glad I came down, for she had fallen into a kind of depression, and she was imagining that I was too ill to leave Baltimore.

Montgomery is really very lovely now: The sunshine is warm but pleasant, and the gardens are in full bloom. I have heard most of the tragedies though, and tomorrow I am beginning my walks with Marie Alexander[2] through the older parts of town we used to love.

Is there anything I should know about the contract with Doubleday, Doran?[3] I'll write you about it when it comes in.

I miss you so.

S.

The absinthe cocktails are the most marvelous ones you have ever mixed! If only you were here to enjoy them with us—

[1]Charles Teed Pollard, Jr., the kindly and well-loved Montgomery physician, was a member of the U.S. Medical Advisory Board and had been in charge of fighting the yellow fever epidemic that raged through Montgomery in 1897.

[2]Sara's girlhood friend.

[3]Doubleday was to publish Sara's novel *The Making of a Lady*.

H. L. MENCKEN
1524 HOLLINS ST.
BALTIMORE

April 21st, 1930

Darling Sara:-

Your telegram about the book made me leap and cavort like a gazelle. I am ten years younger, and at least nine times as sinful. Now to spit on your lovely hands and make ready for No. 2! But first I must hear all about it.

The contract will probably be the standard model, and hence all right. Take whatever advance payment it offers, and if none is offered don't object. The one thing to be scrutinized closely is the section about movie and talkie rights. If you are in doubt, wire me the whole section by night letter and I'll advise you.

Don't let any news of the acceptance get about in Montgomery. Publishers like to make such announcements themselves. I assume that the book will be scheduled for Fall publication. If so, it will go to the printer in a few weeks, and the proofs will be coming along by July. You have a great thrill ahead—the sight of your first book. All I ask is that you keep God's mercies in mind, and give yourself to continued prayer, and avoid the vain-glory of this world.

You should send a note to La Glasgow, thanking her for her good offices. Who Nash may be I don't know. He is probably a newcomer, and sounds somehow English.[1]

All my love, and two billion kisses, and three more cheers. I am more proud of you than ever.

H.

[1]The American writer of light verse, Ogden Nash, came to his metier after a spotty early career. At this time he was in the advertising department of Doubleday, Doran and Company.

H. L. MENCKEN
1524 HOLLINS ST.
BALTIMORE

April 23rd, 1930

Dearest Sara:-

The Nash telegram is really superb.[1] The book must have floored him. Well, why not? It is full of capital stuff, and I think the rewriting improved it 1000%. Doubleday handles fiction quite as well as any other publisher in the country. When the contract comes in, let me hear briefly by wire just what is in it. The important points are:

What royalty does it offer?

What advance payment, if any?

How is the revenue from movie and talkie rights divided?

The normal royalty on a novel is 10% on the first 5000, and 15% thereafter. It should begin with the first copy. In special cases a publisher may propose that the first 1000 or 2000 copies carry no royalty, but this is not such a case. The movie rights may be worth far more than the book rights. It is usual, if a publisher negotiates for their sale, for him to take part of them, but it must not be too much. In the old days it was common to take 50% or even more.

Mrs. Bixby showed up yesterday after horrible alarms.[2] She had met Hamilton Owens in Washington, and told him precisely when she was to reach Baltimore, but he neglected to pass the word to me. So the party was assembled without the guest. However, she popped in just in time. My sister and I had her on our hands until 5 P.M. I put in the evening working on the Buchholz catalogue—a fearful job.[3] To add to my miseries, my stenographer botched the first batch of cards and I had to revise them and send them back. I have already marked up about 3000 titles, with all the larger publishers still to come.

I surely hope that the doctors find your mother better than she thinks she is. I suspect that your long absence has had something to do with her illness. She must have worried about you dreadfully. Now that she sees you well she will probably begin to improve. Don't tell her that I am growing bald and deaf! Represent me as a handsome young man!

Hamilton Owens has decided to go to West Chester, so there will be four of us. I shall proceed to N.Y. Sunday evening and have a session with Goodman. The next night I am to dine with the Quirks, and then again with Goodman, along with Sherwood, the man who wrote "The Road to Rome."[4] The interstices will be filled up with palavers with the Knopfs. The magazine needs serious attention.

I miss you horribly. Every evening I find myself planning to call you up. You are far too lovely to be real. I'll have to get used to believing it.

Yours,

H

[1]Ogden Nash's April 19 telegram read: "Finished reading Making of a Lady at 2:30 this morning. Congratulations to you for writing it and to us for getting it. Certainly one of the richest books I have read in months."

[2]Possibly the wife of Harold Bixby, administrator of Baltimore's Civilian Conservative Corps. The family would not be living in Baltimore until 1933.

[3]Mencken and Heinrich Buchholz were editing a catalogue entitled "The 10,000 Best American Books in Print." As it was not a financial success, the project was dropped after the first number.

[4]Robert Emmet Sherwood's first play in 1927. In 1930 he came out with *Waterloo Bridge* and *This Is New York*.

ALS

SARA HAARDT

April the twenty-second, 1930

Darling,

It was so nice to have your letter today. I miss you terribly. But I console myself with the thought that you'll be away all of next week, and part of the next. You'll have a lovely time in West Chester. Give my love to Dorothy and to Joseph.

It is unmistakably warm here but I feel very well. And it is perfectly lovely. Out here, along the sidewalks, the Mexican primroses are blooming, with a blossoming chinaberry ever so often.

I shall call Grover Hall tomorrow, and ask him to save the country papers for me. They should be rich in Americana with the revivalists all going.

I wonder if I should change the names of *Oak Park* and *Boguehomme* in "The Making of a Lady." They exist, of course, in Montgomery, and I fear there'll be the usual unpleasantness for my family to contend with. It will be a terrible nuisance, and I'd rather not, for there are no other names as typical.

Are you well? I begin to feel like work, and I'll probably dig in after a day or so. Darling, I love you . . . love you. . . .

Sara

ALS

SARA HAARDT

April the twenty-third, 1930

Darling,

You are so precious to write to me about the contract. It hasn't come in yet, but I'll write you the minute it does. How I miss you!

This morning I cooked a thirteen pound ham and did two Check-List notes, and took the sun cure. I feel a million times better for the sunshine. We must have a tiny place in the country some day!

Will you send me an autographed copy of "Treatise on the Gods" for Grover Hall? He has had the most ghastly time. His wife has had what he calls a nervous breakdown but it sounds more like she is insane.[1] He hasn't been able to leave her for two years, he hasn't even taken a vacation, and he's in a really dreadful state of mind. He wants to review "Treatise on the Gods" for the *Advertiser*.[2]

Darling, darling, I love you so . . .

Sara

[1]Claudie McCurdy English Hall was indeed suffering a nervous breakdown; in 1934 she was institutionalized.

[2]Hall's complimentary review appeared on June 1, 1930

H. L. MENCKEN
1524 HOLLINS ST.
BALTIMORE

Thursday, April 24, 1930

Dearest Sara:-

I rather think that it will be advisable to change [the] names of Oak Park and Boguehomme. Get as far away from them as you can. I suggest Smith Heights and Oakhurst, or something of the sort. It would be folly to expose your people to unnecessary annoyance.[1] The names are probably mentioned so seldom that you can correct them in proof. But you will be charged for such corrections. It might be well to select your names, send them to Nash, and ask him to have them made in the office when the MS. is prepared for the printer.

The weather here is very cold. I was at the Woollcotts last night with Pearl, and the temperature was 32 degrees. On my sleeping porch it was only a degree or two higher. All the gardens are paralyzed, and Spring begins to seem a long way off. Marie[2] was in alarm that her new Ford would be frozen.

Somehow, I fear that the party at West Chester will be a flop. I doubt that Buchholz and Henry[3] hit it off with some of the West Chester men. They will like Johnny Hemphill,[4] but not Way,[5] Murtha[6] and the rest. I hope Joe doesn't invite Harold.[7]

I am grinding away at the catalogue of 10, 000 books. My stenographer is already half used up. But she can tackle the business at her leisure while I am away.

I love you more every minute.

H

[1]To protect herself, Sara inserted a prefatory note in her book which read that the names of towns, streets, and outlying districts were taken from regions of Alabama, Georgia, and Mississippi. The name "Boguehomme" was omitted, and "Oak Park" was changed to "Eden Park," but apparently too late for the writer of the cover jacket, who mentioned "Oak Park" repeatedly.

[2]Marie Woollcott.

[3]Dan Henry.

[4]Joseph Hergesheimer's cousin-in-law. Hemphill, a lawyer, used his legal expertise to advise Hergesheimer in his dealings with publishers and movie producers. At the time he was running for governor of Pennsylvania. Despite Mencken's general dislike of politicians, he viewed Johnny Hemphill as *the* civilized man of West Chester, the only one with "no Babbitt qualities."

[5]Channing Way, owner of a small insurance office.

[6]Charles Murtagh, a Philadelphia lawyer.

[7]Harold Baldwin, a local contractor. Mencken had often criticized Hergesheimer for surrounding himself with "rich nonentities."

H. L. MENCKEN
1524 HOLLINS ST.
BALTIMORE

April 25th, 1930

Dearest:-

After all my qualms—my sister greeted the news with cheers.[1] She seemed to be genuinely delighted, and swept away all my uncertainties about herself with lordly gestures. Plainly enough, she thinks you are a swell gal. Well, so do I. I feel immensely relieved, and am as happy as the boy who killed his father. I am leaving before my brother comes home. My sister says that he will be delighted—that his admiration for you is colossal. So we seem to have got around the first corner without breaking a leg.

The Evening Sun is in an uproar over a piece I wrote on Monday.[2] There are loud whoops for a public apology. So I must rush to the office before going to the station.

I bust with love!

Yours,

H

[1] Mencken had just told Gertrude about his intention to marry Sara.

[2] "Purifying the Movies," Mencken's article on the Hudson bill for movie censorship, had appeared in the April 14 issue of the newspaper. Later, William Sheafe Chase, the moral reformer, would answer Mencken's article in a letter to the editor, defending the bill. His response appeared May 27, 1930, on the editorial page.

ALS

SARA HAARDT

April the twenty-sixth, 1930

Darling,

Gertrude is a dear. I had the most charming letter from her. I am writing her but I hope you tell her again how much I admire her, and how lovely it will be for me to be close to her. I suspect that we will both depend on her greatly. . . .

I am so happy I am dizzy. You're the most perfect person in the world,—I adore you. . . .

Sara

H. L. MENCKEN
1524 HOLLINS ST.
BALTIMORE

Thursday, April 25, 1930

Dearest Sara:-

Some time ago Hugh Young sent me his "Practice of Urology," an immense work in two volumes. Last night, dipping into it, I encountered this:

"The operation of nephrectomy in tuberculosis is one of the most satisfactory in surgery. We have recently had a series of 111 consecutive cases without a death, and the results obtained are generally all that can be desired. . . . The most remarkable disappearance of lesions in the bladder and ureter occurs after simple removal of the diseased kidney. . . . The persistence of a sinus or fistula in the loin is a disagreeable and not so infrequent sequel, but it rarely lasts a long time. . . . Bidgood has recently studied 89 cases in our series, and finds that in 18% the wound broke down after operation. This complication has had little effect, apparently, on the ultimate results, but is a serious matter for the patient, since it incapacitates him for weeks or months after he would otherwise be well."

This should console you!

Let me have a sworn report on that ham. Get in a competent committee and have it tested!

A copy of the Treatise for Hall goes to you by this mail. It is too bad that he is in such difficulties. His ordinary day's work is very heavy, and with a crazy wife on his hands it must be almost impossible. Please give him my regards. Tell him I'd have sent him the book direct, but hesitate to circulate such literature in a Christian country.

I am off for West Chester in a few hours. Pearl is laid up with one of his headaches.[1] Thus the party is reduced to Hamilton Owens, Buchholz, Dan Henry and me. I shall be careful about the booze. My tummy has been skittish for a week past. I'll get to N.Y. by Sunday night. Don't forget to mark PERSONAL on any letter you send to me there. Otherwise, the Yiddish ladies may open it.

I have got nearly half way through the catalogue.

I am dreadful lonesome for you, and love you endlessly.

Yours,

H

¹Just as Mencken incessantly suffered from hay fever, Raymond Pearl suffered from migraine.

ALS
SARA HAARDT

April the twenty-sixth, 1930

Darling,

It was so nice to have your letter this morning. The contract still hasn't arrived; I'll telegraph you when it does.

I know your lunch party was lovely. It makes me homesick to think about it! I miss you every minute. The country is really lovely, and it is nice to see my family, but I'd welcome the sight of Maryland soil.

Yesterday we had open fires going all day; luckily there was no frost. I hear on every side that the South is going bankrupt but it looks immensely prosperous. John complains building is at a standstill but he seems to keep busy.¹

I'm blocking out some work. I haven't attempted to write anything but a few Check List notes. I've used up all my books. You have accomplished wonders, as usual. I wish I were there to help you with the book list; it would be an interesting job.

Mayfield called up yesterday and invited me to Tuscaloosa, but I won't go. When do you go to Virginia?²

I miss you and love you so.

Sara

¹Sara's brother was in real estate.
²Mencken had been planning to visit the Troubetzkoys in Charlottesville.

ALS
SARA HAARDT

April the twenty-sixth, 1930

Darling,

How I wish I were at the Dower House with you tonight! I know you've had a lovely time. It is just a week since I left you, and it seems a million years. I doubt if I can stick it out much longer. My mother seems better—she is writing to you—but we haven't a great deal to say to each other. And it is a fact that most of my contemporaries are dead or scattered. . . .

It continues unnaturally cool here. Today is Memorial day, but there were only six veterans down from the Soldiers' Home to march in the parade.

The ginger beer arrived, and John and I stormed the express office but there was no stirring the Confederates on a holiday. Thank you so much for sending it, and the magazines and the books!

Darling, I miss you so . . .

Sara

ALS

THE AMERICAN MERCURY
730 FIFTH AVENUE
NEW YORK

April 28, 1930

Dearest Sara:

The week-end at West Chester was crowded and busy. Friday night Joe gave a stag dinner and all hands got overdoses. Saturday night there was a big dinner *and dance* at the Pickering Hunt. The band played continuously from 8 PM to 2 AM and I damn nigh went crazy. We rolled into bed at 3:30 yesterday. Johnny Hemphill gave a farewell lunch party at the Corinthian Yacht Club on the Delaware—very nice. Hamilton Owens came to N.Y. with me and is at the Algonquin. The Knopfs are here, and so I am busy.

Johnny Hemphill is to be nominated by the Democrats for governor of Pennsylvania and I have promised to stump the Pennsylvania Dutch for him in October.[1] You are to come along! It will be a great show.

Joe dug up two Alabama women in Tuscaloosa, and had them at the party Saturday. One is a Mrs. Calybow of Birmingham. The name of the other I forget. I gathered that Joe got on rather badly in Tuscaloosa. But more of this when we meet.

My sister is really enthusiastic. You have a good friend there! And I love you endlessly. When are you coming back?

Yrs.,
H

¹Hemphill lost the election.

ALS

SARA HAARDT

April the twenty-ninth, 1930

Dearest,

The copy of "Treatise on the Gods" has just come in. You couldn't have done anything that would give Grover Hall more pleasure. Thank you so much. . . . He and his young son Grover¹ called Sunday. They are hoping to get away this summer, if they can persuade Mrs. Hall to go.

Pauline Gilmer Henderson was here to lunch today, which means that she arrived at eleven and left at five. I was completely exhausted, despite the fact that she is very charming. But she still lives on a plantation where protracted visits are a live tradition.²

It is warm today, with the first hint of Summer. I am eager to hear about your visit to West Chester. I know you enjoyed seeing the Goodmans in New York.

Darling I miss you so. . . . And love you more and more. . . .

Sara

¹Like his father, Grover Hall, Jr., left school before graduating and entered journalism, becoming editor of the Montgomery *Advertiser* in 1947. Although he was forced to live under the shadow of Grover Hall, Sr., he became a leading critic of the prime political power of the time, and a spokesman on the race issue. When the Montgomery *Advertiser* changed owners in 1963, Hall was ordered to write an editorial that he felt compromised his principles, refused, and was fired by the publisher. He then moved to Washington, D.C., and became a syndicated columnist. He died of cancer in 1971.

²Pauline Gilmer, wife of William Grey Henderson, the state director of the Works Progress Administration, resided on a plantation about ten miles from Montgomery, near the Tallapoosa river bridge past Gunter Field. The pecan orchard of "Henderson Clover" continues to thrive.

~

ALS

SARA HAARDT

April the thirtieth, 1930

Darling,

It was so sweet to have your letter today. You *did* have a busy time in West Chester! It all sounds very pleasant except the dance, and I confess that I can no longer endure long bombardments of jazz. Mayfield tells me that Joseph was with her eight days, and that she never succeeded in tearing him away from the reigning belles to view the remains of the Confederacy. But that is as it should be.

I was in town this morning and left Grover a copy of your book. He was terribly pleased. You would love his office. There are huge lithographs of Stonewall Jackson, General Lee, Grover Cleveland, and Al Smith on the walls; and underfoot there is an assorted debris of ashes, paper, stamps, old typewriters and matches. I gathered up a pile of country papers and you'll receive the clippings very shortly.[1]

The weather has been delightful and I have enjoyed the sunlight but I want to come back to you. When are you going to Virginia, and will you be away long? I thought I would stay on until you returned to Baltimore.

Gertrude is perfectly marvellous. But I have always thought that! We must have her with us a great deal.

I did not tell Mamma until after I had received her letter. She is delighted, of course. I am forwarding the letter to you in this mail. She has always admired you greatly, and in addition to that—she is convinced that you are responsible for getting me into hospital in time to save my life.

I am terribly happy, and I worship you more every minute.

Sara

[1]As time went on, much of the activity of *The American Mercury* was being left to Angoff. The "Americana" section weakened because Angoff disliked putting it together, and gradually the punch and wit that Mencken had put into the section gave way to a weak assortment of clippings. As usual, Sara continued to send whatever she could find from the local Southern newspapers.

~

ALS

THE AMERICAN MERCURY
730 FIFTH AVENUE
NEW YORK

May 1, 1930

Dearest Sara:

I'll be out of this Gomorrah in an hour, and on my way back to the Free State. It has been a dull week—in fact, worse than usual. Last night, Boyd, Goodman and I went down to Forsyth Street, near the City Hall, to drink some beer reported to be swell. It turned out to be vile, and so we proceeded to Union Hill, N.J. There even worse stuff was on tap, and we switched to California white wine. One bottle of it was enough, and we actually finished the evening drinking water. When I got back to the hotel I couldn't sleep. Water is surely not a suitable drink for a man of my years and learning.

Boyd seems sober and reports that he is hard at work. Goodman is busy with a new play. His daughter has come to work in the Knopf office, and Blanche reports that she is doing very well.

I like to recall the old days before you set out on your travels, and we were together. They seem long ago! But soon you'll be back.

All my love!

H.

H.L. MENCKEN
1524 HOLLINS ST.
BALTIMORE

May 1st, 1930

Dearest Sara:-

I am half wrecked, but still alive. I got to New York after two late nights at West Chester, and added four more for good measure. Last night I was very tired, but the rising temperature made it hard to sleep. I'll turn in early tonight and take a nap tomorrow afternoon. That will fit me for the ceremonies at the club on Saturday.

I had a long palaver with the Knopfs, and we discussed the American Mercury situation at length. As a result some of the things that have wasted time, energy and money are to be abandoned, and we are to follow an easier and better programme.[1] I feel very much relieved. I offered to let all salaries be suspended until profits began to roll in again, but they refused. Altogether, the air is cleared and everything looks pleasant.

I miss you like hell. It seemed desolate to get back to Baltimore and not call you up. But you are NOT to think of coming back until your mother is better and ready to let you go. Take it easy: you have a lot of work ahead of you! My sister and brother seem to be delighted. They are always very nice about everything. I might have staggered Joe with the news, but refrained. He got very tight on Friday night and again on Sunday afternoon. In fact, I have seldom seen him so boozy. "The Party Dress" is doing very well, though no one seems to like it.[2] Last night's party with Boyd and Goodman was ghastly. The beer was positively atrocious. Goodman says he is going to begin brewing again.[3] I surely hope he does, else my liver is doomed. Directly opposite his house in 10th street is the main warehouse of the German-American Importing Company, with shelves full of real German malt and hops.

Item: I am hopelessly mashed on you.

Yours,

H

[1] *The American Mercury* had been on the decline since 1929. In March 1930 Nathan was "fired" from the magazine. In May a cheaper paper began to replace the imported, the cover regularly featured a square box calling attention to its more notable articles, Mencken began to bargain with prospective contributors, "Notes and Queries" was replaced by "The Soap Box" department, serials began to be represented, and the percentage of satirical essays diminished, all in an effort to boost sales for the magazine.

[2] Joseph Hergesheimer's meteoric rise to prominence had reached its pinnacle in 1922. He had produced up to sixty novels and novelettes for popular magazines, including George Lorimer's *Saturday Evening Post*, and Hollywood paid extravagant prices for his novels. In the late 1920s Hergesheimer began to have some difficulty getting his work published; by the mid 1930s he found it almost impossible. The critics complained that his writing lacked the relevance and social consciousness that was being demanded from authors during the Depression years.

[3] An avid beer maker, Goodman had gone to Europe in 1925 to procure some yeast from Munich's Lowenbrau brewery to use in his and Mencken's brew.

ALS

SARA HAARDT

May the third, 1930

Darling,

When are you going to Bethlehem? You are so sweet to say that you will meet my train, and I fear it will arrive early in the morning.[1] I shall need your help to get me off, I'm coming back with a dozen Dresden cups that Mamma has given us in my hands, and another bag packed with china and silver. I'll probably stay through this coming week and come back the early part of next,—if you will be in Baltimore.

I am planning to work at the Capitol every day next week, if I can stand the heat. It has suddenly turned warm but John has promised to haul me up in the morning and call for me at noon. I want to get all the stuff on the Confederate expedition I can, so I can do an article on it sometime soon.

Mayfield is coming over from Tuscaloosa this afternoon. I have talked with her twice over the telephone. I am dining with the Pollards tomorrow and the Houghtons[2] Monday. I may go down to the Meriwether place at the end of the week.

I had a long letter from Willie Barton,[3] at Vanderbilt, wanting to know my sources for the article in the *Mercury* about Pickett. The scandal, apparently, was new to him.

Darling—I miss you so. And love you . . . love you . . . love you.

Sara

[1] The *Crescent Limited* was arriving at 6:35 in the morning, but the two other trains that also arrived in Baltimore came in at 2:00 and 3:00 a.m. "I am distressed at the hour," Sara wrote Mencken, remembering, perhaps, how Mencken couldn't meet her train when he first knew her in the early 1920s. "If it is too outlandish, don't attempt to meet me."

[2] Mary Houghton, a classmate of Sara's from Goucher College.

[3] Author, lecturer, and clergyman William E. Barton of Vanderbilt University had gained an international reputation as an authority on Lincoln.

H. L. MENCKEN
1524 HOLLINS ST.
BALTIMORE

May 3rd, 1930

Dearest Sara:-

The clippings are sublime, especially the very long one—too long, alas, to be printed. No doubt the author has been tarred and feathered by now. I am writing to Hall. . . .

The town seems empty without you. If I went into the neighborhood of Read street I'd bust into tears. When may I call you up? Some afternoon next week? Tell me the time in God's time. I assume that you use Central time in Montgomery. Here we are on Daylight time.

A note from Rosalie Hamilton says that the Treatise is swell.[1] Can it be that she has ceased to be a Christian woman? The Jews still rage, but the war seems to be almost over.[2]

The new cover of the Mercury looks swell. In fact, it is super-swell. I think it is 100 times as good as the old one. Now for a proper shade of green. That job is for Knopf.

I love you.

Yours,
H

[1] *Treatise on the Gods* had been published in March; by the end of the year its sales exceeded 13,000 copies and it would go into nine reprints by 1945. Mencken then revised it, and a paperback edition of this text continues to be sold today.

[2] Mencken's book on religion had caused an uproar, not only among Christians, who said the "upholder for Darwinism" had produced a Bible for "village atheism" and "boobs," but among the Jewish population, who cited a paragraph in the 300-page publication as an example of anti-Semitism. Despite the harsh words, Knopf wrote Mencken happily, everybody was still buying the book.

ALS

SARA HAARDT

May the fifth, 1930

Dearest,

Can you call me Thursday night, after eight o'clock? It is not so expensive after that and the wires are clear.

It is frightfully warm here but I'm getting a little work done at the Capitol. You have a lovely time in Virginia.

I went up to the White House[1] with Marie Alexander and Catherine Steiner[2] to see the battleship quilt. It was so hot we nearly swooned but it was worth it.

I wish I were meeting you at the Schellhase tonight.

> All my love
> Sara

[1]The "White House of the Confederacy," home of Varina Howell and her husband, Jefferson Davis.
[2]Sara's childhood friend.

H. L. MENCKEN
1524 HOLLINS ST.
BALTIMORE

May 5th, 1930

Dearest Sara:-

Hooray! I'll be at the Hauptbahnhof to meet you, early or late. Let me know when you arrive as soon as you choose your train. I am going to Charlottesville on Friday morning, but shall be back by Sunday night. If you get in on Monday I'll be here. But don't land on Tuesday the 13th! Or leave!

It has turned hot here, and the turtles have come out, and all the windows are open, and I have put in a few licks in the yard, cleaning up. I'll have to be diligent during the next few days to get my work done. Last night I did one editorial for the Mercury. I hope to finish the other two today, and to tackle The Library tomorrow. I only hope that no more visitors pop up.

Joe was somewhat vague about Tuscaloosa, and hinted that he had a bad time. But maybe I misunderstood him. He is in liquor at the moment. My carcinomas broke loose after three days in West Chester and four in New York, but I am now all right again. Last night I sat at Schellhase's with Buchholz, seeing your ghost behind every Seidel. The affable serving maids all inquired for you.[1]

I'll be dumb with joy when I see you.

> As ever,
> H

¹Sadly, old Anna, the senior waitress at Schellhase's, would die in a few months, on July 14, and never see her two favorite customers wed. Mencken and Sara would go see her for the last time a few days before her death.

H. L. MENCKEN

1524 HOLLINS ST.

BALTIMORE

May 6th, 1930

Dearest Sara:-

The cotton bale came in safely: even the seed-pods were intact. It goes among the heirlooms! I have been grinding away all day at routine work, with an hour and a half's interval in the yard. My hands are a mess and I am sunburned a bright red. The weather is infernally hot—above 80 all day. Yesterday it was 92. But I finished my Editorial last night, and made it four pages instead of three. Such are the effects of your inspiration, even at a distance of 800 miles! For the first time this year I shed my shirt last night, and worked in my undies. Tonight I have the electric fan operating.¹

I hope to hear from you tomorrow that I may call you up during the afternoon. My voice, I fear, has begun to crack. But it will be restored when I see you next week. Patterson refuses to transport any liquor in his car, so I can't take a bottle of wine to old Troubetzkoy.² What a country!

But I love you!

Yours,

M

Kiss Mayfield's hand for me.

¹In the space of four days, before embarking on his trip, Mencken would have written three separate editorials for *The American Mercury* and completed all the reviews for "The Library" department, as well as his weekly Monday article for the Baltimore *Evening Sun*. For Mencken, the reason for such competence was simple: "Thus I can leave with my desk clear," he wrote Sara.

²Prince Pierre and Princess Amélie Rives Troubetzkoy. Amélie Troubetzkoy was a celebrated beauty and writer of the 1890s, and a playwright of the 1920s.

~

ALS

SARA HAARDT

May the seventh, 1930

Dearest,

It was so wonderful to hear your voice tonight. And Gertrude's! Kiss her for me.

I went in the backwoods for furniture today and bought a chest with a marble top to keep sherry in for $25; walnut book shelves with glass doors for $10; a rosewood stand for $25 (this is the most adorable thing you have ever seen—it is 150 years old—); a sideboard (200 years old, put together with wooden nails) for $50; and a mahogany secretary for $100. I had enough money to pay for all of them except the secretary. I hope you like them, darling. They really are very sweet and terribly cheap. If you don't like them I can sell them in Baltimore for a lot more. The secretary is a dream, and in perfect condition. I thought I would sell the desk I have for $125 to Mr. Murphy[1] for the secretary is a much better piece. I am shipping them by freight together with a rosewood ottoman that Mamma has given up.

Philippa could hear your voice clearly in the living room tonight. She sends you her love, and says you are divine.

Darling—darling, it will be so sweet to be with you again.

Yours,
Sara

[1] An antique dealer who had a secondhand store on Antique Row, on Howard Street.

H. L. MENCKEN
1524 HOLLINS ST.
BALTIMORE

May 9th, 1930

Dearest Sara:-

It was lovely to hear your voice last night. Now for Thursday! I'll be at the Hauptbahnhof by 6 A.M., to make sure that I don't miss you!

Today two of the letters you sent to me in Paris came in. They evidently got there after I had left. Why the French kept them so long I don't know. But it is good to have them, even so.

I am off for Virginia in half an hour. Yesterday I picked up a bit of lumbago, probably by sitting before an electric fan all day. At first it seemed like a sprain, but now it is clearly lumbago. However, it is not bad, and no doubt it will pass. We are driving down to Charlottesville and I'll be comfortable. I had planned to take a bottle of Rhine wine to old Troubetzkoy, but Patterson vetoes it. They search cars in Virginia, and he is afraid of losing his Lincoln.

I love you.

Yours,
M

H. L. MENCKEN
1524 HOLLINS ST.
BALTIMORE

Sunday night, May 12, 1930

Dearest Sara:-

I have just got in from Charlottesville—175 miles by road. The trip turned out to be very pleasant. The temperature on the mountain top last night was 68, with no wind and a full moon. Mrs. Hyde had to go to Washington, so Hyde,[1] Patterson and I had the place to ourselves. We gabbled until nearly 2 A.M. and then rolled in to sleep like sailors. Yesterday we called on the Troubetzkoys. Their place is really marvellous. But more about it when we meet.[2]

I'll be on the station platform when your train rolls in, barring acts of God and the public enemy. If it were 3.30 instead of 6.35 I'd be there too. You will get such a hug as no Christian white woman has ever suffered. I am crazy to see you.

I think 6.35 is 7.35 here. But I'll call up President Atterbury, of the Pennsylvania, and make sure.

I love you!

Yours,
H

[1]Henry Hyde, Washington correspondent for the Baltimore *Evening Sun*.
[2]The Troubetzkoys lived in a 250-year-old mansion that would have delighted

Sara. Leading to the house was a drive bordered by tall box woods that gave off a sharp, clean scent and made the ride dark and secluded. Emily Clark was a frequent visitor, and in a letter she described it to Joseph Hergesheimer: "Miss Amélie's grandfather was twice Minister to France, and the drawing room is full of things that her grandmother brought back. It has a bare, polished floor, huge mirrors and darling stiff chairs around the walls. There are French paintings and funny French gift books, and the most delicious faded green and gold curtains, on carved brass rods, brought from Paris . . . and clocks and vases under glass. . . . All over the rest of the house France and Italy are mixed with Colonial Virginia in the most startling way. . . . The furniture is modern, pink and white. It looks like something very good to eat. . . . She won't have electric light put in, but uses lamps and candles. The lawn is one of the most beautiful I know, like England with views of the mountains everywhere, enclosed in a box, and there is a terraced garden on the other side of a high box wall. . . . And the white columns in the front extend throughout the east and west wings, as well as the porch. To me there's more atmosphere about this place than many of the others, because, though it hasn't bullet marks and all that, so many charming people had a wonderful time here."

Once Sara pulled into town she immediately began to prepare her and Henry's new home on 704 Cathedral Street. The preparations would take months. "The lovely Sal is hard at work in the new Palazzo Mencken," Henry wrote to Mayfield in August, "nailing down carpets, washing windows, gilding the chandeliers, and getting my brewery in order. What a gal she is! I begin to believe that I am doing well to give up on that rich widow in Hoboken, N.J. . . . Next year, if I am lucky at dice, I hope to take her abroad, and show her the jails where so many Menckenii suffered in the past."

ALS

THE AMERICAN MERCURY
730 FIFTH AVENUE
NEW YORK

May [?], 1930

Dearest Sara:

Dorothy Hergesheimer and Alice Logan[1] popped up at the Algonquin last night just as I was leaving for dinner. I dropped in on them for a moment and took them a pair of gin rickeys. They were in town for the theatre, and go back today. They report that Joe has been boiled ever since the stag party, and that he is far decenter and more amiable than he was during his year on the water-wagon.

I had dinner with Eddie Wasserman, a beau of Blanche's, along with Dashiell Hammett,[2] an old Baltimorean, and 2 women.[3] The party was very pleasant, but I cleared out at 12:30, just as more people were coming in. Blanche had gone home long before.

Tonight I am dining with the Van Vechtens,[4] and Texas Guinan[5] is to be on hand. It will be an honor and a pleasure to see that lovely creature again. Tomorrow I am going to a new beer-house with Goodman. He swears the beer is good. Good or bad, I can stand it once. And then will come Thursday, and I'll be on my way back to you.

How I wish you were here with me now!

Yrs.,

H.

[1] Alice Barbour, wife of John Hubbard Logan, professor of history at Rutgers.

[2] A former operative for the Pinkerton National Detective Agency and now considered the father of hard-boiled detective fiction. Hammett's first story was published in October 1922 in Mencken and Nathan's *The Smart Set*. His stories in *Black Mask* magazine (begun by Mencken and Nathan) helped bring about a major movement in detective fiction by bringing it away from genteel detectives solving crimes to rough, believable private eyes dealing with common crooks. In 1930 Knopf published *The Maltese Falcon*, bringing Hammett instant fame and prosperity, and four years later *The Thin Man*, one of his most famous novels, would appear. In late 1930 Hammett began working sporadically for motion picture studios until the end of World War II.

[3] Hammett would not meet the playwright Lillian Hellman until the winter of 1930–1931, when he was in Hollywood.

[4] Fania Marinoff (Mrs. Carl Van Vechten) was an actress.

[5] A Manhattan nightclub hostess of the 1920s (her greeting, "Hello, sucker," became a byword).

ALS

THE AMERICAN MERCURY
730 FIFTH AVENUE
NEW YORK

May [?], 1930

Dearest Sara:

I was a bit in error. The total up to Saturday was 8530, not 8420. And orders are still coming in. So we'll eat regular meals during November and December, and maybe buy some gin!

The Van Vechten party was very nice, and there was much pleasant talk of you. La Guinan got into an automobile accident, and so didn't show up. Fania had a bowl of gumbo that was divine. I am to get the formula from her. Dinner lasted from 8 o'clock until 10:30. I still feel somewhat stuffed, but put my confidence in God.

I'll entrain tomorrow at noon and shall call you up at the same time before 6. Do we meet in the evening? I surely hope so. Last Sunday now seems a year past.

I love you!

Yrs.,
H.

ALS

THE AMERICAN MERCURY
730 FIFTH AVENUE
NEW YORK

June [9], 1930

Dearest Sara:

Dinner with the Menckenii[1] last night was very dull, and when I got back to the hotel I was so used up that I couldn't sleep. So I feel middling rocky today. But I'll be all right by tonight. The weather here is infernal—muggy and hot. I hate the town more and more.

The Haneses are here and I am to lunch with them tomorrow, if there is time, I shall look in at Sloan's and see what is offered in the way of odd rugs.

The telephone rings all day here and every bore in America is on the job. I live in hopes that Madeline Boyd won't discover that I am here. As far as Boyd I hear nothing from him. Van Vechten and Fania are sailing Wednesday and Nathan the next day.

I love you.

H.

¹Mencken's cousin Harry P. Mencken, an obstetrician and gynecologist, lived in Long Island City.

ALS

THE AMERICAN MERCURY
730 FIFTH AVENUE
NEW YORK

June [?], 1930

Dearest Sara:

The trip to the country with the Knopfs blew up, and so I had dinner with Sister Lillian, her sister Dorothy, and Mr. George. Then to Gasha Heifitg's¹ house with Blanche Knopf: his wife is Florence Vidor.² So the day was devoted to artists of the screen. I rolled in at 12, sober but very sleepy, and slept like a log. Now for home and thou!

I'll call you up tomorrow (Thursday) in the afternoon. If you have anything under way *don't stay in*. In any case I'll see you at 9 o'clock—and give you such a buss as you never heard tell of.

I love you

H.

¹Jascha Heifetz, the violinist.
²Actress of the silent screen, and first wife of director King Vidor.

ALS

SARA HAARDT

June the tenth, 1930

Dearest,

It was so sweet to have your letter today. I have a million things to talk to you about. The shower is being installed. I have seen the paperhanger, and have a sample of paper for your rooms; I'm waiting for you to come home to tell you about the linoleum; the coffee table from New York has arrived; the sideboard at Mr. Murphy's is very nice—we'll look at it together. . . . And there are a dozen other things I've attended to. . . . It is all very thrilling, and I think the place is going to be sweet. And it will be perfect with you!

I am dining with Gertrude and August tomorrow night. We will miss you! I'm taking the image for the garden over, and we shall take a drive after dinner.

You are so wonderful, and I love you so much.

                                                            Sara

                                                            ALS

SEVEN HUNDRED AND FOUR CATHEDRAL STREET
BALTIMORE, MARYLAND
                                   August the twelfth, 1930
Darling,

Here is your first letter to come to Cathedral Street. You were so precious last night. I love you.

                                                            Sara

Sara and Mencken were married on August 27.

1931

During his first full year of marriage Mencken did not desist from the routine he followed while he had been a bachelor. He continued to travel to New York to edit The American Mercury; *in May, as was his custom, he attended the Bach Festival in Bethlehem, Pennsylvania; and each Saturday night he met with members of the Saturday Night Club. But increasingly he withdrew from social obligations and immersed himself in his life with Sara. Together, they roamed through antique shops or secondhand stores, looking for Victorian goods. At home, he worked on a scholarly work (*Treatise on Right and Wrong*) while Sara typed out her short stories and articles. In December Mencken became the center of controversy when he wrote an article for the Baltimore* Evening Sun *crying out against a lynching on Maryland's Eastern Shore, with the result that Eastern Shore merchants boycotted Baltimore goods. By the end of the year the Menckens decided to go on vacation.*

ALS

THE UNION MEMORIAL HOSPITAL
BALTIMORE, MD.

Monday [March 9 1931]

Henry dear

This is my first real letter.[1] Like Miss Suckow[2] I couldn't tell you yesterday how much I appreciate your being so nice to Mayfield. You are such a dear. The Mexican cigarettes came and I had my first one, a wonderful new kind—with a gold tip that smelled like your cigars.[3]

It is terribly hot here. I nearly melted on the porch this morning. If it would only get cooler I would try to work. I hope you have a lovely time in New York.

> My devotions
> Sara

[1]Sara had pleurisy. In an uncharacteristic scrawl, Sara found the energy to write a brief note to Mencken.

[2]Dissatisfied with the publicity and other operations at Knopf, Ruth Suckow had switched from her first publisher and began having her books published by Farrar & Rinehart. Here Sara may be making an allusion to what she and Mencken might have thought was Suckow's ingratitude.

ALS

THE UNION MEMORIAL HOSPITAL
BALTIMORE, MD.

March the tenth [1931]

Darling,

Last night my temperature was normal for the first time (it was your kiss).

I love you . . . love you . . . love you and miss you so.

> Sara

the pear blossoms are out.

~

[TELEGRAM]

MARCH 11 1931 12:20 PM

WESTERN UNION
NEW YORK, NY
MRS H L MENCKEN

424 UNION MEMORIAL HOSPITAL

YOUR NEWS IS SWELL AND I AM DELIGHTED   I'LL SEE YOU BY FOUR
THIRTY TODAY   TONS OF LOVE

H.L.M.

ALS

SEVEN HUNDRED AND FOUR CATHEDRAL STREET
BALTIMORE, MARYLAND

Thursday, [April 23] 1931

Darling,

It was so sweet to have your letter. I miss you terribly—every
minute.

I feel very well today. It is cold and clear and I am going down
town. Constance Black is coming in for tea.[1]

Your rooms have had a Spring cleaning. The shower curtain will
be up when you return.

I hope you have a lovely time. Please take care of your precious self.
When you come home I am going to see about you.

I love you so
Sara

[1]Constance Hoffmeister Black, wife of Harry Black, a member of a family
who owned substantial stock in the *Sunpapers*.

ALS

SEVEN HUNDRED AND FOUR CATHEDRAL STREET
BALTIMORE MARYLAND

Friday, [April 24] 1931

Dearest,

It is lonelier and lonelier without you. I went out to the hospital
last night with August. Gertrude is fine; she sits up a little longer

each day but she is not planning to leave until she can walk for some distance.

Marjorie Nicolson is in town for the Robertson inaugural.[1] They are conferring Ph.D.'s upon Mrs. Hoover[2] (!), Lizette Reese[3] and Florence Sabin.[4]

I went down town yesterday and bought you a new shower curtain and a new soap dish for your bathroom. Bessie[5] and Carrie[6] are moaning at your absence.

August is lunching with me on Sunday when we go to the hospital again. We have 4 noble surprises for you.

I kiss you and kiss you

and

kiss

you.

S.

[1]David Allan Robertson was being inaugurated as president of Goucher College at the Lyric Theatre that afternoon.

[2]Lou Henry Hoover, wife of the president, received an honorary doctorate of laws for her work on social welfare and translations.

[3]Lizette Woodworth Reese, Baltimore poet (and one of the few whom Mencken admired) received a doctorate of literature.

[4]Florence Rena Sabin, formerly of Johns Hopkins University, received an honorary doctorate of laws for her research on blood.

[5]Bessie Lee Poindexter worked for Sara and Mencken until Sara's death. To her, 704 Cathedral Street "was so much like home."

[6]Carrie, the cook, would later be replaced by Hester Denby.

ALS

HOTEL BETHLEHEM

BETHLEHEM, PENNA.

May 15, 1931

Darling:

No more of these solo flights! I miss you too much. The first day's sessions were dull—and there is no beer![1] What is music coming to? Our rooms in the hotel are 8 × 6—exactly like that pen in Quebec. But we'll be out by 6:10 PM.

I'll call you up at 5:30 PM E.S.T. on Monday.
I love you.

H.

¹During the Prohibition years Mencken boasted that he could find beer within
ten minutes of his arrival in any town, but this year at the Bach festival he and
Alfred Knopf were stumped. Toward the end of their stay a taxi driver overheard
Mencken's complaint and dropped them off at the right place. They rang a bell,
a door opened a crack, and one eye glared out. Mencken pointed to the scores
of the *B Minor Mass* they were carrying and asked politely, "Can you do anything
for two poor, thirsty musicians?" The door opened wide, the two were let in,
and they were told to turn left. At the end of the hall they found a bar serving
good beer and thick sandwiches, "at ridiculously modest prices," wrote Knopf
years later. "Henry was enchanted."

[TELEGRAM]

MAY 17 1931 2:14 AM

WESTERN UNION
NEW YORK NY
MRS H L MENCKEN

HOTEL AMBASSADOR ATLANTIC CITY NJ
   IF YOU NEED MONEY FILL OUT THE BLANK CHECK AND HAVE THE
HOTEL CASH IT   I WAS WRONG ABOUT THE BEER   IT TURNED OUT
TO BE EXCELLENT   ALFRED AND I JUST GOT IN   I MISS YOU DREAD-
FULLY

H.L.M.

ALS

THE AMBASSADOR
ATLANTIC CITY
Sunday afternoon [May 17, 1931]

Darling,
   It was so sweet to have your telegrams. I have missed you and missed
you. Nothing ever is anything without you.
   Jessie¹ has just left for New York on the 5:25. We had a very quiet
time, sleeping and riding up and down the boardwalk. The weather
has been fair but with a high wind blowing—until today. It is like
the day we arrived, and I am homesick for you.

I'll be waiting for you Wednesday night.. It will be precious to be with you again.

Kisses . . . and Kisses

S.

¹Jessie Lee Rector, Anne Rector Duffy's mother, owned an antique store in New York. She often visited Anne in Baltimore and became a friend to Sara as well. While Mencken was with Alfred Knopf in Bethlehem, Samuel Knopf had arranged for Sara and Mrs. Rector to stay at the Ambassador Hotel in Atlantic City for a week. "It is a cheap Coney Island," Sara wrote to Mayfield about the resort, "but I have low tastes and enjoy such things."

ALS

MAY 17, 1931

DARLING:

. . . THIS AFTERNOON, I CALL YOU UP. HOW LONG IT SEEMS! AND HOW DAMNABLY I MISS YOU!

H.

ALS

SEVEN HUNDRED AND FOUR CATHEDRAL STREET

BALTIMORE, MARYLAND

November the twenty-fifth, 1931

Darling,

This is dreadful. I have been wandering around here as if I expected to collide with your ghost. Next time I'm going with you!¹ I'm writing this on your desk that has been washed with Ivory Soap and waxed. I must say that the process has brought out the elegant grain of the wood. . . .

It has turned cold here with a rising wind. I hope to get over to the Peabody this afternoon—and back to talk to you.

I love you

love you

love you

S

¹Sara often went with Mencken to New York, where they stayed in the Dorothy Parker Grand Suite at the Hotel Algonquin.

1932

In January, the Menckens took a two-and-a-half-week Caribbean cruise on the North German Lloyd Bremen. In June and July Mencken reported on the Republican and Democratic national conventions, both held in Chicago, and collected his observations in Making a President; a Footnote to the Saga of Democracy. Franklin Delano Roosevelt, the governor of New York, defeated Herbert Hoover for the presidency by 472 electoral votes to 59 and took with him a Congress with large Democratic majorities in both the Senate and the House. In 1932 Knopf elected Mencken to its board of directors. Whenever he was away, Mencken missed Sara dreadfully, and they exchanged loving letters. After two years of marriage, newspapers announced, Mencken, Famed Bachelor, proved to be a model husband. "It stands to reason that a bachelor would make a good husband," Sara told reporters. "I think a bachelor is apt to be more thoughtful of his companion . . . he never accepts his wife as part of the household." Meanwhile, the Depression grew worse.

[POSTCARD]

Regalia of Grand Cyclops K.K.K.
Original now in U.D.C. Chapter Room, at Florence, Alabama.

New York
May 10, 1932

Having a swell time. Everyone is treating me swell. On all sides I
hear regrets that you are not along. Many send you their regards.

A Friend

ALS

June the eleventh, 1932

Darling,

It was so sweet to hear your voice today. I ordered a spray of white roses sent to the Emmanuel Temple, from Mary Johnston. She is sending our card special delivery. I know old Mr. Knopf's death will be a shock to his family but it seems a blessing when he might have lived and suffered.[1] I suppose the old man was happy in his last days. Didn't he celebrate his seventieth birthday last Saturday?

The Hearst papers are shouting extras every hour about the Lindbergh case.[2] It is really too extraordinary.

The window is finished, and the man has promised the Venetian blinds for your office and bedroom on Monday. But the house is so lonely without you! I miss you terribly—more than I can tell you, and love you . . . love you.

Sara

[1]Samuel Knopf had died suddenly that morning, one week after his seventieth birthday.

[2]Charles Lindbergh's infant son had been kidnapped from his home near Hopewell, New Jersey, on March 1. Six weeks after the kidnapping, on May 12, extras announced that the baby was dead.

THE BLACKSTONE

CHICAGO

Sunday, June [12], 1932

Darling:-

If you haven't written a note to Alfred, do it. He will be fearfully upset for a week or two, but after that he will recover his wits. My belief is that life will be much easier for him hereafter.

I miss you horribly, and it seems at least a week since I left Baltimore. The weather here is superb—clear skies, a stiff wind from the lake, and a temperature of about 60. Paul is putting in the day visiting his relatives, and Hyde and I have been plodded around the hotels, viewing the celebrities. The story is still flat. Nothing will really happen until tomorrow night, when all of the delegations are in. I met Wm. Allen White this morning, and found him looking pale and puffy. He has some liver derangement and is plainly in dubious shape. All the Washington correspondents are here, and all of them are full of hot news, none of it true.

I may get home a day sooner than I calculated. I have hired a preacher to pray for it.

I love you.

Yours,

H

On June 14, toward noon, the twentieth Republican national convention would get under way at last, with, Mencken observed, "the usual brief moments of glory for nonentities." Herbert Hoover, his prestige already weakened by the Depression, was the outstanding nominee of the Republican party, but as Mencken foresaw, the outcome of his election would "depend largely upon the man the Democrats nominate. If they are as foolish as they were in 1928, and name a candidate as vulnerable as Al Smith, it will be excellent news for Dr. Hoover. But, if showing sense for once, they put up a man who has no inconvenient strings tied to him, and is of pleasing personality, and knows the tricks of national politics, then Dr. Hoover had better take a new lease on his old home in London and prepare to reënter the mine stock business."

ALS

THE AMERICAN MERCURY
730 FIFTH AVENUE
NEW YORK

June the twelfth, 1932

Darling,

This day has been dismal without you. It has rained, a fine drizzle, since early morning, and the house is as quiet as a tomb. . . .

I have been sleeping in your room, and today I typed my story in your office. I'll do a few Check List notes to ease my mind, and then go down to the Pratt library for the material about shells.[1]

Darling, darling, I love you and miss you so.

Sara

[1]Sara's article, "Shells of Fond Memory: The Pleasant Pasttime of Collecting Shell Ornaments," appeared in *Country Life*, November 1932.

ALS

June the thirteenth, 1932

Darling,

It seems ages since I saw you last. I dined with the Blacks. Harry Black was in the pool when I arrived, and he spent the rest of the evening (until 9:30! when I departed) trying to get Chicago on the radio. He called up the *Sun* a dozen times, and was altogether absorbed in the news. . . .

Things here go on as usual. Miss Handy[1] comes and goes and predicts a revolution before we are done. . . . Carrie is enjoying the temporary blower the gas company has installed . . . it is hot during the day but fairly cool at night.

I love you

love you

Sara

[1]Ethalinda Handy, Sara's nurse, periodically came in to give Sara a massage and take care of her needs.

THE BLACKSTONE

CHICAGO

Monday, June 13, 1932

Darling:-

These preliminary days are horribly dull. The place swarms with whisperers full of news that isn't so. I am always glad when the actual convention begins, and the show begins to unroll. We have very good seats, and a convenient office under the stand, with a telegraph machine of our own. I sent the Ev. Sun a piece last night about the booze situation.[1] But real news will begin to run tomorrow.

Last night Paul, Douglas and I went to a beer party given by one of the Tribune men. We thought we were in for a dull time, but it turned out a very pleasant affair, with really excellent beer. Paul and I were back at the hotel and in bed by midnight, and I slept until 9 this morning. So we are getting plenty of rest. But standing around all day in the hotel lobbies, listening to the wiseacres, is hard on the legs.

We have cards on four or five clubs, some of them very convenient. Today Paul and I had lunch at the Chicago Club, the great roost of the Chicago Babbitts. I had a superb dish of pigs' feet, and a slice of watermelon.

I miss you dreadfully, and every day that passes seems another week. If I can manage it I'll leave here Thursday night, and get to Baltimore Friday night. But I may be stuck until Friday. In any case I'll certainly wait on you by Saturday night.

I love you twice as much!

H

'The one subject that the delegates had been talking about since they came to town was the issue of Prohibition. "At Kansas City [in 1928] all of the salient statesmen of the party talked dry, even while they guzzled wet," Mencken wrote in his dispatch to the Baltimore *Evening Sun*. "But now many of them are leaping on the beer wagon with shrill hosannas, and every hour or so a new convert is announced. If platforms were settled in hotel lobbies there would be nothing left to do save play 'The Star-Spangled Banner' and open the saloons." Chicago, it turned out, had laid in a plentiful supply of liquor, but at exorbitant prices. For example, gin, which in Baltimore sold for five to six dollars a gallon, was being sold for fourteen dollars and fifty cents a gallon. Bourbon and Scotch were even higher. Surprisingly, beer was no exception. "The ordinary Canadian brews," Mencken reported, "which now sell in Baltimore for $7 a case of twenty-four bottles, cost $12 here. The local product, which grades down from a wishy-washy helles [light beer] to an almost undrinkable bilge, brings from $5 to $7 a case. These prices are causing a widespread lifting of eyebrows, for most of the visitors came to town expecting to find beer flowing like water at very neat prices. Moreover, figuring that Canada was only across the street, they counted on filling themselves with hard liquor at a cost considerably below the common level. But it is not so, alas, alas.

"The booticians put the blame upon what they call, with polite euphemism, the syndicate. The syndicate, though the Capones are behind the bars, is still functioning powerfully, and its main purpose seems to be to keep up the profits. The retailers are left only a small margin, and so they cannot cut prices materially. If they protest their supplies are withdrawn altogether and their business is ruined. A few of the bolder among them sometimes turn to outlaw bootleggers, who run the stuff in from Canada by motor boat and are content with more modest profits. But any speakeasy operator who is known to dally with such bootleggers is apt to have his place bombed and his head cracked, to say the least. For the syndicate believes in law enforcement, and it enforces its own laws much more effectively than the prohibition agents enforce those of the State and nation."

Thus, while Chicago had the quantity, it could not match the quality of Baltimore and New York. "This, however, is not ruinous during a National Convention," Mencken concluded. "Politicians, in general, are not fastidious, and most of those from the interior, especially the drys, are ready to drink anything that burns, at the same time giving thanks to God."

[POSTCARD]

June 13, 1932

The sheriff has invited me to see a candidate burned on Thursday. This is the electric chair room in the county penitentiary. It looks very sanitary.[1]

H

[1]Mencken had bought this postcard showing the barbershop at the Blackstone, crossed out its identification, and labeled it "Death Chamber." The footrests on the chairs were, of course, a place for the chaplain to kneel.

ALS

June the thirteenth, 1932

Darling,

I forwarded you a letter from old Mr. Knopf. It came with the flap of the envelope open, and I read it, as it was addressed to both of us, and sent it on. It is rather weird to receive a letter from a dead man at the exact hour his funeral is being preached, and containing such a sentiment.[1]

The weather continues rainy and cool here. I go to the hospital tomorrow to see Richardson. In the evening I am having a dinner party: the Clevelands,[2] the Duffys, and Charlie O'Donovan.[3] We hope to hear the business of the convention over the radio.

It was so sweet to have your letter this morning. You are so dear to me—you will never know. The house is dreary beyond words without you. Both Carrie and Bessie have inquired about your health, and when you are coming home.

I have sent Angoff some mail. Not much has come in.[4] I am holding a few pieces for you.

I love you

love you

love you

Sara

[1] Samuel Knopf had written the letter the day before his death, and it was mailed June 11. The letter thanked them for remembering his recent birthday anniversary, particularly with "such wonderful cigars," and concluded: "I hope to be here to reciprocate on your seventies."

[2] Richard Folsom Cleveland was a Baltimore lawyer and the son of President Grover Cleveland.

[3] Pediatrician.

[4] Throughout the early 1930s Mencken began to devote increasingly less time to the *Mercury*; for the most part, Angoff took care of the contributors and some of the mail. Nonetheless, Mencken became alarmed by the financial plight of the magazine and made an effort to vary its contents. But by 1932 the periodical had been dismissed by many of its former supporters, and one critic wrote that Mencken's articles now aroused "about as much controversy as the daily reports of the weather man." Mail that had once piled high on Mencken's desk now came in dwindling numbers.

THE BLACKSTONE
CHICAGO

Tuesday, June [14], 1932

Darling:-

The show is on, and a fourth of it is already over. It is low-down and shabby. I put in two hours in the convention hall this noon, writing my story from the stand, and now I am off to the Congress Hotel, to see the fight over Prohibition in the platform committee.

You would be proud, as a Christian woman, of my conduct. I went to bed last night with only half a cocktail in me, and so far today I haven't had a drop. Maybe I'll tackle a few beers after work tonight, but certainly not more.

Many of the old-timers are here. Wm. Allen White is pale and pasty, and looks very ill. Old Abbott,[1] of the Christian Science Monitor, is on crutches. I can bear the sight. Lippmann,[2] Will Rogers, Brisbane,[3] etc., are also on hand.

I refuse to count the days. It is already far too long.

H

[1] Willis J. Abbott, editor of *The Christian Science Monitor*.

[2] American political analyst, journalist, and author of books of predominantly political topics, Walter Lippmann had called Mencken "the most powerful influence" in America in 1926.

[3] Arthur Brisbane, chief editorial writer for William Randolph Hearst's newspapers. Upon Brisbane's death in 1936 Hearst asked Mencken to replace him (which Mencken politely declined).

WESTERN UNION PRESS

Wednesday, June [15], 1932

Darling:-

The letter from the old man really gave me a turn. It is dated June 10th, the day before his death. Probably it was the last thing he wrote.

We are plugging along comfortably, and are all in good shape. The real uproar begins this afternoon, with the platform fight. I incline to think that it will peter out. Republicans never fight one another. . . .[1]

I have been feasting on the Chicago delicatesies, mainly whitefish and pigs' feet. They serve pigs' feet here at the principal hotels. The town is not proud. . . .

I am weary waiting to see you. It now begins to seem like years. But I still hope to clear out on Friday night.

I love you.

Yours,

H

[1]That is, Mencken used to say in his articles, "except behind closed doors."

ALS

June the sixteenth, 1932

Precious,

I am delighted at the idea that I shall see you a day sooner. I have missed you a million times more this time.

I missed you so last night when the Duffys were here. Carrie cooked a lovely mess of soft shelled crabs and I used some of your boughten beer. I would have rather had your own, because I like it so much better, but I didn't know which brew to take. . . .

It now looks as if Senator Tydings[1] will put Ritchie[2] in nomination. Dick Cleveland is going as a delegate.

I liked your picture. You look like a collegiate beside Paul Patterson and Henry Hyde. The postcards were wonderful, and go in my memory book between two sachets of lavender.

All my love dearest.

Sara

[1]Millard Evelyn Tydings, the United States senator from Maryland.
[2]Maryland's Governor Albert Ritchie was one of the Democratic nominees for president.

~

June the twenty-first, 1932

Darling,

If I weren't patriotic, and a born Democrat, I'd be weeping. I could scarcely bear for you to go this time. It was so sweet to have you back, and the house is so lonely without you.

I love you . . . love you . . . love you . . . love you

l
o
v
e

y
o
u

These are kisses

x x x x x x x x x x x x x x x x x x x x x x x x x x x x x x x x x x x x x

x x x x x x x x x x x x x x x x x x x x x x x x x x x x x x x x x x x x x x

1,000,000,000,000,000,000,000,000,000

Sara

After a subdued convention, Hoover unanimously won the Republican nomination. The platform approved by the Republicans was the longest in the party's history. Among other topics, it encouraged the enforcement of Prohibition, and it viewed unemployment relief as a matter for private agencies and local governments to handle. With the nation in the midst of the Great Depression, the Democratic party had its best chance for victory since 1912. Mencken was now on his way back to Chicago to cover the Democratic convention.

~

ALS

THE AMERICAN MERCURY
730 FIFTH AVENUE
NEW YORK

June [21], 1932

Darling:

I couldn't wait for the Chicago train to read your note. What a grand gal you are! I am happier every day. And I love you more.

Stick to the taxi company. It can find those keys if it tries. Getting a new set would be a great nuisance. I'll send the driver some money when I return.[1]

It is horribly hot here. But there is some breeze on the 11th floor of the Algonquin Palace, and I shall turn in early to enjoy it. Tomorrow I am going out to Purchase for the night. Then Chicago.

A million smacks.

H.

[1] Mencken apparently left his keys in the taxi. When the driver returned the keys Sara gave him three dollars, and, she told Mencken, "he was overcome. The Yellow Cabs have come down to 25 cents for the first 3 1/2 miles, and I see in the paper that the Independents have dropped to 15 cents."

ALS

Friday, June Twenty-fourth, 1932

Darling,

It was so sweet to hear your voice this morning but I couldn't tell you how much I loved you, because Miss Handy was in the room. Did you guess it?

August and I called on Mary[1] last night. She was moaning some but her nurse told me that she was getting along beautifully. The wound is draining but the drainage is perfectly clear. Dr. Stewart[2] thinks she can go home in a week.

We went down to Hanover Street[3] from there, and I got you some noble attentions. I gave August a rickey[4] and we agreed to go out and see Mary on Sunday. I invited him to dinner. Carrie will be away but

Bessie says she can fry chicken. The weather has been marvelous for two days. I do hope it stays cool for you in Chicago.

A million kisses

Sara

[1] Charles Mencken's wife.

[2] Probably Dr. Eleanor B. Wolf Stewart, a Goucher alumna and resident physician of gynecology at Johns Hopkins Hospital. Her husband, Dr. George W. Stewart, was a noted surgeon.

[3] The location of many of Baltimore's antique stores, especially H. H. Runkles, Sara's favorite stop.

[4] A gin rickey.

The Democratic national convention was about to begin. Among the candidates for nomination were Franklin D. Roosevelt, Al Smith, James Reed, and Albert Ritchie.

WESTERN UNION PRESS

Saturday, June [25], 1932

Darling:-

It was horribly hot and muggy when we got in this morning, but there is a thunder-storm this evening, and the night promises to be comfortable. I had a grand sleep on the train. This afternoon I put in three hours listening to imbecile speeches in the platform committee, and then spent an hour with Bishop Cannon.[1] I wrote an interview with him for the Sunday Sun (morning). If you missed it, get a copy and keep it for me. The old boy had very little to say, but he admitted categorically that the Prohibitionists have got a dreadful licking. I saw Ritchie this morning, and also Cleveland. Cleveland was full of discontent. I told him that I thought it would be well for him to dodge seconding Ritchie. With a big fight ahead some other and better chance for him to show himself should pop up. But Ritchie was eager to have Cleveland as his second. I left the two of them palavering on the subject. . . .

My guess is that the convention will be over by the end of next week. Roosevelt is making steady gains. I saw Al Smith this morning. He is only a shell of his former self. His old stock company of Jewish intellectuals is on hand, advising him as badly as in 1928. I think he will blow up by Monday, and that Roosevelt will thus make a sweep. But if it doesn't happen Ritchie has a good chance. He seems to have made a great many friends. Scores of delegates are for him as second choice.

It will seem so long until I see you again. How I love you.

H

[1]The most controversial Methodist bishop of his era, Rev. James Cannon, Jr., had been the spirit behind the Anti-Saloon League of America and chairman of the executive committee of the World League Against Alcoholism. In 1928 he had chaired the Southern Anti-Smith Democrats. In later years, he and his wife would visit Mencken and Sara at their home.

WESTERN UNION PRESS

Sunday night, June [26], 1932

Darling:-

My cigars and the Panama punch arrived safely. In fact, one package was here when I got in and the other bobbed up an hour later. Thus I have plenty of Uncle Willies. This afternoon Paul, John Owens[1] and I went on a yachting party for a couple of hours. It was very pleasant, for the town was horribly hot, and the lake was much cooler. We had lunch aboard and got down a few Scotch highballs. I am sending a piece for tomorrow, dealing with the collapse of Al Smith.[2] If he shows any sign of reviving in the morning I'll kill it. In any case an introduction for it will have to come from the stand. Inasmuch as the session doesn't open until noon—which means 12:30 or 1 o'clock—the introduction will probably miss all the early editions. But it will be in the late financial edition.

I am somewhat beset by visitors, but we manage to keep most of them out. Hyde and I called tonight on Amon G. Carter, the Texan who shot out my window at Houston. We found him quite sober. He swore that he had left his firearms at home.

The Maryland people, seeing that Al Smith is apparently done for, are trying to make terms with Roosevelt. I suppose the upshot will be that Ritchie will be promised the Attorney Generalship. I begin to believe that Roosevelt can be elected.

And I love you more than ever.

H

¹John Whitefield Owens, editor of the Baltimore *Sun* and contributor to the *New Republic*. He and Hamilton Owens, both Marylanders, were only very remotely related.

²Franklin Roosevelt had been one of Alfred E. Smith's warmest supporters, nominating him for the presidency three times, but then Roosevelt replaced Smith as governor of New York and ran for president himself. As a result, the relationship between the two men had cooled. Many of the Catholic voters would not forgive Roosevelt for "stealing" the nomination from Al and remained steadfastly faithful: "Let them nominate him and see what happens" was the common sentiment. "He will be beaten worse than Al. He won't carry a single big State"—but for the most part opinion ran against Smith. "The tragedy of the convention is the collapse of Al Smith," Mencken wrote for the June 27 issue of the Baltimore *Evening Sun*. "Four years ago, even in the face of crushing defeat, he stood forth as the dominant personage of his party, but when he leaves Chicago this time it will be to join such ghosts as John W. Davis, of Wall Street, W. Va., and the Mr. Cox who ran so evanescently in 1920, and whose front I now forget.

"As these lines are written it is the gossip that he still plans to take the floor and deliver a powerful tirade against Roosevelt. If he does so he will be very badly advised. For the more powerful his tirade the more good it will do to Roosevelt and the more damage to Al Smith.

"Roosevelt himself, of course, is anything but popular, either in the convention or outside. I can recall no candidate of like importance who ever had so few fanatics whooping for him. His followers here are as silent as if they were up to something unpalatable to the police. The small band of Garner men [John Nance Garner, later nominated for vice president] . . . from Texas is making at least ten times as much noise.

"If there are any Roosevelt buttons on tap I have not seen them, and Roosevelt portraits are so scarce that Ritchie portraits outnumber them at least ten to one. The whole Roosevelt fight is being carried on in a curiously stealthy and *pianissimo* manner.

"The reason is plain enough. It is that at least a majority of the Roosevelt men are really not for Roosevelt at all, but simply against Al Smith. They want to get rid of Al, once and for all time, some of them because they believe more or less rationally that he has become a liability to the party, but most of them, I suspect, because they are still Ku Kluxers at heart. Al represents something that they can't understand, and hence view with suspicion. He is, by their peculiar standards, a foreigner, an idolator and a generally dubious character. In 1928 he led some of them down to defeat and disaster and forced the rest into a party treason that they are still ashamed of. So they are against him—and any stick is good enough to beat a dog with. . . .

"But the Al of today is no longer a politician of the first shop. His association with the rich has apparently wobbled him and changed him. He has become a golf player. In a championship match with the whole country looking on he has been outsmarted by a former manager of prize-fighters. It is a sad spectacle."

THE BLACKSTONE
CHICAGO

Monday, June [27], 1932

Darling:-

The first session, as usual, was very tiresome. The key-noter whooped along for more than two hours. I left the hall in the midst of it, and had lunch in a speak-easy nearby. The only thing they had to eat was a meat-ball sandwich, but it was pretty good, for the bread was a hard French loaf and the meat was very well flavored. I had sent in about a column last night, but I added another column from the stand. The last part of it was not filed until after 3, so it must have missed all save the six star edition.[1] After adjournment I came here and took a nap. I slept more than an hour, and feel very good. Tomorrow night I am going to dinner with Fishbein at the Tavern Club, along with Hugh Young and Dean Lewis.[2] The club is on the 20th story of a building overlooking the lake and is very cool. We were there last night, and almost shivered.

I am glad that Mary is doing so well. Don't let her groans alarm you. She is apt to groan when she is uncomfortable. A letter from Gertie says that she is having a grand time.

Day after tomorrow it will be a week since I left. Too long!

I love you.

H

[1] Most of Mencken's stories were pieced together in stages as Mencken tried to capture the story from different points of the convention (and he was everywhere); often they had to be revised again and again as facts changed. The conventions offered him a good show, but what never got into the papers were the long and tiresome hours the reporters had to endure while waiting for something of newsworthy interest to print. "Last night more than 10,000 people sat on hard chairs for four hours, while a depressing succession of bad speakers roared into the microphone," he reported at one point. "This oratory was bad

almost beyond description, but it must have been measurably less bad over the radio, with a comfortable chair to sit in and a cold bottle of home brew on the side table."

[2]Dean DeWitt Lewis, surgeon-in-chief of Johns Hopkins Hospital.

ALS

June the twenty-eighth, 1932

Precious,

It rained this morning, a perfect tropical deluge, like the morning we spent in Port Antonio. Now the humidity is rising in clouds and the thermometer is steadily climbing. . . .

Your piece about Al Smith was marvellous. James Bone's[1] stuff leaves me cold. Obviously he is befuddled by the thing but what of it.

I am getting a little work done in spite of the heat. Not much mail has come in for you. I have sent all I could to Angoff.

It was lovely to have your letters this morning. It has been a week since I saw you, and it seems a million years.

All my love to you, darling.

Sara

[1]Jim Bone, a London editor of the *Manchester Guardian* with which the Baltimore *Evening Sun* had a news exchangement, was covering the National conventions.

THE BLACKSTONE

CHICAGO

Tuesday, June [28], 1932

Dearest:-

A tiresome day. I began a piece for the Evening Sun at 8.30 and had to revamp it before the last take was in the Sun office. Then the facts shifted again, and I had to go over it a third time. And then a fourth change followed from the stand. God knows what the poor copy desk made of it—probably a horrible mess. It had to do with the impending combats on the floor.[1] Last night I sent in a longish interview with Col. Patrick H. Callahan, the only known Irish Catholic dry. The old boy loosened up in fine style, and damned everybody, including the Jesuits. He sees that Prohibition is in a state of complete collapse, with no mourners.[2]

This evening I am going to a dinner given by Fishbein, editor of the Journal of the American Medical Association.[3] A big gang of quacks, including many I know. It will be short, for we'll probably have an evening session. I had vaccine No. 9 put in ten minutes ago.[4] No reaction so far.

I begin to believe that we'll be here a week more, which is very unpleasant. When I get back at last, never again.

I kiss you a million times.

H

[1]The Democratic Convention for 1932 promised to be a "battle royal" with four big fights: the chairmanship battle between Roosevelt and Al Smith, the platform fight between the two factions of wets, the rules for nominations, and the nominees themselves. Within 24 hours, Mencken predicted, "the air will be full of hair and ears."

[2]Prohibition was dying a much quieter death than anyone had expected. The country was tired of the twelve-year restriction, save Colonel Patrick H. Callahan of Louisville, Kentucky, one of the last survivors of the bloc of Irish Catholic Prohibitionists. Mencken asked Callahan if he thought that Prohibition, supposing that it was saved, would ever be enforced. "I suppose it would take a Mussolini," he replied. "We don't seem to have one at the moment, but maybe we'll get one later on. However, even a Mussolini could hardly make a clean sweep of it. The country-club people will probably go on boozing until the end of time. The best prohibition can hope to accomplish is to save the poor man. It saves him by making drink too expensive for him." Mencken then asked the colonel what he thought would follow Prohibition, supposing that the Eighteenth Amendment was repealed. "That," said the colonel, somewhat gloomily, "is a hell of a question. Only God knows what the answer is."

[3]Morris Fishbein, one of the founders of the American Medical Association, had been giving Mencken philological studies for Mencken's work on the American language, as well as writing articles for *The American Mercury*.

[4]Robert Anderson Cooke, a physician and allergist from New York, had been trying to devise a new hay fever vaccine. Mencken was only too happy to be used as a guinea pig in the hope that the nuisance would finally disappear.

THE BLACKSTONE
CHICAGO

Wednesday, June [29], 1932

Darling:-

This has been another jumpy day. I put in all morning and half the afternoon hanging about the resolutions committee, waiting for the vote on the Prohibition plank. This meant writing two separate stories, the first of which had to be killed. It was done in six or eight pieces, and the second in three. All this is hard work, but I somehow like it. It is pleasant to turn reporter again. But I shouldn't want to do it every day.

I met a man last night who said his wife was a friend of yours. His name seemed to be Arant, and his wife was Lucille MacNeill[1] or something of the sort. I also met Ruby Darrow. She told me she thought you were a pearl of purest ray serene, and a swell looker. I agreed fully, and then some. Old Clarence begins to look frayed. . . .

Your letters are the loveliest ever heard of. I love you endlessly.

The weather here is hottish, but the nights are cool. Last night Paul and I put in a good eight hours.

H

[1]William Douglas Arant, of the law firm Bradley & Arant, of Birmingham, had recently married Letitia McNeel in 1929.

THE BLACKSTONE
CHICAGO

Thursday, June [30], 1932

Dearest:-

Poor Ritchie seems to be lost. In all probability, Roosevelt will be nominated either tonight or tomorrow. If he is, we should be clear of this job by Friday night, and ready to leave for home Saturday afternoon. I wired you this afternoon, asking you to hold all mail.

The last two days will seem a century!

H

[TELEGRAM]

JUN 30 1932 5:30 PM

WESTERN UNION
CHICAGO ILL
MRS S MENCKEN

704 CATHEDRAL ST BALTO
  PROBABLY HOME SUNDAY MORNING   HOLD ALL MAIL   LOVE
H.

THE BLACKSTONE
CHICAGO

Friday, July [1], 1932

Dearest:-

I probably wired too soon. The damned idiots locked horns last night, and were at it until nine this morning, and now it begins to appear that they may go over the week-end. After getting only five hours sleep Wednesday night, and no nap yesterday, I went into the all-night session last night, and stuck to the end. When I got back here I had some stuff to write, so it was nearly noon before I got to bed. I slept until 5:30, and have just had breakfast—6:15 P.M. But I feel very good, and hereafter it will be easier. It is a swell show, and I enjoy every minute of it, even at 4:30 A.M.

I'll wire you from the hall tonight. If the thing ends I'll start for home immediately. These long separations are simply dreadful. We must keep together hereafter. I love you so much.

H

The presidential balloting began in the middle of an all-night session. The first roll call began at 4:30 a.m. Roosevelt received a clear majority of 666 1/4 votes on the first ballot, compared with 201 3/4 for Smith (770 votes were necessary for nomination). Of side interest was the shift of Oklahoma's votes from its governor to Will Rogers. The final roll call adjourned at 9:15 a.m., with 945 ballots given to Roosevelt.

Prohibition had also been the subject of intense debate. The organized dry forces, headed by Daniel A. Poling of the National Prohibition Board of Strategy, demanded to seek a dry candidate for president. Meanwhile, rival Democratic candidates were unable to unite, and on the third ballot a change by the California and Texas delegates finally gave Roosevelt the nomination. At once Roosevelt launched a campaign which took him 12,500 miles, delivering some 200 speeches. His emphasis on the Depression and the "forgotten man" won him the support of many influential progressive Republicans, but equally effective was his demand to end Prohibition. "Like most other politicians," Mencken observed, "Hoover greatly underestimated the public fury against Prohibition," and once Roosevelt gave his October 26 campaign speech in Baltimore, the single magic word "beer" brought forth cheers. By the time the nation came to vote, Roosevelt would defeat Hoover in a sweeping upset, carrying all but six states with 57 percent of the popular vote compared to 40 percent for Hoover.

ALS

August 27, 1932

Darling,

You are the dearest husband in the world and I love you more every day.

A million kisses on our second anniversary.

Your loving wife,
Sara

ALS

THE AMERICAN MERCURY
730 FIFTH AVENUE
NEW YORK

September [7?], 1932

Darling:

. . . The chiropractors were naturally delighted to hear that the vaccines had cured me. I am to have a shot a month all Winter. Next summer the doses will be increased, but they will be fewer than this year. Cooke says that after 2 or 3 years he hopes to stop them altogether. His experience is that the cure then becomes permanent.[1]

Not a line from you. How are you? I hope the brethren are not making you uncomfortable.

I love you.

H.

¹"Henry is almost cured of his dread malady," Sara wrote to Blanche Knopf about Mencken's hay fever, "but like all cures he is reluctant to admit it."

ALS

H. L. MENCKEN

704 CATHEDRAL ST.

BALTIMORE

September [19], 1932

Darling:

I have written to your mother, telling her where you are.¹ I thought she might hear of it and be worried.

It is horribly lonely here. Last night I turned out at 10, and went to a movie. It was dreadful. I'll see you Thursday—six months away!

H.

¹Once again, Sara was recovering from pleurisy at Johns Hopkins Hospital.

ALS

Tuesday, September the twentieth, 1932

Darling:--

The X-rays were perfectly clear. Dr. Hamburger says there was not even a sign of the pleurisy. He seemed very pleased with them, which is nothing compared to the way I felt.

Duff came in hospital yesterday, and had his knee operated today. He was on the table nearly three hours, and he must be pretty sick. The doctor said a lot of fibroid tissues had grown around the cartilage, and all and all, it was a very messy job. Poor Anne has been almost crazy.

Be sure to write to Duff. His room is 509; he is just above me.

I was in the sun an hour and a half today. I am burnt a beautiful lobster red.

I love you and miss you so.
Kisses

x x x x x x x x x x x x x x x x x x x x x x x x x x x x x x x x x x x

x x x x x x x x x x x x x x x x x x x x x x x x x x x x x x x x x x x

1,000,000,000,000,000

Sara

[TELEGRAM]

SEP 21 1932 4:47PM

WESTERN UNION
NEW YORK NY
MRS H L MENCKEN

409 UNION MEMORIAL HOSPITAL

WELL WHAT DID I TELL?   ALWAYS TRUST THE OLD WISEACRE   THE
WEEK IN THE SUN WILL MAKE YOU PERFECT   AM TELEGRAPHING TO
ANN   LOVE

H.L.M.

ALS

October the seventeenth, 1932

Darling,

Miss Glasgow stayed on an hour after you left, she examined all the pin-boxes and all the other Victorian ornaments. It is raining dismally today. Miss Handy was in this morning, and I shall go to Hollins Street at five.

How I miss you! The house is impossible without you.

I shall type my story in the morning. Mary Richardson[1] is coming in the afternoon.

I read one of Joseph's Palm Beach stories last night in an old *Saturday Evening Post*. It was excellent, as good, in parts, as *The Three Black Pennies*. If he had re written them for Alfred I can't see why he should hesitate to publish them. After all, he publishes worse almost every time he publishes an English novel, which is on an average of once a week. But that, I suppose, is distinctly his affair.

Jim Tully sent us a picture of himself taken beside a huge owl. So Hollywood goes intellectual once again.

I love you

love you

Sara

¹Wife of Dr. Richardson, Sara's doctor.

On November 1 The American Spectator, *(subtitled "A Literary Newspaper") appeared on the newsstands. The magazine, edited by George Jean Nathan, Ernest Boyd, Theodore Dreiser, James Branch Cabell and Eugene O'Neill, included contributions written by Clarence Darrow, Ring Lardner, Van Wyck Brooks, Havelock Ellis and Lincoln Stevens. The editorial read that the magazine had "no policy in the common sense of that word. It advocates no panaceas; it has no axes to grind; it has no private list of taboos." The magazine was greeted with acclaim; Mencken may have felt that many of his allies were deserting him.*

---------- ~ ----------

1933

Few letters remain for 1933: it was a year of ups and downs. In March the Menckens spent a week at Sea Island, Georgia, and visited Sara's home in Montgomery; Sara's short story "Absolutely Perfect" was printed in the O. Henry Memorial Volume for 1933; and she was invited to speak before the International Writer's Conclave and the National Council of Women on What Women Authors Have Done in the United States in the Last Hundred Years—in an address lasting ten minutes or less (an invitation, incidentally, which Sara declined). Prohibition finally ended its fifteen-year reign on April 17, and in December Mencken resigned as editor of The American Mercury. *By the end of 1933 the circulation of the magazine had dropped from 77,277 copies to an all-time low of 23,000.*

[TELEGRAM]

OCT 18 1933 9:08 PM

WESTERN UNION
NEW YORK NY
MRS H L MENCKEN

704 CATHEDRAL ST BALTO
  HOPE IT DIDNT DRIVE YOU OUT OF THE HOUSE[1]   CALLED YOU AT
EIGHT FIFTEEN NO ANSWER   AM ALIVE AND WELL
                              H.L.M

¹That same evening Mencken had given a radio interview with William Lundell on NBC. The topic, simply, was beer. The interview was staged as if Mencken and Lundell were enjoying a conversation at an American hofbräuhaus while being served beer by two waiters named Otto and Emil. Most likely Sara went to listen to the program with her friend Anne Duffy, who lived only two blocks away. Over the airwaves, Sara could hear the clinking of seidels and her husband telling America: "Well, I don't think my wife has any reason to complain because you know what the effect of bootleg liquor is. If a man drinks too much of that he hollers and fights and goes home and scares his wife half to death by trying to kill her. Whereas a beer drinker goes home and scares her half to death by trying to kiss her."

In 1932 Mencken had voted for Roosevelt not so much for the candidate himself but as a vote against Hoover. Throughout 1933 Mencken expressed almost an admiration for Roosevelt and spoke of him in positive terms, calling him "one of the most charming of men" and admitting confidence in his intentions: "He is not an inflated pedagogue with a messianic delusion, but a highly civilized fellow." His "courage" and "enterprise," after four years of "the pathetic mud-turtle, Lord Hoover," Mencken found, was "refreshing."

But as Roosevelt began to lead the United States in a wholly new style of government, Mencken—albeit mildly—began to look at the omnipotent Roosevelt dictatorship with a growing sense of alarm. The tune had changed, he wrote; as he watched Roosevelt assume powers unheard of in previous presidents, Mencken warned the nation they were entering "a time to be wary." The fact that Congress was passing laws to order was never concealed; never before had the American government so closely resembled the British system of ministerial leadership. Roosevelt, "let us remember, is only one man, and can't do everything for himself: he must depend on others . . . ," Mencken wrote. "The danger lies in what those others may do, once a dictatorship is really in effect. Who believes that they will always act prudently, moderately, and sensibly? Certainly no one who has any acquaintance with the course of dictatorships in the past, whether in this country or elsewhere.

"Always they resolve themselves into huge bureaucracies, and a bureaucracy is a public menace in direct ratio to its power. In normal times it annoys us devilishly without doing us much serious damage, but when it has Authority with a big A behind it it invariably puts on a circus in the grand manner. The bureaucrat begins, perhaps, by doing only what he conceives to be his sworn

duty, but unless there are very efficient four-wheel brakes behind him he soon adds a multitude of inventions of his own, all of them born of his professional virtuosity and designed to lather and caress his sense of power." With Roosevelt came a host of federal establishments: an AAA, FCA, PWA, FERA, NRA, CCC, TVA, HOLC, RFC and CWA—a concept of government, Mencken later said, of "a milk cow with 125,000,000 teats." If Roosevelt wanted to be a Good Samaritan, Mencken thought, then it should be remembered that the Good Samaritan charged nothing for his service and did not run the patient into debt.

The nation had been accustomed to Mencken's attacks on government when it had been riotously living throughout the twenties; it had a different impact on those Americans who were undergoing the Depression.

1934

Once again in January the Menckens went on a cruise, this time for a two-month voyage to the Mediterranean, thereby inadvertently missing Mrs. Franklin D. Roosevelt's invitation for Sara to meet with her and become a member of the Committee on the Institute of Women's Professional Relations. Mencken's book Treatise on Right and Wrong *went on sale in the bookstores. Sara's short story "Little White Girl" appeared in Edward O'Brien's collection of* Best Short Stories of 1934, *and she was listed in the 1934–1935 edition of* Who's Who in America. *In the early autumn, Sara traveled to Montgomery to say good-bye to her mother, who lay dying. Sadly, it was also Sara's own farewell to the South: it would be her last visit.*

MRS. H. L. MENCKEN
704 CATHEDRAL STREET
BALTIMORE, MARYLAND

July 18, 1934

Darling,

I miss you and miss you, and love you so. Today is warm but there is a nice breeze blowing. I wish you could come out; I know you would like it.[1]

Gertrude wants a hammock. If you could find one easily, please send it to her; there is very little that she will let me do.

Perhaps if you go to Lewis J. Conger, in New York, you could ship her a garden table and chairs to match. Get deck chairs, and an iron table. She really needs these. Lewis J. Conger ships everything, and would gladly ship them here.

I am amazed at how much Gertrude has accomplished. She enjoys it here, and it really is very comfortable. She could use the garden furniture, and it is all marked down now. Perhaps you could get it in Baltimore; they deliver out here.

Kisses and kisses

I love you   love you

Sara

July 18, 1934

weeds

me taking the sun

¹Gertude had bought a farm near Frizzelsburg, in Carroll County, and named it Choice Parcel.

~

ALS

MRS. H. L. MENCKEN
704 CATHEDRAL STREET
BALTIMORE, MARYLAND

Thursday, July 19, 1934

Henry darling,

Your stamps and note came today. What a darling you are! I am so sorry the old poop has descended upon you.[1] Tell him you are going out of town.

It is hot here today, but there is a cooling breeze blowing. I took the sun for 20 minutes.

Please pay Hester $17[2] and Beatrice $10 when you go to New York. Don't let either one see what the other one gets.

I hope you can come out here when you return. I am sure you would enjoy it.

Millions of kisses. . . .

Sara

Also give Hester $5 in cash when you go to N.Y. for groceries to be had in the house when we return from here.

[1]Sara was probably referring to Heinrich Buchholz, a frequent visitor.

[2]Hester Denby would later follow Mencken back to 1524 Hollins Street after 1935 and cook for him and August. In 1948 she was violently stabbed to death by her daughter, who also (unsuccessfully) tried to kill her own young son. Her death filled Mencken with sadness, not only because he had lost a friend, but because one of his last remaining links with Sara had gone.

H. L. MENCKEN
704 CATHEDRAL ST.
BALTIMORE

Sunday, September 2, 1934

Darling:-

This is a lonely life, being a grass-widower. When I came in last night the house seemed like a morgue. And it was worse when I got up this morning—an hour late, for I had forgot to set the alarm. I didn't go to Hollins street, but August is coming to lunch, and we'll then go to Frizzelsburg. If we get back in time I'll put in a couple of hours on the book.[1]

Old Gustav was somewhat happier last night, but still uneasy.[2] His daughter's pneumonia turned out to be pleurisy, and she has been tapped for it. She is better, but still pretty ill. The old boy has had nothing but trouble for two years past.

You don't need it, but I append a certificate that I love you. And to excess! These four years, in fact, have made me your slave, and by the time we have gone ten I'll be in a completely lost and abject state.

I have packed two boxes for Betty,[3] and shall go to Howard street tomorrow and try to get the missing tops and bottoms. There is no mail tomorrow—Labor Day. But I must go to the office to see Paul.[4]

Let me hear at once how your mother is. And give her my devotion. And remember me to all the others.

Yours,
H

[1]Mencken was then engaged in his fourth edition of *The American Language*.

[2]A graduate of the Leipzig and Peabody conservatories, the German composer Gustav Strube had been conductor of the Boston Symphony Orchestra before he moved to Baltimore in 1915 to raise the musical prestige of the city. He became conductor of the Baltimore Symphony Orchestra and elevated it to new heights. Shortly thereafter he met Mencken and became, as he put it, a "deckhand" of the Saturday Night Club, with fiddle, baton, and pen. About Mencken's piano playing, Strube commented: "All the time he plays the wrong notes. Always down he pressed the pedal. He criticizes our performances as if he were music editor of the *Elysian Mercury*!" Strube had retired in 1930 but left a national legacy, typified by the spirit behind Arthur Fiedler's Boston "Pops" held each summer.

[3]Betty Hanes. The Menckens were planning to stay a few days with the Haneses at their home in Roaring Gap, North Carolina. Mencken was planning to meet Sara's train at Winston when she was due northward.

[4]Paul Patterson. Now that Mencken was no longer editor of the *Mercury*, he had time to give to the *Sunpapers*. That year he had been elected to its board of directors.

On September 2 Sara took the train south to visit her mother.

[TELEGRAM]

SEP 3 1934 8:20 AM

WESTERN UNION
BIRMINGHAM ALA
H L MENCKEN

704 CATHEDRAL ST
  TRAIN TERRIBLE   FOOD TERRIBLE   FIFTEEN CHILDREN UNDER FIVE YEARS OF AGE IN CAR   ARRIVED SAFELY   PHILIPPA AND YUTCH[1]   SEND LOVE   GOING TO MONTGOMERY TUESDAY

SARA.

[1]The nickname for Philippa's husband.

H. L. MENCKEN
704 CATHEDRAL ST.
BALTIMORE

Monday, September [3], 1934

Darling:-

Your telegram is just here. As I write a fife-and-drum corps is playing outside: it is Labor Day. August and I went to Frizzelsburg yesterday, and stopped in the village to see a couple of innings of baseball. It was pretty good, and we enjoyed it. Gertie's place begins to look luxuriant. All the flowers are in bloom, and the sun-flowers are at least 9 ft. high. She explained her sheep scheme, and it sounds plausible, if not exactly practicable. It will not cost much to fence her pasture. Two of her springs have been dug out, and the lower field is now shipshape and almost dry. The springs will water the sheep. In the lower woods some steers were pastured and Vickey[1] took after them, thus reverting to Bach. We couldn't haul her up until she was worn out. There were ten or twelve steers, but they all ran.

Gertie had a severe attack of hay-fever yesterday morning, but was better by the time we arrived. The country made me sniffle a bit, and this morning I had Baker put in a vaccine. He told me that he could find nothing suspicious in your record. He is to consult Richardson when Richardson returns in a few days. They will go over the whole business together.

Baker says that hay-fever is bad this year, and that it began on the 20th. But mine has been very light, and I haven't lost a minute's time.

My devotion to your mother. Tell Wick I have some stamps for him, and shall send them anon.

The house was gloomier than ever last night. I sat with Buchholz for an hour or two, but couldn't get enough aboard to drown my loneliness. But we meet two weeks from today!

Yours,
H

¹Probably Gertrude's dog.

H. L. MENCKEN

704 CATHEDRAL ST.

BALTIMORE

Tuesday, September [5], 1934

Darling:-

The injection yesterday gave me a good lift. It is hot today—78 degrees with 71% of humidity—but I feel pretty good. I sneezed only once this morning.

Return the rotogravure clipping within. I have duplicates of the others. Hearst is still bathing me in goosegrease.¹ I only hope his flow of money is not cut off.

The house begins to be tomblike. At meals there is no one to caution me against eating fast—and so I dawdle along for half an hour. And in the evenings I almost shiver. Such are the effects of love upon even a war hero.

I am writing to Betty Hanes today, saying that we'll be at Winston on Monday, September 17. I fear she is cutting corners pretty closely, and that it will be better to meet her on the 18th. I am asking her to wire to me as soon as she lands on the 14th.

I tried to find bottoms for her milk-glass today, but failed. However, I picked up a swell rabbit for her, with ruby eyes. It is a big piece, and quite unusual. I got it from the little fellow who has taken over Turner's place.[2]

I love you excessively.

Yours,

H

[1]Mencken had been asked to contribute at different times to the New York *American*, one of Hearst's newspapers, but he only began to do so in 1934, submitting small weekly articles on some aspect of American English. The articles were also printed in eight other Hearst satellites throughout the United States. Mencken continued to write philological articles for the newspaper until May 20, 1935.

[2]"Turner" probably refers to Lee Turner, the bootlegger to Baltimore's elite both during and after Prohibition times.

H. L. MENCKEN

704 CATHEDRAL ST.

BALTIMORE

Wednesday, September 6, 1934

Darling:-

Not a word from you so far, save the telegram. If there is no letter tomorrow morning I'll begin to pitch and heave. It now seems a month since you left, and the house begins to be as lonely as the ruins of Carthage. Hester made me a mess of vegetable soup yesterday, and I got down three plates. This was at lunch, and I had to take a nap. But when I riz up I felt fine, and got through a hard day's work. . . .

Tonight I am going down to Highlandtown with Buchholz to try Hausner's beer.[1] But I hate to think of coming home to the empty house. This love business wears me down.

Yours,

H

[1]In 1926 the Bavarian emigré William H. Haussner had opened a small eating house on Eastern Avenue in Highlandtown. It was little more than a short-order place but it attracted attention because Haussner did his own cooking. He had been the manager of several leading restaurants in the hotels of Europe, including the Rathskeller in Frankfurt, which was frequented by the former kaiser. In a

few years Haussner and his wife began buying row houses on Eastern Avenue and Clinton Street, and in 1934 they opened a restaurant there. The restaurant served typical German and Baltimore cuisine, and its walls were lined with rare objects of art, including paintings by Rembrandt and Van Dyck.

ALS

September the fifth, 1934

Darling,

I came down from Birmingham yesterday (Tuesday) and found your letters here. It was such a comfort! The older McClellans came home the night before. So you know. Monday, being a holiday, Yutch was around most of the day, and I didn't have much time with Philippa. However, she managed to tell me enough to cast me down: Mamma is really critically ill, and I marvel that she gets around at all. I'll see Dr. Pollard but I imagine he'll tell me that he is fearful of putting Mamma to bed—she would probably never get up. As it is, she'll drop over one day, as her mother did before her.

Kelley is marvellous, and does practically everything.[1] She will, of course, have to have some help when she starts to school.

Johnnie was in this morning. His business is picking up beautifully but he is working night and day which won't hurt him.

Wick is quite grown and sends you his love. He has improved marvellously, being with Johnnie.

The weather is perfect. I wore my fur coat suit down on the train. It is marvellously cool today.

I may telephone you from Johnnie's, just to hear your voice. This sort of thing really gets me.

I hope everything at the apartment is going well. I love you, love you. . . .

Sara

Philippa's baby is really darling.[2] He has very *blue* eyes and a head shaped like yours.

[1]Sara's younger sister, Mary Kelley.
[2]Philippa's son, Tommy.

ALS
September the fifth, 1934

Darling,

It was such a comfort to hear your voice . . . your letters came this morning, and you are a dear.

Dr. Pollard says Mamma's blood pressure was 230; it has gone down a little bit. She is very feeble indeed—you would not recognize her.

I am lunching with the Pollards Saturday; dining with the Rias and Grover Hall Sunday. This has all played me out: it is such an effort keeping up a front to Mamma, and being sweet to people I really don't care about. I'll be so glad to get home to you.

I got the light and telephone bills, and I am paying them. *The Current Digest* wants permission to reprint my article in the *Household Magazine*. I am writing to them. . . .

If you can send me an extra hundred dollars, I'll make it up to you some day. There are a few little things I would like to get for Mamma, and I feel this will be my last chance to do anything for her. She and Kelley live simply but the prices have gone up here, and I'd like to buy her a few delicacies—her diet is limited.

I was with Dr. Hannah[1] at Johnnie's last night. He was an intern at the Union Memorial when your mother was there, and attended her. He spoke beautifully of her.

I love you
love you
Always
Sara

[1]William Sessions Hannah.

H. L. MENCKEN
704 CATHEDRAL ST.
BALTIMORE

Thursday, September [6], 1934

Darling:-

I was so sorry last night to hear that your mother was so ill. Are you sure she is getting the right attention? If not, you must see that she does. It bucked me up to hear your voice. The day had been very long and lonely. But I finished my Vanity Fair article[1] in the evening, and it is now on its way to Crowninshield.[2] During the night I awoke with a violent sneezing fit—the first and only one I have had this year. I had gone to bed with the window up and the wind blowing on me. I shut it down, and there was no more sneezing. I have been pretty comfortable today, and in addition to handling my mail and putting in an hour at the Peabody I have written my Sun article, and hope to work on the book this evening.

I was amazed this afternoon to hear Mayfield's voice on the telephone. She is at the Stafford, and says she sprained her ankle this morning.[3] I invited her to lunch tomorrow, and shall hear what she has to say. She is going to New York in the afternoon.

No letter from you yet. It seems a year. I love you.

Yours,
H

[1]"Why Not an American Monarchy?" appeared in the November issue of the magazine.

[2]Frank Crowninshield, editor of *Vanity Fair*.

[3]Sara Mayfield apparently had suffered a series of misadventures en route from Tuscaloosa to New York by Greyhound bus. On Wednesday, September 5, her imported hand trunk was thrown down from the bus, burst open at the Atlanta terminal, after which it was left out in the rain, set down in the mud at Richmond, and, she wrote the executive offices of Greyhound, "generally subjected to ill usage." On the trip from Washington to Baltimore the bus collided with a streetcar on a corner of M Street, and Sara sprained her ankle.

H. L. MENCKEN
704 CATHEDRAL ST.
BALTIMORE

Friday, September [7], 1934

Darling:-

Mayfield was here for lunch. She looks pretty well, but is very thin. She says she has been running a 600-acre plantation near Tuscaloosa, and that she closed the year with $650 profit. She has also finished a novel and has taken to sculpture. Now she is joining the advertising department of a distillery in New York, and will have a flat there with Jim Mayfield. She stayed until 3 o'clock, and then went on to New York. There was no sign of her sprained ankle.

The weather is dreadful here today—78 degrees, 85% of humidity, and a drizzle falling. I am glad you are not here—but then again I shorely ain't!

Yours,
H

H. L. MENCKEN
704 CATHEDRAL ST.
BALTIMORE

Friday, September 7, 1934

Darling:-

A long letter from Hergy today. Lorimer[1] has turned down his new novel[2] and he is in the dumps.[3] He says he is sick with some sort of infection—probably the same impetigo. Why the quacks don't cure it I can't make out. He says he is in no state for a party at West Chester. I am surely not eager to go there. Later on in the Autumn it will be better. . . .

One week more, and I'll be getting ready to come down to Winston. And there you will be! I miss you dreadfully. And love you twice as much as ever before.

Yours,
H

Hester reports that the washwoman's bill is low this week because you are not here. But I am paying her the usual amount. She needs it.

[1]George Horace Lorimer, editor of *The Saturday Evening Post*.
[2]*The Foolscap Rose*. The novel itself was diffuse and disconnected.
[3]Hergesheimer concluded his letter by sending Mencken and Sara "almost all the regard I have left for the human race." In time, Hergesheimer would become paralyzed for hours by the confrontation of a blank page, and in the last fifteen years of his life he wrote virtually nothing.

H. L. MENCKEN
704 CATHEDRAL ST.
BALTIMORE

September 10th, 1934

Darling:-

I am so distressed to hear about your mother. Certainly she must be very uncomfortable. You must buy her whatever she needs and will like. I enclose a check. Please tell her I am thinking of her.

The weather here continues damp and unpleasant. Temperature this morning: 78. Humidity: 80. I stayed at home last night, and felt like a sailor cast away on a desert island. Tonight I must bust out with Buchholz.

Raymond Swing, who was in Berlin in 1916 and was very kind to me, is now in Washington as correspondent for The Nation.[1] We must ask him and his wife to come to dinner as soon as we are back home. I am writing to him.

I must get to work on my Liberty article tonight.[2] Yesterday I did another piece for the N.Y.American,[3] and also got in some licks on the book.

The Current Digest reprint will be very good advertising. Say yes by all means. My experience is that such reprints often bring in more mail than the original articles. . . .

How I love you!

Yours,

H

[1]American journalist and radio news commentator. Swing had been a war correspondent in Berlin for the *Chicago Daily News*. In 1935 he became the first American news commentator of American affairs for the BBC, and later for American and Canadian networks.

[2]"Why Nobody Loves a Politician" appeared in the October 27 issue of *Liberty* magazine.

[3]"Counter-Words: Common Coins of Speech Worn Smooth and Thin," for September 17.

~

ALS
September the eleventh, 1934

Darling,

It has turned very warm here, the usual September weather. I had a pleasant time at the Hilton Rice's[1] last night: Grover Hall was the only other guest. He seems somehow to have been caught in this awful life down here: he is drinking too much, and is otherwise not his old self.

Your story of Mayfield is interesting. I don't believe a word she said but I am glad you had her to luncheon.

Mamma continues the same, save that she is never as well in hot weather. It is all extremely depressing, darling. I can scarcely get away from her for a few minutes at a time which is not like her at all. It has been rather hectic, trying to see other people too. . . .

How glad I'll be to see you. I shall fall on your neck, and never leave you.

A million kisses. I miss you so!

Sara

It is difficult to write, there are so many interruptions.

[1] Clark Hilton Rice, a pediatrician and specialist in psychology and nervous disorders, also contributed short stories to popular magazines.

H. L. MENCKEN
704 CATHEDRAL ST.
BALTIMORE

Thursday, September 13, 1934

Darling:-

My birthday ran true to form. That is, the weather was hot, muggy and uncomfortable, and I had a sneezing bout in the late evening. But today I feel pretty comfortable, and so the vaccine scores again. If there is any sneezing later in the day I'll have Baker give me another injection tomorrow—NOT today, for today is the 13th.

Last night I went to Paul Patterson's house for dinner, with Lew Douglas, the late director of the budget.[1] Present: John Owens, Harry Black and Fred Essary.[2] A pleasant dinner, and some interesting talk.

Douglas, of course, knows all the ins and outs of the New Deal. I left early and was in bed by 11:30.

This morning came a letter from young Teddy Roosevelt.[3] It appears that he was struck all of a heap by my Liberty article on crime.[4] Can it be a flirtation? In his autobiography, published a few years ago, young Teddy denounced me as a scoundrel.[5] . . .

I am very uneasy about your mother. She will need this and that after you leave. Why not arrange with Kelley to send her enough money every week to pay for these things? We can manage it. Your mother must have what she needs. She must be made comfortable. Find out from Kelley what all this will cost, and tell her that you will send the money.

I am crazy for a sight of you. It will seem a week from the time I get to Winston to the time you roll in.

Yours,

H

[1]In an attempt to rally conservative support for his administration, President Roosevelt appointed Lewis William Douglas as director of the budget on March 4, 1933. Douglas found his views of economy in conflict with those of the president and resigned from office on August 31, 1934.

[2]Head of the *Sun*'s Washington bureau.

[3]The young Theodore Roosevelt, Jr.

[4]"What to Do with Criminals," published in the July 28 issue of *Liberty*, supported the death penalty.

[5]In his book, *All in the Family* (1929), Roosevelt had written: "We throw away the modern books of the sniggering nasty type, whose authors, like H. L. Mencken, have too little ability to attract attention to themselves except in the fashion of a stink cabbage." Later, Theodore Roosevelt, Jr., would be writing Mencken friendly letters, in one of them praising Sara's writing.

Once Sara finally did arrive in Winston, Mencken and the Haneses found her pale, tired, and weak, on the verge of another serious illness. By the time the Menckens returned to Baltimore Sara had to be put to bed.

~

ALS

SEVEN HUNDRED AND FOUR CATHEDRAL STREET
BALTIMORE, MARYLAND

Sunday, October 7, 1934

Darling,

I will miss you more than I ever have. You are such a dear, and I love you so much.

Please have a nice time in New York and forget me a little but not too much. I'll be counting the minutes until you are back.

I worship you.

Sara

Kisses

x x x x x x x x x x x x x x x x x x x x x x x x x x x x x x x x x x x x x x

1,000,000,000,000,000,000,000

ALS

HOTEL ALGONQUIN
NEW YORK

Tuesday, October [9], 1934

Darling:

Swell news! I begin to believe in medicine again.[1] But take it slowly. Why wouldn't this be a good time to lay out your book?

I spent a pleasant evening at Purchase with Alfred. Blanche remained in town. We had a good dinner, and went to bed early. The country is really heavenly. All the poplars and beeches are turning, and the woods are full of color. But, as usual, we turned out a bit too early this morning. We drove out and in, and missed 5 or 6 trucks, culverts, etc. by inches.

I have a note from Philippa about the bulbs. I'll send them to Gertie Thursday.

I have 6 or 7 engagements today, and am on the jump. But not too jumpy to remember thou with kindest personal regards.

H.

[1] Sara was at Union Memorial Hospital. Among Mencken's friends rumors circulated that Sara was pregnant. She was actually ill with pleurisy, but on this day she was feeling somewhat better.

ALS

SEVEN HUNDRED AND FOUR CATHEDRAL STREET
BALTIMORE, MARYLAND

October the ninth, 1934

Darling,

Your note was sweet. I can't begin to tell you how much I miss you. The whole day and night are empty.

This is another lovely day, though warmish. I am going out on the bridge this morning and afternoon too.

Everything is going smoothly. Anne was out yesterday; she is getting more nervous as the time goes.[1]

The hall is almost full but there are plenty of nurses and the food is good.

How I miss you! If I ever get home with you again I'll never leave you.

Until Thursday, a million years—

Sara

[1]Anne Duffy was pregnant. Her daughter, Sara Anne, was named after Sara.

[TELEGRAM]

DEC 5 1934 11:34 AM

WESTERN UNION
NEW YORK NY
MRS H L MENCKEN

704 CATHEDRAL ST
HOME AT THREE THIRTY

H.

Mencken was rushing home to Baltimore. Three days later he had to be in Washington, D.C., to address the Gridiron Club, made up of Washington-based newspapermen, senators, cabinet members, governors, industrialists, and prominent publishers, on the inequities of Franklin D. Roosevelt's New Deal. Roosevelt was to follow with his own speech.

Never comfortable with giving speeches, Mencken practiced his address before

Sara, trying in vain to memorize it, until she advised him to read it instead. By the time he gave the speech before the club he felt comfortable and began a relatively harmless and good-humored address to the president and his peers, addressing them as "Fellow Subjects of the Reich" (he had previously crossed out the words "Fellow Victims of the More Abundant Life"). He spoke of the poverty the nation was facing; he related anecdotes; he told a few jokes.

Roosevelt followed. Flashing a wide smile, he launched into a speech criticizing journalists. As the speech went on it dawned on everyone that the president was quoting from works written by Mencken himself. Throughout the speech he kept calling Mencken "Henry" and speaking of him as an old friend. Nonetheless, it was plain to Mencken and others that Roosevelt had been harboring some of these things for a long while. At the end of ten minutes, Roosevelt flashed a grin to his "old friend, Henry Mencken," shook hands with him, and was wheeled out of the room.

Two weeks after the event, Roosevelt explained in a letter to the journalist Arthur Brisbane: "I did not really intend to be quite so rough on Henry Mencken but the old quotations which I dug up were too good to be true, and I felt in view of all the amusing but cynically rough things which Henry had said in print for twenty years, he was entitled to ten minutes of comeback." The comeback, however, was never forgotten by Mencken; for him, it was public humiliation.

To add to matters, Sara's mother died on Christmas Day, and Sara herself was ill with pleurisy. Thus, the year ended on a note that fulfilled Mencken's own sarcastic prediction of doom. "I feel it in my bones that 1934 is going to be a fortune year," Mencken had written to Dudley Field Malone at the end of 1933. "To this end I have instructed my chaplain to pray powerfully." He was right.

1935

Throughout the early months of 1935 Sara had begun revising her short stories and planning work on a novel, but in late March she returned to Johns Hopkins Hospital. At first there was no clear diagnosis; Mencken knew only that her trouble was "something in the order of influenza."

ALS

MRS. H. L. MENCKEN
704 CATHEDRAL STREET
BALTIMORE, MARYLAND
Sunday, March the thirty-first, 1935

Darling

I believe my temperature was actually normal this afternoon. Miss Handy—who looks ten years older—came in and we had a talk about the South. I told her I would call her after talking to Ben Baker about coming home.

This has been a dreary day indeed. I don't like the idea of your being in the house alone, and not feeling well. Darling, please, please, be careful, and at the first time of fatigue, go to bed, or better still, come home.

I'll try to get out and call you tonight. If I fail, you'll know Old Hawk-Eye, the head-nurse, has her eye on the telephone.

Do write me how you feel. I love you, love you

Sara

H. L. MENCKEN
704 CATHEDRAL ST.
BALTIMORE

April 1st, 1935

Darling:-

Baker tells me that your temperature has been down for two days. Grand news! A couple of days of sunlight, and you'll be ready to sign off. If only the weather were decenter!

My larynx and trachea are sore, but Baker could find nothing in the bronchial tubes. He ordered me to lie low, and this afternoon I took a long nap. Tonight I shall go to bed early, with a big slug of whiskey aboard. He found my blood pressure to be 130—very good for an old boozer.

I wired to all of the New York brethren. My trip there can wait a few weeks. I probably won't go until it is time for the next hay-fever shot.

The house is horribly lonely and gloomy. When you come home I shall yell.

I love you.

H

ALS

MRS. H. L. MENCKEN
704 CATHEDRAL STREET
BALTIMORE, MARYLAND

April the second, 1935

Darling,

I seem to be holding my own. I was out on the porch this morning for two hours, and the sun was really warm. I have missed you terribly, and felt dreadfully about your being in the house alone when you didn't feel well.

Ben Baker says you are in excellent shape except for your cold. He says he made a thorough examination of your chest. Your blood-pressure is only 8 points higher than mine. Well, it will be a joy to see you again! . . .

I hope my temperature stays down. Ben Baker has been going over my X-rays and my chart. He says he can find nothing in the X-rays.[1]

I love you, dearest one.

Sara

[1]Rather ironically, tuberculosis of the lung, which Sara always believed would take her in the end, did not trouble her.

[TELEGRAM]

APR 30 1935 6:51 PM

WESTERN UNION

BALTIMORE MD

H L MENCKEN

HOTEL ALGONQUIN 58 WEST 44 ST

PLEASE CALL K S WHITE OF NEW YORKER[1]   IMPORTANT   SHE HAS YOUR PROOF READY AND IS GOING TO PRESS THURSDAY   MISS YOU TERRIBLY

SARA.

[1]In an effort to prime the pump, Mencken wrote a series of language pieces for *The New Yorker*. Upset over Sara's illness, Mencken had submitted one article which was so confused that Katharine Sergeant White, the managing and fiction editor, was forced to return it.

As the weeks progressed, the Menckens exchanged letters with a real estate broker and found a summer home located at Turtle Pond, in the Adirondacks, and made plans to move in on June 1. But as April continued, Sara was no better.

~

H. L. MENCKEN
704 CATHEDRAL ST.
BALTIMORE

[April ?], 1935

Darling:-

In view of the weather I think it would be foolish to go to New York today. I feel pretty good but there is still some soreness, and I think I had better lie low. I'll see you tomorrow.

How I miss you!

Yours,
H.

H. L. MENCKEN
704 CATHEDRAL ST.
BALTIMORE

April [?], 1935

Darling:-

This needs no special adjustment. Simply hook the end of the thin wire to the valve of the radiator, or to the radiator itself, and plug the power wire in on your light. You will then bathe in art.

The house is a desert.

H

This was the last letter Sara would receive from Mencken. Thoughtful as ever, Mencken had brought Sara a record player to cheer her up at the hospital. For a few weeks she sat up and despite her dizzy spells continued to write notes for her novel and letters to her friends. Toward the end of May Dr. Benjamin Baker diagnosed that Sara had meningitis, with tubercular bacillus in the spinal fluid. During her last days she slept peacefully, waking up and then falling asleep again, while Mencken sat by, watching her fight "magnificently in the shadows."

Sara died on May 31, 1935.

NOTES

~

THERE ARE FEW STUDIES ON THE WORK of Sara Haardt. None are of any major length. William T. Going gives a brief summary of Sara Haardt's work and personality in "Zelda Sayre Fitzgerald and Sara Haardt Mencken," in *Essays on Alabama Literature* (University, Alabama: The University of Alabama Press, 1975), pp. 114–141. See also William T. Going, "Two Alabama Writers: Zelda Sayre Fitzgerald and Sara Haardt Mencken," *Alabama Review*, January 1970, pp. 3–29. Both are helpful. Durard le Grand, editor of the Birmingham *Post Herald*, in his article "Alabama Poorer for Neglect of Mrs. Mencken" (June 14, 1969) calls for the need of a study of Sara Haardt's works. M. K. Singleton's *H. L. Mencken and the American Mercury Adventure* (Durham, North Carolina: Duke University Press, 1962) mentions Sara Haardt's articles. For a personal view on Sara an unpublished report by Larry Yeatman gives a brief glimpse into Sara's Goucher years. At least three biographies on Mencken devote a chapter or more to Mencken and Sara's courtship, marriage, and married life. The first on the list is Sara Mayfield's *The Constant Circle: H. L. Mencken and His Friends* (New York: Delacorte Press, 1968). This gives an entertaining firsthand view, but unhappily, since most of it is derived from personal memory, the biography is not well documented. William Manchester's *Disturber of the Peace: The Life of H. L. Mencken* (New York: Harper and Brothers, 1950) and Carl Bode's *Mencken* (Carbondale, Illinois:

Southern Illinois University Press, 1969) give a thorough and comprehensive picture of Mencken and Sara's courtship and married life. But it is on Carl Bode's book that all subsequent studies on Mencken and Sara's married life must rest. Much of it consists of interviews with people who are no longer living. In addition, Carl Bode touches upon Sara Haardt's writing. Other books that have been essential to my introduction and annotations are cited in these notes. Those works or institutions which I have cited the most often are listed below, with their abbreviations:

Ala	The William Stanley Hoole Special Collections Library, the University of Alabama.
AN 1925	*Autobiographical Notes 1925* were written by Mencken to help Isaac Goldberg in his biography, *The Man Mencken.* They are deposited in the Mencken Room at the Enoch Pratt Free Library, Baltimore.
AN 1941	*Autobiographical Notes 1941–* These are miscellaneous autobiographical notes Mencken composed from 1941 on. There are no page numbers. They are deposited in the Mencken Room.
Bode	Carl Bode, *The New Mencken Letters* (New York: The Dial Press, 1977).
C. Bode	Carl Bode, *Mencken* (Carbondale: Southern Illinois University Press, paperback reprint, 1973).
EPL	The Enoch Pratt Free Library, Baltimore.
Forgue	Guy J. Forgue, *Letters of H. L. Mencken* (New York: Alfred A. Knopf, Inc., 1961).
MdBG	The Sara Haardt Mencken Collection, the Julia Rogers Library, Goucher College.
MdBJ	Special Collections, the Milton S. Eisenhower Library, the Johns Hopkins University.
SH	*Sara Powell Haardt Mencken, 1898–1935.* Mencken

compiled a scrapbook on Sara and deposited it in the Mencken Room at the Enoch Pratt Free Library.

SS   The autobiographical sketch, "Southern Souvenir," was written by Sara Haardt in January or February 1935, a few short months before Sara Haardt's death. It was never published. It is in manuscript form in the Mencken Collection at the Julia Rogers Library, Goucher College.

SECTION I

Page

1   Mencken defined love: These quotations are taken from the "Sententiae" section of *A Mencken Chrestomathy* (New York: Alfred A. Knopf, 1949), pp. 619–621.

1   As for Sara: Sara Haardt, *The Love Story of an Old Maid* (Girard, Kansas: Haldeman-Julius, 1927), p. 32.

2   Although Mencken wrote: Mencken, *Minority Report* (New York: Alfred A. Knopf, 1956), p. 281.

2   Mencken's relationship with: Ibid., p. 228.

2   "A bad writer": *AN 1925*, p. 192. EPL.

3   Long after the: Van Wyck Brooks, *Days of the Phoenix: The Nineteen Twenties I Remember* (New York: E. P. Dutton and Co., 1957), p. 163. Sherwood Anderson, writing to Mencken from New Orleans in 1925, discovered, "Everywhere I went they asked me first—What do you think of Mencken?" Charles E. Modlin, ed., *Sherwood Anderson, Selected Letters* (Knoxville: University of Tennessee Press, 1984), p. 72.

3   In his maturity: Ray Lewis White, ed., *Sherwood Anderson's Memoirs, A Critical Edition* (Chapel Hill: The University of North Carolina Press, 1969), p. 369.

4   As one of: Carl Bode, "Mencken in His Letters," *On Mencken*, John Dorsey, ed. (New York: Alfred A. Knopf, 1980), p. 242.

4   In many ways: Mencken, "Preface," *Southern Album*, by Sara Haardt, H. L. Mencken, ed. (New York: Doubleday, Doran & Co., Inc., 1936), p. xviii.

4   Of her work: Mencken, "Prefatory Note," *Sara Haardt: Clippings of Short Stories and Articles Contributed to American Magazines and Newspapers, 1918–1935*, Vol. I. MdBG.

Page

5   At the same: Frederick C. Hobson, Jr., *Serpent in Eden: H. L. Mencken and the South* (Chapel Hill: The University of North Carolina Press, 1974). For his discussion, see pp. 147–169.

5   In a letter: Mencken to Philip Goodman, May 1, 1933. Forgue, p. 365.

5   During the lecture: Mencken to Philip Goodman, May 9, 1923. EPL.

6   Afterwards, she would: Sara Haardt (SH) to H. L. Mencken (HLM), August 22, 1923. MdBG.

6   Her first letter: SH to HLM, May 20, 1923. MdBG.

6   After experiencing what: SH to HLM, May 26, 1923. MdBG.

6   Mencken, meanwhile, ate: HLM to SH, April 1, 1925. MdBG.

7   His friends, editors: *Ingenue Among the Lions: The Letters of Emily Clark to Joseph Hergesheimer*, Gerald Langford, ed. (Austin: The University of Texas Press, 1965), p. 54.

7   Then there was: My interview with Mrs. Hamilton Owens, March 22, 1985.

7   And what of: *AN 1925*, p. 192. EPL.

7   "No unmarried woman": *AN 1925*, p. 192. EPL.

7   Incautiously, he remarked: "Why I Remain Unmarried," Philadelphia *Ledger Syndicate*, March 11, 1926.

8   The truth, in: Joseph Hergesheimer, "Mr. Henry L. Mencken," *The Borzoi 1925* (New York: Alfred A. Knopf, 1925), pp. 105–106.

8   There was also: *Ingenue Among the Lions*, Gerald Langford, ed., p. 59.

8   She enjoyed the: Gloria Swanson, *Swanson on Swanson* (New York: Random House, 1980), p. 182.

9   "You may resent": Mencken to James Cain, July 25, 1944. NYPL.

9   She chided Mencken: All the letters between Mencken and Marion Bloom: EPL.

10   James Cain wrote: Roy Hoopes, *Cain* (New York: Holt, Rinehart & Winston, 1982), p. 194.

10   The writer and: Letter from James Tully to Sara Haardt, September 8, 1929. *SH*, p. 173. EPL.

10   His letters to: HLM to SH, March 17, 1924. MdBG.

10   The bauble, it: HLM to SH, March 21, 1924. MdBG.

11   He mixed his: HLM to SH, March 8, 1924. MdBG.

11   Finally, when she: HLM to SH, March 4, 1925. MdBG.

11   There were her: Interview with Isabelle Diffenderfer, April 27, 1978. (Yeatman)

11   She had, as: Mencken, "Preface," *Southern Album*, pp. xxii–xxiii.

11   It was this: Letter from R. P. Harriss to Sara Mayfield, January 25, 1929. Ala.

Page

12 Nearer to home: Letter from John Haardt to Sara, February 1, 1924. *SH*, p. 134. EPL.

12 That Mencken was: Letter from James Cain to Sara Mayfield, August 19, 1968. Ala.

12 She believed that: Sara Haardt, "Career Germ," *Notes, by Sara Haardt 1927–1935.* MdBG.

13 However, it must: San Francisco *Chronicle*, November 20, 1926. Interview with Mencken.

13 The letter written: HLM to SH, September 29, 1927. MdBG.

13 She was a: Mencken, "Confederate Notes," the Baltimore *Evening Sun*, December 22, 1922.

13 To anyone observing: C. Bode, p. 282.

13 Cro-Magnon man: "H. L. Mencken to Wed Young Author," New York *Herald Tribune*, August 3, 1930.

14 (she was noted): *Donnybrook Fair, 1921* (Goucher College Yearbook), p. 69. MdBG.

14 (Although Sara's outlook): HLM to Sara Mayfield (undated), 1927. Ala.

14 "We have substantially": Sally MacDougall, "Mencken the Perfect Husband," New York *Herald Tribune*, August 17, 1930.

14 New York was: Mencken, "On Living in Baltimore," the Baltimore *Evening Sun*, February 16, 1925.

14 He went on: MacDougall, Ibid.

14 "in human relationships": Mencken, "On Living in Baltimore," Ibid.

14 And he added: Ibid.

15 Although Emily Clark: *Ingenue Among the Lions*, Gerald Langford, ed., p. 54.

15 "the first Christian": SH to HLM, July 23, 1923. MdBG.

15 Sara, with her: John E. Rosser, "H. L. Mencken: The Bad Boy of Baltimore," *Real America*, September 1933.

15 Successful friendships and: Mencken, *AN 1925*, p. 191. EPL.

15 "Neither of us": Memphis, Tennessee, *Press Scrinitar*, August 9, 1928.

15 When they married: Ibid.

15 Unlike Sara, he: *Ilnesses 1912–1948.* EPL.

16 As she put: Sara Haardt, "Sara Haardt, Wife of H. L. Mencken, Conquers TB Four Times," *The Fluoroscope*, May 1935.

16 Mencken's publisher, Alfred: Letter to me from Mrs. Alfred Knopf, February 1, 1985.

16 "It always amazed": Mencken, "Prefatory Note," *Notes by Sara Haardt 1927–1935.* MdBG.

17 He put it: *AN 1941-.* EPL.

Page

17   He thought "my": *AN* 1941-. EPL.
18   (Indeed, she was): Letter from Lucy Lester to editors, June 11, 1926, from
       Thomasville, Georgia. *SH*, p. 44. EPL.

SECTION II

20   "When you've battled": Sara Haardt, *The Fluoroscope*, p. 5.
20   It was her: Haardt, *SS*, p. 1. MdBG.
20   It was taken: Haardt, *SS*, p. 10. MdBG.
21   Venetia, her daughter: *SS*, p. 2. MdBG.
21   When she compared: *SS*, p. 2. MdBG.
21   It was not: My interview with Ida Haardt, October 1, 1983.
21   "Pressed butterfly": Sara Haardt, "Soulrise," *Kalends*, January 1919, p.
       13.
22   There were other: My interview with Ida Haardt, October 1, 1983.
22   After Venetia died: *SS*, p. 13. MdBG.
23   Her teacher would: Letter from Margaret Booth to Goucher College, June
       1916. Admissions file at registrar's office, Goucher College.
23   (Sara usually responded): Sara Mayfield, *The Constant Circle: H. L. Mencken
       and His Friends* (New York: Delacorte Press, 1968), p. 24.
23   It is a: Sara Haardt, "Commencement," *Southern Album*, p. 133.
24   Against "the powdery": Sara Haardt, "Dear Life," *Southern Album*, p. 279.
24   For Sara, these: Sara Haardt, Ibid.
25   In the ballroom: Sara Haardt, "Zelda Fitzgerald," unpublished manu-
       script, *Articles and Movie Scenarios 1927–1935*. MdBG.
25   It worked for: My interview with Catherine Steiner, October 2, 1983.
25   "Before 1905 or": Sara Haardt, "Zelda Fitzgerald," pp. 2–3. MdBG.
26   By herself or: Sara Haardt, "Joe Moore and Callie Blasingame," *The Smart
       Set*, October 1923, p. 109.
26   She ventured also: Sara Haardt, "Southern Credo," *The American Mercury*,
       May 1930, p. 108.
26   More often, Sara: Ibid., p. 105.
26   Years later, she: Ibid.
26   But at the: Ibid.
27   "I trembled ecstatically": Ibid., p. 110.
27   "Through the web": Ibid.
28   "The characteristics of": Anne Huebeck Knipp and Thaddeus P. Thomas,
       The History of Goucher College (Baltimore: Goucher College, 1938), p. 549.
28   It was also: *Donnybrook Fair* 1921, p. 69. MdBG.

Page

33   "Why this sentimentality": Haardt, "Dear Life," *Southern Album*, pp. 272–273.

SECTION ·III

34   In it Mencken: Mencken, "The Sahara of the Bozart," *Prejudices: Second Series* (New York: Alfred A. Knopf, 1920), p. 136.

34   He mocked what: Ibid., pp. 142, 137.

34   These criticisms were: Virginius Dabney, *Liberalism in the South* (Chapel Hill: The University of North Carolina Press, 1932), p. 387. Nor did their denouncing end there. During the single year 1926 more than 500 separate editorials upon the sayings and actions of H. L. Mencken were printed in the United States, and at least four-fifths of them were unfavorable. Sara helped gather most of them together for Mencken's collection, *Menckeniania: A Schimflexicon* (Alfred A. Knopf, 1928).

34   "The Sahara of the Bozart": Fred C. Hobson, Jr., *Serpent in Eden: H. L. Mencken and the South* (Chapel Hill; The University of North Carolina Press, 1974), p. 28.
    1-46 Early in 1921: Emily Clark, *Innocence Abroad* (New York: Alfred A. Knopf, 1931), p. 112.

35   "One might suggest": Frances Newman, "On the State of Literature in the Late Confederacy," New York *Herald Tribune* Books, August 16, 1925.

35   She made the: Hobson, p. 58.

36   Mencken had become: Hobson, p. 32.

36   It is interesting: Wilfred A. Beardsley to H. L. Mencken, June 5, 1935. *Sara Haardt Mencken: Letters and Telegrams After Her Death*. MdBG.

36   The motivation for: Sara Haardt, editorial, the *Kalends*, February 1918, p. 47. MdBG.

36   In another editorial: Sara Haardt, editorial, the *Kalends*, April 1920, p. 15. MdBG.

37   "It has a": HLM to SH, June 5, 1923. MdBG.

37   Buoyed by his: SH to HLM, June 24, 1923. MdBG.

37   When this was: SH to HLM, July 7, 1923. MdBG.

37   "Joe Moore and": Haardt, "Dear Life," *Southern Album*, p. 274.

37   *The American Mercury*: HLM to SH, August 17, 1923. MdBG.

38   The post-World War: W. H. A. Williams, *H. L. Mencken* (Boston: Twayne Publishers, 1977), p. 96.

38   If there seems: Charles A. Fecher, *Mencken: A Study of His Thought* (New York: Alfred A. Knopf, 1978), p. 208.

38   In his letters: HLM to SH, August 17, 1923. MdBG.

Page

38   He also added: HLM to SH, August 24, 1923. MdBG.

39   Sara responded enthusiastically: SH to HLM, August 22, 1923. MdBG.

39   Unfortunately, the topics: Ibid.

39   She finally told: Sara Haardt, *The Fluoroscope*, p. 13.

39   Just one year: H. L. Mencken, "Violets in the Sahara," the Baltimore *Evening Sun*, May 15, 1922.

39   To which he: Ibid.

40   There she observed: Letter from President William Westley Guth, of Goucher College, to Sara Haardt, September 16, 1927. *SH*, p. 54. EPL.

40   Mencken himself was: HLM to SH, April 18, 1925; April 25, 1925. MdBG.

40   She complained that: HLM to SH, April 11, 1925. MdBG.

41   His explanation of: H. L. Mencken, "Arnold Bennett," *Prejudices: First Series* (New York: Alfred A. Knopf, 1919), p. 38.

41   Her aim, instead: H. L. Mencken, "Theodore Dreiser," *A Book of Prefaces* (New York: Alfred A. Knopf, 1917), p. 136.

41   Recognizing its originality: HLM to SH, September 22, 1927. MdBG.

42   On April 27: HLM to SH, April 27, 1927. MdBG.

43   He had the: HLM to SH, May 5, 1927. MdBG.

43   Sara promptly set: HLM to SH, June 13, 1927. MdBG.

43   He advised her: HLM to SH, October 17, 1927. MdBG.

43   "Every writer of ": H. L. Mencken, "Notes in the Margin," *The Smart Set*, November 1920.

43   He continued his: H.L. Mencken, "Appendix from Moronia," *Prejudices: Sixth Series* (New York: Alfred A. Knopf, 1927), p. 303.

43   The fact that: HLM to SH, October 26, 1927. MdBG.

43   Privately, he wrote: Mencken to Jim Tully, November 13, 1927. Bode, p. 216.

44   Perhaps Maugham, Waugh; HLM to SH, October 10, 1927. MdBG.

44   "Her adventures there": Mencken, "Preface," *Southern Album*, p. xvi.

44   "The truth is": SH to HLM, November 6, 1927. MdBG.

44   To cheer her: HLM to SH, November 11, 1927. MdBG.

44   "This letter is": SH to HLM, October 26, 1927. MdBG.

45   "He's probably lying and exaggerating": SH to HLM, Ibid.

46   Mencken felt that: Mencken, "The Anatomy of the Novel," *The Smart Set*, 1914, p. 153. "The better the novel, indeed, the more man approached Everyman and the more the background overshadows him."

46   "First, I know": SH to HLM, July 7, 1923. MdBG.

46   "Lay on! You": HLM to SH, July 10, 1923. MdBG.

47   "Get plenty of": Ibid.

Page
47 Yet it is not: "Sara Haardt's *The Making of a Lady*," *The New York Times Book Review*, October 1930, p. 5.
48 Sara Haardt's experiment: Mencken, "Preface," *Southern Album*, p. xix.
48 He knew the: HLM to Mary Parmenter, February 18, 1936. NYPL.
48 "I am being": Hobson, p. 177.
48 "I think the": Dolly Dalrymple, "Mr. Mencken's Verbal Arabesques," the Birmingham *News-Age Herald*, March 26, 1933.
49 It would almost: Sara Haardt, "Ellen Glasgow and the South," p. 134.
49 Sara had written: Sara Haardt, "Southern Credo," p. 103.
49 "For all her": Edith H. Walton, "Miss Haardt's Stories: *Southern Album*," *The New York Times Book Review*, March 8, 1936, p. 7.
49 "No overwhelming genius": Sara Haardt, "Youth in the Cotton Belt," *Brentano's Book Chat*, August 1927, p. 67.

Section IV

50 When the news: Baltimore, Maryland, *News*, August 4, 1930.
50 Now, with the: Ibid.
50 Naturally, everyone was: Ibid.
50 The Mobile, Alabama: The Mobile, Alabama *News*, August 6, 1930.
50 Sara, now labeled: The New York *Herald*, August 5, 1930.
50 For weeks these: Memphis Tennessee *Press Scrintar*, August 28, 1930.
50 "I can only": Ibid.
50 Among Sara's friends: Letter from Adele Conmadine to Sara Haardt (undated), 1930. *SH*, p. 179. EPL.
50 Dorothy Hergesheimer, who: Edgar Kemler, *The Irreverent Mr. Mencken* (Boston: Little, Brown & Co., paperback edition, 1963), p. 238.
51 Anna, he said: Letter from James Cain to Sara Mayfield, August 19, 1968. Ala.
51 She also "could": Mencken, *AN 1941-*. EPL.
51 George Jean Nathan: The New York *Telegram*, August 13, 1930.
52 "I see no": H. L. Mencken, "On Falling in Love After Forty," John M. Wheeler Syndicate, December 21, 1927.
52 In a letter: HLM to Lillian Gish, August 9, 1928, Bode, p. 225.
52 During 1928 Mencken: Sara Mayfield to Sara Haardt, September 25, 1928; Mary Parmenter to Sara Mayfield, February 2, 1929. Ala.
53 As he stood: Mayfield, p. 137.
53 "Harry is worried": Letter from Gertrude Mencken to Sara Haardt, April 26, 1930. *SH*, p. 176. EPL.

Page

55 "Sara is moving": Mencken to Philip Goodman, August 4, 1930. Bode, p. 245.

55 "The musical engineers": Mencken to Max Broedel, August 20, 1930, Bode, p. 246.

55 He came to: Ibid.

55 To his secretary: Mencken to Edith Lustgarten, July 28, 1930, Bode, p. 244.

55 Together, Mencken and: The Baltimore *Evening Sun*, August 22, 1930.

55 The man who: Savannah, Georgia, *Press*, August 4, 1930.

55 Finally he took: Letter from Herbert Parrish to H. L. Mencken, August 19, 1930. MdBG.

56 (on ceremonial occasions): Alistair Cooke, *Six Men* (New York: Alfred A. Knopf, 1977), p. 91.

56 "Sara is out": Mencken to Blanche Knopf, September 4, 1930, Forgue, p. 321.

56 In postcards to: Sara Haardt to Elsa G. Hayden. *Sara Haardt Mencken: Letters and Telegrams.* . . . MdBG.

56 "Ida, come tell": My interview with Ida Haardt, October 1, 1983.

56 Often this would: Letter from F. Scott Fitzgerald to Sara Haardt Mencken, October 5, 1933. *SH*, p. 200. EPL.

56 The visitors who: Theodore Maynard, *The World I Saw* (Milwaukee: The Bruce Publishing Company, 1938), pp. 283–285.

57 Whenever he went: Mencken, "Preface," *Southern Album*, p. xx.

57 From Chicago, where: HLM to SH, June [12], 1932. MdBG.

57 ("My wife can"): H. L. Mencken, "Beer," Radio interview with William Lundell, NBC, October 18, 1933. Mimeo text. *Radio Addresses 1933–1937* EPL.

57 She told reporters: Savannah, Georgia, *Press*, August 4, 1930.

57 Sara Haardt, *Diary and Memorandum Books*. MdBG.

58 Years later, Mencken: The sheet of music and Mencken's comments are among the letters between H. L. Mencken and Sara Haardt, MdBG. The translation from the German is by James J. MacMahon, Emory University.

58 There were visits: Sinclair Lewis to H. L. Mencken, June 2, 1935. *Sara Haardt Mencken: Letters and Telegrams.* . . . MdBG.

59 "The trouble with": Mencken to Philip Goodman, Jan. 19, 1932. Forgue, p. 338.

59 In it he: "Confidential Information," *The Caribbean Caravel, Newssheet Aboard S.S. Columbus, North German Lloyd*, January 25, 1932.

59 "The business of": Mencken to Philip Goodman, January 16, 1932, Bode, p. 260.

Page
60 ("The perfumes there"): Ibid.
60 Years before, Sara: Marcella Miller DuPont, "Heroic Days and Hours with Henry Mencken," *Menckeniana*, Summer 1966, p. 5.
60 Nonetheless, there were: SH to HLM, April 22, 1930. MdBG.
60 "Gentlemen: My attention": Letter from Marie Bankhead Owen to Virginia Archives and History (nonexistent), June 8, 1933. The Department of Archives and History, Montgomery, Alabama.
60 Ibid.
61 "Five o'clock tea": "Distinguished Visitor," Birmingham *News-Age Herald*, March 26, 1933.
61 As Mencken would: H. L. Mencken, "Off the Grand Banks," the Baltimore *Evening Sun*, September 7, 1925.
62 "As for Egypt": Bode, "Mencken in His Letters," Dorsey, ed., pp. 271–272.
62 The trip had: My interview with Ida Haardt, October 1, 1983.
62 "I was going": Sara Haardt, *SS*, p. 3. MdBG.
62 The North was: Ibid., p. 9. MdBG.
62 She asked herself: Ibid., p. 10. MdBG.
63 "She can read": Mencken to Estelle Bloom Kubitz Williams, November 19, 1934, Bode, p. 330.
63 With Sara bedridden: As Mencken was to write to his friend, Dan Henry: "Christmas is always an unlucky time at my house, and so I look forward to it with dread and am seldom disappointed." HLM to Dan Henry, December 31, 1934. EPL.
63 On May 23: Mencken to F. Scott Fitzgerald, May 23, 1935, Forgue, p. 391.
63 (To which Fitzgerald): F. Scott Fitzgerald to Mencken, undated. *Sara Haardt Mencken: Letters, Telegrams. . . .* MdBG.
63 Mencken politely declined:Mencken to Fulton Oursler, May 18, 1935, Bode, pp. 352–353.
63 In one of: Letter from Sara Haardt to Sara Mayfield, undated. Ala.
63 On the evening: Mencken gave the lecture at the Hamilton Street Club, at 6:30 p.m. Letter to John Calvin French, May 9, 1935. The French Collection, MdBJ.
64 He wrote that: Letter to John Calvin French, May 3, 1935, The French Collection, MdBJ.
64 "Sara has meningitis": Mencken to Max Broedel, Bode, p. 354,
64 Accompanied by Gertrude: Ibid.
64 Mencken summed up: Hamilton Owens, "A Personal Note," Forgue, pp. xi–xii.

SECTION V

64 Biography fails, Mencken: Owen Arthur James Hatteras (pseudonym, H. L. Mencken), *Pistols for Two* (New York: Alfred A. Knopf, 1917), p. 1.

65 It is, needless: Ibid., pp. 1–2.

65 Mother and daughter: *SS*, p. 6. MdBG.

65 Inevitably, they spoke: *SS*, p. 7. MdBG.

65 "Even when I": Ibid.

65 "She heard what": Ibid.

65 She maintained that: Ibid., p. 8.

66 And some of: E. H. Walton, *The New Republic*, May 27, 1936, p. 79.

66 "At last I": Sara Haardt, "Dear Life," *Southern Album*, pp. 284–285.

67 "And yet, despite": Sara Haardt, "Literary Life in the Cotton Belt," pp. 35–36.

67 "If I had": H. L. Mencken, "Preface," *Happy Days* (New York: Alfred A. Knopf, 1940), p. ix.

67 Sara Haardt was: My interview with Lillian Gish, March 6, 1985.

67 For years Mencken: Mencken to Sara Mayfield, September 10, 1937. Ala.

67 Every year Mencken: Mencken to Sara Mayfield, June 6, 1938. Ala.

68 "I was fifty-five": Mencken, *AN 1941-*. EPL.

68 "The life of ": Sara Haardt, "The First Lady of the Confederacy: Varina Howell, Wife of Jefferson Davis" (book review), New York *Herald Tribune Books*, February 5, 1928.

68 Theodore Dreiser's letter: Letter from Theodore Dreiser to H. L. Mencken, June 4, 1935. *Sara Haardt Mencken: Letters, Telegrams.* . . . MdBG.

68 When Mencken returned: Roy Hoopes, *Cain* (New York: Holt, Rinehart & Winston, 1982), p. 273.

69 In a preface: H. L. Mencken, "Prefatory Note," *Notes by Sara Haardt 1927–1935*, MdBG.

69 Accompanying him would: C. Bode, p. 303.

BIBLIOGRAPHICAL NOTES
TO THE LETTERS
1923–1935

Throughout my annotations I have drawn upon various sources. Those from which I have paraphrased or made direct quotes are *Nowhere at Home: Letters from Exile of Emma Goldman and Alexander Berkman*, Richard and Anne Maria Drinnon, ed. (New York: Schocken Books, 1975); James Hall Bready, "Strube's Muse Struck After 'Peace Overture,' " the Baltimore *Evening Sun* (February 3, 1946); Emily Clark, *Ingenue Among the Lions: The Letters of Emily Clark to Joseph Hergesheimer*, Gerald Langford, ed. (Austin: The University of Texas Press, 1965); Philip Goodman, "A Week in Paris with Mencken;" New York *World* (August 18, 1930); Edgar Kemler, *The Irreverent Mr. Mencken* (Boston: Little, Brown & Co., paperback reprint, 1963); Sara Haardt's works: "Jim Tully," *The American Mercury* (May 1928); "Good-bye," *Scribner's* (December 1934); "Sara Haardt, Wife of H. L. Mencken, Conquers T.B. Four Times," *The Fluoroscope* (May 1935); "Heart of Hollywood" (unpublished manuscript), *Articles and Movie Scenarios 1927–1935* (MdBG); Letters to Blanche Knopf and H. L. Mencken and received from Grover Hall, Paul de Kruif, Ogden Nash, and Lillian Welsh are deposited at the Julia Rogers Library, Goucher College, and in *Sara Powell Haardt Mencken:* 1898–1935, the Enoch Pratt Free Library, and at the Mayfield Collection, Ala. Letters from Joseph Hergesheimer to H. L. Mencken are at the Harry Ransom Humanities Center, the University of Texas at Austin; Letters quoted between Sara Mayfield, Sara Haardt, H. L. Mencken, and Mary Parmenter are at the Mayfield Collection, the Amelia Gayle Gorgas Library, the University of Alabama; many of these are also cited in Sara Mayfield's *The Constant Circle* (New York: Delacorte Press, 1968); the letter from Sara Mayfield to Mr. E. G. Smith, Teche Greyhound Lines, is also in the Mayfield Collection, Ala.; Alfred A. Knopf, *Friends and Authors*. H. L. Mencken's works that are cited are: "Preface," *Southern Album* (Garden City, New York: Doubleday, Doran & Co., 1936); "Beer," Radio Interview with William Lundell for NBC, *Radio Addresses 1933–1937* EPL; "New York," the *The Smart Set* (September 1923); Newspaper articles from the Baltimore *Evening Sun* May 30, 1923–March 13, 1933; Letters to and from Samuel Knopf, Dudley Field Malone, Theodore Roosevelt, Jr., and Marvin C. Ross, and his speech for the Gridiron Club are at the NYPL; his letters to and from Sara Haardt are at MdBG; all other letters cited are from Carl Bode, *The New Mencken Letters* (New York: The Dial Press, 1977), and Guy J. Forgue, *Letters of H. L. Mencken* (New York: Alfred A. Knopf, 1961); articles describing Mencken are from the Columbia (South Carolina) *Record* (November 9, 1924); Los Angeles *Negro Paper* (November 5, 1926); Fort Worth *Press* (June 20,

1928); Houston *Post Dispatch* (June 22, 1928); Houston Texas *Chronicle* (June 23, 1928); Julia Blanshard, "After Two Years of Marriage, Mencken, Famed Bachelor, Proves Model Husband," St. Paul, *The Cloverleaf American Review* (August 1932); Richard Meryman, *Mank: The Wit, World, and Life of Herman Mankiewicz* (New York: William Morrow and Company, 1978); George Jean Nathan, *The Intimate Notebooks of George Jean Nathan* (New York: Alfred A. Knopf, 1932); Marjorie Nicolson's letters are from the Neilson/Nicolson Correspondence (letters from and to President W. A. Neilson, Smith College), Archives, Smith College; H. L. Mencken, *Sara Haardt Mencken: Letters and Telegrams at Her Death*, MdBG.; William H. Nolte, *H. L. Mencken: Literary Critic* (Middletown, Connecticut: Wesleyan University Press, 1966); Franklin D. Roosevelt's letter to Arthur Brisbane is from the Franklin D. Roosevelt Library. Hyde Park, New York; Theodore Roosevelt, Jr., *All in the Family* (New York and London: G. P. Putnam's Sons, 1929).

APPENDIX

—————————— ~ ——————————

SARA HAARDT TO Sara Mayfield, April 24, 1930 (The Mayfield Collection, Amelia Gayle Gorgas Library, The University of Alabama). In *The Constant Circle* (New York: Delacorte Press, 1968), Sara Mayfield has written: "In April {1930} Sara went down to Montgomery to tell her family that she was to be married. On her arrival there, she called me in Tuscaloosa that her novel, *The Making of a Lady*, had been accepted for publication and asked me to come to Montgomery at once; she had something to show me and something to tell me. When I told her that it was impossible for me to get away just then, I thought she seemed irked and said so. . . ." (p. 157). The letters between Sara Haardt and Sara Mayfield in the Mayfield Collection seem to tell a different story. Apparently, it was Sara Mayfield who repeatedly asked Sara Haardt if she could come up from Montgomery and visit her in Tuscaloosa, to which Sara Haardt responded: "You are very sweet to invite me to Tuscaloosa, but I am terribly tired after my session with my novel, and I am having to return to Baltimore sooner than I thought for Dr. Richardson to resume some treatments he had started. I have heard none of the gossip, or whoever you say people there are talking about. . . . I am moving out of 16 W. Read {street} in August. . . . the medical faculty say I have to have a lighter apartment. So I must return and start house-hunting in that neighborhood. . . . I'll probably have to leave Baltimore sometime in the summer if the weather gets too hot" (April 24, 1930). In *The Constant Circle* (p. 157) Sara Mayfield gives a long quotation of an undated letter Sara Haardt wrote to her (it simply says "Thursday"; it was probably written May 1, 1930), but it is full of deletions. The excerpts that are deleted in Mayfield's book read: *"Thank you again for your invitation to Tuscaloosa. I'd love to come, except that I look like hell, and for the complications here.* [Sara's mother was very ill; this is explained at the top of the letter.] *Let me hear your plans.* I'm certainly not 'mad' whatever you mean by that. Old loves, as my old friend Langdon used to say, are hard to down." [The italics are mine.] Finally, Sara Mayfield decided she would travel to Montgomery herself and visit Sara. The account Sara Mayfield gives reads: "When I did drive over to Montgomery, I discovered it was not 'Southern Credo' that she had called me over to see or the babble she proposed to discuss. It was her engagement ring that she wanted to show me and her future plans she intended to tell me about" (p. 157). Sara Mayfield then describes how the two of them went shopping for antique furniture and other ornaments, discussing the upcoming marriage (p. 158). But Sara Haardt's letter, thanking Sara Mayfield for her visit, does not acknowledge any confidences had been shared: "Thanks a lot for your letter. I enjoyed your visit so much, but surely you know this. I hope that I'll be able to get around more the next time I come down. I'm leaving here the early part of the week. In a way I hate to go" (May 8, 1930). The letter mentions that she spoke with Mencken and what the temperature was in Baltimore. On May 11, 1930, Sara Haardt wrote another letter to Sara Mayfield, this time from Baltimore: "I won't move for another month or so—I'll certainly let you hear when. The address is 704 Cathedral Street." It seems that, contrary to what has been written in *The Constant Circle*, Sara Haardt did not inform Sara Mayfield of her plans to wed Mencken until July, when Mencken was also informing his closest friends. The letter Sara Haardt wrote of her engagement is undated, but Sara Mayfield does acknowledge that the letter was sent in July and quotes it in full in her book (p. 160). In another letter, written by Sara Haardt and dated July 31, 1930, she thanks Sara Mayfield for her telegram and letter, wherein Sara Mayfield had expressed her surprise and excitement of the news (that letter is undated, 1930, and is at the Enoch Pratt Free Library).

~

So what does one make of the seeming discrepancies? Sara Mayfield may have mistaken Sara Haardt's unusually withdrawn letters as a sign of aloofness or even anger, when in fact Sara Haardt was trying to be cautious by not letting her wedding plans get into the newspapers. Sara Haardt was so cautious, in fact, that she rented the apartment on 704 Cathedral Street in her name only, so as not to arouse any suspicion that she and Mencken were about to be married. Sara Haardt's other letters to Sara Mayfield in the collection are open and unreserved, showing the warmth and friendship the two women shared. It may be that, owing to the seven-year difference in their age, Sara Haardt looked upon "little Sara" as a younger sister who might, in her excitement, inadvertently leak the news. And it may also be that, in later years, when Sara Mayfield was writing about Sara Haardt and Mencken for *The Constant Circle*, she might have felt hurt at being excluded and not being the first to know of Sara's and Mencken's plans, and so glossed the story.

ACKNOWLEDGMENTS

‿

THE DESIRE TO WRITE ABOUT the literary relationship and love between H. L. Mencken and Sara Powell Haardt goes back to when I was an undergraduate at Goucher College. There are many individuals and institutions I would like to thank, and this page seems to be one of the happiest places in which to express my gratitude.

At the outset I would like to thank Averil J. Kadis and the Trustees for the Estate of H. L. Mencken at the Enoch Pratt Free Library in Baltimore. It is difficult for me to make an adequate acknowledgment to them, for it is the Estate that gives *carte blanche* to quote from the letters of H. L. Mencken and Sara Haardt and other unpublished manuscripts. Without their permission this book could not have been written. My thanks also to Neil R. Jordahl, Director of Humanities at the Enoch Pratt Free Library, for his unfailing assistance throughout the many months I spent at the Mencken Room at the library, a haven that I found to be, in the words of Alistair Cooke, "for the comfort of sinners and for the astonishment of the virtuous." Betty R. Kondayan, Head Librarian of the Julia Rogers Library at Goucher College, generously granted me the privilege of working there and provided me with materials, and I can only say that without her I would have never been able to work as freely as I did. Because the germ of this work was originally based on my master's thesis, "Sara Haardt, H. L. Mencken, and the Sense of Place," while I was a graduate student at

Emory University, I am indebted to my advisor, Floyd C. Watkins. He not only provided me with sound counsel but had faith in me and in my project, and for that I shall always be grateful. Among those I especially wish to please are Charles A. Fecher, who generously read an early draft of my introduction and made many valuable suggestions, and Robin P. Harriss, for his many kindnesses. My thanks also to Carl Bode, for his encouragement. To all of the above, my deepest thanks.

Of those I interviewed and corresponded with, all were generous in sharing with me their impressions of Sara Haardt and H. L. Mencken. It seems that the memory of Mencken and Sara struck a special chord, and almost all were, if not at the outset, eager to share their memories of these two exceptional people. As the book progressed, many were kind enough to let me speak to them again and again. In alphabetical order, those I wish to thank are as follows: Selma van Leer Adler, Benjamin Baker, Alice Braunlich, Mary Ross Flowers, Lillian Gish, Emerson Greenaway, Norton Gesner, Marion Gutman, Ida and Philippa Haardt, R. P. Harriss, Ellen C. Masters, Mrs. Hamilton Owens, Catherine Steiner, Isabel Yates. I hope that, in its final form, this book does their memories of Mencken and Sara justice.

Through the years many other individuals have helped me generously in my work, and I owe many thanks to the following for information, advice, loan of letters, and every other kind of assistance: Mrs. J. W. Athey; Edmund Berkeley, Jr., Curator of Manuscripts at the University of Virginia; and the Vestry at St. James Protestant Episcopal Church, executors of the estate of Emily Clark Balch, for kindly giving me permission to quote from her letters to Joseph Hergesheimer and from her book, *Innocence Abroad* (Knopf, 1931); Amy Bernstein; Robin M. Carlaw; Timothy D. Cary; William R. Emerson; Nancy Engelhardt; Florence DeLibera; Vince Fitzpatrick: Maida Goodwin; Arthur J. Gutman; Mrs. John Haardt; Mr. and Mrs. P. Hamburger, Jr.; Steven Hahn; Dallett Hemphill, Esq., for kindly giving me permission to quote from the letters of Joseph Hergesheimer to H. L. Mencken; Cathy Henderson; Shirley Horowitz; Jackie Jiles; Marie Keipart; Jacques Kelly; John Kish; Mrs. Alfred Knopf; Joyce H. Lamont; Cecil Y. Lang; Elenore Linsmayer; Janette S. Mayfield and James J. Mayfield IV, for kindly giving me permission to quote from the Sara Mayfield Collection at the Amelia Gayle Gorgas Library, the University of Alabama; Hilary and Marcia Lee Masters; James V. McMahon, director, German Department, Emory University, for his translations; Craig David Miller (a special thanks); Edward C. Moore; Julia Morgan; Betty Morrison; Ms. Julie Haydon Nathan, for kindly giving me permission to quote from *The Intimate Notebooks of George Jean Nathan*; Edward Pattillo; Eugenia Rawls; Jane A. Rosenberg; Otto Schellhase, Jr.; Gerald Shorb; Barbara Simons; James Stimpert; John B. Stinson; Marilyn B. Sullivan; Joan Snyder; Mary Schultz; Evelyn Schroedel; Andrew Tauber; Raymond Teichman; Abigail Toffel; Barbara Waybright; William Weiler; Wesley L. Wilson; Daniel T. Williams; Joanne K. Woods; Narcie Woolf. All of them have made the writing of this book easier by their ready assistance and thoughtfulness.

For their excellent reproductions of the photographs shown in this book, my thanks to: Gaither Scott of the Hughes Company and John Parker and his team at Artography Labs, Inc. in Baltimore, Maryland. For granting permission to use his photographs, I am grateful to: Mrs. Aubrey Bodine, for use of her husband's photographs; the estate of Carl Van Vechten; and the Peale Museum, Baltimore City Life Museums, the A. Aubrey Bodine Photographic Collection.

A large number of libraries and other institutions helped me during my research, and I am grateful to the following organizations and their staff members: The State of Alabama Department of Archives and History, Montgomery; The Amelia Gayle Gorgas Library, the University of Alabama, Tuscaloosa; Auswartiges AMT in Bonn, the Federal Republic of Germany; the Embassy of the Federal Republic of Germany, Washington, D.C.; the Julia Rogers Library, Goucher College, Towson; the Enoch Pratt Free Library, Baltimore; The Alan Mason Chesney Medical Archives, The Ferdinand Hamburger, Jr., Archives, and The Milton S. Eisenhower Library, all part of the Johns Hopkins University, Baltimore; The Museum and Library of Maryland History, the Maryland Historical Society, Baltimore; The New York Public Library, New York; The Franklin Delano Roosevelt Library, Hyde Park; Smith College, Northampton; The Harry Ransom Humanities Research Center at the University of Texas at Austin; Tuskegee Institute, Tuskegee; Vanderbilt University, Nashville.

Permission to quote from Mencken's published work was granted by Alfred A. Knopf, Inc. The publishers of other writers are acknowledged at the beginning of this book.

A special debt of thanks to both Joe Beck, Esq., of Kilpatrick &

Cody, and to Robert S. Schlossberg, Esq., of Morgan, Lewis, & Bockius for their time, and expert legal advice. A special thanks, too, to Barry Marc Goldman, Esq., of Hansell & Post. His generosity, thoughtfulness, advice and support has been invaluable—I cannot thank him enough.

To Leon Livingstone, Professor Emeritus of the State University of New York at Buffalo, who reviewed an early draft and made timely and helpful suggestions: I am grateful for his advice; thanks go as well to my agent, Patrick Delahunt, of John Schaffner Agency, and my editor, Thomas Ward Miller, of McGraw-Hill, for their invaluable help. Last, but certainly not least, to my typist, Natalie Neviaser, for her efficiency and patience.

And finally, I am indebted to my parents, William L. and Maria A. Rodgers. My father and mother were my confidants: both listened, both inspired. Their support has been behind every moment of this and various other undertakings of mine, and I shall always find I do not have quite enough words to thank them for their encouragement, wisdom, and good humor.

MARION ELIZABETH RODGERS
Bethesda, Md.

INDEX

Abbott, Ellis, 405, 406n
Abbott, Leonard, 191
Abbott, Lyman, 192n
"Absolutely Perfect," 492
Adams, John Haslup, 296, 298
"Alabama," 40, 209–210, 215, 241n
Alexander, Marie, 437, 453
"All in the Family," 228, 234n,
    240n
Altgeld, John Peter, 178
American Credo, The (Mencken and
    Nathan), 137n
American Language, The (Mencken),
    16, 57, 64, 84, 85n, 498n
American Mercury, The, 3, 22, 47,
    57, 94, 101, 102–103n, 104–
    105, 118, 140, 167n, 241n, 249n
    Americana section in, 105n, 214n,
        448n
    Angoff at, 186n, 194, 196, 197
    in censorship case, 245–247, 249,
        250, 251
    Check List reviews in, 277, 278
    decline of, 449–450, 475n, 492

American Mercury, The (cont.)
    departure of Nathan, 171n, 174n,
        186–187, 198–199,
        202
    first number of, 104–105, 106n
    founding of, 37, 84, 86, 88
    influence of, 38
    libel suits against, 286n
    offices of, 116n, 117
    pay rate of, 88n
    success of, 111n
Americana, 213, 214n
Americanization of Edward Bok, The
    (Bok), 179n
Anderson, Sherwood, 3, 191–192,
    193n, 227
Angoff, Charles, 40, 186n, 194,
    196, 197, 215, 448n, 475n
Anti-Saloon League, 398n, 481n
Arant, William Douglas, 486n
Arrowsmith (Lewis), 192n, 197, 205,
    292n
Asbury, Herbert, 245n
Associated Press, 382n

ABOUT THE AUTHOR

MARION ELIZABETH RODGERS, a writer and Mencken scholar who has worked with National Public Radio and Georgia Public Television, is the editor of *The Impossible H. L. Mencken*. She is presently at work on a biography of H. L. Mencken. She lives in Baltimore, Maryland.